Craufurd Tait Ramage

Drumlanrig Castle and the Douglases

With the early History and Ancient Remains of Durisdeer, Closeburn, and Morton

Craufurd Tait Ramage

Drumlanrig Castle and the Douglases
With the early History and Ancient Remains of Durisdeer, Closeburn, and Morton

ISBN/EAN: 9783743419704

Manufactured in Europe, USA, Canada, Australia, Japa

Cover: Foto ©ninafisch / pixelio.de

Manufactured and distributed by brebook publishing software (www.brebook.com)

Craufurd Tait Ramage

Drumlanrig Castle and the Douglases

DRUMLANRIG CASTLE

AND

THE DOUGLASES:

WITH THE

EARLY HISTORY AND ANCIENT REMAINS

OF

DURISDEER, CLOSEBURN, AND MORTON.

BY

CRAUFURD TAIT RAMAGE, LL.D.,

AUTHOR OF "NOOKS AND BY-WAYS OF ITALY," "BEAUTIFUL THOUGHTS
FROM LATIN AUTHORS," "BEAUTIFUL THOUGHTS FROM FRENCH
AND ITALIAN AUTHORS," "BEAUTIFUL THOUGHTS FROM
GERMAN AND SPANISH AUTHORS," ETC.

DUMFRIES: J. ANDERSON & SON.
HODDER AND STOUGHTON, 27 PATERNOSTER ROW, LONDON, E.C.
1876.

TO THE

REV. DAVID OGILVY-RAMSAY

OF WESTHALL.

Rev. Sir,

Admiring the catholic spirit, the zeal and unflagging attention, which you have shown in the performance of your duties since your appointment as Minister of Closeburn, I cannot refuse myself the pleasure of inscribing to you this small volume, as a mark of esteem and respect. It contains the Early History of the Parish over the spiritual interests of which you have been placed, and where I trust you may be long spared to labour in your holy calling.

Believe me to remain,

Rev. Sir,

Your very sincere well-wisher and friend,

CRAUFURD TAIT RAMAGE.

PREFACE.

This small volume consists of an account of the Parishes of Durisdeer, Closeburn, and Morton, in Upper Nithsdale, which appeared in the *Dumfries and Galloway Courier*, with some scattered notices of Burns which I had recorded in the pages of *Notes and Queries*. As it is the result of considerable research, it has been thought proper to place it in a more permanent form than the pages of a weekly journal. An attempt has been made to bring together everything that could throw light on the early races that inhabited these parishes. *Tumuli*, cairns, stone and bronze celts, coins, remains of ancient camps, place-names—the most enduring and probably the most important of all the means of illustrating the races that have occupied a country—have been pressed into service, though, to do justice to the subject, a knowledge is required much more encyclopædical than one man can be expected to possess. The history of a country can only be reached through its individual parts: it is only by descending to particulars, and by recollecting that the bygone ages of the world were actually filled by living men, that the true character of ancient times can be thoroughly elucidated. Each portion of our country, each parish, has a story of its own, which lies at the foundation of all national history. These parishes, on which an attempt has been made to throw light, contain the first chapters of the history of Gael and Saxon, and even of the Norse rovers.

Each wave of race that swept across our country left its mark on hills and streams: the tread of the Roman legions can almost be heard as they made their way laboriously through our marshes and forests; early charters show the gradual approach of our feudal system; the mythic Arthur is not unknown among us; the heroic Bruce still lives by his place-names; Kirkpatricks, Mandevilles, and Douglases

"Fight and sing
Their scornful way across the stage of Time."

I am quite aware of the shortcomings of which I may be accused, but the far-distant period with the history of which I have been engaged, enveloped as it is in the mist of ages, must be my excuse for any mistakes into which I may have fallen. When the Drumlanrig charters have been placed before Scottish investigators of ancient times in the clear and able manner that the learning and knowledge of Mr. William Fraser, of the Register Office, who is now engaged in their illustration, will enable him to do, then the basis which has been laid by a pretty minute examination of its Inventory will enable future antiquarians to give a more complete history of this upper vale of Nithsdale. I have not failed to examine all the chartularies of monasteries that contain references to these parishes; and in saying so, I must not omit to acknowledge the courtesy of John Gilchrist Clark, Esq., of Speddoch, in allowing me access to his valuable library. I was thus able to have before me the works published by the Bannatyne and other Clubs, and without an examination of these the account would have been still more imperfect than it is.

I have to thank many others of my friends for placing at my disposal whatever information they possessed; and it has been not one of the least of the pleasures attending on these investigations, that everyone to whom I applied, even though they were personally unknown, was ready to assist me in whatever way I pointed out.

INDEX.

	PAGE
Æ	175, 242
Agincourt, Battle of	37
Agnes, Black	316, 346
Alexander II., Charter of	179, 191
Alexander, Rev. John	165
Alison, John	64
Angus, Earl of	40, 79
Anne, Queen	19
Annoltoun	76
Ardoch	45, 142
Ariosto	101
Arthur, King	100
Augustine, St.	110
Auchenskeoch	142
Auchenskew	142
Auchinleck	173
Aufrica	186, 315
Auldgarth	176, 384
Avenel, Roger de	194
Bacon	253, 267
Baird, Family of	213-217
Baitford	99
Balagan, Family of	98
,, House	100
Ban	142
Bardi	176

	PAGE
Barony of Briddeburg	179, 198
,, of Drumlanrig	2, 155
,, of Durisdeer	95, 155
,, of Enoch	88, 155
,, of Halydean	228
,, of Kylosbern	178
,, of Morton	308
,, of Tibbers	181
Barscar	176
Beeches	32, 249
Bell of Durisdeer	121
,, of Kirkbride	114
Bellybucht	307, 330, 331
Belstane	140
Bennet, Rev. Andrew	231
,, Rev. George	231
Black Douglas	4, 96
,, Minister of Closeburn	175, 181
Blackwoodhead	43
Blare, James de	75
Blind Harry	104
Boat, old	243
Bondington, Walter de	58, 194
Borthwick, Sir William de	4
Bos Scoticus	25
Boundaries of Durisdeer	151
,, of Kirkbride	151
,, of Morton	330
Boyle, Lady Mary	11
Breadalbane, Family of	6
Breadislee, Johnnie of	34
Briddeburg, Barony of	179, 198
,, Chapel of	239
Bridge, Drumlanrig	22
Bridget, St.	112, 181
Brown, Dr. John	107, 158
Brownhill	267
Bruce, Robert	196

INDEX.

	PAGE
Brus, William de	191
Brysone, James	112, 123
Buccleuch, Charles, Duke of	58
,, Henry, Duke of	58
,, Walter, Duke of	1, 56, 58, 335
Buchanites	238, 240
Burlington, Earl of	12
Burning of Drumlanrig Gates	46
Burns in Closeburn	251, 270
,, Letters to J. M'Murdo	67
,, Letter to S. Clark	73
,, in Morton	360
,, on Fair of Dalgarnock	219
,, on Gateslack	159
,, on Woods of Drumlanrig	30
Cairns	169
Capenoch	162
Carron	102, 157
Carson, Dr.	251
Castlehill	98
Celt	141, 167
Celtic Dyke	102, 137
Census, Ecclesiastical	247
Chamberlains	64, 74
Chapels	118, 181, 233, 237
Charles I.	45
Charters	3, 5, 7, 75, 95, 111, 179, 191, 198
Chillingham	26
Church of Closeburn	174
,, Dalgarnock	219-223
,, Durisdeer	108, 121
,, Kirkbride	112
,, Kirkpatrick	232
,, Morton	324
Cist	139
Clark, John Gilchrist, Esq.	73, 121
Closeburn, Castle of	182

		PAGE
Closeburn, Church of		174, 223, 232
,, Heights of		240
,, Lochs of		242
,, Minerals and Manufactures of		245
,, Ministers of		229, 231
,, Origin of Name		174
,, Population of		247
,, Rivers of		241
,, Stipend of		229
,, Traditions of		185
,, Valuation of		248
,, Woods of		349
Clouden		101
Coins		145, 233
Cole, Viscount		218
Collace, Peter		225
Colvyle, Robert de		4
Combination Poorhouse		346
Communion Cups		121
Comyn, Red		196
Copper Kettle		312
Corse, Rob's		197
Corsehillend		328
Coshogle, Family of		38, 43, 44, 74, 84
,, House		84
Covenanting Times		126
Cowfaddoch		237
Crairie Know		119
Cramond		100
Cranston, James		150
Crawick		100
Crichope Linn		241
Crichton, Major Thomas		73
Croal Chapel		233-235
Cuthbert, St.		110
,, Well of		110
Dalgarnock, Origin of Name		173

INDEX.   xiii

		PAGE
Dalgarnock, Church of		219-223, 315
Dalpeddar		101
Dalrymple, Family of		65
,, James de		76
Dalswinton		103
Dalveen Castle		87
,, Family of		44, 85
,, Origin of Name		142
,, Pass of		159
,, Upper and Lower		135
Darcongal, Abbey of		101
David I.		177
David II., Charter of		119
Deer Camp		105, 306
Defoe		127
Deil's Dyke		102, 137, 169, 305
Denmark, Prince George of		19
Discipline, Book of		41
Discomfit, Gutter		241
Donegal		312, 324
Douglas, Family of Coshogle		74-85, 316
,, ,, of Dalveen		85-87
,, ,, of Dornock		397
,, ,, of Drumlanrig		36-63
,, ,, of Holm Hill		8, 312, 322
,, ,, of Morton		317, 323, 348
,, ,, of Morton Mains		317, 323
Douglas, Archibald		64, 65, 321
,, Charles, Duke		2, 55
,, Charles, Earl of Drumlanrig		55
,, Lord George		53
,, Lord Henry of Drumlanrig		55
,, James de, Lord of Dalkeith		345
,, Sir James		200
,, James, Earl of		2, 45
,, James, Duke of		2, 54
,, Lady Jane		12, 55
,, William, First Duke		2, 53

		PAGE
Douglas, William, Fourth Duke		2, 53, 56
,, Sir William of Hawick		42
,, William, Earl of		2, 45
,. William of Fingland		65
,, Brown, Esq.		320
,, Gresley, Esq., of High Park		321
Douglas Vault		111
Dour		143
Dow		136
Dressetland		44
Druidical Circle		169, 305
Drum		142, 307
Drumlanrig Castle		6, 46, 50
,, Woods of		29, 33, 34
,, Bridge of		22
,, Gardens of		20
,, Wild Cattle of		25
,, Plundered by the English		35
Dryfe's Sands, Battle of		205
Duchess' Drive		157
Dunduff		143
Durisdeer, Castle of		97, 103
,, Church		108
,, Communion Cups		121
,, Heights of		132
,, Means of Communication		153
,, Ministers of		122
,, Poor of		157
,, Population of		156
,, Stewart Family of		95-97
,, Streams of		157
,, Valuation of		155
Duvenald		314
Earncleugh		143
Earncrag		173
Earthquake		234
Edgar		314, 324

INDEX.

	PAGE
Edward I.	114
Egidia	88
Elfin Pipes	141
Enoch	143
,, Castle of	94, 103
,, Menzies of	88
Enterkine Path	127, 159
,, River	158
Esk	143
Ettrick Loch	242
Ewart, Family of	379
Fairies	29
Fairy Knowe	306
Fell	308
Ferguson, Family of	350-351
Fergusson of Craigdarroch	39, 166
Firs, Scotch	22
Flint, Kirsty	266
Flodden, Battle of	2, 39, 76
Foles-streme	108
Font, Kirkbride	114
,, Dalgarnock	221
,, Kirkpatrick	232
Forrester, Sir Adam	4
Forts	106
Fraser, Janet	339
Gallows Flat	22, 311
Garant	102
Gardens of Drumlanrig	20
Garrock	173
Garth	176
Gateslack	159
Gill	307
Gillespie, Dr.	250, 265
Gladstone, Mrs. Stuart	74
Glennie, Stuart	100

	PAGE
Glenmarlin	100
Grampian Club	109
Gregory, St.	110
Grey Mare's Tail	241
Grierson, Dr., Museum of	141, 160, 166, 167, 247, 249, 362-369
Grinling Gibbons	9
Gullet Spout	241
Gwenever	100
Harkness, Family of	131-134
Harkness, Thomas, Martyr	132
Halydean, Barony of	228
Hassock, House of	9
Heads	146
Hel,	145, 241
Heriot's Hospital	7
Herries, Lord	41
Hill-Burton, Dr.	184
Hills of Closeburn	240
,, Durisdeer	152
,, Morton	331
Holestane	144
Holles	144
Holmhead	181
Hope, Lady Elizabeth	35
Holywell	110
Horsley, Bishop	231
Humby	145, 176
Humma	176
Hunter, Family of Balagan	98
Hunter, Dr. John	148, 250
Hyde, Chancellor	15
Hyde, Lady Catherine	10, 15
Ingleston, Oak at	34, 145
James I., Letter of	5
James VI.	45, 80

INDEX. xvii

	PAGE
James, Duke of Queensberry	2, 54
James, Second Earl of Queensberry	10, 45
Jock and the Horn	10, 21
Johnnie of Breadislee	39
Jones, Inigo	7
Judgment Thorn	311
Keith, Robert de	200
Kemp's Grave	306
Kettleton	307
Kingstand Burn	197
King's Stone	197
Kirkbride, Church of	112
,, Ministers of	122
Kirkpatrick, Family of Alisland	386-389
,, ,, of Closeburn	189
,, ,, of Friar's Carse	386
,, ,, of Kirkmichael	391
Kirkpatrick, Adam	194
,, Alexander	203
,, Charles	210
,, Duncan	195, 196
,, George	202
,, Humphrey	201, 202
,, Ivone	177, 190
,, James	210
,, Robert	209
,, Roger	189, 195, 196, 198, 203, 205
,, Stephen	195
,, Thomas	198, 202, 203, 204, 205, 209, 210
Kneller, Godfrey	13, 15, 19
Knights Templar	120, 237
Knockconey, Moss of	81, 82
Kulenhat, Adam de	195
Kylosbern	174
Lag	136
Lagdow	105, 136

	PAGE
Langside, Battle of	43
Laurie, Bonnie Annie	65, 66, 348
Laurie, Simon S., Esq.	300
Law	175
Lawson, Mrs.	268
Legendary Tales of Drumlanrig Castle	28
Leitch, 'Water-Colours of	15
Lely, Peter	12
Lennox, Earl of	40
Liddel's Moat	101
Lime Tree	33
Living in Early Times	149
Lochaber Axe	142
Lochmaben, Battle near	38
Long Gun	132
Lowthers	106, 144
Lukup	7
Lyndesay, Sir James de	4
Lyon, Dame Jean	79
Maccuswell, John de	194
M'Gachen	98
M'Michael, Daniel	135
M'Murdo, Family of	66, 72, 393
Mandeville	177, 186
Manrent, Bond of	40, 204
Mar, Earl of	11, 104
,, Burn of	158
Marlborough, Duchess of	15
Mary, Queen	19
Maxwell, John	67
Maxwell, W.	73
Maxwell, Sir George, of Pollock	46, 49
Menoc,	143, 160
Menteth, Family of	211-213
,, Sir Charles G. S., Bart.	212
,, Sir James	212
,, John de	200

Menzies, Family of	88-94
Merlin	101
Meyners, Family of	88
,, Robert de	88, 194
Mid Cairn	169
Ministers of Closeburn	229-231
,, of Durisdeer	122
,, of Kirkbryde	122
,, of Morton	325
Moat of Balagan	137
,, of Gateslack	139
,, of Hawick	138
,, of Liddel	101
,, of Mark	138
,, of Merkland	139
,, of Tynwald Hill	138
Morton, Castle of	309-312, 317
,, Church of	324-326
,, Entrenchments of	306
,, Heights of	331
,, Minerals	335
,, Ministers of	325
,, Poor of	330
,, Population of	329
,, Roads of	332
,, Schools of	328
,, Streams of	331
,, Topography of	330
,, Valuation of	334
,, Woods of	332
Mundell, Alexander	278
,, Robert	278
,, Family of	188
Murray, Adam, of Drumcrieff	83
Museum	362-369
Myres	145
Napier, Barbara	78

	PAGE
Napiers,	76
Neidpath	33
Ninian's Well, St.,	238
Nith Bridge	333
,, River	157
Norsemen	175
Oak at Doocot Knowe	32
Oaks at Drumlanrig	22, 32
,, at Lochwood	32
,, in Peat Moss of Ingleston	34
,, at Closeburn Castle	249
"Old Mortality"	352-359
Orkney, Earl of	90
Osbern	174
Osbernston	174
Paintings in Drumlanrig Castle	10
Panbride	112
Pedder Crook	102
Peithwyr	101, 102
Penbane	142
Penbreck	173
Pennirsax	191
Penpont, Presbytery of	301
Penzerie, Douglases of	38
Perth, Duke of	19
Picts' Wall	102, 169, 305
Picture Gallery	9
Poldivan Stream	193
Polly Stewart	254-264
Postal Communication	147
Pottis Shank	169
Priest's Pool	22, 120
Queensberry Property	61
,, ,, Value of	63
Queensberry Hill	100, 242
Quincey, Roger de	194

	PAGE
Rabbling	117
Rae, Rev. Peter .	8, 20, 22, 119, 163
Rain-fall .	160
Ramage, C. T.	296
Ramsay, Allan	115
Ramsay, Rev. D. Ogilvy	247, 303
Randolph	312-315
Red House	79, 319
Rankine, Sir John	109
Reid, Dr. Alexander	351
Riddell on Consistorial Law	57
Ridding .	307
Robert II.	75
Rob's Corse	197
Rogers, Dr. Charles	315
Romans in Closeburn	170
Roman Camp in Durisdeer	105
,, Road in Closeburn	171
Rothes, John, Earl of	19
Roubilliac	110
Roxburgh, Earl of	227
Runic Cross	141
Russell Prizes	339
Rhymer, Thomas the	9
Sampsoune, Annie, Witch	78
Sanquhar Castle .	103
Sark, Battle of	37
Scar	176
Scotch Firs	22
Scott, Lady Mary	11
Scott, Sir David .	38
Scot, Walterus	175
Scott, Sir Walter	28
,, Sir Walter of Branxholm	40
Seton, Alexander de	200
Seymour, Lady Jane	11
Shaw, John	145, 165

	PAGE
Shaws	175
Shepherd, Views by	18
Silver, Sir William	109
,, Sir James	109
Somerset, Duchess of	19
Souter's Seat	241
Stewart, Family of	95
,, Polly	254, 264
,, William	184, 251, 254
Suicides, Bodies of	107
Tankerville, Earl of	26
Templand of Shaws	237
Terregles House	41
Thomas the Rhymer	9
Thorn Tree of Kirkbride	116
Thornhill	336-346
Thorscleugh	143
Thurlow, Lord	16
Tod, John, of Craigieburn	83
Tod, The Rev. Thomas	83, 124
Topach Cairn	169
Traditions	185
Traquhair, John, Earl of	10
Trees in Drumlanrig	32, 33
Tripoli Ambassador	19
Tumuli	168
Tybaris, Barony of	6, 181
,, Castle of	103
Tynron, Woods of	8
Urns at Wallace Hall	171
Urus Sylvestris	25
Vault, Douglas	381
Vanora	100
Villiers, Frederick Ernest, Esq.	217
Virgin Mary, Altar of	111

	PAGE
Waddel, Rev. Mr.	67, 74
Wald-path	144, 153
Wallace, Sir William, in Closeburn	195, 197
,, ,, in Durisdeer	103
,, ,, Kist of	197, 241
Wallace Hall School	270-303
Walpole, Horace	16
Watchman Knowe	312
Well, Bruce's	197
,, Catherine's	238
,, St. Cuthbert's	110
,, Francis	244
,, Holywell	110
,, King's	197
,, Mary's	328
,, My Lady's	238
,, Moses	238
,, St. Ninian's	238
,, St. Patrick's	328
,, Physic	244
,, Town Cleugh	244
Wharton, Lord	35, 40
White Hose	132
White Neck	82
Wild Cattle	25
William of Orange	18
Wilson, Elias	126
Witchcraft	78
Woods of Drumlanrig	29, 33
,, of Durisdeer	148
,, of Neidpath	33
,, of Morton	332
Wordsworth	33
Yew Trees	22
Young, Peter	109
Yorstoun, Family of	72, 378

EARLY HISTORY OF DURISDEER.

It has been well said of the Douglas family by an old poet,

> "So many, so good, as of the Douglases have been,
> Of one Sirname were ne'er in Scotland seen,"

and as a proof of the truth of this remark it will be observed that the branch of Drumlanrig has continued to flourish down to the present time with all the freshness and vigour of its early days. For many centuries its thews and sinews were at the service of Scotland against its old enemies, and in these piping times of peace its representative is still in the front rank, leading the way in every praiseworthy enterprise that can improve his countrymen and advance their real interests. The Douglas branch, from which his Grace the Duke of Buccleuch and Queensberry is descended, was planted here five hundred years ago, when the first of the Stewarts was near the close of his reign, and while many other noble families have sunk and disappeared, the Drumlanrig shoot has maintained its ground, and at the present moment stands out prominently before Scotland, illustrating the truth of the observation of Ben Jonson—

> "I would have you
> Not stand so much on your gentility,
> Which is an airy and mere borrow'd thing
> From dead men's dust and bones: and none of yours
> Except you make and hold."

War had its hero in Sir William Douglas, who fell at the battle of Flodden with so many of his brave countrymen; peace had its supporter in Duke James, who carried by his energy and prudence the union of the two kingdoms, to which the present prosperity of Scotland must in a great measure be ascribed; while Duke Walter of Buccleuch passes on the torch which has been handed to him by his ancestors to others, who will equally feel with those who have gone before them—

> "*Genus et proavos, et quæ non fecimus ipsi,
> Vix ea nostra voco.*"

> "The deeds of long descended ancestors
> Are but by grace of imputation ours,
> Theirs in effect."

BARONY OF DRUMLANRIG.

The barony of Drumlanrig, which became the home of this family, belonged at an early period to the great Douglas family, as is shown in a charter of Drumlanrig muniment room. "By David II., King of Scots, a new grant and confirmation to William, Lord Douglas, knight, of all lands, revenues, and possessions belonging to him at that time, in his own right or in right of his uncle, James, Lord Douglas, or of his father, Archibald de Douglas, knight, particularly his lands of the barony of Drumlanrig, with all the liberties and appurtenances, as granted to him and to his wife Marguerite, the King's cousin, by (the lady's brother) Thomas, Earl of Mar, November 13th, in the twenty-eighth year of David's reign, which was 1356."

This is, I believe, the earliest notice in any charter of

this barony, so that it can be traced back to 1356, but a few years after this there is a charter under the great seal by Robert II., dated 28th May, 1374, granting to James Blair the lands of Corshoggyl (Coshogle) in this barony.

The barony stretched from the Marr Burn, close to Drumlanrig Castle upwards along the western side of the river Nith into Sanquhar parish, including some lands on the eastern side of the river, and also others in the parishes of Dunscore and Penpont. So far as I have observed in old documents the following lands belonged to it, but there may have been others which have not come under my notice:—Glenym, Fardine-Malloch, Dalpeddar, Auchensow, Auchingreuch, Castle-Gilmour, Muirhouse, Powgaun (Polgowan), Arkland, Dalgoner, Balagan, Coshogle, Benzery, Benans, Corsfarding, Ellioc.

We find it conferred by James, Earl of Douglas and Marr, on his son, Sir William de Douglas, who became the first Baron of Drumlanrig. This grant is "*Gullielmo de Duglas, filio nostro et heredibus suis de corpore suo legitime procreandis,*" by charter without a date, but which was necessarily granted before 19th August, 1388. The lands are "the entire barony of Drumlanrig, lying in the shire of Dumfries, with the Milns, woods, fishings, the right of jurisdiction, those of hawking and hunting, and all other rights belonging to the barony, except the right of regality only, which Earl Douglas reserves to himself, making a free gift of the rest as a fee of him and his heirs by serving as a knight in their host, *nomine albe firme. Testibus Domino Archibaldo de Duglas, domino Gallovidie, Jacobo de Duglas, domino de Dalkeith, Jacobo de Lindesay, domino de Crauford, Willelmo de Lindesay, Roberto Colvyle, Willelmo de Borthwick, consanguineis nostris, Militibus,*

Adamo Forrester, Adamo de Hop-pringle, Alano de Laudre, cum multis aliis."

It is not without interest to see who were the witnesses to this deed, and on examination it will be found that they were the most important personages in the realm.

Archibald de Douglas, Lord of Galloway, was third Earl of Douglas, and popularly known as the *Grim*. He surpassed all Scotchmen of his age in civil wisdom, prowess, and hardy enterprise, in the extent of his acquisitions, and his wealth. The dark visage and stern countenance of Archibald the Grim is thought to be well depicted in a painting still to be seen in Drumlanrig Castle, though it may be doubted whether any representation of this bold baron can have come down to us.

James de Douglas, the next witness, was Lord of Dalkeith, and succeeded his uncle in his extensive property, obtaining a charter from David II. in 1368 of the barony and castle of Dalkeith. He was married to Agnes de Dunbar, sister of the Earl of March.

Sir James de Lyndesay, of Crawford, seems to have been taken at Otterburn, as Richard II. issued an order 25th September, 1388, to Henry de Percy, Earl of Northumberland, "*quod Jacobum de Lyndesay de Scotia, chivaler, jam noviter captum de guerra per nostram partem, nullomodo deliberari faciatis.* (Rym. Fœd., vii., 607.)

William de Lyndesay, brother of Sir James de Lyndesay.

Robert de Colvyle (Colvill) had a charter of the barony of Ochiltrie in Ayrshire from King David II., was lord of Oxnam, with lands in Dumfriesshire, which he forfeited.

Sir William de Borthwick, an ancestor of Lord Borthwick.

Sir Adam Forrester, a wealthy burgess, was a friend of David II. and Robert II., from both of whom he received charters confirmatory of many lands. He was taken prisoner at the battle of Homildon, 1402.

Notwithstanding this array of witnesses, the date was omitted to be added, rendering the deed of no effect; and to confirm its legality as far as it could be, Sir William obtained from John de Swintoune and his wife, Marguerite, Countess of Douglas and Marr, the mother of James, second Earl of Douglas, a recognizance of the foregoing grant, by their faithful promise never to call it in question, that so the barony of Drumlanrig might be freely possessed by the above William de Douglas and his descendants, according to the concession of his father, the Earl, dated 5th December, 1389. To make the grant doubly sure, he obtained another confirmation by James I. in a letter of which the original is elegantly engrossed on vellum with the King's own hand, and preserved in the charter-room of Drumlanrig, in these words:—" James, throu the grace of God, Kynge of Scottis, till all this lettre hereis or seis, Sendis gretynge. Wit ye that we haue granntit and be thir present lettre grannts a special confirmacion in the mast forme, till our traiste and wele belofit cosyng, Sir William of Douglas of Drumlangrig, of all the lands that he is possessit and Charterit of within the kyngdome of Scotland; that is to say, The Landis of Drumlangrig, of Hawyke, and of Selkirke; the which Charter and possessions, by this Lettre we confirm, and will for the mair sickerness, this our confirmacion be formabilli after the fourme of our Chaunsellere and the Tenor of the Charteris seled with oure grete sele in tyme to come. In witness of the whilkis thir presentis Lettre we wrote with oure proper hande under the Signet ussit in seling of our Lettris, as now at Croidoun the last day of Novembre, the yeir of oure Lorde 1412."

DRUMLANRIG CASTLE.

This was no doubt from the first the manor-house of the barony, though it is curious that it should have been set down at its very extremity, so near to the boundary that an arrow-shot could easily have been sent into the adjoining barony of Tybaris, which belonged to the great Earls of March, and latterly to the Maitlands of Lethington. One might almost imagine that it was the same feeling that actuated the head of the Breadalbane family, who, when some of his friends expressed surprise that he should place his mansion at the extremity of his land, coolly answered, "We'll breast yont;" and so surely enough both families have "breasted yont," as in all directions the Douglases added to their possessions till the eye could scarcely light on a spot which they did not call their own.

At what period a baronial residence was erected at this spot it is impossible to say, but it would scarcely be in existence before the barony was made over about 1388 to Sir William Douglas, the founder of this branch of the Douglas family. It was built on the southern edge of the barony, and close to the Castle of Tybaris, which probably existed at a much earlier period. Tradition hands down that there were two houses previous to the later castle, and this may have been the case though we have no written records to prove it. The site was well chosen on the end of a Drum or long ridge of a hill, looking down on a small glen, through which flows the Marr Burn, and having an extensive view of the whole valley of the Nith, closed in by the distant Criffel. Within the present castle some remnants of the more ancient building are to be found in the south-east corner, where the dungeon once existed, at present turned to a more joyous purpose, furnishing the guests of the noble proprietor with wine "that maketh the heart glad." The castle in its present quadrangular form is believed to have been on the design of Inigo Jones, but this can scarcely be, as that celebrated architect died in 1651, and the castle was not begun till 1679, nearly thirty years after the death of Jones. The origin of this idea is its resemblance to Heriot's Hospital in Edinburgh, which was thought to have been designed by Jones. There is, however, no certain proof that even Heriot's Hospital was his design.

Be this as it may, there is a plan made of wood, with proper elevations, which it is evident the master of the works, Mr. Lukup, had closely followed, but whether this was an original plan of his own there is no means of knowing. I have been told that some one saw in a foreign library or picture gallery plans of a building like Drumlanrig Castle, and that it proved that Lukup designed this building, but this is too vague a statement to allow us to place dependence upon it. The castle was begun to be built in 1679, and seems to have been finished in 1689, under the direction of William, the first Duke of Queensberry. There had, however, been a castle here so early as 1492, as it is mentioned in the following charter of James IV., dated Edinburgh, 19th May:—

"*Rex concessit Gul^{mo} Douglas filio et heredi app. Jac. Dowglas de Drumlangrig, Terras et Baroniam de Drumlangrig cum castro (Castle) de Drumlangrig et Molendinum, eorundem,*" &c. This is probably the first notice of a baronial residence on this site. The earliest date found at present at Drumlanrig is 1645, on a separate stone in the garden. This was the very year that James, second

Earl of Queensberry, was fined so heavily by the Long Parliament.

Duke William seems to have regretted the expense, as tradition hands down that he denounces in writing on the bundle of accounts a bitter curse on any of his posterity who offered to inspect them. "The Deil pike out his een, wha looks herein," but at all events, the expense must have been great, and that it kept the noble proprietor in difficulties is proved by an amusing anecdote told by the late Miss Clerk Douglas of Holmhill. She had a letter addressed by the Duchess of Duke William imploring Archibald Douglas, her ancestor, and at that time Chamberlain, in most pathetic terms, to send her some small sum to purchase a silk gown, as she was penniless.

It is a stately building, and when seen embosomed amidst the green foliage of a summer's day it is a striking object. The quarry, from which the earlier houses were built, is believed to be on the western side of the river, near the bridge, where a loch is now found. The present castle was chiefly constructed from stones quarried from the opposite side. It is soft freestone, and the sharp lines of the carving have begun to disappear. The walls have sunk in some parts, and it has been necessary to clasp them firmly with iron bars. Rae, in his Manuscript Account of Tynron, when he refers to the woods of that parish, says that Mr. Lukup told him "that when the house was building Sir Robert Grierson of Lag gifted to Queensberry eleven score of tall stately oaks out of Craignee wood for joists to the said house, and could spare a good cut off the thick end of them." These joists were obliged to be replaced a few years ago, as the ends had given way, and the centre of the drawing-room had sunk as much as six inches. The greater part of the wood, however, was found to be quite sound, and as hard as stone; it being supposed that the ends had suffered by the housemaid's pails of water, which had sunk down through the floor. There was a picture gallery running along the northern side of the castle for one hundred and forty-five feet, and in which the Highlanders spent a night in 1745 on their retreat from England. The room was ornamented by carving in wood by the celebrated Grinling Gibbons, and this carving is now found partly in the dining and partly in the drawing room. In early times the castle was known as the house of the Hassock, and there was an old couplet predicting the fall of the family of Douglas in which this name appears:—

> "When the Marr Burn rins where man never saw,
> The House of the Hassock is near a fa'."

This stanza has been ascribed to Thomas of Ercildoun, or, as he is better known, the Rhymer; but it is more likely to have been of a much later date, and to have originated about or shortly after the time of the religious troubles in Scotland in the time of Charles II., and may be regarded not so much as a prophecy, but rather as a bitter exclamation, in which "the wish was father to the thought." The answer to this malicious poetaster is found in another couplet, which runs thus:—

> "He who stands on the Hassock hill
> Shall rule all Nithsdale at his will."

The prophecy of the fall of the family was considered by the superstitious as likely to be fulfilled when this Marr Burn was diverted from its original channel into a ditch, familiarly called the race, which, after many a turning and winding, delivered its waters at Jock and the Horn (and also a part of them fountain-wise through the Horn) over a steep, jagged rock, and thus formed a cascade opposite to the south front of Drumlanrig Castle, and, of course, within view of the dining-room and drawing-room windows. It was when this race was made by order of Lady Catherine Hyde, the Duchess of Duke Charles, that it was thought the first half of the prophecy was being fulfilled, and many imagined that the latter half would also be found to be true at no distant date. Indeed, it was thought to be so by the superstitious when Duke William died in 1810 without issue, and the property passed to the noble family of Buccleuch.

PAINTINGS IN DRUMLANRIG CASTLE.

In the dining-room are the following:—

1. Earl of Traquhair. He was the father of Lady Margaret, wife of James, second Earl of Queensberry, and mother of the first Duke. He stood high in favour with Charles I., who created him a Peer, 19th April, 1628. He joined in the attempt in 1648 to rescue Charles, and was made prisoner at the battle of Preston, being sent under a strong guard to Warwick Castle, where he was confined four years. Being at last released, he returned home, where he suffered extreme poverty, and died September, 1659. Lord Clarendon (Hist. Rev., i., 108) says:—"The Earl of Traquair was, without doubt, not inferior to any in that nation (Scotland) in wisdom and dexterity; and, though he was often provoked by the insolence of some of the bishops to a dislike of their overmuch favour and too little discretion, his integrity to the King was without blemish, and his affection to the

Church so notorious that he never deserted it till both it and he were overrun and trode under foot, and they, who were the most notorious persecutors of it, never left persecuting him to the death."

2. Earl of Marr. This is John Erskine, ninth Earl, the husband of Lady Mary Scott, eldest daughter of Walter, first Earl of Buccleuch. He was a staunch Royalist, was at the battle of Philiphaugh, 19th September, 1645, and escaped with Montrose to Marr, where he raised forces for the King's service. For this he was fined 24,000 merks, and soldiers were quartered on his estate. He succeeded his father 1654, but his estates continued under sequestration till the restoration, during which time he lived in a cottage at the gate of his house at Alloa. He died in September, 1668.

3. Lady Jane Seymour, married to Lord Clifford, youngest daughter and co-heiress of William, second Duke of Somerset. Lord Clifford was eldest son of first Earl of Burlington. Their daughter, Lady Mary Boyle, was wife of James, second Duke of Queensberry, and is buried at Durisdeer, where her husband erected a magnificent mausoleum to her honour, recording his attachment in the following affecting terms:—

"*Mariæ, Ducissæ Queensberriæ et Doverni, &c., quæ paternâ stirpe e Burlingtonii et Cumbriæ, maternâ vero Somerseti et Essexiæ familiis prælustribus oriunda generis splendorem morum suavitate temperavit, animi magnitudine auxit, Et severiorem virtutem honestis ingenii et formæ illecebris, Jucundam reddidit et benignam Marito amantissimo dum variâ Rerum vice exerceretur, In secundis decus, in dubiis stabilimen, in asperis solamen, Curarum Thalami et consiliorum sanctissimum depossitum, Conjugi incomparabili Jacobus Dux Queensberriæ et Doverni,*

"*Eâ spe et hoc unico solatio, quod sub eodem marmore ubi hos caros deposuit cineres,*

"*Suos depositurus sit, Hoc monumentum extrui jussit. Obiit Londini, Octobris 2, 1709.*"

"To Mary, Duchess of Queensberry and Dover, &c., who, being sprung on the father's side from the very illustrious families of Burlington and Cumberland, on the mother's from those of Somerset and Essex, tempered the splendour of her lineage by a winning disposition, heightened it by greatness of spirit, and rendered by the seductive allurement of her wit and beauty her sterner virtue pleasing and acceptable to her most loving husband, while he was engaged in the ever-changing affairs of State, in prosperity an ornament, in 'straits a very present help,' in adversity a comfort, in the cares and councils of domestic life a most faithful partner, to his matchless wife, James, Duke of Queensberry and Dover, has caused this monument to be erected, with this hope and only solace, that under the same tomb, where he has placed these beloved ashes, he will place his own. Died at London, 2nd October, 1709."

The painting of Lady Seymour, afterwards Countess of Burlington, is by Sir Peter Lely. Here, as in many other of Sir Peter's pictures, we have the graceful posture of the head and the delicate rounding of the hands.

4. The Earl of Burlington. This is the first Earl, grandfather of Lady Mary Boyle. It was painted by Sir Peter Lely.

5. Lady Jane Douglas, second daughter of James, second Duke of Queensberry, &c., married 5th April, 1720, to Francis, Earl of Dalkeith, afterwards Duke of Buccleuch, dying 31st August, 1729. Her grandson, Henry, Duke of Buccleuch, succeeded as heir of entail to the Dukedom of Queensberry and great estates in

Dumfriesshire in 1810. This painting is by Sir Godfrey Kneller, and has less of the mannerism that is so conspicuous in many of his works, though here too we have the oval of the head greatly lengthened.

6. William, last Duke of Queensberry, was third Earl of March, born 16th December, 1725, and succeeded his cousin in 1778 as fourth Duke of Queensberry, thus uniting in his person three distinct peerages. His Grace was well known on the turf and in the circles of fashion, and after possessing a peerage for eighty years, died at London, 23rd December, 1810, in the eighty-sixth year of his age, unmarried. In him terminated the male line of William, first Duke of Queensberry; the descendants of John, Earl of Ruglen; and of William, Earl of March. The titles of Duke of Queensberry, Marquis of Dumfriesshire, Earl of Drumlanrig and Sanquhar, Viscount of Nith, Torthorwald, and Ross, Lord Douglas of Kinmount, Middlebie, and Dornock, with the barony of Drumlanrig and other extensive property in the county of Dumfries, devolved in terms of the patent, 1706, and in virtue of an entail executed by the second Duke, on Henry, Duke of Buccleuch, the heir of line of the Queensberry family, who was thenceforward designed Duke of Buccleuch and Queensberry. The titles of Marquis and Earl of Queensberry, Viscount of Drumlanrig, Lord Douglas of Hawick and Tibbers, devolved on the heir male of the family, Sir Charles Douglas of Kelhead, Bt., in terms of the patents 1628, 1633, and 1682, along with the baronies of Tinwald and Torthorwald and other estates in Dumfriesshire. The titles of Earl of March, Viscount of Peebles, and Lord Douglas of Neidpath, Lyne, and Munard, devolved on the Earl of Wemyss. It seems not to be known by whom this painting was executed.

PAINTINGS IN DRAWING-ROOM.

1. Henry Douglas, Earl of Drumlanrig, eldest son of Charles, third Duke of Queensberry, born 30th October, 1722, was educated at Winchester College,

"When Bigg presided and when Burton taught,"

and at the University of Oxford. He entered the army and distinguished himself so much that Charles Emmanuel, King of Sardinia, ordered his ambassador in London to wait on the Duke of Queensberry to thank him for the services performed by his son. He married, 24th July, 1754, Lady Elizabeth Hope, eldest daughter of John, second Earl of Hopetoun. After passing some weeks in Scotland, he proceeded with his bride towards England, and riding before the carriage was killed by the going off of one of his own pistols, near Bawtrey, in Yorkshire, 19th October, 1754, in his thirty-second year. This painting is said to be by Sir Godfrey Kneller, but this is quite impossible, as Sir Godfrey died in 1723, one year after the birth of the Earl. It is difficult even to conjecture the name of the artist who executed this painting and that of his wife, Lady Elizabeth Hope, as after the death of Sir Godfrey there is a great gap where there is no celebrated artist. Sir Joshua Reynolds was indeed coming into notice about 1754, and it is just possible that these two paintings may be by Sir Joshua.

2. Lady Elizabeth Hope, eldest daughter of John, second Earl of Hopetoun, married to Henry, Earl of Drumlanrig, never recovered the shock of her husband's sad death, and dying childless, 7th April, 1756, in her twenty-first year, was buried with her husband at Durisdeer. This painting is also said to be by Sir Godfrey Kneller,

but there is the same objection as in the case of the picture of her husband.

3. The Duchess of Marlborough. There is a doubt respecting the individual represented by this picture, but if it be Sarah, Duchess of Marlborough, then it is likely to be by Kneller, as it is believed to be. Her hair was of a pale honey colour, and doubtless of a very pure and rich tint. There is a pathetic anecdote respecting her hair, how being once in a towering rage with her husband, who admired her hair as her chief ornament, she, to spite him, cut off her abundant tresses, laid them on a table in an ante-room, where the Duke found them and put them in his cabinet, where, after his death, she discovered them among his most valued treasures. There are several portraits of this lady at Althorpe, in which her hair is always of this auburn colour.

Ante-chamber to Drawing-room.—Chancellor Hyde. This is Edward Hyde, the great historian of the Rebellion, Earl of Clarendon, and Lord High Chancellor of England, who died 9th December, 1674. It is the representative of a thoughtful old gentleman, but who was the artist is unknown. It is likely to have been Sir Peter Lely or Sir Godfrey Kneller.

Sitting-room of Duchess.—A variety of views of Drumlanrig Castle, in water colours, taken from different points, by Leitch.

Morning-room.—Lady Catherine Hyde, wife of Duke Charles, was second daughter of Henry, Earl of Clarendon and Rochester, celebrated for her beauty, wit, and sprightliness, by Pope, Swift, and other poets, particularly by Prior in his well-known ballad beginning—

"Thus Kitty, beautiful and young,
 And wild as colt untam'd."

At the funeral of the Princess Dowager of Wales, 1772, her Grace, walking as one of the assistants to the chief mourners, occasioned these verses by Horace Walpole, Earl of Oxford—

> "To many a Kitty Love his ear
> Would for a day engage;
> But Prior's Kitty, ever fair,
> Obtain'd it for an age."

This picture in the morning-room has an interesting anecdote connected with it. When the Duchess was seventy-five years of age, Lord Thurlow, at that time Attorney-General (1776), had gained the Douglas law-suit, in which she took a warm interest, and from a feeling of gratitude for his services, she agreed, at his request, to sit for this picture for him. It descended from him to a grand-niece, Mrs. Brown. At her death it was left by her to her nieces, the Misses Ellis. It remained with them till the last of them died in 1860, when it was sold. It was bought by the Duke of Buccleuch from the executors of the Earl of Chatham. The picture represents the Duchess as still possessing in her advanced years great beauty, showing eyes of sparkling brightness, and a most winning expression. The artist is unknown. There was a copy of this picture at Drumlanrig, now in his Grace's business-room, but it is Hyperion to a Satyr when compared with the original. The head is curiously enveloped in a white kerchief.

In the same room there is another picture of the Duchess over the fire-place, which must have been painted when she was many years younger, and is a fine representation of her lovely face. In this, too, her head is covered, though not in the same way. In the main staircase there is a marble bust of the same Duchess.

Lady Catherine Hyde must have possessed from her earliest years great beauty, as she inspired poets, great and small, to sing her charms. In Lord Lansdowne's Poems (Cooke's Edition, p. 31) we find that George Granville, Lord Lansdowne, wrote three poems on this lady, entitled as follows:—"Lady Hyde having the Small-pox soon after the Recovery of Mrs. Mohun," "Lady Hyde sitting at Sir Godfrey Kneller's for her Picture," "Lady Hyde." The first four lines to "Lady Hyde" run thus:

> "When fam'd Apelles sought to frame
> Some image of th' Idalian dame,
> To furnish graces for the piece,
> He summon'd all the nymphs of Greece."

There is another poem, "On Lady K. Hyde's Picture done by Sir Godfrey Kneller," by an unknown writer. As Sir Godfrey died in 1723, Lady Catherine could only have been, at the very most, sixteen years of age when this picture was painted. It runs thus:

> "By milk-white Doves, as drawn of old,
> Venus, the Queen of Love,
> Sr Godfrey's paintings to behold,
> Descended from above.
>
> "When to the earth ye goddess came,
> Pleas'd and surpriz'd the same,
> Thy labours, Kneller, and thy Fame
> Salsb'ry and Ranelagh;
>
> "Fixt on Miranda, streight she cries
> Astonisht, Here I trace
> No modern shades, no mortal eyes,
> Apelles' art, my face.

"But soon as her mistake she found
 (I swear by all that's pretty),
I thought the goddess would have swoon'd
 To hear 'twas Lady Kitty.

"Poor Venus! I must fairly tell her
 (What cannot be deny'd),
Apelles is outdone by Kneller,
 As Venus is by Hyde."

I have not been able to discover who is now the possessor of this celebrated picture of Kneller, unless the second picture in the morning-room be the picture referred to.

The Duchess was a keen politician, and the following anecdote is still prevailing amongst us. On an election day she and the Duke were driving from Drumlanrig Castle to Dumfries, and on passing Closeburn saw Sir Thomas Kirkpatrick (who was on the opposite side of politics) hastening on before them, when the Duchess called out in her usual lusty way to the coachman to drive with all his might, "else Tam o' Closeburn," she exclaimed, "will get before us and lick the butter off our bread;" upon which the Duke mildly replied, "Why, my lady Duchess, let me tell you that the Kirkpatricks were belted knights of Closeburn when we were but spitten lairds of Drumlanrig." This anecdote is quite in keeping with the kindly character of his Grace, who is still known in the district as the "guid Duke Charles."

In the morning-room there are a number of views of Drumlanrig from various points by Shepherd, and also among them a representation of a Welsh legend, "The Fairies comb the Goat's beards to make them tidy for Sunday."

Principal Staircase.—King William of Orange. At the bottom of the staircase there is a painting of King

William on a white charger, after the battle of the Boyne, 1st July, 1690. This picture was transfixed by the bayonets of the Highlanders in 1745, as they returned from England on their way to the north. The marks are still to be seen. The artist is Sir Godfrey Kneller.

King William and Queen Mary. These pictures, found in the staircase, are believed to be by Sir Godfrey Kneller.

Queen Anne and Prince George of Denmark. These are also supposed to be by Sir Godfrey Kneller.

A Tripoli Ambassador. This picture, also believed to be by Kneller, represents the Ambassador drawing his sword when he was threatened to be imprisoned for debt. It is possibly the best work of art in Drumlanrig Castle.

At the time that Pennant visited Drumlanrig about 1770 there seem to have been paintings, which have disappeared, unless some of them now to be found there have got mis-named in the course of time. He mentions "The first Duchess of Somerset, half length, no cap, with a small love-lock."

"John, Earl of Rothes, Chancellor of Scotland, in his gown, with the seals by him. He was in power during the cruel persecutions of the Covenanters in Charles II.'s time, and discharging his trust to the satisfaction of the Court was created Duke of Rothes, a title that died with him." May this painting not be what is now considered Chancellor Hyde?

"A head of the Duke of Perth, in a bushy wig: a post-abdication Duke, a converted favourite of James II., and Chancellor of Scotland at the time of the Revolution, when he retired into France."

"George Douglas, Earl of Dumbarton, in armour, great wig and cravat. Instructed in the art of war in the armies of Louis XIV., was General of the forces in Scotland under James II., dispersed the army of the unfortunate Argyle. A gallant officer, who, when James was at Salisbury, generously offered to attack the Prince of Orange with his single regiment of the Scottish Royal, not with the hope of victory, but of giving him such a check as his Sovereign might take advantage of; James with equal generosity would not permit the sacrifice of so many brave men. Dumbarton adhered to the King in all fortunes, and on the abdication partook of his exile."

"General James Douglas, who, in 1691, died at Namur."

"Earl of Clarendon, son of the Chancellor, half length, in his robes."

GARDENS.

The gardens of Drumlanrig Castle are a great attraction at all times, but in the beginning of autumn they show to more advantage than at any other period of the year. If we look from the southern front of the castle down upon the gardens, we have, in addition to the green sloping banks, the beautiful configuration of flower-plots in the finest harmony. It is astonishing when taste presides and wealth is at command how much beauty the skilled hand of the designer may elicit by the simplest contrivances. It is not, however, now for the first time that Drumlanrig has been famed for beautiful gardens. About the beginning of last century they were equally the object of admiration. The Rev. Peter Rae, in his Manuscript History of Durisdeer, thus describes them in his time (1700-1740):—"The gardens of Drumlanrig are very beautiful, and the rather because of their variety.

... The regular gardens, with one designed to be made on the back of the plumbery, the outer court before the house, and the house itself make nine square plots of ground, whereof the kitchen garden, the court before the house, and the garden designed make three; my lady Duchess's garden, the house, and the last parterre and the flower garden make other three, that is nine in all, and the castle is in the centre. Only as to the last three, the westernmost is always more than a story above the rest. As to these called irregular gardens, because the course of the Parkburn would not allow them to be square, they are very pretty, and well suited to one another. They call one part thereof Virginia, the other Barbadoes; there goes a large gravel walk down betwixt them from the south parterre to the cascade." This cascade is no longer in existence, but within the recollection of the present generation the remains of it, with a leaden figure of a man, who was well known as "Jock and the Horn," could be seen. The gardens were still in existence in their original form in 1772, when Pennant passed through Scotland. He refers to them thus:—" In the gardens, which are most expensively cut out of a rock, is a bird cherry of a great size, not less than 7 feet 8 inches in girth; and among several fine silver firs one $13\frac{1}{2}$ feet in circumference." It is difficult to understand what Pennant means when he says that the gardens were cut out of a rock. There must, indeed, have been a great deal of expense incurred in levelling and making the ground, but there does not appear to have been much rock, if any, to blast. The bird cherry or *gean* (French *guigne*) no longer exists, nor any large silver firs; there is, however, a fine specimen of the common Scotch fir close to the side of the old cascade, which measures nearly eleven feet of girth at the base, and in Auchenaight wood there are two Scotch firs of remarkable size. "Particulars of No. 1—height, 64 feet; length of bole, 11 feet; girth of bole, 8 feet 6 inches; spread of branches, 48 feet; contents, 170 cubic feet; altitude, about 320 feet above sea level. Particulars of No. 2—height, 50 feet; length of bole, 17 feet 6 inches, girth of bole, 8 feet 10 inches; spread of branches, 51 feet; contents, 100 cubic feet; altitude above sea level, 300 feet." (Journal of Agriculture, 1865.)

Some of the yew-trees are still larger, one of them being twelve feet and a half in girth; but these yews do not grow from a single stem, shooting up with a number of stems from the root. An oak, which grows on the edge of what is known as the Gallows Flat, is probably the oldest tree in Drumlanrig park. There are some old beech-trees in the park, but though they may seem to claim a greater age from their girth, the oak grows at a much slower rate.

DRUMLANRIG BRIDGE.

This bridge is one of the oldest over the Nith, though Dumfries Old Bridge may be of a still earlier date. There is no tradition as to its building; it is shrouded in the mist of ages. There are no documents to show at what period it was erected. Possibly it may owe its origin to the ecclesiastical authorities in olden times. Below it there is the Priest's Pool, and Priest's Holm, showing that they were close to it. The earliest notice of the bridge is found in the MS. account of Durisdeer by Peter Rae, who speaks of it thus:—"It has been constantly reported that one of the priests of the chappell below Enoch town built Drumlanrig bridge, and this I am apt to believe; the rather that a gentleman told me that William, Duke of Queensberry, declared to him that he could find no documents that any of his family built it. This bridge, then, seems to be very old, and may well be reckoned among the monuments of antiquity in this parish and country. The building of this bridge was truly *bonum opus*, a good (though I do not say, in the Popish sense, a meritorious) work. It is certainly a great blessing to the country, who have occasion to travel that way both about their civil and religious concerns, and has been the means to save the lives of many; that river not being fordable within two miles above, and a mile below it, save only in great drought. This bridge consists of two arches, though at the top of it it is not much higher than the ground next to it at each end. The east side of the mid pillar had been founded on a frame of wood, which old men told me was carried down the river about forty years before it was repaired. The stones of that part were fallen off almost as high as the arch, and the ledges on both sides were down; yet, notwithstanding carts went along it, and I have travelled that way even while it was in that ruinous condition, as everybody did who had occasion. William, Duke of Queensberry, having resolved to have a bridge of one arch about half a mile further up the river at the end of the avenue opposite to the front of his house, would not be persuaded to repair this; but James, Duke of Queensberry and Dover, after the Union, appointed the Earl of Glasgow, Sir W. Douglas of Kellhead, Archibald Douglas of Cavers, and W. Douglas of Dornock, commissioners of his affairs in Scotland, anno 1703. They agreed with William Lukup (who built the castle) to repair this bridge. For which end he made a large box of deals, which enclosed the said pillar and the arch on the east side, and employed country people to throw out the water and wait on it night and day to keep it dry till he searched down and founded that part of the pillar upon the rock, which he told me was sixteen feet beneath the ordinary surface of the water; clasping the stones all along as they came up to the rocks upon which the pillar stands with in-band clasps of iron to some firm stones in the pillar, till the work was finished, which is done so exactly that it is not discoverable where the old and the new work are joined. He also put ledges upon it, so that it is now an excellent stone bridge, as good as at its first erection."

After a period of one hundred and sixty years, during which scarcely anything was done to the bridge, it began to show symptoms of decay, and to require to be thoroughly overhauled. The Duke of Buccleuch determined at his own expense to put it into a proper state, and gave directions to Mr. Howitt, clerk of the works at Drumlanrig, to take what steps might be necessary for this purpose. In 1860 this was thoroughly accomplished by renewing the spandrils, wing walls, and parapets. When the old arches were uncovered it was curious to find that it must have stood long without what is called a roadway, as the crown of the arches had every appearance of well-worn stairs. This shows that it must have been used for many years merely for foot passengers.

Though it was now repaired at the sole expense of his Grace, this bridge was regarded in the seventeenth century as a bridge which ought to be maintained at the expense of the county, as we find an Act of Parliament passed 17th September, 1681, "in favour of the Shire and Burgh of Dumfries anent a custome upon the water of Nith," in which the Estates of Parliament "doe statute and ordaine that the customs and import of all goods and bestiel . . . at Portract foord and all upwards to the march of Kyle shall hereafter be uplifted by such as shall be appointed by the Earl of Queensberry and the Commissioners of the Shire for repairing and maintaining the bridge of Drumlangrig, wherein the said Burgh of Dumfries is to have no interest."

WILD CATTLE IN DRUMLANRIG PARK.

In the beginning of last century there was a herd of these cattle roaming at large in the park, descendants, as is supposed, of the Urus Sylvestris. Pennant in his tour gives an interesting account of their appearance about 1770, when he saw them as he was passing through Scotland :—" In my walk about the park, see the white breed of wild cattle, derived from the native race of the country, and still retain the primeval savageness and ferocity of their ancestors; were more shy than any deer; ran away on the appearance of any of the human species; and even set off at full gallop on the least noise, so that I was under the necessity of going very softly under the shelter of trees or bushes to get a near view of them. During summer they keep apart from all other cattle; but in severe weather hunger will compel them to visit the out-houses in search of food. The keepers are obliged to shoot them if any are wanted; if the beast is not killed on the spot, it runs at the person who gave the wound, and who is forced, in order to save his life, to fly for safety to the intervention of some tree. These cattle are of a middle size, have very long legs, and the cows are five-horned; the orbits of the eyes and the tips of the noses are black, but the bulls have lost the manes attributed to them by Boece." It was a peculiar habit of the mothers to cover their young offspring with the withered leaves which abounded in the park. There is a tradition that about a hundred years ago the whole stock was sold and driven off *en masse* to Chillingham, the seat of the Earl of Tankerville, in Northumberland, *via* Durisdeer and the Wald-path, and as they were rather an unruly drove, they were accompanied to the confines of the county by almost all the men and dogs in the surrounding district. It does not, however, appear that they were conveyed to Chillingham, as, on communicating with Mr. Jacob Wilson, the agent of the Earl of Tankerville, he says:—"In reply to your queries with reference to the wild cattle in this park, I may inform you that their origin cannot be correctly traced, but we have direct evidence of their having been here for more than 400 years; therefore, the theory of their having come from Drumlanrig is evidently incorrect. Besides, fossilized bones of this animal have also been discovered in this neighbourhood." What became of this herd is thus unknown, nor is there any tradition at what period they were introduced. There were herds to be found in various parts of Scotland and England. Fitz-Stephen, who lived in the twelfth century, speaks of the *uri sylvestres* which in his time inhabited great forests in the neighbourhood of London; and at a later period (fourteenth century), Robert Bruce was nearly slain by a wild bull, which attacked him "in the great Caledon Wood," but from which he was rescued by an attendant. They are still to be found in the park round Hamilton Palace, and the Bos Scoticus may be considered to be a genuine wild animal still existing in the midst of civilization.

In the *Naturalists' Cabinet*, 1806, I find the following paragraph:—

"The cows of this species, at the time of parturition, seek out some sequestered retreat, where they conceal their young for a week or ten days, occasionally going to suckle them. The calves, if approached by anyone, clap their heads close to the ground and lie like a hare in form to hide themselves. This seems a proof of their native wildness, and is corroborated by the following circumstance related by Dr. Fuller, author of the 'History of Berwick.' He found a hidden calf of about two days old, very lean and weak, but on his stroking its head it got up, pawed two or three times like an old bull, bellowed very loud, retreated a few steps, and bolted at his legs with all its force; it then began to paw again, bellowed, stepped back, and bolted as before; but being aware of its intention, he moved aside and it missed its aim and fell, and was so very weak that though it made several efforts it was unable to rise. The noise it had made, however, had alarmed the whole herd, and our author was compelled to retire.

"It has been remarked that when an individual of this species happens to be wounded, or is growing weak and feeble through age and sickness, the rest of the herd set upon it and gore it to death."

It is remarkable that in the old "Niebelungen Lied" of the twelfth century the two kinds of great wild oxen recorded as having been slain in the great hunt of Worms are mentioned under the same names, which we find given them by the Romans, showing that the

Romans had borrowed them from the Teutonic people who then inhabited Germany:—

"Dar nach schluch er schiere einen Wisent und einen Elch,
Starcher Ure vier, und einen grimmin schelch."

"After this he straightway slew a Bisn and an Elk,
Of the Strong Uri four, and a single fierce schelch."

It will be recollected that Scott in his Ballad of Cadzow Castle thus depicts the image of the great Urus in the full vigour of life:

"Mightiest of all the beast of chase
  That roam in woody Caledon,
Crushing the forest in his race,
  The mountain bull comes thundering on.
Fierce on the hunter's quiver'd hand,
  He rolls his eye of swarthy glow,
Spurns with black hoofs and horns the sand."

LEGENDARY TALES OF DRUMLANRIG CASTLE.

Like all old baronial residences, this castle was believed to be haunted by the ghosts of the dead. The most alarming legend was connected with what was known as the "Bloody Passage," where a foul murder had been committed, and the very spot was marked out by the stains of blood which no housemaid's scrubbing could obliterate. It is the passage on the south-side of the castle running above the drawing-room, from which a number of bed-chambers enter. Here, at midnight, the perturbed spirit of a lady, in her night-clothes, parades, bewailing her sad fate, but by whom she had suffered tradition tells not. There is also a haunted room on the east side of the castle, on the fourth story from the ground, where in former times fearful noises used to be heard. It is curious that there was discovered in later times a large aperture running above a passage from this room, and this might have enabled parties to play tricks to alarm strangers. But Drumlanrig was not only frequented by ghosts; its gardens were visited by fairies, who were often seen dancing in the gloaming in the glade opposite to "Jock and the Horn." All these superstitious notions are pretty well got rid of, though they still linger in the minds of the ignorant.

WOODS OF DRUMLANRIG.

During the greater part of last century the castle was surrounded by trees of great age, which attracted the attention of Smollett, as he was passing towards the north. He speaks in enthusiastic terms of the beauty of the country and its umbrageous groves. These woods, however, were doomed to destruction by the last Duke of Queensberry (old Q.), it is believed to spite the noble family who were to succeed him, and at the beginning of this century they had nearly disappeared. They were proceeding to be cut down before 1796, if the following poem, which is said to be by Burns, be genuine. According to M'Kie in his edition of Burns (vol. ii., 378), this poem first appeared in a newspaper, introduced by the following note:—"Though the beauty of the following verses cannot be adequately estimated by those who are unacquainted with the scenery which it was their object to celebrate, yet it is presumed they possess merit sufficient, independently of all adventitious circumstances, to recommend them to the notice of every true lover of the simple and sublime in nature. They were found written on a window-shutter of a small inn on the banks of the Nith soon after the finest scenes that were perhaps to be met with in the south of Scotland had been sacrificed to sordid avarice. Burns is supposed to have been the author; and by his most ardent admirers we believe they will not be thought unworthy the pen of the immortal Bard :"—

> "As on the banks o' wandering Nith
>   Ae smiling morn I strayed,
> And traced its bonnie howes and haughs,
>   Where linties sang and lambkins play'd,
> I sat me down upon a craig,
>   And drank my fill o' fancy's dream,
> When, from the eddying deep below,
>   Uprose the genius of the stream.
>
> "Dark, like the frowning rock, his brow,
>   And troubled, like his wintry wave,
> And deep, as sighs the boding wind
>   Among his eaves, the sigh he gave:
> 'And came ye here, my son,' he cried,
>   'To wander in my birken shade?
> To muse some favourite Scottish theme,
>   Or sing some favourite Scottish maid?
>
> "'There was a time, it's nae lang syne,
>   Ye might hae seen me in my pride;
> When a' my weel-clad banks could see
>   Their woody pictures in my tide;
> When hanging beech and spreading elm
>   Shaded my streams sae clear and cool,
> And stately oaks their twisted arms
>   Threw broad and dark across the pool;
>
> "'When, glinting through the trees, appeared
>   The wee white cot aboon the mill,
> And peacefu' rose its ingle reek,
>   That slowly curling clamb the hill.

>   But now the cot is bare and cauld,
>   Its branchy shelter's lost and gane,
>   And scarce a stinted birch is left
>   To shiver in the blast its lane.'
>
> " 'Alas!' said I, 'what wofu' chance
>   Has twin'd ye o' your stately trees?
>   Has laid your rocky bosom bare?
>   Has stripp'd the cleading aff your braes?
>   Was it the bitter eastern blast,
>   That scatters blight in early spring?
>   Or was't the wil'fire scorched their boughs,
>   Or canker-worm wi' secret sting?'
>
> " 'Nae eastlin blast,' the sprite replied;
>   'It blaws na here sae fierce and fell;
>   And on my dry and halesome banks
>   Nae canker-worms get leave to dwell.
>   Man! cruel man!' the genius sigh'd,
>   As through the cliffs he sank him down,
>   'The worm that gnaw'd my bonnie trees—
>   That reptile wears a Ducal Crown!'"

The property came thus denuded of its beautiful clothing into the possession of Duke Henry of Buccleuch in 1810, and he at once began to replace what had been thus recklessly destroyed. Some of the old trees in the park had escaped the hand of the destroyer, and I have been told that it was in the following way:—The Earl of Dalkeith, afterwards Duke Charles, and father of the present noble Duke of Buccleuch and Queensberry, happened to be in Dumfries in command of the Dumfriesshire Militia, when he heard that an English company had bought the whole trees of the park to carry them off as a mere commercial speculation. The Earl of Dalkeith entered into communication with this company and bought back the trees, and it is in this way that they were rescued. I have, however, heard a different account that they had been bought by tradesmen in the neighbourhood, and that they were only saved by the death of the Duke taking place before they could be cut down, and that these parties lost the money which they had paid. The late Sir Charles Menteth used to say that he had bought the oak tree near the castle to save it. The trees are chiefly limes, beeches, elms, and sycamores, with three or four oaks. The finest oak in the park is on the west side of the road at Doocot Knowe. Its height is $83\frac{1}{2}$ feet; length of bole, 24 feet; girth at base, 23 feet; do. 4 feet from base, $14\frac{1}{2}$ feet; spread of branches, 90 feet. There is another at the foot of the hill, close to the castle, which is 14 feet at the base. There are some old oaks at Lochwood, in Annandale, which are thought by Mr. M'Nab of the Botanical Garden, Edinburgh, to be probably not less than 500 years old. Their stems are from 9 to 17 feet in circumference, and the trees are from 30 to 50 feet in height, with an average spread of branches of 68 feet. All the trees are in a decayed or dying condition, and are covered with evergreen ferns, which give the wood in winter a wonderfully beautiful appearance. If Mr. M'Nab be correct in his calculation as to the age of these Lochwood oaks, then these Drumlanrig oaks were planted in 1374, before the Drumlanrig branch of the Douglas family was settled here. They continue in robust health, and may yet continue to flourish for another five hundred years. In Drumlanrig Park there are some fine beeches. No. 1, on the west side of the road from Doocot Knowe, leading to Drumlanrig Bridge, height, 89 feet; length of bole, 15 feet; girth at base, 25 feet; do. 4 feet from base, 16 feet; spread of branches, 93 feet. No. 2, growing on the east end of flower garden, height, 86 feet; length of bole, 13½ feet; girth at base, 23 feet; do. 4 feet from base, 14½ feet; spread of branches, 106 feet. Sycamore, growing 150 yards north-east from the castle (old Plumbery), height, 97 feet; length of bole, 23 feet; girth at base, 29 feet; do. 4 feet from base, 16 feet; spread of branches, 81 feet. Lime tree, growing about 20 yards north-east from old Plumbery, height, 91 feet; length of bole, 7 feet; girth at base, 23 feet; do. 4 feet from base, 15¼ feet; spread of branches, 75 feet.

Even to the day of his death old Queensberry continued to destroy the woods on all his estates. The parish of Sanquhar to the present day shows the course he was pursuing. The cutting ended at his death, and at that time one side of the banks of the Yeochan (Euchan) was cleared, and the other had not been overtaken. The wood on the uncleared side still exists.

It was not only the woods of Drumlanrig that he destroyed, but the banks of the Tweed at Neidpath, in Peeblesshire, suffered in the same way. Wordsworth passed along the banks of the Tweed in 1807, and was so provoked by what he saw that he indited the following poem equally severe as that of Burns:—

> " Degenerate Douglas; oh, the unworthy Lord!
> Whom mere despite of heart could so far please,
> And love of havoc (for with such disease
> Fame taxes him) that he could send forth word
> To level with the dust a noble horde,
> A brotherhood of venerable Trees,
> Leaving an ancient dome and towers like these
> Beggared and outraged! Many hearts deplored
> The fate of these old Trees; and oft with pain
> The traveller, at this day, will stop and gaze
> On wrongs which Nature scarcely seems to heed:

> For sheltered places, bosoms, nooks, and bogs,
> And the pure mountains, and the gentle Tweed,
> And the green silent pastures, yet remain."

It will require centuries to replace the ancient woods of Drumlanrig, though as much has already been done as the space of sixty years can effect. There is a fine avenue of lime trees running from the castle, and it is handed down by tradition that the ground was being levelled and the trees planted with an intention by Duke Charles to carry it forward for upwards of a mile in front of the castle, when his son Henry, in 1754, was so sadly deprived of life. The father was so overcome with grief by the unfortunate occurrence that he put a stop to these improvements, and it was not till a century afterwards that the idea was carried out to a certain extent by the present noble proprietor. In primitive times the whole parish would be covered with wood, and wild animals, such as the wolf and red stag, would roam around. In the beautiful ballad of "Johnnie of Breadislee" we are told how

> "Johnnie busk't up his gude bent bow,
> His arrows ane by ane,
> And he has gane to Durisdeer
> To hunt the dun deer down."

On the 29th August, 1818, there was dug from a morass on the farm of Ingleston an oak, embedded in peat and black to the core, one of the original trees that had given the name of Dair to the parish. The trunk was 65 feet in length, and as there was a splinter of 14 feet on the butt end, and no appearance of roots, it is probable that it may have been many feet longer. The girth $32\frac{1}{2}$

feet from the boughs was 9 feet 10 inches, and as both the bark and white wood were decayed, it must originally have been nearly 12 feet in circumferenee, and have contained at least 500 feet of wood. Ten cartloads of its wood were conveyed to Drumlanrig Castle, and much besides was distributed among the neighbouring inhabitants. The wood was sent to London, and it now forms the dining-room table of the castle.

DRUMLANRIG PLUNDERED BY THE ENGLISH IN 1549.

The border raids are well known, but Upper Nithsdale lay at such a distance from England that it might have been considered tolerably safe, and yet Lord Wharton contrived in the summer of 1549 to make a raid into Durisdeer and carry off from Sir James Douglas of Drumlanrig twenty-four score or 480 oxen and cows. This is probably one of the most serious cases of wholesale robbery on record, and is told in Pitcairn's Criminal Trials (vol. i., part i., p. 348). "1550, March 17. Richard Latymer of that Ilk convicted of treasonable fire-raising and burning the town of Durisdeer in company with Sir Henry Quhertoune (Wharton), Englishman, and his accomplices, in the month of March, 1547. Item, for art and part of treasonable fire-raising and burning of the lands of Auchincassel and Tibberis, in company with the said Henry Quhertoune, Englishman, and of art and part of the violent Stouthreif and 'Hereschip' of the poor tenants of these lands, 'reiving' from them 5000 oxen, cows, and sheep, together with all their goods, utensils, and household stuff, to the value of £3000 or thereby; committed in the month of December, 1547: Item, for art and part of the theft and concealment of xxiiij^{xx} oxen and cows from Sir James Douglas of Drumlangrig, Knicht, in company with the Bells and the English, manifest thieves and traitors, furth of the lands of Kirkhoip (Kirkup), and driving the said cattle to England and there disposing of them, committed in summer, 1549, &c." Sentence—"To be drawn to the gallows and hanged, and his body to be quartered, and that his heritages, lands, and provisions, and all his goods, moveable and immoveable, shall be forfeited and escheated to the Queen to be applied to her use." The raid was no doubt intended to punish Sir James for refusing to join the English faction at a time when most of the proprietors of Dumfriesshire submitted nominally to the English rule.

> "Behold, behold, from out the shadowy Past
> Our Scottish fathers start! They start, they come
> With onward ages, around their lifted heads
> A troubled glory, as they fight and sing
> Their scornful way across the stage of time!"—*Aird.*

DOUGLASES OF DRUMLANRIG.

It is not difficult to trace with considerable accuracy the personal history of this family, as it took a prominent part in all the public transactions of the period, and whether it were a negotiation for peace, a hostage for a captive king, or the more stirring events of war, there we are sure to find a Douglas actively employed. They were a strong-boned, hot-blooded race, born leaders of men, and the heads of the family never failed to hold their ground against all comers. It is a most remarkable circumstance that from 1388 down to 1778 son succeeded to father without a break in the male succession—a unique occurrence, I believe, in the noble families of any country. Every head of the family was a bold, energetic man in the troublous times of these four hundred years.

1. Sir William de Douglas, the first Baron of Drumlanrig, was son of James, Earl of Douglas and Marr, killed at the battle of Otterburn, 19th August, 1388. He had a grant of this barony from his father, as we have already stated. Sir William was employed in all the important affairs of that period, being joined in 1416 in commission with the Earl of Athole and other nobles to treat with the English about the release of King James I. (Rymer's Fœdera), but the negotiation was without effect. In 1420, when the English carried King James over into France to try whether his presence might not induce the Scotch in the service of the French to pass over to the English, Sir William proceeded to France to wait on his Sovereign, receiving a safe conduct from the King of England, but with this remarkable proviso that he should do nothing prejudicial to him or his dear father, the King of France. Sir William was knighted at the coronation of James in 1424, and it is said that he lost his life at the battle of Agincourt in 1427. He married Elizabeth, daughter of Sir Robert Stewart of Durisdeer and Rosyth, by whom he had at least one son, who succeeded him.

2. William Douglas, his son and heir, is mentioned as one of the hostages sent to England in 1427, for the redemption of King James I. He distinguished himself at the battle of Sark in 1448, when the English were signally defeated by Earl Douglas and Hugh, Earl of Ormond. William, Earl Douglas, was his superior, and refused to enter him in form, notwithstanding the King's mandate, addressed to the Earl and exhibited to him for that effect,

June 7th, 1451. There is a protocol of a notary, certifying a protestation by the Baron, among the old documents of Drumlanrig. He died in 1458, leaving by Janet, his wife, daughter of Sir Herbert Maxwell of Caerlaverock, a son.

3. William Douglas of Drumlanrig, who distinguished himself at the siege of Roxburgh, where James II. was killed in 1460 (Crawford's Peerage). He was also present in 1463 at Alnwick, where the French garrison was relieved by the Earl of Angus. He died in 1464, leaving by his wife Margaret, daughter of Sir William Carlyle of Torthorwald, a son.

4. Sir William Douglas, who was killed in the Royal army in the engagement with the Duke of Albany and the Earl of Douglas, near Lochmaben, 22nd July, 1484. There is a charter by James III., dated 7th June, 1482, to the use of this Baron, upon his own resignation, and also to his wife, Elizabeth Crichton, and the heirs-general of that marriage, but in failure of such heirs to the heirs-general of the resigner. "The lands are Nether Dalpeder, Glennyn, and divers other parts of the Barony of Drumlanrig, then held in chief of the Crown, not of Earl Douglas, as formerly." He married Elizabeth, eldest daughter of Sir Robert Crichton of Sanquhar, by whom he had issue, James; Archibald, ancestor of the Douglases of Coshogle; George, ancestor of the Douglases of Penzerie; John, vicar of Kirkconnel; Margaret, married to John, second Lord Cathcart; Janet, married first to William, Master of Somerville, secondly to Sir Alexander Gordon of Lochinvar; Elizabeth, married son and heir-apparent of James Campbell of Wester Loudon.

5. James Douglas married in 1470 Janet, eldest daughter of Sir David Scott, ancestor of the Duke of Buccleuch. There is a letter of reversion granted to him by Grierson

of Kepanoch, in respect to some land in Drumlanrig barony, then under pledge to Kepanoch for payment of £20 Scots, September 1, 1490. He died in 1498, leaving issue, a daughter, Janet, married to Robert Grierson of Lag, and a son.

6. Sir William Douglas, who fell at the battle of Flodden, 9th September, 1513. We find him assisting Lord Maxwell in 1508 in driving Lord Sanquhar, Sheriff of Nithsdale, from Dumfries, where he held rule in the King's name, and though he was brought to trial at Edinburgh, 30th September, 1512, along with John Fergusson of Craigdarroch and his son Thomas, he and his accomplices were acquitted. We find the following engagement entered into by Sir William, dated 4th June, 1509, showing an intimate alliance with the Maxwells:—" Obligation by Sir William Douglas of Drumlanrich, Kn., for himself, his heirs, executors, and assignees, whereby on the narrative that John Maxwell had become bound that Sir Robert Maxwell, Kn., his son, should marry Janet Douglas, daughter of Sir William, and to infeft the said Sir Robert and Janet and the lawful heirs of their bodies in the lands of Hesildene, Tydwood, and Humby, extending to a 25 merkland, in the barony of the Mernys and shire of Renfrew, and in other lands specified in the barony of Caerlaverock (Glencapil, Glenhowane, and the merklands of the Langside) extending to 25 merkland, the said Sir William bound himself to pay to the said Lord Maxwell the sum of one thousand pounds at the term specified in the bond. Dated at Gleneslane, 4th June, 1509." Sir William married Elizabeth, daughter of Sir John Gordon of Lochinvar, and besides James, who succeeded him, had Robert, who was Provost of Lincluden, and Collector-General of the Superplus of the Teinds in Scotland.

7. Sir James Douglas, the eldest son, is first brought under our notice 13th September, 1518, in the following "Bond of Manrent" to Lord Robert Maxwell:—"Be it kend till all men be thir present lettres, me, James Dowglace of Drumlangrig, to becumin man and servant, and be thir present lettres becumis man in speciale retinewe, manrent and servis, till ane noble lord, Robert Lord Maxwell, to be with hym in peac and in weir, manrent and servis befoir and aganis all thame that levis and dee may, for all the days of my life, myne allegiance till oure soverane lord the King and his governour alenerly exceptit, and I sall geif my said lord the best counsale I can, geif he only askis me, and I sall keip his counsale secrete geif he only shawis me, and sall nouther heire, see, nor wytt ony manner of scaith, hurt, or harm to my said lord, but I sall stop and lett it at all my utir power, and geif I may nocht stop it I sall incontinent warn hyme thairof, and salbe redy nycht and day, lait and air, to do my said lord servis all tymes, quhat tyme I happen to be warint by my said lord or his writing, to this my bond and lettres of manrentship subscrivit with my hand, my proper sele is affixit at Dumfries, 13th September, 1518,

"JAMES DOWGLAS of Drumlanrik, wyth my hand."
(Book of Caerlaverock.)

Sir James was engaged with Sir Walter Scott of Branxholm in his attempt to rescue James V. out of the power of the Earl of Angus,—June, 1526. We find Sir James joining the party of the Earl of Angus in 1543 (Keith i., 33), and in the warlike proceedings of those times between the Earl of Lennox—Lord Wharton on the one side (The Lennox, by Mr Fraser, 1874), and Angus on the other—there is a letter from Angus dated

Drumlanrig, 22nd February, 1547-8, to Lennox, saying that he had heard that Lennox was about to attack the Laird of Drumlanrig, and begs to know whether his attentions towards himself and his friends in this journey were favourable. The result of this is seen in what I have already stated as to the plundering of the lands of Sir James in 1549. In 1552 Sir James was appointed a commissioner to meet commissioners from England for making a division of the debateable land on the borders (Keith i., p. 58). He was knighted by the Duke of Chatelherault, Regent of Scotland, and in 1553 appointed guardian of the western marches with a full power of justiciary, which office he discharged for many years with great wisdom and prudence. On the 27th January, 1561, he signed, with many others of the nobility, in the Tolbooth of Edinburgh the first Book of Discipline. He took part in 1567 against Queen Mary when she was taken at Carberry. After the Queen's defeat, Sir James, as told by Lord Herries himself in his "History of the reigns of Mary and James VI.," saved Terregles House, which had been devoted to destruction, in the following way :—"The Lord Herreis' hous of Terregles, the Regent gave full orders to throw it doune. But the laird of Drumlanrig, who was the Lord Herreis' uncle, and much in favour with the Regent, told that the Lord Herreis wold take it for a favour if he wold ease him of his pains, for he was resolved to throw it doune himselfe and build it in another place. The Regent sware he scorned to be a barrowman to his old walls! And so it was safe."

When Mary revoked her resignation of the crown of Scotland in favour of her son in 1568, she speaks very bitterly of Sir James Douglas and his son, with many others who took part against her. "The cowert traitour, the

Laird of Craigmillar, quhome we had in sic credit as our awin hart and nevir denyit his reasonabil sute; the dowbill flattering traytour Maister Johne Hay quhome we promotit fra ane puir semple clerk to ane abot and pryour; the bishope of Orkney quhome we promotit thairts fra ane puir clerk; the hell houndis, bludy tyrantis without saullis or feir of God, zung Cesfurd, Andro Ker of Faldonsyde, Drumlangrig, zunger and elder, the fibill tyrant Mynto, the schameles boutchour, George Douglas." (The Lennox papers by Mr. Fraser, vol. ii., 437.)

In those wild and troublesome times we find "Old Dumlanrig," as he is called, taken prisoner in 1571, by David Spence, Laird of Ormiston, acting no doubt for the government of the day. It is thus noticed in Calderwood (vol. iii., p. 105):—"Upon Saturday, the 23rd June, old Dumlanrig was taken, as he was riding home for some bussinesse betwixt him and the Lord Hereis and others, who were at variance. The Lord Hereis appointed to meete him at the same place where the Laird of Wormeston lay waiting for him. Young Dumlanrig and Applegirth escaped narrowlie." Old Dumlanrig not being certain whether his son had escaped or not, sent to him the following singular epistle:— "Willie, Thow sall wit that I am haill and feare. Send me word thairfoir how thow art, whether deid or livand? Gif thow be deid, I doubt not but freindis will let me know the treuth; and gif thow be weill, I desyre na mair," &c. He showed this letter to his captors, that they might be sure it contained no treason, and to save his purse he sent it with the letter, desiring the messenger to deliver it to his son.

Losing his only son, Sir William Douglas of Hawick, in 1572, and having as male heir only a grandson to inherit his large property, he resolved to take steps to convey it in the way in which he wished it to go. He executed a Tail-bond, 11th March, 1574, by which he entails his property on the heirs-male of his family as follows:—"In failure of his grandson James and his issue-male, on his special friend and cousin, Robert Douglas of Coshogle, next on James, son and heir of David Douglas of Baitford, and lastly on James Douglas, son of Patrick in Morton. To them and to their issue-male he gives the power of redeeming from the daughters of his grandson James by the payment of 20 lib. Scots and no more, whatever estate might devolve to them as heirs-general to him." (Drumlanrig Charters.) He was married first to Margaret Douglas, third daughter of George, Master of Angus, sister to Archibald, sixth Earl of Angus, by whom he had three daughters: 1. Janet, married first to Sir William Douglas of Coshogle, secondly to John Charteris of Amisfield; 2. Margaret, married to John Jardine of Applegirth; 3. Nicholas, married to James Johnston. Having divorced his first wife, he married secondly Christian Montgomery, only daughter of John, Master of Eglinton. They had four daughters and a son, Sir William Douglas of Hawick, who died before his father in 1572. This Sir William commanded a force of 200 horse at the battle of Langside, 1568, against Queen Mary. (Calderwood.)

(8) Sir James Douglas, his son, succeeded his grandfather in 1578, being very active in suppressing disturbances on the borders, and died 16th October, 1615. On the 23rd October, 1593, at Blackwoodhead, he enters into a bond with Robert Maxwell of Castlemilk and Thomas Kirkpatrick of Closeburn, binding themselves to stand firmly by each other in the

execution of the Royal Commission against Sir James Johnstoun of Dunskellie. (Calderwood's History, vol. v., p. 256.) He accompanied Lord Hay with nearly 2000 men in a forage in Annandale, taking away a great booty of goods, 17th October, 1595. (Colville's Letters, p. 184.) There seems to have been a great dread in the Douglas family of their property passing out of the direct male line, for we find another Tail-bond by this Sir James, 11th May, 1604, in which "he entails it on himself and his issue-male, but in failure of such issue, on Sir Robert Douglas of Coshogle and his issue-male, next to Hugh Douglas of Dalveen and issue-male, and in failure of all, to the nearest heir-male of the resigner, a Douglas by name and carrying the arms of this family of Drumlanrig." (Drumlanrig Charters.)

He married Mary, eldest daughter of John, fifth Lord Fleming, and had issue two daughters and four sons. William, the eldest son, was accused, 21st December, 1611, of taking captive William Kirkpatrick of Kirkmichael, and keeping him prisoner at Drumlanrig. "Dilaitit of the invading and persecuting of William K. of K., and for usurpation of our soveraine lordis royall power and authoritie in taking him captive and prissoner at Dressetland (in Closeburn), and thairfrom transpoirting him to the place of Drumlanerig, quhair he was detenit; and keiping him in close prissone within the Tower of Drumlanerig for the space of six or seven dayis or thairby, he being our soveraine lordis frie lege, committit upone the fyftene day of July, 1610 yearis: And for contravening of our soveraine lordis Actis of Parliament in beiring and weiring of hag buttis and pistolettis." (Pitcairn's Criminal Trials, iii., 213.) William Kirkpatrick, however, declared by letter that he was not prisoner, but honourably entertained, having free liberty to pass where he pleased at the place of Drumlanrig, and thus William Douglas was relieved of the accusation. His other children were Sir James Douglas of Mousewald, David Douglas of Ardoch, George Douglas of Pinzierie, and two daughters, Janet married to William Livingston of Jerviswood, and Helen to John Menzies of Castlehill.

9. Sir William Douglas, who succeeded his father in 1615, entertained James VI. at his house of Drumlanrig, 1st August, 1617, and was created a peer by Charles I. with the title of Viscount of Drumlanrig, Lord Douglas of Hawick and Tibberis, 1st April, 1628. At the coronation of Charles I. in 1633, His Majesty was pleased to advance the Viscount of Drumlanrig to the title of Earl of Queensberry, 13th June, 1633. By a charter under the great seal of Scotland, dated 7th July, 1636, in favour of William, Earl of Queensberry, in life-rent, and James, Lord Drumlanrig, his son and his heirs in fee, of the earldom and estates of Queensberry, the same are now erected into one whole and free earldom, lordship, barony, regality, &c., to be called, then and in all time thereafter, the Earldom of Queensberry and Lordship of Drumlanrig.

He married Isobel, daughter of Mark, first Earl of Lothian, by whom he had James, his successor, William Douglas of Killheed, Archibald Douglas of Dornock, and two daughters, Margaret married to James, Earl of Hartfell and Janet to Thomas, Lord Kirkcudbright; he died on 8th March, 1640, and was succeeded by his son.

10. James, the second Earl of Queensberry, was served heir to his father, 20th May, 1640, took the part of Charles I. in the civil wars, and was on his way to join Montrose after the battle of Kilsyth in August, 1645,

when the leading men of the district of Glencairn intercepted and took him prisoner. He was fined heavily by the Parliament in 1645. Drumlanrig was attacked in 1650 by Colonel Kerr and a number of gentlemen who had espoused the side of the Parliament, among whom was Sir George Maxwell of Pollok. The gates were burned, the ground wasted, and the tenantry ruined. In 1661 the Earl claimed redress from Parliament against these gentlemen, whose names had been forwarded, and they were compelled to pay proportionately a sum of £2000 sterling for the damage that had been sustained. The Earl was fined a second time by Cromwell. He died 1671.

The following letters refer to this attack on Drumlanrig in 1650:—

"James, Viscount Drumlanrig, to Sir George
"Maxwell of Pollok,

"Sanchwher Castle, 23rd February, 1661.

"SIR,—Upon my petitioun to His Majestie's Commissioner and Parliament, it pleased theme to give warand for citing such persones as were accessorie to the barborous and unworthie usage my father receaved from Gilbert Ker and those who were associat with him in Anno 1650, by burneing his gates, waisting his groundis, and rwining his tennentis. And though amongst the rest yow were there, yet your intrest in my Lord Cancellor made me so tender of your concernement, that I wold not bring your name in publict for so base ane act till once I spoke with yowre selfe, and endevored ane amicable setelment with yow. To which effect I have procured ane warand from my Lord Cancellor (whereof receave ane double heir enclosed) for your coming to Edinburgh, notwithstanding of any proclamatioun to the contrare. The bearer will show you the principle warand, but cannot leave it with yow, in regard it must be made use of to severall others, who, upoun that same acompt, are to come to towne. Sir, if you intend to take away this diference betwixt us in ane freindlie way, I shall expect to sie yow at Edinburghe betwixt and Seterday nixt, March, 2. But if agayne that tyme at fardest yow are not come there to treet with me, I hope yow will hold me excused if I take such ane course to make yow come as will neither tend to your credit nor advantage, and (if possiblie it can be shunde) is in nowayes intendit, Sir, by your affectionat freind and servant,

"DRUMLANRIG.

"To the Laird of Pollok—Maxwell.
"Haist. Haist."

"Sir Archibald Stewart of Blackhall to James,
"Viscount Drumlanerig.—28th Feb., 1661.

"MY LORD,—I have seen a letter of youris direct to my sone-in-law, the Laird of Pollok, proposeing his comeing to Edinburgh betwext and Saturday at night, being March 2nd, for treating in that injurie my Lord, your father, receaved in the burning of the gates of his house and otheris, in the year 1650. My Lord, I certainly know that, examin the bussiness well, yeale find that neither then, nor many dayes before, he was either in those pairties or with that pairtie. So his owne innocence pleading his defence, your Lordship is much freed from my sollicitations, then which (if need were) I could not use one more persuasive then the zeal he caryed to the service of your deceased noble grand-father, my Lord Traquair, and the esteem yourselfe perchaince knowes in parte he conferred upon him. All I now supplicat is that, if it cannot be proven that he was either with that pairtie or in that place the time quhen the injurie was done to your fatheris house (as I know it cannot be proven, for he was then at home), I hope your Lordship will not put him to the needless pains of coming to Edinburgh because of some weightie affairis, both his and mine, quherewith he is necessarily pressed. But if your Lordship command his attendance, he shall come in however so innocent he be. But, my Lord, the sad occasion qvhich drave me so suddainly from Edinburgh, as it hath taken me up, so for some time him also, so that I have presumed to keep him here till I know your Lordship's pleasure. Howsoever I shall continue your Lordship's most humble servant,

"A. S. BLACKHALL.

"Ardgowan, last February, 1661."

"For my noble Lord, my Lord Drumlanerig.
"Sir George Maxwell of Pollok to James, Viscount
"Drumlanerig.—31st March, 1661.

"MY LORD,—I was not a little surprised reading your letter of the 22nd February, but then I found the ground to be some misinformation, as if I had been one of those from quhom, my Lord, your father receaved the injuries therein mentioned and complained on; then which there can be no greater mistake, I being both then and many dayes before not near Drumlanerig—I believe some scores of miles. And, albeit, from the undeserved respects vouchafed at all occasions from some of your

Lordship's nearest relations, I did perswade myselfe that the knowledge and notice of my innocence would redeem me from further trouble and molestation; yet, if Blackhall's advice, or rather his commandis, for my stay a day or two till he should know your Lordship's pleaseour, had not prevailed (for his interest in your Lordship soe doth I perceive improve to a deall of confidence) I had not failed to give attendance day and place prefixed to me. If I have in this simplicitie transgressed, I crave pardon. If your Lordship's cammandis be renewed, I shall without delay obey to be with your Lordship within a day or two; albeit, I doe freely confess my desire to lurk at home, if it may be consistent with your Lordship's pleasure. And if, after examination there shall none be found to prove my being there (as sure I ame none without ane egregious mistake can or will assert) to moderate the power of those commandis (quhich by the law, as well of affection, as subjection does challenge obedience on my parte, quhen I call to mind the memorie of your relatione) were not only a signall profe of your owne justice, but also much strengthening of the obligations due from, my Lord, your Lordship's most humble servant,

"G. M. NEATHER POLLOK.

" Pollok, Friday, last Feb., 1661,
" For my noble Lord, my Lord Drumlanrig."

It is right to say that Sir George continued to maintain that he had not been present. "Being questioned (27th July, 1661) by the Commissioner at Ayr regarding the injuries complained of by the Earl of Queensberry and his son, he declared that he knew nothing of the marching of these forces into Nithsdale; that in company with some gentlemen from Ayr he had gone to Sanquhar, where they had lived in an inn, paying for all they got; that there were then no forces in the house; that he had gone thence to Dumfries and stayed eight days; and then having left the forces with a resolution to march into England, had not returned till on his way to Dumfries, when having heard that some gentlemen were in Drumlanrig, and that the forces were marching to the western parts, he went there and remained from eight of the clock at night till seven next morning, and then heard for the first time that the gates had been burned some days before." (Copy declaration at Pollok.) It is not surprising that such a declaration should not have cleared him from giving countenance to the party who had committed the attack, and accordingly we find that his proportion of the damage was assessed at £1044, 9s. Scots money.

It is not without interest to see the parties who had been employed in this attack on Drumlanrig, and from whom redress was claimed. The list is from a copy marked on the back "Anent Drumlangrige, 1662," in the possession of John Fullarton, Esq.

"The roole of the Remonstrators that burnt the gaits of drumlangrig and plundered and waisted the Lands." (The above title is written on the outside of the folding.) "A list off persones who are to be perseued by the Earle of Queensberie and my Lord drumlangrig before the parliament for besiging and fyring the house of drumlanrig, waisting and distroying the Lands of the haill tennents belonging to the saids noble Earle and Lord in away taken ther cornis cattell and other plenishing in Anno, 1650, in the moneth of October."

"Wariston, Sr John Chieslie, Gilbert Ker, Laird of

Colston (Collieston), Sr Andrew Ker of Greinhead, William Ker of Newtoun, the Laird of Cesnok, the Laird of Cunninghamehead (Glencairn family), the Laird of Rowalland, the Laird of Pollock, Maxwell; the Laird of Corsbie, Fulerton; the Laird of Glanderstoun, Capitane Giffeand, William Dounie, ther Clark; Robert Achison, ther Comissar; Andrew Broun, ther Chirurgian; John Gordon, Cap., wha burnt the gaits; Harie Cunynghame, Livetenant; William Glendinning; Laird of Park, Mure; Laird of Park, Hay; Georg Porterfield and John Grahame; Provest of Glasgow; Mr. John Sprucill; two Roberts, sons to Stephen of Wicketshaw; Major Shaw, of Sornbeg and his troop, who was grivious wher ever the came; the Laird of Fail, elder and younger; the Laird of Craufurdland (in Glencairn) and his troop; the Laird of Pinkell (Boyd), the Laird of Stair (Dalrymple?), the Laird of Blair; Heugh Walace of Uinderwood with ane troop; Laird of Kirkhill (Kennedie) with ane troop; the Laird of ——; Cunynghame of Hill of Beith with his troop; Sir James Stuart; the Laird of Dolphintoun, Borland, Cunynghame, Hamilton of Grainge, Ringand Cleugh (Kingancleugh?); the Laird of Kinhilt and his troop; the Lord Cathcart, the Laird of Allinshaw, Mr. Heugh Cathcart, John Crafurd, baillie of Air, Gilmylner Croft; John Gordon of Boghall; the Laird of Culzeane; Craigoch, Kennedie; James Kenedie, son to Culzean; William Colville, in Uckltree; Robert Cathcart, son to Drumjonard; Grimmot, Shaw; the Laird of Coushreg (Boyd); the Laird of Kirkmichell (Kennedie); Thomas Kenedie, his brother; the Laird of Auchendrain; Thomas Campbell, in Glasgow; James Hamelton, laite bailie ther; Patrick Bryce, maltman ther; John Johnston, merchant ther; Umphray Colquhoune, ther; Thomas Paterson, merchant, yr.; James ——, merchant in Glasgow; Rot. Simsone in Edinburgh. *Ministers*—Mr. Patrick Gillespie, Mr. William Adaire, Mr. John Nevay, Mr. Thomas Naile, Mr. Gabrill Maxwell, Mr. Matthew Mouat, Mr. James Rouat, Mr. William Guthrie, Mr. John Fullerton, Mr. Gilbert Hall, Mr. Georg Hutchison, Mr. Alex. Blair, Mr. David Bruce, Mr. Heugh Campbell, Laird Adamtoune and Laird of Carnehill, Wallace."

These are the parties from whom the Earl of Queensberry and his son claimed to be reimbursed for the heavy losses they had sustained; and as they had been severely fined by Cromwell for their attachment to the Royal cause, we cannot be surprised that they should try to make their opponents, when the whirligig of time brought its revenge, feel what they themselves had suffered in worldly circumstances. It is curious to observe how few in Dumfriesshire had taken part against them so far as the names show. We have possibly Copland of Colliestoun, if the Laird of Colston refers to that family and not to the family of Sir William Broun, Baronet of Colston, as he is designated. The Laird of Crawfordland, in Glencairn, belonged, I believe, to the family of the Earls of Glencairn. A number of the merchants of Glasgow had joined in the raid into Dumfriesshire and suffered for their zeal. There were fourteen clergymen, but, so far as I know, little is known as to their history.

The Earl married first, Lady Mary Hamilton, third daughter of James, second Marquis of Hamilton, without issue; secondly, Lady Margaret Stewart, eldest daughter of John, first Earl of Traquhair, Lord High Treasurer of Scotland, by whom he had nine children, William, his successor; Lieutenant-General James Douglas, who died at Namur in 1691; John, killed at the siege of Treves, 1675; Robert, killed at the siege of Maestricht, 1676; five daughters, Mary married to Alexander, Earl of Galloway; Catherine to Sir James Douglas of Kellhead, Bart., and had issue; Henrietta to Sir Robert Grierson of Lag, and had issue; Margaret to Sir Alexander Jardine of Applegirth, Bart., and had issue; Isobel to Sir William Lockhart of Carstairs, Bart., and had issue. Dying on 15th August, 1671, he was succeeded by his son.

11. William, third Earl of Queensberry, born 1637, was in 1667 sworn of the Privy Council to Charles II., and on the removal of Sir George Mackenzie was on 1st June, 1680, made Justice-General, then six months afterwards appointed Lord High Treasurer of Scotland and Governor of Edinburgh Castle, on the 3rd November, 1684, he was created Duke of Queensberry, Marquis of Dumfriesshire, Earl of Drumlanrig and Sanquhar, &c. He continued in equal favour with James II., by whom he was appointed Lord High Commissioner in the first session of Parliament 1685; the same year he and James, Earl of Drumlanrig, were made Lords-Lieutenant of Dumfriesshire, Kirkcudbright, and Wigtown.

However, when it became evident that James was resolved on re-establishing the power of the Pope, and was preparing to do away with the penal laws against Popery, the Duke drew back and refused to join in such proceedings. He was therefore deprived of all his public employments and withdrew to private life, where he spent his time in overlooking the erection of Drumlanrig Castle.

He married Isobel, daughter of William, Marquis of Douglas, by whom he had James, his son and heir; William, Earl of March; and Lord George, a young nobleman of great hopes, who died in 1693; and a daughter Anne, married to David, Earl of Wemys. He died at Edinburgh, 28th March, 1695.

12. James, second Duke of Queensberry, was born 18th December, 1662, and after studying at the University of Glasgow travelled over the Continent. On his return in 1684 he was appointed by Charles II. one of the Privy Council and Lieutenant-Colonel of a regiment of horse commanded by Lieutenant-General Graham, the notorious Claverhouse. He continued to occupy these situations till 1688, when, disapproving of the measures of King James II., he gave up all connection with the court. He joined the Prince of Orange at an early period, and was appointed by him Colonel of the Scots Horse Guards, and was also sworn one of the Privy Council. On the death of his father he was made Lord Privy Seal and one of the extraordinary Lords of Session. On the accession of Queen Anne to the throne he was made Secretary of State, and it was chiefly through his exertions that the union of Scotland and England was accomplished on the 16th January, 1707. As a token of her approval Anne created him a peer of Great Britain by the titles of Baron Ripon, Marquis of Beverley, and Duke of Dover. He died 6th July, 1711, and was buried at Durisdeer.

He married the Lady Mary Boyle, fourth daughter of Charles, Lord Clifford, eldest son of Richard, Earl of Burlington and Cork, by whom he had four sons and three daughters: William, the eldest, was born at Edinburgh in May, 1696, and died seven months after: James was born in London in November, 1697, and died before his father: Charles, born at Edinburgh, 24th November, 1698, and in 1707, for the great services of his father and ancestors, was created Earl of Solway: George was born at London in February, 1700, and died at Paris in 1724: of the daughters, Lady Isobel, the eldest, was born at London, 1698, and died at Edinburgh: Lady Jane was married to Francis, Duke of Buccleuch, then Earl of Dalkeith, and died of the small-pox, 1729: Lady Ann married the Hon. William Finch, his Majesty's Envoy at the Hague, and brother to the Earl of Winchelsea, dying 1741.

13. Charles, third Duke of Queensberry, born at Edinburgh, 24th November, 1698, was Gentleman of the Bedchamber to King George I. in 1720; likewise to Frederick, Prince of Wales, in 1758. He married in 1720 Lady Catherine Hyde, daughter to Henry, Earl of Clarendon and Rochester, by whom he had a daughter, Catherine, who died young; and two sons, Henry, Earl of Drumlanrig, born 30th October, 1722, married 10th July, 1754, to the Lady Elizabeth Hope, daughter to the Earl of Hopetoun, but was killed by the going off of his own pistol on his journey from Scotland to London, October 20th following; and Lord Charles, who was born 17th July, 1726, and represented the county of Dumfries from 1747 (succeeded Sir John Douglas, Bart.) to 1754, when his elder brother was unfortunately killed, and he succeeded to the title of Earl of Drumlanrig. Being the eldest son of a Scots peer, he was obliged to vacate his seat, and was succeeded in the representation by James Veitch of Elliock.

It is a curious circumstance that, though the Queensberry family, now represented by the Duke of Buccleuch, possess a very extensive property in Dumfriesshire, the only member of the family during one hundred and seventy years who has represented the county should have been this Earl of Drumlanrig. This is a sufficient answer to those who seek a cause of complaint against the present representative of the family as overbearing the county by his great influence. No doubt he exercises great influence, but it is from that, of which he cannot denude himself, if he would, his high and unselfish character and the feeling entertained by his numerous supporters that he has only the best interests of his country at heart and is a safe guide to follow.

The Earl of Drumlanrig, who had gone to Lisbon for his health, and was there during the great earthquake, having narrowly escaped the fate which met so many others, returned to England and died October, 1756. Duke Charles died 22nd October, 1778, without any issue surviving him.

14. William, third Earl of March and Ruglen, who was born 16th December, 1725, succeeded in 1778 as fourth Duke and Marquis of Queensberry; he died unmarried 23rd December, 1810, when his titles of Earl of Ruglen, &c., became extinct; those of Earl of March, &c., devolved on the Earl of Wemys; those of Duke of Queensberry, &c., on Henry, third Duke of Buccleuch, as heir of line of the first Duke, the heirs-male of his body being extinct; and those of the Marquis of Queensberry, Earl Queensberry, Viscount of Drumlanrig, Lord Douglas of Hawick and Tibbers, entailed by the patent of the first Marquis, the first Earl, and their heirs-male whatsoever, descended to Sir Charles Douglas, Bart., the lineal representative of Sir William, second son of William, first Earl, and the nearest heir-male of the last Duke. It was on the death of Duke William that the new entail of James, Duke of Queensberry (patent dated 17th June, 1706), came under consideration, when it was found that, whatever might have been the intention of Duke James,

a separation of the Dukedom and higher title from the Marquisate must take place. When we look at the wording of the provision or reservation, which was to the following effect in the deed of resignation, " that there, moreover, shall be no *prejudice to us* (*the resigner*) nor *our forsaid aires* of *tailzie*—of *any* of our *former* titles, *honours*, &c., formerly granted to *us*, and our *predecessors*," it is scarcely possible to doubt that Duke James intended to cover by these words the whole of his titles and honours, and to regrant them to his new heirs. It seems to be a curious instance of a draughtsman failing to carry out in unmistakeable language the intentions of his employer.

Riddell on Peerage and Consistorial Law (vol. ii., p. 668, 669) refers thus to this curious subject:—" In the case of the Marquisate of Queensberry, decided the 9th of July, 1812, that dignity, the Viscounty of Drumlanrig, and a subordinate Barony, were found to remain with the original heirs, even in the face of an actual resignation and regrant of the other, and principal family dignities, in favour of *new* heirs—with a general reference to, and salvo in behalf of, the latter, of any honours and dignities, &c., ever conferred upon the grantee and his family— merely because the former were not specified *nominatim*. And this, although there could be no doubt of the intentions of the resigner to make (under due authority) a total settlement of his honours and estates, *simul et semel*. Neither was there, as has been supposed, at the time any reservation of the Marquisate of Queensberry to the old heirs. And, accordingly, it so happens that their representative, the heir-male, inherits that dignity and the relative ones mentioned without a particle of the resigner's land, while his entire territorial patrimony, and more exalted titles of Duke of Queensberry, Earl of Drumlanrig,

&c., now, in virtue of the resignation and regrant in 1706, centre in the Buccleuch family, the heirs-female. The law here, justly enough, is strict and scrupulous."

It was thus that on the death of William, fourth Duke of Queensberry, the noble family of Buccleuch succeeded to the Dukedom. Riddell is wrong in saying that no part of the property went with the Marquisate, as the Marquis of Queensberry now inherits upwards of thirteen thousand pounds per annum of the old Queensberry property.

15. Henry, third Duke of Buccleuch, who was born 13th September, 1746, succeeded his grandfather in 1751, and also succeeded, as stated above, as heir of line in right of his grandmother to the titles of Duke of Queensberry, Marquis of Dumfriesshire, Earl of Drumlanrig and Sanquhar, Viscount of Nith, Torthorwald, and Ross, and Lord Douglas of Kinmount, Middlebie, and Dornock. He married on 2nd May, 1767, Lady Elizabeth Montague, only daughter, and at length sole heir, of John, Duke of Montague.

16. Charles-William-Henry, his eldest surviving son, born 24th May, 1772, succeeded as fourth Duke of Buccleuch and sixth of Queensberry, 11th January, 1812. He married in 1795 the Hon. Harriet-Katherine Townshend, daughter of the first Viscount Sidney, and had issue, besides the present Duke, two sons and six daughters. He died 20th June, 1819.

17. Walter-Francis Montague-Douglas-Scott, fifth Duke of Buccleuch and seventh of Queensberry, succeeded when he was in his minority, being born 25th November, 1806. He was educated at St. John's College, Cambridge, where he took the degree of M.A. in 1827. His high character and great wealth place him in the front

rank of the British Nobility, and by the wisdom and prudence of his conduct on all occasions he has succeeded in gaining an influence in Scotland that more than equals the authority once wielded by his ancestor, Duke James of Queensberry. He is High Steward of Westminster, a Governor of the Charter-house, Lord-Lieutenant of Midlothian and Roxburghshire, and Captain of the Queen's Body-guard in Scotland. He held the posts of Lord Privy Seal and Lord President of the Council in Sir Robert Peel's second administration in 1842-6. He leads the way in agricultural improvements in Scotland, and spares no trouble or expense to bring his estates up to the highest state of cultivation. The generous patron of arts and literature, his Grace received the honorary degree of D.C.L. from the University of Oxford.

He married in 1829 Lady Charlotte-Anne Thynne, born 1811, daughter of Thomas second Marquis of Bath, and has issue: 1. William-Henry-Walter, Earl of Dalkeith, K.T., born 1831, married 1859 Lady Louisa-Jane Hamilton, third daughter of James, Duke of Abercorn, and has issue (Walter-Henry, Lord Eskdaill, born 1861; Hon. John-Charles, born 1864; Hon. George-William, born 1866; Hon. Henry-Francis, born 1868; Hon. Herbert-Andrew, born 1872); 1858 Lord-Lieutenant of Dumfriesshire, M.P. for Midlothian from 1853 to 1868, and again in 1874.

2. Lord Henry-John, M.P. for Selkirkshire from 1861 to 1868, 1868 M.P. for South Hampshire, born 1832, married 1865 Hon. Cecily-Susan, youngest daughter of John, second Baron Wharncliffe, and has issue.

3. Lord Walter-Charles, born 1834, married 1858 Anna-Maria, daughter of Sir William-Edmund Cradock-Hartopp, Bart., and has issue.

4. Lord Charles-Thomas, Captain R.N., born 1839.

5. Lady Victoria-Alexandrina, born 1844, married 1865 Schomberg-Henry, ninth Marquis of Lothian, and has issue.

6. Lady Margaret-Elizabeth, born 1846.

7. Lady Mary-Charlotte, born 1851.

Such is a short sketch of the Douglas family of Drumlanrig from 1388, and it is curious to observe that during four hundred years the property descended from father to son without a break to 1778, when Duke Charles died without male issue, and was succeeded by his cousin William, third Earl of March, who was descended from Lord William Douglas, second son of William, first Duke of Queensberry. It is not less interesting to watch the gradual accumulation of property in the family during that long period, and to find that, while other families sunk in the social scale, they kept afloat, retaining, I believe, nearly every acre of land which once came into their possession. It has been said that these bold barons were not over-scrupulous as to their mode of acquisition, but I do not think—and I have examined the question with some care—that any properties were acquired without a fair value being paid for them.

In the Appendix (No. 1) will be found a pretty accurate account of their acquisitions in each century during four hundred years, and the families from whom they were acquired. It does not appear, as far as I have been able to discover, that "Old Q." added much, if anything, to the Queensberry property. The present noble family have added small patches here and there to make it more symmetrical.

The question now arises—What is the yearly value of the Queensberry property in Dumfriesshire, such as we show it in the Appendix to have been? and this may be approximately reached by the Valuation Roll of 1873. We have calculated it by adding together the properties now enjoyed by the Duke of Buccleuch and Marquis of Queensberry. These properties continued to be united till the death of William, last Duke of Queensberry, when the new patent granted by Queen Anne, 17th June, 1706, came into operation and separated the titles and property.

The following is the approximate rental of the separate properties of the Duke of Buccleuch and Marquis of Queensberry. It is collected from the Valuation Roll (1873) of the different parishes and is only given as an approximation of the present value of the old Queensberry property. The portion in Mouswald parish, which was sold in 1832 by the late Marquis to pay for the building of Kinmount House, has also been added.

PROPERTY OF DUKE OF BUCCLEUCH IN DUMFRIESSHIRE.

	£	s.	d.
Canonbie,	16,027	19	0
Closeburn,	3,080	0	0
Dornock,	842	0	0
Dryfesdale,	1,423	0	0
Dunscore,	20	0	0
Durisdeer,	9,285	15	0
Eskdalemuir,	6,554	12	0
Ewes,	4,534	14	6
Glencairn,	3	18	6
Hoddam,	853	2	0
Keir,	2,340	0	0
Kirkconnel,	9,965	0	0
Kirkmichael,	4,827	0	0
Kirkpatrick-Juxta,	882	0	0
Carry forward,	£60,639	1	6

Brought forward,	£60,639	1	6
Langholm,	4,654	14	6
Middlebie,	1,623	5	0
Moffat,	878	15	0
Morton,	6,697	17	8
Penpont,	5,992	5	3
Sanquhar,	12,101	4	8
Burgh of Sanquhar,	693	10	0
Tynron,	2,924	0	0
Westerkirk,	3,344	3	4
	£99,548	16	11

PROPERTY OF MARQUIS OF QUEENSBERRY.

Cummertrees,	£1,601	3	1½
Lochmaben,	524	10	0
Mouswald,	3,382	10	0
Tinwald,	2,253	4	0
Torthorwald,	4,792	10	0
	£12,553	17	1½
Property of Duke of Buccleuch,	£99,548	16	11
Property of Marquis of Queensberry,	12,553	17	1½
Total,	£112,102	14	0½
Approximate Annual Value of Land taken by Railway,	1,000	0	0
	£113,102	14	0½

It is, however, to be borne in mind that some portion of these estates was sold to the railway companies for the construction of their works, but it could scarcely be one-tenth of the valuation now put on the railways in the several parishes. Possibly the agricultural value of the land sold might be £1000 per annum, and therefore we have to add this sum to the sum total, as I have done above. Then, again, there requires to be deducted what belonged to the Buccleuch family in Dumfriesshire before they succeeded to the Queensberry property. The property lay in the north-east of the county, and according to an old Valuation Roll of 1671, nearly the whole parishes of Canonbie, Ewes, Eskdalemuir, and Langholm belonged to the Buccleuch family, amounting at present to somewhat about £31,772. We have also to deduct the annual value of the lands bought by the Dukes of Buccleuch since 1810, which may amount to £5000. We thus have—

Queensberry Property—total,	£113,102 14 0½
Deduct Buccleuch Property,	36,772 0 0
	£76,330 14 0½

This may be considered an approximation to the present annual value of the Queensberry property, as possessed by the last Duke of Queensberry.

Since the calculation of the value of the property belonging to the Duke of Buccleuch in Dumfriesshire was made, an official valuation with respect to the owners of lands and heritages in Scotland has been issued by Parliament, and the precise value of the Duke of Buccleuch's property in Dumfriesshire is there said to be £97,530, with an acreage of 253,514, which is somewhat less than the value which I had calculated it to be, whereas the property of the Marquis of Queensberry is given as £13,384, with an acreage of 13,243, somewhat more than I had calculated it to be. My calculation, however, is sufficient for the purpose for which I intended it.

CHAMBERLAINS OF THE DUKES OF QUEENSBERRY FOR THE LAST TWO HUNDRED YEARS.

The earliest Chamberlain whose name I have met with is (1) John Alison of Glencorse, in Closeburn. He acted for William, first Duke of Queensberry, and his name is in bad repute, as he entered heartily into the persecution of the Covenanters (1685-1688), and as is believed in all such cases, something terrible happened to him at the close of his life. He was said not to have been over-scrupulous in obtaining possession of surrounding properties for the Duke, and among other legends, it is handed down that he got his men to drive the Duke's cattle into the outhouses of Tibbers Castle, as if they had been stolen, and then commenced a suit against the Maitland family to deprive them of their possessions. This of course is a mere myth, as the Queensberry family, as I have shown in the Appendix, had been in possession of these lands from 1544, when they were bought from John Maitland of Auchengassel, the son-in-law of Sir James Douglas of Drumlanrig. Alison left no children, and his property of Glencorse, inherited by two nephews, was sold to Duke William, and it has ever since continued to belong to the Queensberry estate. It is now rented at £360 per annum.

2. Archibald Douglas. In the receipts for rents for Drudle and Knowe, I find Archibald Douglas signing these receipts from 1699, but he was most likely appointed on the death of Alison in 1694, though I have no proof of this. He continues to give receipts till 27th July, 1708. He was the great-grandfather of the late Miss Clerk Douglas of Holmhill, and was much respected by

both Dukes under whom he acted. Miss Douglas had letters in which he was addressed "Honest Archibald," showing the affectionate and kindly feelings with which he was regarded by his employers. He was the last inhabitant of Morton Castle. He was the father of William Douglas, suitor of "Bonnie Annie Laurie," and grandfather of Archibald Douglas, who represented the county of Dumfries in Parliament from 1762 to 1774. The following quaint receipt is given by A. Douglas in 1699: "Received from James Hunter in drudall threti one pound and nineteen shillings Scots in pt. of payment of bond granted by him for by-gone rent due. Whitsunday ninety nine years. (Signed) A. Douglas."

3. John Dalrymple of Watersyde, in Keir. He signs receipts from 30th November, 1708, to 13th March, 1730.

4. William Dalrymple of Watersyde. He succeeded his father as Chamberlain, and signs receipts from 1731 to 1748.

In regard to these Dalrymples of Waterside, it has been stated that they were descended from some of the old clergy of Durisdeer, but how this idea originated I am unable to say, as there is no such name among the clergy of Durisdeer in any old documents that have come under my notice. The first of the name that we find connected with this property in Keir is John Dalrymple in 1629, who had a wadsett of Watersyde for 4000 merks from Robert Maxwell, Earl of Nithsdale, and Dame Elizabeth Beaumont, his spouse. He was married to Katherine Thomson, and on the 23rd Feburary, 1630, the property passes to him and his wife by charter to be holden of said Earl. His son John, the Chamberlain, succeeded him, and had a charter, 9th August, 1671, as heir to his father, from John, Earl of Nithsdale. William,

E

the Chamberlain, was retoured heir to his father 17th May, 1737. The estate, which consisted of the 40s. land Watersyde, 7 Merkland of Kirkpatrick (called the Gait) with other lands, continued in the possession of the family for upwards of one hundred years, when it was sold to meet the pecuniary rights of five children. The charter of sale is dated 6th August, 1782, when it was bought by George Hoggan for £4300 sterling.

5. James Fergusson of Craigdarroch. He signs receipts from 1748 to 1763. He was the son of Alexander Fergusson, who was one of the county gentlemen who actively supported King William against the Pretender, representing the Dumfries Burghs from 1715 to 1722. He married in 1709 Ann, daughter of Sir Robert Laurie of Maxwelton—the "Bonnie Annie Laurie" so pathetically sung by William Douglas of Fingland. James was retoured heir to his father, 1st June, 1749, and was father of Alexander Fergusson, an eminent advocate, and the hero of Burns' song, "The Whistle."

6. Robert M'Murdo of Drungans. He signs receipts from 1763 to 1766. The family of M'Murdo can be traced back for a considerable period, being connected with the parish of Dunscore, and giving name to the property of M'Murdiston, according to Mr. Gracie, the genealogist. There is a charter from the Commendator of Melrose, dated 25th July, 1565, to William M'Murday, and his heirs, of the lands of M'Cubbingstoun and Ferdinmakrary (possibly Farding-makrary). Among the lands paying feu-duties to the Abbey, the former is mentioned but not the latter, though Farding-well is given. His son John succeeded him, and he had two sons, Robert and John. From this John sprang the Dumfries members of the family. James, John's

eldest son, succeeded, while the second son, also named John, entering the Church, became minister of Torthorwald, the charge at present occupied by his great-great-grandson, the Rev. J. R. Duncan. He married Mary Muir of Cassencarry, and thus became connected with the Sharpes of Hoddam; and, secondly, Alice Charteris, a member of the Amisfield family. He was father of Robert M'Murdo of Drungans; and by his connection with the above families was no doubt appointed to represent Duke Charles of Queensberry, having become Chamberlain, as we see, in 1763.

Mr. M'Dowall, in his interesting "Annals" of St. Michael's Churchyard, shows the connection of the M'Murdos with the respectable family of Duncan, so honourably known in Dumfries: "The Torthorwald minister had also a son William, whose daughter Anne, born 1745, married in 1770 the Rev. George Duncan, Lochrutton, and thus became the link between the two families;" this George being the father of Dr. Henry Duncan, the founder of the Savings Banks.

7. John Maxwell. He signs receipts from 1766 to 1780.

8. John M'Murdo. He signs receipts from 1780 to 1797.

Mr. M'Murdo was the kind friend of Burns, who was often entertained at his hospitable table at Drumlanrig, from 1788 till the time of the poet's death in 1796. The following letter has been lately discovered by Mr. Waddell, and it was no doubt addressed to Mr. M'Murdo, though the address has been destroyed. It runs thus:—

"Sanquhar, 26th Nov., 1788.

"SIR,—I write you this and the enclosed, literally *en passant*, for I am just baiting on my way to Ayrshire. I have Philosophy or Pride enough to support me with unwounded indifference against the neglect of my more dull superiors, the merely rank and file of Noblesse and Gentry, nay, even to keep my vanity quite sober under the loading of their compliments; but from those who are equally distinguished by their rank and character— those who bear the true elegant impressions of the Great Creator on the richest materials, their little notices and attentions are to me amongst the first of earthly enjoyments. The honour you did my fugitive pieces in requesting copies of them is so highly flattering to my feelings and Poetic Ambition, that I could not resist even this half opportunity of scrawling off for you the enclosed as a small but honest testimony how truly and gratefully I have the honour to be, Sir, your deeply obliged humble Servant,

"ROBT. BURNS."

Mr. Waddell says that "the original of this document is in the possession of Mr. James Graham, Mount Vernon Cottage, Carluke—a most enthusiastic antiquary of fully fourscore—who has very obligingly communicated a copy to me. From subsequent inquiries I learn that it came into Mr. Graham's hands from those of an old acquaintance of his, now resident in England, but who had formerly been confidential servant to Mr. Norman Lockhart of Lee. Mr. Lockhart, when on a visit at Dumfries, received it it from his brother-in-law, Mr. M'Murdo, the Duke of Queensberry's representative at Drumlanrig, to whom it was no doubt originally addressed; and by Mr. Lockhart it was bequeathed as a memorial to his faithful servant. The poet at that time was frequently in Ayrshire, coming and going, before his final settlement at Ellisland, and the letter must have been written on the occasion of his journey to Mauchline, when he went to bring home his bride. It gives additional interest to that journey, so important in his life, and shows him exactly as he was upon the road. It seems, in fact, to be the only letter ever written by him from Sanquhar, although he was often enough there both professionally and otherwise, and once in a very bad humour, as we know, only two months later. But its chief literary interest is in the proof it affords so distinctly that his friendship with M'Murdo, and others of that class, was courted by such persons themselves, and was in no way brought about by any intrusion of the poet."

We find again the following letter of thanks in the following year:—

"Ellisland, 9th Jan., 1789.

"SIR,—A poet and a beggar are in so many points of view alike, that one might take them for the same individual character under different designations, were it not that though, with a trifling poetic licence, poets may be styled beggars, yet the converse of the proposition does not hold that every beggar is a poet. In one particular, however, they remarkably agree; if you help either the one or the other to a mug of ale or the picking of a bone, they will very willingly repay you with a song. This occurs to me at present, as I have just despatched a well-lined rib of J. Kilpatrick's Highlander (a neighbouring blacksmith); a bargain for which I am indebted to you, in the style of our ballad printers, "Five Excellent New Songs." The enclosed is nearly my newest songs, and one that has cost me some pains, though that is but an equivocal mark of its excellence. Two or three others, which I have by me, shall do themselves the honour to wait on your after-leisure: petitioners for admittance into favour must not harass the condescension of their benefactor.

"You see, Sir, what it is to patronize a poet. 'Tis like being a magistrate in Petty-borough; you do them the favour to preside in their council for one year, and your name bears the prefatory stigma of baillie for life.

"With not the compliments, but the best wishes, the sincerest prayers of the season for you, that you may see many happy years with Mrs. M'Murdo and your family—two blessings, by-the-by, to which your rank does not entitle you—a loving wife and fine family being almost the only things of this life to which the farm-house and cottage have an exclusive right, I have the honour to be, Sir, your much indebted and very humble Servant,

"R. BURNS."

In sending Mr. M'Murdo a copy of his elegy on "Captain Matthew Henderson, a gentleman who held the patent for his honours immediately from Almighty God" he thus writes, evidently at the close of a disputed election for Dumfries burghs, which had been keenly contested, and had gone against the feelings of Burns:—

"Ellisland, 2nd Aug., 1790.

"SIR,—Now that you are over with the Sirens of Flattery, the Harpies of Corruption, and the furies of Ambition, those infernal deities on all sides and in all parties, preside over the villanous business of politics, permit a rustic Muse of your acquaintance to do her best to soothe you with a song.

"You knew Henderson—I have not flattered his memory. I have the honour to be, Sir, your obliged humble Servant,

"R. B."

In sending Mr. M'Murdo a copy of the new edition of his poems he writes:—

"Dumfries, 1793.

"Will Mr. M'Murdo do me the favour to accept of these volumes? a trifling but sincere mark of the very high respect I have for his worth as a man, his manners as a gentleman, and his kindness as a friend. However inferior now, or afterwards, I may rank as a poet, one honest virtue to which few poets can pretend I trust that I shall ever claim as mine—to no man, whatever his station in life, or his power to serve me, have I ever paid a compliment at the expense of Truth.

"The Author."

Burns felt keenly the load on the mind of being indebted to another for money, and though his impecuniousness sometimes compelled him to submit, he was no sooner able to pay back what he had borrowed than he hastened to do so. He seems to have been under this obligation to Mr. M'Murdo, and in the following letter we get a glimpse of his feelings:—

"Dumfries, Dec., 1793.

"Sir,—It is said that we take the greatest liberties with our greatest friends, and I pay myself a very high compliment, in the manner in which I am going to apply the remark. I have owed you money longer than I ever owed it to any man. Here is Ker's account, and here are six guineas; and now, I dont owe a shilling to man—or woman either. But for the d——d dirty dog-eared little pages, I had done myself the honour to have waited on you long ago. Independent of the obligations your hospitality has laid me under, the consciousness of your superiority in the rank of man and gentleman of itself was fully as much as I could even make head against; but to owe you money too was more than I could face.

"I think that I once mentioned something of a collection of Scots songs I have for some years been making—I send you a perusal of what I have got together. I could not conveniently spare them above five or six days, and five or six glances of them will probably more than suffice you. A very few of them are my own. When you are tired of them, place them with Mr. Clint, of the King's Arms. There is not another copy of the collection in the world; and I should be sorry that any unfortunate negligence should deprive me of what has cost me a good deal of pains.

"R. B."

Mr. M'Murdo occupied a prominent position in the county of Dumfries, from representing the interests of the Duke of Queensberry. His son, Lieutenant-Colonel Archibald M'Murdo, was an officer in the British army, and his grandson, Major-General W. M'Murdo, C.B., is also known as a distinguished officer, having attracted the attention of the late Sir Charles Napier by his personal intrepidity and great zeal in the Scinde war, more particularly at the battle of Meeanee.

9. Dr. Thomas Yorstoun. He acted as Chamberlain

from 1797 till his death, 7th Dec., 1810, at the age of sixty-two (see Appendix No. 11).

10. Major Thomas Crichton of Auchenskeoch. On the accession of Duke Henry of Buccleuch to the Queensberry property, Major Crichton was appointed Chamberlain in 1811, and continued to act till 1843, when Mr. Maxwell was appointed. Major Crichton died in 1848.

11. William Maxwell, Esq., of Carruchan. He succeeded Major Crichton, and held office till his death in 1863, being cut off in the middle of a useful and honoured manhood. He was heir to the old Earldom of Nithsdale (though the second title of Herries (1489) was adjudged by the House of Lords, in 1858, to William Constable Maxwell), and was thus the last representative of a noble and chivalrous line. For more than twenty years he discharged his important functions with great ability, never failing to command the respect of every one with whom he had to transact business.

12. John Gilchrist Clark, Esq., of Speddoch. He succeeded as Chamberlain on the death of his brother-in-law, Mr. Maxwell, in 1863.

We have seen how Burns was in friendly intercourse with a former Chamberlain, Mr. John M'Murdo, and in Mr. Gilchrist Clark we find another link with our great poet. Mr. Clark is connected with Mr. Samuel Clark, conjunct Commissary Clerk and Clerk of the Peace, with his father for the county of Dumfries, who was on very familiar terms with Burns. It was in his presence that the unfortunate squabble took place respecting the toast proposed by Burns, "May our success in the present war be equal to the goodness of our cause," which was regarded in those excited times as disloyal, and which

Burns himself regretted next morning, imploring Mr. Clark to prevent it, as far as possible, from reaching the ears of his superiors. There is another letter which has lately come to light in Mr. Waddell's magnificent edition of Burns, addressed to Mr. Clark. It is in the following terms:—

"My Dear Sir,—I recollect something of a drunken promise yesternight to breakfast with you this morning; I am very sorry that it is impossible. I remember, too, your oblidgingly mentioning something of your intimacy with Mr. Corbet, our Supervisor-General. Some of our folks about the Excise Office, Edinburgh, had, and perhaps still have, conceived a prejudice against me, as being a drunken, dissipated character. I might be all this, you know, and yet be an honest fellow; but you know that I am an honest fellow and am nothing of this. You may in your own way let him know that I am not unworthy of subscribing myself, my dear Clark, your friend, "R. BURNS."

This letter, without date, but probably written in 1794, is in the possession of Mrs. Stuart Gladstone of Capenoch, the daughter of Burns' bosom friend. Miss Belle Clark, another daughter, was married to Dr. Henry Duncan's eldest son, the late Rev. Dr. George John C. Duncan, minister of a Presbyterian Church in England.

DOUGLAS FAMILY OF COSHOGLE.

As might be expected, there were cadet branches of the noble family of Drumlanrig in the parish of Durisdeer. In those early times fathers had no other way of providing for their younger children except by giving them a portion of land, which it was generally settled by legal deeds should return to the head of the family, if male heirs failed. The Douglas family of Coshogle was a cadet branch, and continued to flourish for many years alongside the parent stem, though it was at last overwhelmed by difficulties, whether brought on by its own follies or by accidental circumstances we have now no means of determining. The earliest notice of the land which gave title to this branch of the Douglas family is found in a charter under the great seal of Robert II., dated at Cumbray, 28th May, 1374, granting James Blare the lands of Coshogle. It runs thus, leaving out the technical parts:—

"*Robertus Rex, &c., Sciatis nos approbasse et confirmasse donacionem illam et concessionem quas recolende memorie dominus Avunculus et Predecessor noster, Dominus David Rex Scotorum illustris fecit et concessit Jacobo de Blare de terris de Corshogyll cum pertinenciis in baronia de Drumlangrig infra Vicecomitatem Drumf. Ten. et Hab. eodem Jac. et her. suis libere, &c.*

"Robert, &c. Know that we have approved and confirmed that donation and concession, which our uncle and predecessor of blessed memory, our Lord David, illustrious King of the Scots, made and granted to James de Blare of the lands of Corshogyll with their pertinents in the barony of Drumlangrig, &c." This charter was only confirmatory of one that had been granted by his uncle and predecessor King David II., so that we can carry the history of this piece of land back to this King's reign (1329-1370). The land is situated in the northern part of the parish, and is now known as Coshogle. Two farms adjoining to Coshogle, namely, Inglistoun and

Annistoun or Annoltoun, were in later times incorporated with this property, and as to these we know also by a charter under the great seal granted by Robert II., that he gave "*Johanni de Walays, Militi, 8 merkl. de Inglestoun et de Annoltoun in bar. de Durisdere.*"

These lands do not seem to have remained long in the possession of the Walays (Wallace) family, as there is a charter granted by Robert Stewart, Lord of Durisdeer, to his kinsman, James de Dalrymple, of the lands resigned to his use by Hugh de Walays, viz., those of Inglistoun and Annistoun, lying in the barony of Durisdeer, &c., dated 20th April, 1398. This family of Wallace of Carnell or Cairnhill in Ayrshire, descendants of the old family of Ellerslie, do not appear to have parted with the whole of this property, as we find in Robertson's "Ayrshire Families" (vol. iii., 70), a return alluded to, dated 12th May, 1596, to William Wallace of Carnell, designed heir to his great-great-grandfather William Wallace of Carnell in the ten merkland of Coshogil, in the barony of Drumlanrich and shire of Dumfries. He is there designed "*hæres Willielmi Wallace de Carnel (qui interfectus est sub vexillo regis in bello de Flouden) abavi.*" This old gentleman had fallen with many others of his countrymen at the battle of Flodden, 9th September, 1513, showing that the patriotic feelings of the great Wallace still animated his descendants. A hundred years pass without mention of these lands, but on 16th April, 1495, there is a charter granted by the superior, William Stewart of Rosyth, as Baron of Durisdeer, to Archibald Napier of Merchistoun, and his heirs, upon the resignation of John Dalrymple, sometime of Laich, so that for one hundred years the Dalrymples had kept possession of the land. Then we have the resignation of Merchistoun himself,

21st November, 1509, in favour of his eldest son, Alexander, younger of Merchistoun, and another by Merchistoun, the younger, in favour of himself and his betrothed wife, Isabel Little, 18th March, 1562. Then there is a precept of Clare Constat and seisin of the above lands, granted by Stewart of Rosyth to Mungo Napier, brother and heir of Alexander, the younger of Merchistoun, 20th April, 1573, and lastly Mungo's resignation of the lands to Stewart of Rosyth, with a seisin in favour of Robert Douglas of Coshogle and his wife, Nicholas Johnstoun, 18th July, 1573. It was in this way that these lands at last became part of Coshogle property. (Drumlanrig Charters.)

As to the origin of the Coshogle branch of the Douglases, both Douglas in his "Peerage," and Hume of Godscroft in his "History of the House of Douglas," agree that the first was Archibald, son of Sir William Douglas of Drumlanrig, who was killed in the engagement with the Duke of Albany, 22nd July, 1484. Hume says that he married "one Pringle of the house of Galashiels, who bore to him twelve sons; and after his death she was married to one Carnel Wallace, and bore twelve more to him also." Where Hume obtained this information about his wife he does not tell us, but her marriage to a Wallace is not unlikely when we know that they possessed property so near to Coshogle.

The earliest notice of the family in old charters as connected with Coshogle is a seisin, 20th March, 1545, of the church lands and mill of Kirkbryde, which lay close to their property, by John Menzies of Enoch, to the use of William Douglas of Coshogle for life, and to his son James in fee, with a confirmation of all by the Rector of Kirkbryde as superior, 25th May, 1546. Now, this William may very well have been either son or grandson of Archibald above-mentioned. Next we have special service of Robert of Coshogle, as heir to his brother James, 30th July, 1594. This is the Robert who is called "special friend and cousin" by Sir James Douglas of Drumlanrig, when he executed the tail-bond of 1574, and was named by him as first to succeed to the Queensberry property if his grandson died without male issue.

It is curious to find about this period one of this family accused of witchcraft, and condemned to be burned on the Castlehill of Edinburgh. The trial is found in Pitcairn's "Criminal Trials" (vol. ii., 242), and shows the strange infatuation that possessed all classes of society in those days. "1591, May 8.—Barbara Naipar, spous to Archibald Douglas, burges of Edinburgh (brother to the Laird of Carschogill), Dilaitit of sindrie poyntis of wichcraft, contenit in Dittay gewin in aganis hir be Mr. David M'Gill of Cranstoun—Ryddell, advocat to our soverane lord. Verdict. The Assyse, be the mouth of Robert Cuningham, chancillor, ffand, pronunceit, and declarit the said Barbara Naipar to be fylit, culpabill and convict of the seiking of consultation from Annie Sampsoune, ane wich, for the help of Dame Jeane Lyonne, Lady Angus, to keip hir from vometing quhen sche was in breedin of barne. Item, for the consulting with the said Annie Sampsoune, for causing of the said Dame Jeane Lyonne, Lady Angus, to love hir, and to gif hir the geir awin hir agayne, and geiving of ane ring for this purpois to the said Anny, quhill sche had send hir ane courchie (kerchief) of linning and swa for contravening of the Act of Parliament, in consulting with hir and seiking of hir help, being ane wich, &c." The result of all this was that "Dome was pronunceit against Barbara Naipar," the sister-in-law of the Laird of Coshogle.

This Dame Jean Lyon, eldest daughter of John, eighth Lord Glamis, was married first to Robert Douglas, younger of Lochleven, and was mother of William, Earl of Morton; secondly, in 1586, to Archibald, eighth Earl of Angus; thirdly, to Alexander, Lord Spynnie (Douglas Peerage).

William, son of Robert, was served heir to his father in the lands of Inglistoun, Annistoun, and Coshogle, 28th March, 1623. He became a baronet, and is known as Sir William Douglas of Coshogle. The recognition by Sir James of the right to succeed to the Queensberry property placed the family in a marked position, and was probably the cause of their ruin. Rae, in his manuscript account of the parish of Morton, tells us that Sir William bought from the Earl of Morton the barony of Morton, and built a house below Thornhill to the south-westward of that place, and sometimes resided there. This was commonly called the Red House. Adversity seems to have followed close on the heels of his prosperity, for we find, ten years after he had got the property from the Earl of Morton, a deed of resignation and a contract of sale to the Earl of Queensberry of the barony of Morton. We thus find that the Coshogle family had to part with their rich possessions in Morton, and to make them over to the Drumlanrig branch of the Douglases. This was the time that the greater part of Morton parish merged in the Queensberry property. A more detailed account of the connection of the Coshogle family with the barony of Morton is found in the history of Morton.

The families of Drumlanrig and Coshogle were closely allied, as Sir William of Coshogle was married to Janet, daughter of Sir James Douglas, who had executed the tail-bond of 1574, and they still continued with the same friendly feelings towards each other, as I find that his grandson, Sir James Douglas of Drumlanrig, though he had four sons—Sir William, who succeeded him in 1615; Sir James Douglas of Mouswald; David Douglas of Ardoch; and George Douglas of Penzarie—not satisfied with this array of issue (male), executes a deed in 1609, in which he states that "in failure of such issue" he leaves his large property "to Robert Douglas, son of Sir William of Coshogle, and his issue (male); next to Hugh Douglas of Dalveen; and in failure of all, to the nearest heir of the resigner—a Douglas by name, and carrying the arms of the family of Drumlanrig." Then follows an enumeration of the lands included in the Queensberry property. These friendly feelings of the families, however, did not continue. As years rolled on they became gradually estranged, the Coshogle family probably soured by going back in the world after such bright prospects in their earlier history. The star of Drumlanrig continued to shine with resplendent lustre, as the family had been honoured with a visit by King James VI. in 1617, while that of Coshogle paled before it. There was still the wild blood in this border family, and it broke out at this time in a little petty war between the families. It was a mere trifle that brought them to blows, but in all probability there had been a variety of irritating questions which are unrecorded. The story is told by Pitcairn (Letters of James VI.), and is not without interest, as showing that the law was still set at defiance by men of rank and property in the south of Scotland.

On the 12th May, 1621, we are told that "a small private war between the Lairds of Drumlanrig and

Coshogle came to a bearing this day at the moss of Knockonie. This moss belonged to David Douglas, brother to Drumlanrig; but Coshogle had always been allowed to raise peats from it for his winter fuel. The two lairds having fallen into a coldness, Coshogle would not ask this any longer as a favour, but determined to take it as a right. Twice his servants were interrupted in their operations, so he himself came one day to the moss with his son Robert, and thirty-six men or thereby, armed with swords, hagbuts, lances, corn-forks, and staves. Thereafter, the Laird of Mouswald (Sir James Douglas), a brother of the proprietor of the moss (who was absent), sent a friend to remonstrate, and to urge upon Coshogle the propriety of his asking the peats "out of love," instead of taking them in contempt. The Coshogle party returned only contemptuous answers, "declaring they would cast peats there, wha wald, wha wald not." Some further remonstrances being ineffectual, Drumlanrig himself, accompanied with friends and servants, came upon the scene, showing that he had the royal authority to command Coshogle to desist. But even this reference failed to induce submission. At length the Laird of Mouswald, losing temper, exclaimed, "Ye are ower pert to disobey the King's Majesty's charge—quickly pack ye and begone." "Immediately ane of Coshogle's servants, with ane great kent (staff), strak Captain Johnston, behind his back, twa great straiks upon the head, which made him fall dead to the ground with great loss of blood. Then Robert Douglas, son of Coshogle, presentit ane bended hagbut within three ells 'to the Laird of Drumlanrig's breast, which, at the pleasure of God, misgave. Immediately thereafter, Robert of new morsit the hagbut, and presentit her again to him, which shot missed him at the pleasure of God. Robert Dalzell, natural son to the Laird of Dalzell, was struck through the body with ane lance, who cried that he was slain; and some twa or three men was strucken through their clothes with lances, sae that the haill company thought that they had been killed, and then thought it were time for them to begin to defend themselves." This was done so effectually that Coshogle's party was driven from the field with the loss of one of their men. There was a mutual prosecution between the families, but as they contrived to make up the quarrel between themselves out of court, the law took no notice of their outrageous proceedings.

Sir Robert Douglas, the son of Sir William, was a remarkable shot, and once when a reaver called White Neck was driving off along the pass of Dalveen a number of his cattle, he made signs from the hill of West Side Height that he would shoot him if he did not stop, but the distance was so great that no attention was paid to his signs, when Sir Robert fired, and the robber dropt into a pool, which is still known as White Neck's Pool.

The moss of Knockconey is on the borders of Coshogle property, belonging probably to David Douglas of Ardoch, third son of Sir James, who had succeeded to his grandfather in 1578. The original lands of the family still continued in their possession, but Sir William seemed to have sunk deeper into debt. The Coshogle family had got hold of the church lands and mill of Kirkbride, with the lands of Thurston, but they were mortgaged to Douglas of Dalveen, then conveyed to Menzies of Auchensell, and lastly the whole passed into the possession of the Earl of Queensberry, and so registered 12th June, 1634. I am unable to follow this elder branch further, except that Christian, a daughter or grand-daughter of Sir William, married Adam Murray of Drumcrieff, in 1652, and a descendant of hers, the Rev. Thomas Tod, is found minister of Durisdeer.

Adam Murray of Drumcrieff=Christina, d. of
   Retoured to his father in | Sir William Douglas of
   1692. | Coshogle.

Robert suc. in 1702.
    ob. S.P.
1. Anna M. Coh.=Geo. Johnstone
              of Girthhead.
         Arch. and Wm.
2. Nicholas Murray, Coh.=John Tod, tenant in
                         Craigieburn.

Arch. Tod, heir portioner =
   Sas., 13 April, 1713.
Rob. Tod, heir portioner.

  Rev. Thos. Tod of Craigieburn,
    Minister of Durisdeer.

The history of Archibald, uncle to Sir William, can be traced to a later period with some degree of accuracy. In those days, when the old Catholic Church had brought itself into disrepute, the vultures flocked to the dead carcase, and the laity tried to lay hold of the lands that had been accumulating in the hands of Churchmen for many centuries. Here we have an example of it, as we find a seisin granted by the Prebend of Durisdeer to Archibald Douglas, brother of Robert of Coshogle, of three 16-parts of the glebe and church lands belonging to the Rectory, and lying in the barony of Durisdeer, 14th October, 1569, with a confirmation by James VI. to Archibald, 19th May, 1585; also another to his son John, with 6 acres of ground called the Vicarland, and the right of pasturage, 19th March, 1612; then seisin of the whole granted by the above John to Archibald Douglas, in Enterkinefoot, 8th July, 1612. Then we find a precept of Clare Constat by Charles, Duke of Queensberry, as superior, for giving seisin of these lands to James Douglas, the great-grandson and heir of that John above-mentioned, 24th June, 1714. It may be added, that this Coshogle branch never recovered its position in the country.

COSHOGLE HOUSE.

There was a mansion-house here belonging to the family of Douglas, situated on the hill overhanging the Enterkine burn, a little way above the farm-house. Fifty years ago portions of the walls were still remaining, at least 6 feet high, and the buildings seem to have occupied not less than an acre of ground. Like all old keeps, it had been a strong building, as the walls were fully 6 feet thick. Nothing of all this now remains, as the stones have been scattered in all directions to build dykes, and we are only reminded of the ancient mansion by a stone built into the gable of a neighbouring cottage, about 2 feet long by 18 inches broad. At the top are the letters R.D.—N.J., with a coat of arms and 1576 inscribed. The letters represent Robert Douglas and his wife Nicholas Johnstoun. This Robert Douglas was called by Sir James Douglas of Drumlanrig his "special friend and cousin," and appointed in the tail-bond of

1574 to succeed to the Queensberry property if Sir James' grandson died without male issue.

DOUGLAS FAMILY OF DALVEEN.

Another cadet branch of the Drumlanrig family was the Douglas family of Dalveen, but what was the connection it is not possible with any certainty to determine. I would suggest that they may be sprung from Sir William Douglas, the first Baron (1388) of Drumlanrig, who married Elizabeth, daughter of Sir Robert Stewart of Durisdeer. Though no other son than William, who succeeded him in 1427, is mentioned, he may have had other children; and as Dalveen may have been the dowry of his mother, nothing is more likely than that the second son may have inherited his mother's portion. That the family must have been closely allied with the Douglas branch of Drumlanrig is proved by Hugh Douglas of Dalveen being appointed by Sir James of Drumlanrig, in the tail-bond of 1604, to succeed to the Queensberry property in case of a failure of other male heirs. They appear first in charters towards the end of the fifteenth century, for at least four generations, in connection with property in Durisdeer, though they seem to have hung on in that quarter till a later period, as Rae speaks of the death of Hugh Douglas of Dalveen and his lady, and of their being buried in Kirkbryde Churchyard. The first notice of the family is in a charter by Douglas of Dalveen, resigning the lands of Castlehill, Muircleuch, and Upper Dalveen, to John Menzies of Castlehill, 5th March, 1492. Then we have a grant made by Stewart of Rosyth to Hugh Douglas of Half-pennyland (Hapland), 6th August, 1500, and grants containing the 5 lib. land of Upper Dalveen. In the Terregles Inventory (No. 286) we have a "charter by Robert Douglas, Provost of Lincluden, with consent of the chapter thereof, in favour of Hugh Douglas of Dalwena, of the salmon-fishings in the Nith belonging to the provostry, in the barony of Drumsleit and Stewartry of Kirkcudbright, dated 10th September, 1558," and again (No. 288), "charter by Robert Douglas, Provost of Lincluden, in favour of the same Hugh of the lands of Fuffok and others in the Stewartry" of same date. Hugh did not retain these possessions as he resigns them (Nos. 299, 300, 301), 21st June, 1563, in favour of John Johnstoun, writer in Edinburgh. Then we hear of Stewart of Rosyth, as superior, granting seisin to William, son and heir of Hugh, of the lands of Upper and Nether Dalveen, Gateslack, Hapland, Enterkinefoot Mill, and the merkland of Muirhouse, 13th March, 1567. Then we have grants in favour of Archibald of Dalveen, the brother and heir of William, containing the whole of these lands, 23rd Oct., 1578; then again, in favour of Hugh, the brother and heir of Archibald, 21st Nov., 1590. He is succeeded in these lands by Hugh, the son and heir of the last Hugh, 9th Nov., 1607. The state of the country about this time is shown by a trial, which is given in Pitcairn's Criminal Trials (vol. iii., 270), where this Hugh of Dalveen pursues to the death, for the murder of his father, a Gilbert Johnnestoun, brother to Gawin Johnnestoun in Annand-holme. The trial is thus given (15th July, 1614):—

"Dilaitit, accuset, and persewit be Hew Douglais of Dalwein, as sone, Sir Robert Dowglais of Carschogill, as neir kinsman, of umq^{le} Hew Dowglais of Dalwein, fer airt and pairt of the thifteous steilling, conceilling, and away-taking, under silence and clud of nycht, furth of the landis and Maines of Dalwein, of threttie-sax heid of ky and oxin, pertening to the said ump^{le} Hew and his tennentis; committit be him, and utheris his complices, commone and notorious thevis, rebellis, and fugitives, upone the 28th day of August, 1597 years: And siclyk, ffor airt and pairt of the crewall Murthour and slauchter of the said umq^{le} Hew Douglas of Dalvene, in the following and redding of the said guidis, at the tyme foirsaid." He was found guilty and ordered to be hung on the "Castle-hill" of Edinburgh "quhill he be deid."

The family obtained from the Crown the church lands of Durisdeer, 6th May, 1608. They thus possessed a considerable property in the parish of Durisdeer, but like all the other cadet branches of Douglas, they got into difficulties, and William, son of the above Hugh, was obliged to part with all his possessions, 3rd Sept., 1633, to the Earl of Queensberry. They disappear from our sight at this time, except what Rae says of them above. As it was possible that some record of the family might have been found in Kirkbryde Churchyard, the tombstones have been examined there, but if any such ever existed they have disappeared.

DALVEEN CASTLE.

This mansion was situated near the present farmsteading of Nether Dalveen, and must have been of considerable size. One wing still existed in the memory of the present inhabitants, being of a square form, about 30 feet outside the walls, with a vault below, and an outside stone stair. It was taken down in 1836 to furnish materials for the present house, but the coat of arms belonging to the Douglases of Dalveen, and the date 1622, are still to be seen, carefully preserved in the walls.

These are all the families of Douglas who possessed property in the parish of Durisdeer, but all their lands were eventually bought by the Drumlanrig branch, and they are now merged in the great Queensberry estate. There were, however, other families of some importance, of which I shall now proceed to give an account, though it can only be of an imperfect nature, as they have long ceased to be connected with the parish.

MENZIES FAMILY OF ENOCH.

This family possessed a small barony lying between the Nith and the Carron, immediately opposite to Drumlanrig Castle. It is first noticed about 1327, when it was granted along with the barony of Durisdeer to Egidia, daughter of Sir James Stewart, High Steward of Scotland, and consisted of the lands, as far as old documents show, of Holestane, Blackmyre, Auchensell, Drumcruil, and Sourland.

The family known in early times as De Meyners, passing in the mouth of the Scotch into *Menzies*, and of the English into *Manners*, was of Norman extraction. In a charter of Alexander II. (1232), confirming the barony of Kylosbern to Ivan de Kyrkepatric, one of the witnesses is "Roberto de Meyners." This Robert, or his son, was one of the Regents of Scotland in 1255, during the minority of Alexander III. (Hailes' Annals).

Browne in his History of the Highlands and Clans (vol. iv., 500) says, "The family of Menzies obtained a footing in Athole at a very early period, as appears from a charter granted by Robert de Meyners in the reign of Alexander II. Alexander de Meyners, the son of this Robert, possessed the lands of Weem, Aberfeldy, and Glendochart, in Athole, besides his original estate of Durisdeer, in Nithsdale, and he was succeeded by his eldest son, Robert, in the property of Weem, Aberfeldy, and Durisdeer, while his second son, Thomas, obtained the lands of Fortingal. From the former of these the present family is descended." The arms of Menzies are given by Browne, with the motto, "Will God I shall."

Where Browne obtains this information respecting Durisdeer being the original estate of the family I know not, but the family was, I have no doubt, a branch of an old Norman family, and appears for the first time, so far as I have seen, in connection with the parish of Durisdeer in the time of Robert Bruce (1306-1329), when there is a charter (Robertson's Index, 13) by Bruce in favour of Alexander de Meyners and Egidia Stewart, his spouse, of the barony of Durisdeer. This Egidia Stewart was the daughter of James, High Steward of Scotland (Chalmers' Caledonia, vol. i., p. 585, quoting Robertson's Index, p. 19). Egidia resigned the barony of Durisdeer to her brother, Sir James Stewart, who received a charter of these lands, and another charter to him and his wife of the barony of *Enache* from Robert Bruce. This is the first notice of *Enoch* in any public document which has come under my notice. The family of De Meyners and Stewart of Durisdeer thus became connected as early as the time of Robert Bruce. In the reign of David II. (1329-1371) I have not been able to discover any reference to the family of Meyners in connection with Enoch, but near the beginning of the reign of Robert II. (1377), there is a charter of the whole barony of Enoch to

Robert de Meyners upon resignation of his father, John. John might, therefore, very well be the son of Alexander, husband of Egidia Stewart.

The 11th Dec., 1416, Henry St. Clair, second Earl of Orkney, appoints by will his brother-in-law, David de Meyners, Laird of Weymm, tutor to his son and heir William, afterwards third Earl of Orkney. On the 9th Dec., 1422, we hear of David's wife, Marota St. Clair, as Lady Enoch, giving commission of baillery to John Menzies of Enoch, her son. Sir David had, besides John, a son Cuthbert, who got part of Enoch. Then in the reign of James I. (1424-1437) there is a charter to John of the lands of Edderdamoky and Murynche with the barony of Enoch. John joins with his father in a donation to a monastery of a grant of one carrucate and a half of land in the ville and territory of Culter, forfeited by the late Robert Livingston, burgess of Linlithgow, dated 1449. Then on the 3rd March, 1456, in the reign of James II., we find the same John as one of the jury to serve Margaret Mundeville co-heiress to her father. We hear 12th March, 1478, of Marion de Carrutheris, daughter of Carrutheris of Holmendis in Annandale, spouse of umq[le] John Menzies of Veymme. So John was dead, and on the 4th Nov., 1479, the ward and marriage of his son and heir, Robert, was given up by the Bishop of Aberdeen to Cuthbert, probably her uncle. Robert's wife seems to have been Marion Crichton.

It is difficult to bring together a connected account of the succession of this old family, but what Nisbett in his Heraldry (p. 245) says seems to refer to this part of their history. "Sir David de Mengues (clergymen were called *dominus*, sir, in those days), about 1436, had a son, Cuthbert. There is a reversion of the lands of Auchintinsel (Auchinsell) and Duncrule (Drumcrool) in the barony of Enach, granted by said Cuthbert to John de Meignies, his brother-german, anno 1472. Cuthbert had a feu grant of part of the barony of Enach from John, his brother (Constat, per said reversion), and it is reckoned that the family of Enach and others in Dumfriesshire were descended of him." Nisbett goes on to say, "It is to be observed that before this period there were Menzieses of Enach mentioned; but that these were always the eldest sons of the family of Menzies; they were so called till they got the estate. The predecessor of the present family of Enach was in 1603 called Menzies of Boltachan; for, at that time, Adam Menzies of Boltachan got the superiority of Enach from Menzies of that Ilk. Charta in pub. archiv. ad annum 1603, and from that Adam is Captain Charles Menzies, the representative of that family, lineally descended." The above statement is what Nisbett says, but what follows is a more connected account of the family of Menzies in Durisdeer.

In the reign of James II. we reach a period when charters and public documents were more likely to be preserved, and the family can be traced for two hundred years, till their property is swallowed up in the Queensberry estate. This John, of whom I have spoken above, had a grant by Stewart of Rosyth, the descendant of Sir James Stewart of Durisdeer, of the lands of Upper Dalveen, in the Lordship of Durisdeer, 15th July, 1461. Then there is a charter to Edward de Menzies of Dalveen of the lands called Castlehill of Durisdeer, with the tower, fortlet, 8th Sept., 1489; a seisin to John, son and heir of Edward Menzies, of the lands of Castlehill and Upper Dalveen, 26th Oct., 1492; also, a charter to John

Menzies of Castlehill and his son William, after his own resignation and the resignation of Douglas of Dalveen, of the same lands of Castlehill, Muircleugh, and Upper Dalveen, 5th March, 1493; another to John Menzies in Castlehill of the lands of Muircleugh and Pennyland, lying in the same lordship, 22nd May, 1507. A few years after there is a charter by James IV., dated 2nd Oct., 1510, to Robert Menzies and his heirs-male of the barony of Enoch, with the mill and the altar of the Blessed Mary within the Church of Durisdeer. On the 1st Sept., 1512, Cuthbert Menzies of Auchinsell and John Menzies of Gardenland were witnesses to a charter of confirmation by Robert Menzies of that Ilk to his son and heir Robert, and Christina Gordon, his spouse.—(Drumlanrig Charters.)

There is a long blank in their history during the sixteenth century, and it is not till 8th Sept., 1603, that we find a charter in favour of Adam Menzies of Baltoquhan, of the lands of Enoch, Holstane, Cleughfoot; and again, 26th Nov., 1603, in favour of Duncan Menzies, of Enoch, in the lands of Rerick, &c., Perthshire. Then, six years afterwards, 22nd Aug., 1609, there is a charter of confirmation in favour of Adam Menzies of Baltoquhan, and Margaret Lindsay, his spouse, of the barony of Enoch. James, the son of this Adam, is retoured son and heir, 24th January, 1627, of the barony of Enoch.

It is about this time we come upon a trial in which this family of Menzies is concerned (Pitcairn's Criminal Trials, vol. iii., 442). William Menzies, of Castlehill, is mentioned 8th July, 1618. "Johnne Menzies, and Andro Menzies, brother to William Menzies, of Castlehill; Raulf Dalzell at the mylne of Durisdeer, James Barbour in Colymme, Hector M'Quhynzie in Thornhill, Jonet

M'Rone, spous to John Williamsoun in Dusdeir, Johnne Williamsone, hir spous for his intreis, Maroun M'Rone, sister to the said Jonet. Dilaitit of airt and pairt of the crewall murthour and slauchter, under nycht, of Patrick Douglas, sone to Hew Douglas of Bailiebought; committit the fyftene day of March last, at the gavill of the said Johnne Williamsone's hous, in Dusdeir, in his ganging furth of the town of Dusdeir to the place of Muirtown." The trial is put off, the laird of Dalzell, elder, and William Menzies, Castlehill, becoming pledges for Johnne and Andro Menzies, and Robert Douglas of Cashogil for the entrie of Hectour M'Quhynzie.

Then we come down a hundred years later, and find a William Menzies of Castlehill as heir to his grandfather, Edward of Dalveen, and again as heir to his grandfather, William of Castlehill, 6th Nov., 1677. (Drumlanrig Charters.) The family of Menzies got gradually into difficulties, and like many of the other small properties around Drumlanrig, the barony of Enoch eventually passed into the possession of the Duke of Queensberry, 1708. Here is the closing scene of this family, as told by Rae. "James Menzies of Enoch, with whom I was well acquainted, was married to Katharine Douglas, daughter of Col. William Douglas, second son of William, the first Earl of Queensberry, who disposed to his second son the Lordship of Torthorwald and the lands of Kinmount, called also Kelhead but because of his zeal, his father, who was much of a malignant spirit, found means to deprive him of the former, though his posterity have hitherto retained the other. This lady bore to Enoch several children, particularly these, whom I knew, viz., James, Thomas, Abigail, Agnes, Katharine, and Grizzel. He disposed to his eldest son James, who had a Captain's commission, the barony of Enoch, with the reservation of his own and his lady's life-rent of some part of it, and his son Captain James sold it to James, Duke of Queensberry, anno 1703, and bought the estate of Stenhouse. This barony is now mostly enclosed in a park." It will be observed that the Drumlanrig property was hemmed in very much by this barony, which was bounded by the Carron and Nith.

ENOCH CASTLE.

This castle, of which there are now no remains, was situated on a knoll close to the western bank of the Carron, and must have been of considerable strength in early times. Its site can be distinctly traced on all sides, having been of a rectangular shape, 118 feet by 78. It rises about 80 feet above the stream of the Carron, and to render it more secure, on the south and north the rock had been cut to a depth of about 20 feet with a width of not less than 15 feet. Thus on three sides it was rendered safe by its perpendicular banks. It has been supposed that it was surrounded by water led into a fosse from the higher part of the river, but an examination of the ground will show that this could never have taken place. It was the perpendicular banks that guarded it. The date of its erection is unknown, but Rae says he saw engraved on a stone 1281, and it is likely enough that this may be correct, as the family of Meyners, of which this is a cadet branch, was powerful at that period. It came into the possession of the Douglas family about 1703, and the stones of the castle were employed partly to build a manse at Enoch for the minister of Durisdeer, and partly to erect the park wall at Drumlanrig.

STEWART FAMILY OF DURISDEER.

Another family, which is of royal origin, is found to have possessed property in this parish—the Stewarts of Durisdeer. They possessed a barony of some extent, which is first heard of when it was granted by Robert Bruce, about 1327, to Egidia, daughter of Sir James Stewart, High Steward of Scotland, and consisted of the lands of Castlehill, where the manor-house was situated, Upper and Nether Dalveen, Thirstane, Gateslack, Stanebut, Burngrains, Muirhouse, Hafland, Inglestoun, and Annoltoun (called also Colin and Chapel).

The first of the family who is mentioned in connection with the barony of Durisdeer is Egidia, daughter of James, High Steward of Scotland, who succeeded his father in 1283. She had a charter from Robert Bruce, granting the barony to herself and her husband, Alexander de Meyners, but she resigned it in favour of her brother, Sir James Stewart, who became in this way first connected with the parish. This James commanded his brother's vassals in 1327, in a hostile incursion into England led by Randolph and Douglas.

There is the following charter of Robert II., dated at Perth, 6th April, in the fourth year of his reign (1374):—
"*Robertus Dei gratia rex, &c. Sciatis nos dedisse, &c., dilecto consanguineo nostro Roberto Senescallo de Innermuth, Mil. Omnes et singulas terras baronie de Dorrisder cum pertinenciis infra Vic de Drumf. que fuerunt Alex. de Meyners de Redchell et quas idem Alex. nobis sursum Reddidit et Resignavit. . . . Ten. et Hab. . . . in unam liberam baroniam, &c.*"

It is not easy to trace continuously the connection of

the Stewarts with this barony, but there is an obligation still extant, dated 10th Nov., 1390, at Bruges, "by William de Douglas, Lord of Nithsdale, Robert Stewart, Lord of Durisdere, William Douglas of Strathbrock, and James Douglas of Strathbrock, to pay to Laurence of Prestoun and David Palleyburg, of Edinburgh, £26 13s. 4d. sterling, for money lent in their necessities in the toun of Bruges."

This William, Lord of Nithsdale, was called "the Black Douglas," from the swarthy nature of his complexion. He was the natural son of Archibald "the Grim," and the first Lord of Nithsdale, being of enormous strength. He obtained in marriage Egidia, daughter of Robert II., the fairest woman of her age, getting with her Nithsdale as her dowry. When a truce was made, after the battle of Otterburn, 1388, between England and Scotland, disliking a life of inactivity, he joined the Teutonic knights of Prussia against the pagan natives of their country, and it was no doubt on his way thither that he and Robert Stewart of Durisdeer, his companion in arms, borrowed the money at Bruges to relieve them of their difficulties. Of the Stewarts we hear nothing more, but William de Douglas distinguished himself, was made Admiral of the Prussian fleet, Duke of Prussia, and Prince of Dantzic. He was murdered by a band of assassins on the bridge of Dantzic, in the pay of Lord Clifford, an Englishman, with whom he had had a quarrel. Before he left Scotland we hear of Robert Stewart being joined with him in an expedition into Ireland, to punish some marauding attacks of the Irish. They laid siege to Carlingford, took it, and returned home with great spoil (Hume of Godscroft, vol. i., p. 201).

Then we find a charter in 1398 by Sir Robert Stewart of Durisdeer to his kinsman, James de Dalrymple, of a part of the barony. Sir William Douglas, the first Baron of Drumlanrig (1388-1427), was married to his daughter. The barony belonged in later times to the Stewarts of Rosyth, who were Lords of Durisdeer. There is a charter of James IV., dated Edinburgh, 6th May, 1513, referring to this barony. "*Rex concessit Dav. Stewart, filio Gul. Stewart de Rossith, terras baronie de Durisdere, infra Vic. de Drumf, que quidem terre fuerunt dicti Gul. unite bar. de Rossith, Vic. Perth.*" Here we find that the two baronies of Rosyth and Durisdeer had been united. The following year they seem to have been disjoined, as we find the following charter of James V., in the first year of his reign, dated July 14th, at Edinburgh (1514). "*Rex cum consensu matris suæ Reginæ concessit Henrico Stewart fil. Dav. Stewart de Rossith, &c. Terras et Baroniam de Durrisdere, &c.*"

A portion of the barony of Durisdeer passed in 1573 to Robert Douglas of Coshogle. The last time that we hear of the family being connected with the parish is about 1675, when they made over what remained of the barony to the Earl of Queensberry.

DURISDEER CASTLE.

Though this castle has long disappeared, it was in early times one of the fortresses of the kingdom, as David II. is thought to have agreed to its being dismantled with the Castle of Morton and others, as part of the price of his ransom when he was prisoner in England. The English would not have thought of its destruction unless it had been a serious obstacle in their way. We hear of its being stormed by Sir Roger Kirkpatrick in 1356, along with Caerlaverock and Dalswinton (Hume's House of Douglas). It was situated about a quarter of a mile from the church of Durisdeer, not far from the farm-steading of Castlehill, the place-name recording the vicinity of the old castle. Rae says that the farm-house was built from the old town, "the stones of which were transported to a more accessible place, where they now stand." It was the manor-house of the barony of Durisdeer, belonging to the Stewarts of Rosyth, but not a single stone of it is to be seen on the hill, though the site is pointed out surrounded by a young plantation.

HUNTER FAMILY OF BALAGAN.

The origin of this old family is thus told by Rae in his manuscript history. "When King Robert Bruce was lying with the Scottish army near Glenwharg, and the English army at the moat in Balagan Holm, a man named Hunter, carrying a trumpet, and another named M'Gachen, bearing a pair of colours, came from the Scotch army to the head of the glen called Balagan; the one blew the trumpet and the other flourished his colours in sight of the English army, who, apprehending that the Scottish forces were immediately upon them, were so much affrighted that they fled out of the country. For which achievement King Robert gave Hunter the lands of Balagan, and to M'Gachen the lands of Dalwhat. If this tradition be true, the family of Balagan would appear to be a very old one. The last of them, it is said, usually contended with James Menzies of Enoch for precedency. But the family is now extinct. It terminated with three daughters, one of whom was married to Hunter of Polmoody, in Tweeddale; another to James Graham of

Shaw, in the parish of Hutton in Annandale; and the third to Wm. Charteris of Brigmoor, Commissary of Dumfries." The following are the lands which they possessed, viz. :—Balagan and Drumcrool, with its teinds, and Auchinsell, in Durisdeer; the Kirkland, manse, glebe, bank, and acres of ground in the holm of Penpont; also, Lochar meadow, Boatford, and Glen-whaparock, in the same parish; also, two marks of Tibbers Birks in the barony of Tibbers, and four marks of Drumshinnoch in the barony of Morton (1611-1653). All these lands passed in 1672 to the Earl of Queensberry. In 1685, when the deeds were made out respecting the sale, there is mention of an Ann Douglas, widow of William Hunter, W.S., and there is also notice of a Hunter of Auchenbonny (Auchenbenzie?). James Hunter of Balagan was retoured heir to his father, 31st December, 1661, and on 2nd December, 1664, sold to John Maitland of Eccles the church lands of Penpont.

These Hunters of Balagan were superiors only of the lands of Baitford, as we find a charter of resignation, 9th February, 1611, by Duncan Hunter of Balagan of the 14s. land of Baitford to John Hunter of Baitford, in life-rent, and Thomas, his son, in fee. Then on the 5th March, 1649, a charter by said Thomas Hunter of Baitford to James Hunter, son of John Hunter of Auchinbrache, and Nich. Hunter, his spouse, daughter of said Thomas, and to the heirs of their body, whom failing to Thomas, and the heirs to be holders of Duncan Hunter of Balagan, for the payment of a penny Scots. On the 15th January, 1678, there is a charter under the great seal to James Hunter of the foresaid lands against Hunter of Balagan. On 21st March, 1747, disposition by William, late of Baitford, grandson of said James, to Robert Dalrymple, W.S.

BALAGAN HOUSE.

There was here also a house belonging to the ancient family of Hunter, which was in existence at the beginning of last century, upwards of a mile north-west of Drumlanrig, on the western side of the Marr burn. There are now no remains of it to be found, but tradition has handed down that it stood on the site of the present hay-shed.

KING ARTHUR IN DURISDEER.

It is not without interest to find that this celebrated king and hero, half myth and half real, should have left a place-name in the parish, which is believed to be a reminiscence of his presence in the south of Scotland. There are various spots not far from us which are thought to reveal places connected with his history, and among others, Mr. Glennie in his " Arthuriana" or Arthur Localities (p. 78), thinks that the river Carron is the stream mentioned in the "Book of Taliessin" as the boundary of Garant, and that Caer Rywc, mentioned in another of these poems, probably refers to Sanquhar or Senchaer, the old fort, which is on the Crawick, a name formed from Caer Rawick, as Cramond is from Caer Amond (Four Ancient Books, ii., p. 401). As another proof of his presence among us, I would suggest that Queensberry is a reminiscence of the name of his queen, who was called Quenivere or Gwenever, and popularly Vanora, famous in his history for her bad conduct, while Glen-*marlin* on the Scarr carries us away to the magician Merlin, through whose arts Arthur and all his court are said now to be lying in an enchanted sleep under the

Eildons. This is the Merlin of whom Ariosto, in his "Orlando Furioso" (c. iii. v. 10), thus sings:

> *Questa è l' antiqua e memorabil grotta,*
> *Ch' edifico Merlino, il savio Mago*
> *Che forse ricordare odi tal 'otta*
> *Dove ingannollo la Donna del lago.*

> "This is the ancient memorable cave,
> Which Merlin, that enchanter sage, did make;
> Thou may'st have heard how that magician brave
> Was cheated by the Lady of the Lake."

Holywood has also some place-names, as Mr. Glennie thinks, connected with the story of Arthur, as we find on the left bank of the Clouden—the Cludvein, or Cledyfein, of the poems—the scene of the battle, also commemorated in the Book of Taliessin (i. p. 338), where

> "Lay the Peithwyr prostrate
> At the end of the wood of Celyddon."

This oak forest gave name to the abbey called Darcongal, "oak of St. Connel," known also as *Abbatia Sacri nemoris*, and the battle is no doubt recorded by the eleven large stones in an oval form a little distance from the present bridge. They are situated near the lower end of the sacred grove, and are a record of this battle of Pencoed. The Peithwyr were the Picts of Galloway, whose name has been handed down to us in Dal-*pedder* (peithwyr), which was originally in the parish of Kirkbride, but now in Sanquhar. It is curious to find that these Picts (Peithwyr) had stretched into Cumberland, as we find two place-names near Liddel's Moat, a few miles from

Longtown, still called Peithwyr Crook, now corrupted into Pedder Crook, and Peithwyr Hill, now Petter Hill.

That "boundary of Garant" (Carron), mentioned in connection with Arthur, may not unlikely refer to the "Picts' Wall," or "Deil's Dyke," noticed in "prehistoric times," and which runs on the face of the hills parallel to the Carron up towards its source. For what purpose it was intended it is difficult to say, unless for a mere boundary between different British tribes or races. It is distinctly traced above Gateslack about fifty yards above the point where the hill begins to rise precipitously. It is an earthen mound formed by scooping out the ground on the upper or eastern side, nowhere rising more than about 3 feet, and about 18 inches in breadth. For military purposes it must have been a slight protection, and if so, it must have been to withstand a hostile attack of opponents approaching from the lower ground. Whatever its purposes may have been, it must have cost great labour, though nowhere in this parish does it seem to have been built of stones. It stretches away into Galloway, and respecting it Mr. Joseph Train remarks:—"As it passes from Toregan to Drunandow it runs through a bog, and is only perceptible by the heather growing long and close on the top of it; whereas on each side the soil only produces rushes and moss. Near the centre of the bog I caused the peat to be cleared away close to the dike, and thereby found the foundation to be several feet below the surface, which appeared to me a sure indication of its great antiquity." This ancient wall in Galloway measures 8 feet broad at the base, and is mostly built of rough, unhewn blocks of moor-stone or trap. In this parish it is entirely of earth.

SIR WILLIAM WALLACE IN DURISDEER.

After Wallace relieved Sir William Douglas, the Hardy or Long Leg, as he was called, at Sanquhar Castle, which had been invested by the English, the English fled, according to the metrical story of "Blind Harry," down Nithsdale, pursued by the Scotch under Wallace (chapter vii., p. 307):—

> "Through Durisdeer he took the gainest gate,
> Right fain he would with Southern make debate,
> The plainest way above Morton they hold,
> Keeping the hight, if that the Southerns would
> House to pursue, or turn to Lochmabane."

And elsewhere Blind Harry says:—

> "Thir three Captains he sticked in that stound,
> Of Durisdeer, Enneth (Enoch), and Tybristoun."

We thus see that Wallace took the three castles of Durisdeer, Enoch, and Tibbers, and this must have been about 1297, or the following year. The English seem to have gone down the valley past Dalswinton, where they were defeated with a loss of five hundred men. We are then told—

> "The true Douglas, that I you told of aye,
> Keeper was made from Drumlanrick to Air."

This is possibly the earliest notice we have of Drumlanrig, but whether it refers to the barony or the castle, it is not possible to determine. At all events, it must have been a spot of some importance, as it is noticed as the southern limit of the district assigned to Lord Douglas; likely enough the barony was then in the possession of the Douglas family, as we know that it was some eighty years after.

The account given above is from Blind Harry, who flourished in the fifteenth century. The work is in eleven books, embodying all the traditions about Wallace, and containing many animated and picturesque descriptions, especially of war and battle pieces The only MS. copy known of the work is in the Advocates' Library, Edinburgh, dated 1488.

THE EARLS OF MAR IN DURISDEER.

It is curious to find the title of this northern family recorded by a place-name in this parish, and it no doubt arises from the heiress Margaret, Countess of Mar, who succeeded her brother Thomas, the thirteenth Earl, having married William, Earl of Douglas, who, in her right became fourteenth Earl of Mar, and is designed Earl of Douglas and Mar in several charters. By him she had a son, James Earl of Douglas and Mar, killed at Otterburn, 1388. It was this James that gave the barony of Drumlanrig to his son, the founder of the Queensberry branch. In this way we can trace the origin of the name of the streamlet Marr burn and Marr farm, a little above Drumlanrig Castle. Between Hapland and Inglestone there is a spot called the Mar, and a cleugh called Mar-cleugh. Montague Wood, immediately to the right of the road leading to the Holm, has received its name somewhat in the same way. Lord Montague was guardian to the present noble proprietor, Duke Walter, and to perpetuate his name in connection with this circumstance the wood was so called. At the same time it is right to say that the word Marr may be only a corruption of the Anglo-Saxon *Maera* signifying a boundary, and thus it would mean the boundary between the parishes of Penpont and Durisdeer, which it no doubt is in the greater part of its course. It would apply equally to the Mar-cleugh, which seems to have separated a part of Kirkbryde parish from Durisdeer. There is also in the high ground at the foot of Knockoney Dodd a Mar-burn and Lagnee Mar, near the boundary of Sanquhar and Durisdeer, so that it seems not unlikely that the name may have arisen from the Anglo-Saxon *Maera*, boundary.

DEER CAMP IN DURISDEER.

This Roman camp is situated about half-a-mile above Durisdeer Church, on the right bank of the Kirk burn. The position was well chosen, being at the end of a ridge, where it falls somewhat abruptly, and at some distance from the surrounding hills, so that it could not be attacked from the higher ground. The tower of the Church can be seen, but the view stretches away as far as Tynron Doon, across the Tibbers hill. It guarded the approach from Crawford Muir, and protected the whole valley of the Nith, being able to have communication by fire-beacons with the camp on Tynron Doon. Notwithstanding the wintry storms of seventeen hundred years, the form of the camp is still preserved, and can be traced with perfect accuracy. There is first the rampart formed by the earth dug from the fosse, and on which there would no doubt be palisades. Then there is a fosse which runs round the whole camp, except on the north-eastern side, where there is a piece of level ground 15 feet broad for the entrance. About 40 feet in front of this level ground there has been a small fosse, as an outer defence for the entrance. The site of the camp is considerably above the fosse. The fosse is about 560 feet in extent. The camp, which was a quadrangle, was of no great size, being 120 feet by 80 feet. The interior of the camp had been dug out and the earth piled up at the edges. The track of the old Roman road can be distinctly traced along the bottom of the hill on which the camp stands. It does not seem to have been paved, nor would it be necessary, as there could have been little traffic in this wild region. This road passed on through Crawford Muir, and Rae says that he has seen several miles of the Roman causeway standing through this muir, and indeed the Ordinance Survey shows that it can still be traced.

FORTS.

There are remains of three old forts, one on the east side of the Nith, not far from the spot where the fish creel is placed, and another on Drumcruil farm, and a third near Cleughhead, near the spot called Langknowe. The hill overhanging the Eila, or Priest's Holm, is called Castle Hill, though no remains of a castle can be seen.

THE LOWTHERS.

On the summit of this mountain the counties of Dumfries and Lanark meet, as also the lands of three lairds —the Duke of Buccleuch, the Earl of Hopetoun, and Mr. Irving of Newton—and here, owing to a superstitious feeling, it was the custom up to fifty years ago to bury suicides. Being on the edge of two counties and the borders of three lairds' lands, it was supposed that the spot could legally be claimed by none, as the boundaries of the properties had never been straightened. Dr. John Brown, in his interesting paper entitled "Enterkin," says: —" The bodies were brought from great distances all round, and, in accordance with the dark superstitions of the time, the unblest corpse was treated with curious indignity—no dressing with grave-clothes, no *stricking* of the pitiful limbs—the body was thrust with the clothes it was found in into a rude box, not even shaped like a coffin, and hurried away on some old shattered cart or sledge with ropes for harness. One can imagine the miserable procession as it slunk, often during night, through the villages and past the farm-steads, every one turning from it as abhorred. Then arrived at this high and desolate region, the horse was taken out and the weary burden dragged with pain up to its resting place, and carried head foremost as in despite; then a shallow hole dug, and the long, uncouth box pushed in—the cart and harness left to rot as accursed. The white human bones may sometimes be seen among the thick, short grass; and one that was there more than fifty years ago remembers, with a shudder still, coming—when crossing that hill top—upon a small outstretched hand, as of one crying from the ground; this one little hand, with its thin fingers held up to heaven, as if in agony of supplication or despair. What a sight seen against the spotless sky, or crossing the disc of the waning moon!"

These feelings have happily ceased to exist, and it is now known that suicide is committed scarcely by any but by those who have been afflicted by the will of a Higher

Power with mental derangement, and who are, therefore, irresponsible in their actions.

ECCLESIASTICAL ESTABLISHMENTS.

We are inclined to believe, though we have seen no proof of it, that the Douglas family of Drumlanrig must have had a right of chapelry in their own mansion, as we do not find any separate religious establishment in the neigbourhood of the castle, which could scarcely otherwise have failed to exist. Though no chapel was near to the castle, the united parishes of Kirkbride and Durisdeer had no fewer than seven places of worship: each of them was a centre of Christian civilization, and we are now reaping the fruits of the self-denying conduct of these old priests. Though they degenerated in later times from their pristine purity, we must not forget that Scotland owes a debt of gratitude to the men who sacrificed all the comforts of civilized life, that they might point the way to heaven to the barbarous inhabitants around them.

DURISDEER CHURCH.

At what period this church was founded there are no documents to show, but we may reasonably conclude that it was intended for the family of Stewart, since it is placed near their castle, and on a site particularly inconvenient for the greater number of the inhabitants of the parish. In the thirteenth century John de Huntedon, the rector of the Church of *Duresdeere*, granted to the monks of Kelso a fishing called the Foles-streme in the Tweed, near Berwick (No. 27, Chart. Kelso). The rectory of Durisdeer belonged to the Bishop of Glasgow in the reign of Robert Bruce (1306-1329), and the cure was served by a vicar. During the fourteenth century this rectory was constituted one of the prebends of the chapter of Glasgow, being the prebend of the sub-chantor.

In the "Protocol Register of the Diocese of Glasgow from 1499 to 1510," published by the Grampian Club, there is a curious transaction recorded in regard to this church. On the 13th December, 1505, "Dominus Jacobus Silver" resigns his office of succentor, prebend, canonry, and rectory of Durisdeer, to the Archbishop of Glasgow, who confers them on Sir John Rankine, rector of Hutone (Hutton). On the next day, Sunday, the 14th December, the Dean invests Sir *William* Silver with the office, canonry, prebend, and the Church of Durisdeer, resigned by Rankine, and on the 19th December, the new sub-chantor assigns to Sir James Silver, rector of Balmaclellan, a pension of 40 merks out of his prebend of Durisdeer, subject to confirmation by the Roman Curia.

So late as 1st August, 1570, we find Mr. Peter Young, "pedagogue to the King," presented to the sub-chantorie of Glasgow, and the parsonage and vicarage of Durisdeir, which were vacant, by the decease of Mr. John Hamilton. In a *taxatio* of those prebends during the year 1401, Durisdeer is taxed £3 (Privy Seal Reg., XXXIX, 2); whereas in Bagimont's Roll, drawn up, it is believed, in 1275, it is put down as £8, of course Scots money. In later times we find two-sixteenths of the Church lands granted by a crown charter in 1587 to Archibald Menzies of Dalveen, but like other parts of the parish they eventually merged in the property of the Queensberry family, which agreed, according to Rae, "with the minister to give him and his successors in the office about a hundred merks per annum, in the room of tithes and feus, so that the stipend of Durisdeer (which, beside three chalders of victual, was but eight hundred merks) is now (about 1730) fifty pounds sterling."

The church was probably dedicated to St. Cuthbert, as there is a well below the ford of the Kirkburn that still bears his name. There is another sacred well, called Holywell, a little above Enterkinefoot, giving name to Holywell-cleugh. In many places we find the name of Holywell, and here, no doubt, has often been the site of a Pagan worship, to which, in accordance with Gregory's well-weighed instructions, a Christian import was given by Augustine and his brother missionaries. Gregory, after careful consideration, came to the conclusion that the temples of the idols should not be destroyed, but that the idols should be burnt, and the temples, well sprinkled with holy water, should be supplied with relics, so that the people should continue to flock to the spot where they had been accustomed to meet for religious worship.

The monument in honour of Duke James and his Duchess is highly ornate, perhaps beyond what the simpler taste of the present day would allow. The effigies of the Duke and Duchess are of white marble, and though there be no name of a sculptor on any part of the monument, it is believed that the figures are the work of Roubilliac, who was the most distinguished sculptor of that time.

The Latin inscription to the Duchess evinces the strong affection borne to her by her husband, and the inscription to the Duke states nothing more than the truth, when it records the high honours which he had worthily earned from his country. It runs thus:—

> *Hic*
> *In eodem Tumulo*
> *Cum charissimæ Conjugis Cineribus*
> *Misci (Misceri) voluit suos*
> *Jacobus Dux Queensberriæ et Doverni,*
> *Qui ad tot et tanta honoris*
> *Et negotiorum fastigia,*
> *Quæ nullus antea subditus*
> *Attigit, evectus, Londini,*
> *Fato cessit sexto die*
> *Julii, Anno Christi Redemptoris,*
> *1711.*

"In the same tomb, with the ashes of his most beloved wife, James, Duke of Queensberry and Dover, has desired his own to be mingled, (a man) who having arrived to such and so great a pinnacle of honour and high employments as no subject before had reached, yielded to fate at London, 6th July, in the year of Christ our Redeemer, 1711."

The Douglas vault is beneath this monument, and was opened 16th May, 1836. An enumeration of the coffins will be found in Appendix No. III.

The family of Menzies had an altar in the Church of Durisdeer, which was called "The High Altar of the Blessed Virgin Mary." It is mentioned in the following charter of James IV., 1510, Oct. 2:—"*Jacobus rex., &c., concessit Roberto Menzies de eodem, Mil. et heredibus suis masculis cognomen et arma de Menzies, &c., terras et baroniam de Enache, &c., cum don. Cap. altaris B.*

Virginis Marie ap. ecclesiam par. de Durisdeer." As no chaplain officiated after the Reformation, the patron, Menzies of Enoch, enjoyed the revenues (Privy Seal, Reg. iv., 83), and it continued in that family till the reign of Charles II.

It is curious to find a clergyman in 1596, James Brysone, called of Christ's Church, Durisdeer. He is called the Commissioner of Nithsdale, who seems to have been the commendator or bailie of the Abbey of Holywood at that time; and Brysone gives a discharge to Homer Maxwell of the feus and teinds of the Merkland of Meikle Speddoch, in the parish of Holywood.

CHURCH OF KILBRIDE OR KIRKBRIDE.

The origin of this *ecclesiola*, which is unique in appearance, is unknown, but being close to Coshogle, where many different proprietors have resided, it is likely to have been founded by one of these families. The name was *Kilbride* from the twelfth to the sixteenth century. Curiously enough, in James IV.'s charter in 1507 it is called *Pan*-bride, as synonymous with *Kil*-bride, in the same manner as *Pan*-bride and *Pan*-mure in Forfarshire, where the *Pan* is used for the British *Llan*, church. In the sixteenth century the name of *Kil*-bride was changed to *Kirk*-bride. It was a distinct parish, and was only suppressed towards the beginning of last century, when Peter Rae was translated from Kirkbride to Kirkconnel, and the divisions of Kirkbride were annexed by the Lords Commissioners of Teinds, 19th July, 1727, to the parishes of Sanquhar and Durisdeer. The church was sacred to St. Bridget, an Irish saint, to whose memory we find many churches dedicated, not only in Ireland, but in every part of Great

Britain, though how she acquired this honour is a mystery. In Wales no less than nineteen churches are found dedicated to her. She was the daughter of Cadwrthai, being born in Ulster soon after the establishment of Christianity, and receiving the religious veil in early youth from St. Mal, the nephew and disciple of St. Patrick. St. Bride formed for herself a cell under an oak, called Kildara, the cell of the oak, and subsequently being joined by others of her sex formed a religious community, from which several other nunneries in Ireland derived their origin. She was regarded as the patroness of that country, and is supposed to have lived in the early part of the sixth century, being first mentioned in the Martyrology of Bede. One of the Hebrides near to Islay was called Brigidiani, from a famous monastery built there to her honour.

Tradition also states that she possessed miraculous gifts. Thus it is said that, as her father was opposed to her conversion to Christianity, she left her home and floated on a sod of earth till she came to the river Dovey, in North Wales, and that she there caused the rushes to be turned into trouts (Archæological Journal, iii., 224) for the sustenance of herself and her maidens. It was also common for persons in trouble to call upon St. Bridget, in the belief that she had power to prevent any accident happening to families. Sir Walter Scott (Guy Mannering, page 11) gives an incantation used in times of yore where her name is mentioned—

> "St. Bride and her brat,
> St. Colme and his cat,
> St. Michael and his spear,
> Keep this house fra reif and wear."

Such was the saint to whom this parish was consecrated.

The church is first mentioned in a charter of William, Bishop of Glasgow, in 1240, where it is called "the church of St. Brigid de Stranith" (Macfarlane's Coll. MSS.). It belonged in the reign of Alexander II. (1214-1249) to the monks of Holyrood House, and it was confirmed to them by William, Bishop of Glasgow, in 1240, but seems afterwards to have been relinquished for some other acquisition. It continued a rectory or parsonage till the Reformation. We find Walter de Lillesclif, the parson of Kilbride, swearing fealty to Edward I., and obtaining from him a precept to the Sheriff of Dumfries in September, 1296, for restoring his possessions (Rymer, ii., 723). Its value, according to Bagimont's Roll, about 1275, was taxed at £6 13s. 4d.

The church is now in ruins, but the walls still remain, and I am sure that I express the earnest wishes of the antiquarians of Dumfriesshire that what of Kirkbride now exists should be preserved for future generations. The noble proprietor has caused a substantial wall to be built round the grave-yard. The church has been of small dimensions, being 46 feet in length and 21 feet in width. The door is 2 feet 4 inches, and the window 1 foot 3 inches. The north-west gable has fallen. The font is still there, of very coarse stone, not unlike what is found at Dalgarnock church-yard, and the belfry still exists. The windows were very small, having iron stanchels. The iron frame to hold the baptismal basin is still remaining. The bell was stolen in 1857 and carried off some five hundred yards, and there broken, where the tongue and some fragments were found in a ditch and taken to the Court-house of Dumfries. A portion of it is preserved in Dr. Grierson's museum. There was an old superstitious notion connected with this bell, that whoever meddled with it would undoubtedly come to an unfortunate end. The thieves were not discovered, but likely enough, if we knew the end of the parties, it would be found that the superstition had been in this case a true prediction. There are several tombstones, but there is only one of special interest, erected to a "Robert Ramsay, servitor to Lord Hopetoun, who died December, 1674;" and it has been not unreasonably suggested that we may have here a reminiscence of the grandfather of Allan Ramsay, the author of the "Gentle Shepherd." This is by no means unlikely, as Allan's father was manager of Lord Hopetoun's mines at Leadhills; and I find on inquiry that two hundred years ago the inhabitants, as there was no grave-yard in those high regions, were obliged to convey their dead either to Crawford or Kirkbryde church-yards, which were nearly at equal distances from Leadhills. Old "Sandy Ferguson" of the Holm of Drumlanrig, lately dead, had heard that the Ramsays buried in Kirkbryde, and this confirms the suggestion that we have here a notice of a relative of the poet. In a rockery in front of Morton school-house, there is a piece of freestone which was found near the old church of Kirkbryde, with black-letter characters on it. As was generally the case with church lands, we find that those of Kirkbryde passed into lay hands. In 1541 the Rector of Kirkbryde, with consent of the Archbishop of Glasgow, and of the Provost and Chapter of Lincluden, granted a charter and seisin in favour of John Menzies, brother of Edward Menzies of Castlehill, giving to him and his heirs general the whole church lands of Kirkbryde, making 5 marks, A.E., and lying by annexation in the barony of Drumlanrig, for the payment of 10 marks yearly. They were then passed to Sir William Douglas of Coshogle for life, and to his son James in fee. In the year 1543 we find James Douglas of Drumlanrig obliged to find surety to appear "to underly the law for art and part of the slaughter of Mr. Hector Sinclare, rector of Kirkbryde" (Pitcairn's Criminal Trials, vol. i., part i., p. 329). The church lands came at last into the possession of the Douglas family of Drumlanrig, with the other part of the Coshogle property (Drumlanrig charters). The position of the old church had been well chosen, standing on the sloping side of a green hill, and looking down on the distant valley of the Nith, with the high hill of Criffel in the distance. On the right is a deep glen called "The Lime Cleuch," with bold and precipitous banks; while on the left the Enterkine burn passes through a darkly-wooded ravine.

There is an interesting tradition connected with this parish, which, though I have not been able to verify it, is worthy of being recorded. The Covenanting spirit was particularly strong in this quarter, and it is said that Kirkbryde was the first to throw off the Papal yoke and embrace the Reformed principles. The inhabitants were ahead of the Government, which had not yet declared itself, and not daring to make use of the church, met round an aged thorn, which no longer exists, under which the preacher stood. The tradition goes on to state that this thorn tree of Kirkbryde was, among many other things, excommunicated every year by the Pope. We believe the Papal government to have done many foolish things in its day, but the small parish of Kirkbryde can scarcely be imagined to have attracted its attention so as to have brought down on a senseless object the power of its church artillery. We may dismiss it as one of those curious legends that show the spirit of the times, but which is without foundation.

Another tradition is more likely to be true, as it is quite in keeping with the proceedings in other parts of the country in those days. "Rabbling," as it was called, was a common mode of getting rid of unwelcome clergymen, and something of the kind seems to have happened here, as it has been handed down that six of the stalwart inhabitants appeared before the manse, and so frightened the minister that he ran off and never returned. His name has not been handed down, nor even the exact period of time when it happened, but the story has nothing improbable in it. It may probably have been Robert Lockhart, who molested the parish in 1691.

The Rev. Mr. Porteus in his "History of Sanquhar," gives some curious stories in regard to the feelings of the people in the neighbourhood, when attempts were made to disjoin the parish. Thus: It is said that the Rev. Mr. Gibson, the first day he preached in the united parishes of Sanquhar and Kirkbryde, was struck dumb when attempting to give out the psalm, he having been attacked by paralysis. His offence was that he had declared that it was of no use to keep up Kirkbryde as a separate parish. Abraham Crichton, provost of Sanquhar, had gathered a number of workmen to the spot, declaring, "I'll sune ding doon the Whig's sanctuary;" and, though failing of his purpose, he some time after fell from his horse in Dalpeddar and broke his neck. Being buried in the church-yard of Sanquhar, the provost would not lie, and servant maids could not milk their cows, because Abraham's ghost kept grinning over the kirk-dyke, till Mr. Hunter of Penpont had lain the ghost.

Every one who had any hand in the spoliation of the "Auld Kirk" met with some disaster. An old wife, who carried off an iron "stanchel," or iron bar of a window, fell, along with her cuddy, down Enterkin and broke her thigh-bone. A man who took away a stone for a corner of a steading never wrought more. Taking ill immediately, he soon after died. Then Major Crichton, the chamberlain, said to a farmer, "You may take some of it, if you like, but I'll not touch it." The farmer, on hearing this, is said to have replied, "Weel, we'd better let it alane." Such are some of the traditionary legends respecting Kirkbride Church. It still stands, but unless some substantial repairs be ere long made on it, Time, which spares nothing, will set at nought such superstitious notions and level it with the ground.

I have some doubts as to the correctness of this anecdote in regard to Major Crichton, as it does not tally with what I know to have taken place many years ago. He gave directions to one of the officials at Drumlanrig, long since dead, to have the bell removed for safe custody, but the party receiving the order entreated that he should not be employed in such a dangerous business, and in consequence of this, the bell continued in its original place, till it was stolen and destroyed by tinkers. This anecdote I am able to give from personal knowledge.

CHAPELS.

Besides these two churches, there were several chapels in various parts of the parish, though the names of the saints to whom they were consecrated have passed away. In the beginning of last century, Rae says, that there was one on the west side of Carron water, about half-a-mile below Upper Dalveen, the yard of which was still to be seen in his time, but there was no vestige of the chapel or stones, except what might be found in the walls of the neighbouring houses. The spot is still called Chapel. This may have been the chapel belonging to the Douglas family of Dalveen.

Another of these chapels was immediately on the left hand, after you cross the ford below Enterkinefoot, lying close to the north on a rocky prominence, and respecting which Rae tells, that in his time "the chapel-yard was still entire, being enclosed with a stone dyke, though it is now fallen down; the chapel is still to be seen in the midst of it. This being situate in a remote solitary place, near the head of a steep rock, on the brink of the river, at a considerable distance from any houses, and the grounds about it generally covered with wood, I cannot perceive what use it has been, if it were not intended as penance for a person to stand there alone in a dark winter night." I have little doubt that this chapel had been founded for their own use by the family of Lyndesay, to whom in early times both Humbie and Crarieknowe belonged, and from whom the Douglas family of Drumlanrig bought the property in 1492.

Another of these chapels was at Crarieknowe, which, Rae says, "was there forty years ago. I observed many carved stones on the walls of one of the houses, such as used to be in chapels, and having inquired about them, the people told me that there was anciently a chapel there, which is a little to the westward of this place." There are a few houses at Crarieknowe still, but I do not find that any of the carved stones are to be seen.

The fourth chapel was, according to Rae, "to the east

side of the river Nith below Enoch Tower, at the head of that ground opposite to Drumlanrig Castle, which is called the Priest's Holm or Pool."

On Coshogle farm there is a cleugh called Chapel Cleugh, showing that in ancient times there had been a place of religious worship in this remote spot, though its site is now unknown, and its former existence is only pointed out by the place-name.

KNIGHTS TEMPLAR.

The knights had possessions in the parish, as we find reference in an old charter to a Templeland called Muirhouse.

CHURCHES AFTER THE REFORMATION.

At the Reformation all these chapels, if they had not ceased long before, came to an end and were represented by the churches of Kirkbride and Durisdeer, which were, both of them, at a very inconvenient distance from the larger number of the inhabitants. The patronage of these churches came into the possession of the Queensberry family, and much of their property, as in other parts of the country, went in the same direction. The patronage of Durisdeer Church continued to belong to the Duke of Buccleuch and Queensberry till the abolition of Patronage in 1874. The present stipend is 19 chalders, with £8 6s. 8d. for communion elements. In the return to the House of Commons (March, 1875), the total amount of stipend of Durisdeer is given as £345 14s. 3d., and the total annual value of living from all sources is £399 0s. 11d. The free teinds, according to the Abridged Statistical History of Scotland (1853), were in that year £1207 15s. 8d. The glebe consists of nearly 30 acres, valued at £25 annual value. The manse was built in 1763, having formerly stood at Enoch, and has been often repaired, though the rooms are still of small dimensions and the ceilings low. The church, though it has been often repaired, was built, as the inscription 1699 upon it shows, originally by Duke James in the form of a cross, the north arm of which is the sepulchral monument of the family of Queensberry. There was a steeple about ninety feet high, but, as it got gradually into disrepair and became dangerous, it has been removed. The church has been reseated within the last few years, and is in every way in excellent order, being seated for 540. There were two bells presented by Duke Charles; on one of which was the inscription— "*Ex dono Caroli Ducis de Queensberrie et Dover Parochiæ Dursdear*, 1729." They fell about the year 1825, and were broken. One is still in the church in a dilapidated state, while the other was recast, though it is again cracked. The two silver cups belonging to the Durisdeer communion plate were made, as the marks show, in Edinburgh, in 1620, by George Robertson, the silversmith who made the city mace. The flagons and patens were of pewter, and in a wretched dilapidated state. Two silver cups have been lately (1874) added at the expense of the Duke of Buccleuch, as like in workmanship as is possible to the old cups, and besides his Grace has given two silver patens and a silver flagon, designed under the superintendence of Mr. Gilchrist Clark to match the chalices. All are enclosed in a handsome oaken box made for the purpose.

The following is the list of Ministers in the churches of Kirkbride and Durisdeer:—

MINISTERS OF KIRKBRYDE.

1567—Thomas Weir, reader.
1568—Thomas Macgunzeon.
1571-74—Alexander Myll.
1574-78—William Runcyman.
1579—William Douglas.
1585-91—Simon Purdie.
1615—John Forke.
1634—Robert Blackwood.
1655—Thomas Shields, deprived by the Acts of Parliament, 11th June, and of the Privy Council, 1st October, 1662.
1677—Robert Lockhart. In 1691-1693 he molested the parish, though legally cast out, and prevented them getting another minister.
1689—Thomas Shields returned, and was restored by Act of Parliament, 25th April, 1690.
1703—Peter Rae, clerk to the Presbytery of Penpont and Synod of Dumfries, translated to Kirkconnel, 19th April, 1732.

MINISTERS OF DURISDEER.

1567—Lyon Brown, exhorter.
1570—Peter Young, presented by James VI.
1575—James Lindsay, presented by James VI.
1576—Alexander Brysoun, presented by James VI.
1577—James Beton.

This year the parish of Durisdeer appears in the

proceedings of the General Assembly, for one of its inhabitants having contravened the laws of the church as to marriage. We are told in Calderwood's "History of the Kirk of Scotland" (vol. iii., p. 386):—"In trial of commissioners of counties, Mr. Peter Watsone was delated for mareing Garlais in a privat hous. He alledged Mr. Willocke had done the like there. The Assemblie, in respect of the acts made prohibiting privat celebrations of marriage, ordeaned Mr. Peter to confesse his offence, in transgressing the said acts, upon a Sabbath-day, in the parish kirk of Disdeir, where the parties sould have beene maried in presence of the congregatione and Mr. James Beton, minister: which acts he shall also read in the presence of the people: and to report a testimoniall from the said Mr. James of the performance of this ordinance to the nixt Assemblie."

1578—Hercules Stewart, reader, having under his charge Glencairn, Morton, Penpont, and Tynron.

1579-1601—James Brysone, presented by James VI., was appointed by the Privy Council, 6th March, 1589, as one of the commissioners for the preservation of true religion in Sanquhar or the over-part of Nithsdale. He was a commissioner of Halliwoode in 1600.

1594—Andrew Johnstoun.

1601—Thomas Abernethie, A.M. Left, with the advice of the Presbytery, "for his weill and the weill of the kirk," and went to Hawick.

1607—Robert Henderson, A.M.

1608-1657—George Cleland. Gave xx lib. towards the building of the Library and College of Glasgow, about the 1st of August, 1632. By his latter will he "desyred that my bookis may be equallie divided betwixt my two sons, Mr. John, minister of Stow, and Mr. George, minister of Morton, reservand as many Inglis' bookis as may serve for the use of my wife and her children."

1658—Alexander Strang, A.M. Deprived in 1662. He was called before the Privy Council, 11th August, 1670, for keeping conventicles, which he positively denied, affirming that he waited on ordinances every Sabbath in the parish where he lived, on which he was dismissed. He was cited before them again, 11th August, 1677.

1663—Francis Gordon, appointed by Bishop of Glasgow.

1667—George Shields, A.M., who was at Durisdeer for some years, and then was settled at Hutton; and for serving the cure of Durisdeer he employed Mr. James Hume, who married Mary Kirkpatrick, daughter of Mr. Kirkpatrick of Auchensow. He continued there for several years, and was at length settled at Torthorwald, and thence (1682) transported to Kirkmahoe, where he continued till the Revolution. Next after Mr. Hume, Mr. Shields sent Mr. Forrest to Durisdeer (Rae's MS.).

1679-1683—George Cleland, A.M., the younger, having conformed to Prelacy, was transported from Morton to his father's church of Durisdeer. He had "ane precept granted by the Lords of his Majesty's Exchequer upon the laird of Meldrome, and that as the pryce of a horse quhiche the rebells took from him in 1679."

1683—John Alexander. Ousted by the people in 1689.

1689—Alexander Strang, A.M., above-mentioned, returned to his former charge, but being old and infirm he demitted 27th March, 1693.

1700—Thomas Tod, A.M. He scrupled to acknowledge King William as the lawful magistrate of the kingdom, but at last yielding, he was ordained 5th Sept.,

1700. He threatened separation from the church in 1712, on account of the Oath of Abjuration, but did not. He died 28th June, 1742, in his eighty-fifth year and forty-second of his ministry. His last will and testament, dated 2nd October, 1741, with codicil dated 25th December, 1741, begins in these words—"I Mr. Thomas Tod, Minister of the Gospel at Durisdeer, being inffirm of body but of perfect memory and health and composure of mind, blessed be God; and not knowing what may be the issue of my bodily infirmity, I have thought fit, for preventing differences among my relations after my decease, when at the pleasure of Almighty God the samen shall be, To make my Latter Will and Testament in manner following: And in the first place I leave my soul to God, who gave it, depending upon him for Salvation through the merites of Jesus Christ my blessed Saviour and Redeemer, and my body to be decently interred in the Church-yard of Durisdeer, &c." He mortified 2000 merks to the poor of the parish of Durisdeer and for a school at Townhead of Fardingbank, on the west side of the parish. Birleyhill school was thus originated, and at present (1873) the School Board draws the interest of 1252 merks, being the portion of the mortification which was given for the school, equal to £69 11s. $1\frac{4}{12}$d. sterling, in support of this school. Alexander Bayne, minister of Keir, Robert Hunter in Crawfordstoun, Peter Rae, minister of Kirkconnel, Robert M'Morrine, assistant minister at Durisdeer, and John Graham, postmaster at Moffat, were his executors.

1744—William Cunninghame, A.M. Translated to Sanquhar, 22nd May, 1753.

1754—Robert Greir. Deposed for immorality, 31st May, 1757.

1755—John Johnston.

1771—John M'Kill. Died 1794, in the fifty-fourth year of his age and twenty-third of his ministry. His name is still kept up in the parish, as one of the Maxwells, farmer in Ingleston, is called M'Kill Maxwell.

1794—John Williamson. Died 24th July, 1816.

1817—George Wallace, who was seized with sudden illness in the pulpit, 17th Sept., 1854, and died within one hour, in the sixty-fifth year of his age and thirty-eighth of his ministry.

1855—Henry W. Smith. Translated to Kirknewton, 1862.

1862—Henry M. Hamilton. Translated to Hamilton, 1864.

1865—D. Morrison, M.A. Translated to Dunblane, 1872.

1872—Charles West M'Kenzie.

COVENANTING TIMES.

I cannot close this account of ecclesiastical affairs in this parish without referring to that unfortunate period in the history of our country when the spirit of toleration in religion was little understood or practised by any class or sex in Scotland. Like many other parishes in Upper Nithsdale, the inhabitants of Durisdeer were deeply tinged with reformed principles, and some of them were prepared to brave every danger and submit to persecution even to death rather than bow the knee, as they thought, to Baal. The wilds of Enterkine were often a place of refuge from their enemies, and tradition hands down the name of Elias Wilson, as one of those who saved himself in this way. He lived in a cottage on the farm of Dalveen, and hearing that his enemies were on their way to apprehend him, he fled to a cave. Here he maintained his ground against the dragoons, shooting several, and during the night escaping with his wife to the hills. He succeeded in weathering the storm and lived to see the Revolution. There are now no caves known to the inhabitants of Enterkine, but the persecution may be perfectly true, though Dr. Simpson, from whose " Traditions of the Covenanters " I quote the story, may have been misled in some of the particulars. There can, however, be no doubt respecting the rescue which took place of some Covenanters at Enterkine, who were being conveyed to Edinburgh by a company of dragoons. Defoe's account of the affair and of its wild scene in his Memoirs of the Church of Scotland, is so graphic that we cannot attempt to give it in other language than his homely English:—

" This Entrekein is a very steep and dangerous mountain; nor could such another place have been easily found in the whole country for their purpose; and, had not the dragoons been infatuated from heaven, they would never have entered such a pass without well discovering the hill above them. The road for above a mile goes winding, with a moderate ascent on the side of a very high and steep hill, till on the latter part, still ascending, and the height on the left above them being still vastly great, the depth on their right below makes a prodigious precipice, descending steep and ghastly into a narrow deep bottom, only broad enough for the current of water to run that descends upon hasty rain. From this bottom the mountain rises instantly again, steep as a precipice, on the other side of a stupendous height. The passage on the side of the first hill, by which, as I said, the way creeps gradually up, is narrow, so that two horsemen can but ill pass in front; and if any disorder should happen to them, so as that they step but a little awry, they are in danger of falling down the said precipice on their right, where there would be no stopping till they came to the bottom. And the writer of this has seen, by the accident only of a sudden frost, which had made the way slippery, three or four horses at a time of travellers or carryers lying in that dismal bottom, which, slipping in their way, have not been able to recover themselves, but have fallen down the precipice and rolled to the bottom, perhaps tumbling twenty times over, by which it is impossible but they must be broken to pieces ere they come to stop.

"In this way the dragoons were blindly marching two and two with the minister and five countrymen, whom they had taken prisoners, and were hauling them along to *Edinburgh;* the front of them being near the top of the hill and the rest reaching all along the steep part, when on a sudden they heard a man's voice calling to them from the side of the hill on their left a great height above them.

"It was misty, as indeed it is seldom otherwise on the height of that mountain, so that nobody was seen at first. But the commanding officer hearing somebody call, halted, and called aloud, *What d'ye want, and who are ye?* He had no sooner spoke, but twelve men came in sight upon the side of the hill above them, and the officer call'd again, *What are ye?* and bad *Stand.* One of the twelve answer'd by giving the word of command to his men, *Make ready!* and then calling to the officer said, *Sir, will ye deliver our minister?* The officer answer'd with an oath, *No, sir, an' ye were to be damn'd.* At which the leader of the countrymen fir'd immediately, and aimed so true at him, tho' the distance was pretty great, that he shot him thro' the head, and immediately he fell from his horse. His horse, fluttering a little with the fall of his rider, fell over the precipiece, rolling to the bottom, and was dashed to pieces.

"The rest of the twelve men were stooping to give fire over the body when the next commanding officer call'd to them to *hold their hands*, and desired a *truce*. It was apparent that the whole body was in a dreadful consternation; not a man of them durst stir a foot, or offer to fire a shot. And had the twelve men given fire upon them, the first volley, in all probability, would have driven twenty of them down the side of the mountain into that dreadful gulph at the bottom.

"To add to their consternation, their two scouts who rode before gave them notice *that there appear'd another body of arm'd countrymen at the top of the hill in their front?* which, however, was nothing but some travellers, who, seeing troops of horse coming up, stood there to let them pass, the way being too narrow to go by them. It's true there were about twenty-five more of the countrymen in arms, though they had not appear'd, and they had been sufficient if they had thought fit, to have cut this whole body of horse in pieces.

"But the officer having ask'd a parley, and demanded *What it was they would have?* they again replied, *Deliver our minister*. *Well, sir*, says the officer, *Ye's get your minister, an' ye will promise forbear firing*. *Indeed, we'll forbear*, says the good man. *We desire to hurt none of ye; but, sir*, says he, *belike ye have more prisoners*. *Indeed, have we*, says the officer; *and ye mon deliver them all*, says the honest man. *Well*, says the officer, *ye shall have them then*. Immediately the officer calls to *bring forward the minister;* but the way was so narrow and crooked he could not be brought up by a horseman without danger of putting them into disorder, so that the officer bade them *loose him and let him go,* which was done. So the minister stept up the hill a step or two, and stood still. Then the officer said to him, *Sir, an I let you go, I expect you promise to oblige your people to offer no hindrance to our march.* The minister promised them *he would do so. Then go, sir,* said he, *you owe your life to this damn'd mountain. Rather, sir,* said the minister, *to that God that made this mountain.* When their minister was come to them their leader call'd again to the officer, *Sir, we want yet the other prisoners?* The officer gave orders to the rear, where they were, and they were also deliver'd. Upon which the leader began to march away, when the officer call'd again, *But, hold, sir,* says he, *ye promised to be satisfied if ye had your prisoners; I expect you'll be as good as your word. Indeed, shall I,* says the leader; *I am just marching away.* It seems he did not rightly understand the officer. *Well, sir, but,* says the officer, *I expect you call off those fellows you have posted at the head of the way. They belong not to us,* says the honest man, *they are unarm'd people waiting till you pass by. Say you so,* said the officer. *Had I known that you had not gotten your men so cheap, or have come off so free.* Says the countryman, *An ye are for battle, sir, we are ready for you: still, if you think you are able for us, ye may trye your hand; we'll quit the truce if you like. No,* says the officer, *I think ye be brave fellows, e'en gang your gate."*

The mode in which this rescue took place, as given by Defoe, does not altogether agree with the account of Wodrow (vol. ii., 448), who tells us that the soldiers, when they were required to yield up their prisoners, fired a volley. This was returned, when one of the soldiers was killed and several of them wounded. Six of the prisoners were rescued. There is a possibility, however, that the rescue of which Defoe and Wodrow give an account may have taken place at different times, and in that way may both be correct.

This rescue in July or August, 1684, for Wodrow cannot tell when it occurred, was no doubt galling to the officers of Government, and vigorous measures were adopted to discover the parties who had inflicted the blow. A strict search was made throughout the district, and when this was without effect, public intimation was given in all the churches, in ten or twelve parishes nearest the scene of the rescue, that all above fifteen years of age should meet at New Dalgarnock, now Thornhill. When they assembled, in great numbers, the following questions were asked:—"Do you know who rescued the prisoners at Enterkine? Do you know which way they fled? Do you know where they are at present?" It was soon discovered that two of the leaders of the band were James and Thomas Harkness, of Locherben, in the parish of Closeburn, whose relative still lives in the neighbouring farm of Mitchellslacks. Being seized, they were conveyed to Edinburgh, and condemned to death; but James, with twenty-five others, avoided the execution of the sentence by escaping from the Canongate Jail; Thomas Harkness was not so fortunate, and suffered with others. "They were," says Wodrow, "brought into Edinburgh about one of the clock, and that same day they were sentenced and executed about five of the clock." James lived to 1723, and is buried in Dalgarnock church-yard.

These Harknesses of Closeburn had attracted the attention of the authorities even before the rescue at

Enterkine, as we find in Wodrow (vol. ii., 104) a royal proclamation, dated 5th May, 1684, in which their names are mentioned as avoiding trial "James Harkness, in Locharbain," and as resetters of fugitives "Thomas Harkness in Locharbain or Laight, William Harkness in Mitchellslacks." The dates in Wodrow as to the events in which the names of these Harknesses occur do not agree with his narrative. Their names are in the proclamation of 5th May: the rescue at Enterkine is said to have taken place in July or August—James was imprisoned and escaped, while Thomas was executed on the 5th August. There is no doubt that Thomas suffered martyrdom, but there is something wrong about the dates.

Be this as it may, the Harknesses of these mountainous regions were bold and determined men, worthy descendants of those Scotchmen, who had maintained their country's independence for five hundred years against England. They had fled at the beginning of the persecution to Ireland, but had returned to their native land. James Harkness was known under the *soubriquet* of "Long Gun," and Thomas was called "White Hose." James, when he was pursued by Red Tom, one of Glenæ's men, turned boldly upon him and called out—"Stop there, or I'll shoot you." Red Tom rushed on, when James pulled the trigger and shot him. The spot in Closeburn is still known as Red Tom's Gutter, where he fell; and tradition says that the gutter ran three or four days red blood, and thus got its name. Thomas, the martyr, had a posthumous child born to him, called Thomas, in 1685, whose tombstone, with the following inscription, is found in Dalgarnock church-yard:—" Here lyeth the body of Thomas Harkness, who departed this life on June 3,

1756, aged 71, who was son to Thomas Harkness, who suffered martyrdom in the time of the hot persecution, for the interest of Christ." The descendants of this Thomas cannot be traced. Whether James and Thomas of Locherben and William of Mitchellslacks were brothers, it is impossible to determine with certainty, but the dates would lead me to believe that they were so. From William Harkness of Mitchellslacks we can trace the following pedigree for families who live amongst us.

William Harkness in Mitchellslacks, who is named in a royal proclamation, 5th May, 1684, as a resetter of fugitives, was probably brother to Thomas Harkness of Locherben, the martyr.

The following pedigree does not include all the members of the different families, but only the more prominent individuals:—

William Harkness in Mitchellslacks=
  b. 1646.

| Thomas H., | William H.,=1 Isabel Currie.
  b. 1681,   b. 1689,   =2 Cat. Ferguson.
  d. 1702.   d. 1769.   =3 Grizzel Ewart.

| Thomas H.,=Janet Scott,
  d. 1797.   d. 1782.

| William,=Janet Walker, | John=Janet Harkness
  died 1823. died 1853.   of Mitchellslacks.

| Thomas, | Alexander, | William, | John,
  Writer in   Rector of   Minister of   Principal of
  Dumfries,   Kilmarnock, Fala and   Elphinstone
  d. 1832.   d. 1851.   Soutra,   College, Bom-
                           d. 1841.   bay, for 20 years.

John H.=Janet Harkness,
Mitchellslacks, died 1859,
died 1852, aged 74.
aged 87.

Thomas,=Alison Irving.
Mitchellslacks.

| Walter. | Jessie.=David Macqueen.

(See Appendix No. IV.)

James Harkness of Locherben narrowly escaped martyrdom; the more prominent of his descendants are here given:—

James H. of Locherben,=
b. 1651, d. 1723, aged 72.

| William H.,=Katrin Hoatson,
b. 1697, b. 1696,
d. 1767. d. 1764.

| John, in Holestane,=Margt. M'Cormick,
b. 1710, b. 1719,
d. 1790. d. 1771.

| Margt. | Isabell. | William,=1 Cath. Fairservice.
b. 1754,=2 Elzth. Corry.
d. 1811.

William=Catherine Fairservice.

| John. | Peter. | Jane. | Janet=John Harkness
of Mitchellslacks.

| William=Elizth. Corry.

| Elizth. | Thomas, | Walter, | Christopher,
Baillie of b. 1801. Provost of
Dumfries, Dumfries,
b. 1798. b. 1809.

Another of these old worthies was Daniel M'Michael, born at Dalzien, near Glemmanna, in the valley of the Scaur in Penpont, and living latterly at Blairfoot, a cottage on the farm of Burn, in Morton. This cottage became known as a place where the Covenanters convened for spiritual converse. Tradition tells us that in the beginning of 1685 Daniel was confined to his bed by fever, and was surrounded by a number of his friends, when notice was given that the dragoons were approaching, led by General Dalziel of Glenæ. His friends carried him with them in the direction of Durisdeer, but he was at last obliged to be left, when he was taken and shot at the Pass of Dalveen. He was buried in the church-yard of Durisdeer, where the following epitaph is found:—

"Here Lyes Daniel M'Michel, Martyr Shot Dead At Dalveen By Sir John Dalziel, For His Adhering To the Word of God, Christs Kingly Goverment In His House: And the Covenanted Work of Reformation Against Tyranny, Perjury And Prelacy: 1685. Rev. 12. 11."

> "As Daniel cast was into Lyon's den,
> For praying unto God and not to men;
> Thus Lyons cruelly devoured me,
> For bearing witness to Truth's testimony.
> I rest in peace till Jesus rend the cloud
> And judge 'twixt me and those who shed my blood."

The tradition is that M'Michael had got as far as Nether Dalveen, when he was overtaken and confined in the barn during the night. Next morning he was taken out and three dragoons were ordered to shoot him, but from pity they thrice missed him, when Dalziel, enraged at their conduct, compelled them by threats of immediate death to obey his orders. In 1836, when the present farm-house was being erected, the masons put up a small monument to mark the spot where he was shot, and an iron railing has been placed round the monument to preserve it. The inscription upon this monument is, "Sacred to the memory of Daniel M'Michael, who suffered martyrdom here by Sir John Dalziell, A.D. 1685. Erected 1836."

Another of these worthies was called Dow, and on the banks of the Enterkine, west of Nether Dalveen farm-steading, there is a cairn called Lag-dow, where he had been caught by Grierson of Lag and shot. A few rude stones were placed there to commemorate the spot, which is called Lag-dow. I give this tradition, but I am afraid that it must, like many others of the same kind, be set down as one of the myths, which are often found to have originated in a way for which it is difficult to account. The hill in the neighbourhood has been called from time immemorial Upper and Nether Lagnee. Lag, or Lug, is a Celtic word, found in the Scoto-Irish language, signifying a hollow, which describes with great precision the Castle of Lag, the residence of the Griersons.

While the word was applied to a hollow in a mountain, it occasionally happened that the name of the hollow was extended to the mountain itself, and in this case of Lagnee it seems to have been so. Lag-dow cairn would thus mean the cairn of the black hollow.

PREHISTORIC TIMES.

I have given the history of the inhabitants of this parish during the last thousand years, but of course it had been peopled in ages long gone by, and of that early period we can only gather a slight knowledge from the accidental

EARLY HISTORY OF DURISDEER. 137

discovery of sepulchral remains, and the implements that have been sometimes buried with these bodies. In every parish such discoveries are made, but they have been often destroyed from the ignorance or carelessness of those into whose possession they have come. There are some proofs of the existence of an early race in this parish, and this is not surprising, as its hilly character could easily preserve such ancient remains. The Celtic or Deil's Dyke is seen for two miles close to Glenginny Moor, and again on the opposite side of the Nith bits of it are observed running up towards Nether Dalveen, and then crossing the Carron, along the foot of Pettylung and Castlehill, running up the Kirkburn towards the Waldpath. It continues across Durisdeer Hill, also the hills above Gateslack steading, and onwards to Morton Mains. It appears to be entirely made of earth. It is difficult to imagine for what purpose this dyke, which can be traced for many miles along these hills, could have been intended. Though it may have been higher than it now appears, at no time could it have been a sufficient defence against a hostile attack. Offa's Dyke, in Wales, is of a much more defensible character, and is sufficiently lofty to have been a serious obstacle to a barbarous enemy if guarded by resolute men.

MOAT OF BALAGAN.

Whether what is called the Moat of Balagan is prehistoric it is difficult to say. It is an artificial mound 200 yards to the south of the present farm-house, rising in the middle of a level field to the height of nearly 20 feet. Its diameter at top is 10 yards, extending about 30 yards at base. There is a track round it, mid-way between base and top, very much resembling a carriage drive. There is no appearance of any building having been erected on its summit, and as Druid remains are found at no great distance from it in the parish of Penpont, it is not unlikely to have been used for some religious purpose in early times. Bal and Belstane point to fire-worship.

At the same time, it is to be recollected that the Norsemen were not only settled in the lower parts of Dumfriesshire, along the coast of the Solway, but that place-names show that they had penetrated to Durisdeer, and wherever they settled we know that they carried the customs of their northern fatherland with them, and of all these customs the most sacred were the judicial and legislative assemblies called *Things*. They generally met on some hill or mound, where their deliberations could be carried on secure from lawless disturbance. By far the most interesting of these ancient Westminsters is Tynwald Hill in the Isle of Man, and it is curious to note that the formation of that ancient mound is not unlike this Moat of Balagan. Here we have a circular stage round the mound; in that of the Isle of Man there are four circular concentric stages. The mound is 18 feet in height; that of Balagan is nearly 20 feet. The ancient place of national assembly of Scotland was the Mote Hill at Scone. This hill, perhaps the most interesting historical memorial in Scotland, is said to have been recently removed to improve the view from a drawing-room window. In the midst of the town of Hawick there is a singular conical mound called the Moat Hill, and in Galloway we have also the Mote of the Mark. This Moat of Balagan, therefore, may have been the place of meeting for the Norsemen of Upper Nithsdale.

There is also, about 300 yards west from Gateslack, a hill, called Moat Knoll, situated on a ridge near the junction of the Carron and Hapland burn, which is partly natural and partly artificial. This may also have been used for judicial purposes. The ground has been under the plough for the last forty years, and is called Morris. Mr. Rae of Gateslack recollects seeing a cist discovered about 100 paces from the house, consisting of slabs of native stone, but its contents seemed to have mouldered to dust. In a gravel-pit some little distance from the house there was an urn discovered, which fell to pieces when exposed to the air.

On the outskirts of the parish, to the west, there is a moat at the side of Druidhill burn 1060 feet in circuit. The face, which is sloping, is 200 feet. The trench behind is 124 feet long, 10 feet broad, and 4 feet deep. About 130 yards distant from it, on the opposite side of the burn, and on Merkland farm, within the parish of Penpont, there is another moat of still larger dimensions. It is 1300 feet in circuit, 30 feet high—being in the form of a hillock, flat at the top, somewhat oval in shape. In one direction it is 270 feet, and in another 140 feet. The face, which is almost perpendicular, is 140 feet in height. There is a trench behind it, ploughed a few years ago, 200 feet long, 25 feet broad, and 8 feet deep. There are two ridges extending from the north and south sides of the moat, about 200 feet long and 20 feet high. This moat has Druidhill burn on the east, and Dunduff burn, a tributary, on the north. In the trench, where ploughed, a gold coin was found, which from its inscription seems to have been of the reign of one of the Edwards.

They are both of them natural hills formed into moats by earth piled up, at least on the top, though there is no appearance of a hollow from which the earth had been dug, unless it be the trench, which is not of sufficient depth to afford materials for such masses. They are in too lofty and hilly a situation to allow us to suppose that they were for military operations. The place-name of Druidhill in the neighbourhood would rather lead us to believe that their erection must have been for some religious purpose. We know that in early ages high places were selected for religious worship, it is said, because they were thought to be nearer to the gods, and that on them prayer was more acceptable than the valleys (Lucian De Sacrific, i. 4.). Ancient writers abound in allusions to the worship of the gods upon the hill tops, and we know that some of those divinities took their distinctive names from the hill on which their principal seat of worship stood, such as Mercurius Cyllenius, Venus Erycina, Jupiter Capitolinus. It is, therefore, not unlikely that we have here an example of that primitive worship which in the early ages of the world was so widely spread.

There are some remnants of a tumulus on Cairn Hill, in the north-west of the parish, 1471 feet above the sea level.

BELSTANE.

There is a large boulder rock, called Belstane, about a mile above Drumlanrig Castle, where the ground begins to rise. It may have been transported to its present site during the remote glacial period of Scotland. Its circumference at base is 20 feet, at the top 29 feet. The height on one side is 8 feet, on the other 6 feet. Some of the neighbouring inhabitants remember when they could easily make it rock, but it was displaced between 1824 and 1828 by two lads. The hill immediately overhanging Durisdeer Church is called Belstane

Shoulder, but there is no remarkable stone known to the inhabitants in this quarter, though there is a fine echo. These Belstanes occur in various parts of Scotland. There is a stone so called in Mistylaw Moor, near Lochwinnoch; and another, a farm in Dalry parish, Ayrshire; also, one near the Kirk o' Shotts.

ANTIQUITIES.

In Dr. Grierson's Museum the stone and bronze ages are both represented. The half of a stone celt, beautifully polished, which must have been, when entire, upwards of 10 inches in length and 3 inches in breadth, was turned up in the spring of 1875 by a subsoil plough in a field called Sannyflat, to the west of the road leading to Durisdeer, after passing the bridge over the Carron. There is also a bronze celt of the ruder type, found at a spot called Kirkleys, on Drumcruil farm. It is about 2 inches in breadth, and 5 inches in length. At Kirkleys there is some appearance of military earthworks, but its name shows that it was a spot originally cleared by the churchmen, as *leys* was the open forest glades where the cattle loved to lie.

There have also been found in Durisdeer what is popularly known as Elfin pipes, some of which are to be seen in the museum, and also many whorl-stones, used by housewives as weights at the end of their distaff, but which the superstitious used to regard as charm-stones, and which were kept to drive away diseases from human beings as well as cattle. There is also a fragment of a Runic cross found in Durisdeer, on which is Celtic ornamentation, and of which a drawing is found in the "Sculptured Stones of Scotland," published by the Spalding Club.

The museum possesses also an old flint-lock found at Enoch Castle, and a Lochaber axe found on Drumcruil farm, no doubt one of the axes of the Highlanders thrown away on their retreat in 1745. Five of these Lochaber axes were long kept at Drumlanrig Castle, but during a fire, which took place many years ago, they were burnt, and the iron heads were, I believe, used in the smithy, excepting one that is perserved in the museum. It is nearly the same as that which was found on Drumcruil farm.

DIFFERENT RACES IN DURISDEER.

CELTS.—There are many place-names in this parish that show the presence of a Celtic race in early times. Even the name of the palatial castle is Celtic, Drum signifying a long low ridge, and appearing not only in Drumlanrig but in Drumcruil. Ardoch, being ard-ach, high-lying field, appears in the Irish as Ardagh, and is found in the names of numerous villages, town-lands, and parishes through the four provinces of Ireland. The Irish form is Ard-achadh, high field. Auchen-skeoch, the field of thorns or haw-tree. This appears in the Irish as Aghnaskeagh, Achnaskew, meaning bushy field. In Kirkmichael parish we have Auchenskew, the same word. Dalveen is thought to be two Gaelic words— Dail-whin, the smooth field, and this is certainly not an improper epithet to the beautifully smooth sward now found on these romantic hills. Pen-*bane* and Stran-bane; to the Gaelic or Erse, *ban*, white, we may refer the last syllable in the name of these hills. It appears in many names both in England and Ireland— the Bane in Lincoln, the Bain in Hertford, the Bane in

Down, the Ban-don in Cork, the Ban-oc-burn in Stirling, even the Ban-itz in Bohemia. In all these it implies whiteness, in streams the white foam of the mountain torrent, and in hills their snowy covering. Dun-duff.—Here we have the Gaelic dhu, black, referring to the heathery and mossy appearance. Dhu is often found applied to streams, as Dou-glas in Lanarkshire, Doulas in Radnor, Dou-les in Shropshire, and Dig-gles in Lanarkshire. Earn-cleugh.—In Gaelic earn is eagle, and records the fact that in the early times that bird had frequented the cleugh. In Closeburn the place-name appears near Queensberry, and in Mouswald there is Earn-hurst (Ironhurst), eagle-wood, close to Locharmoss. In Sussex there is Earn-ley, and in Warwickshire Ar-ley, both of which are written Earn-cleah in old Saxon charters. Menoc.—The last syllable of the name of this stream is a corruption of the Gaelic and Erse word uisge, water. It has many phonetic variations, and appears in the names of a vast number of rivers—the Esk in Dumfriesshire and Mid-Lothian, the Esky in Sligo, the Tem-ese (Thames), meaning broad river, the Exe in Ecster, the Ock, which joins the Thames near Oxford, the Oke in Down, Bannockburn, and here Men-oc. Thors-cleuch.—The first syllable in the name of this stream is the Gaelic dwr, water, which is widely diffused over Europe. It is found that there are forty-four ancient river-names which contain the root—the Dour in Fife, Aberdeen, and Kent, the Duir in Lanark, the Thur in Norfolk, Glas-dur in Elgin, the Cal-der, a winding stream in Yorkshire, and here we have Thors-cleugh, the water cleugh. Enoch.—This place-name occurs near Whithorn, where was discovered a highly curious sculptured cross, one of the earliest known of the Christian period (Proc. S. of Antiq., vol. ix., part 2nd). It appears also in the form of Aitnoch, a rock on the Rye, near Dalry in Ayrshire, overhanging a deep ravine, which has been fortified by art on the land side all round by a moat from one part of the precipitous rock to another. This has a great resemblance to the site of old Enoch Castle in Durisdeer. In regard to the etymology of the word, Joyce, in his Irish names (p. 196), shows by a numerous collection of place-names in Ireland that Aenach (the earliest form of Enoch in Durisdeer is Enache) was a place of assembly or meeting of the people; and it is highly interesting to know that at these aenachs was often, if not invariably, a mound or cairn, often many of them, erected to serve a double purpose—1st, that the people at stated periods might meet around them; and 2nd, that the king or chief of the tribe might be interred within them, as well as his successors. Here, then, we may have a place-name recording the place of meeting of one of those early British tribes that occupied the country ere Cæsar landed (B.C. 55) on the southern shore of Britain.

SAXONS.—The Anglo-Saxons have left some place-names showing their presence—wald, wood, Law, from Saxon hlaew, hill, and this idea may also be considered to be found in Low-thers; Inglis-toun; Annoltoun; Al-toun (Auld-toun); Stane-butt; Gate-slacks; Holestane and Holles.—These two place-names contain the same root as Holstein in Denmark, and show the wooded state of the country when the Saxons penetrated into this parish. Holt is the Anglo-Saxon for wood, and Scete is seat or place inhabited, so that it would mean "forest abode."

NORSEMEN.—In the south of Scotland the only Scandinavian settlement on the mainland was in Dumfriesshire.

Here we find more than a dozen names with the suffix by, and others ending in garth, beck, and thwaite. They penetrated up the valley of the Nith, and can be traced by place-names as far up as Durisdeer. We have for instance Humby. The motes, of which there are several in the parish, show also where they had congregated. Myres, also, may be the old Norse myri, signifying a bog, which is a very common term in Cumberland and Westmoreland. Near Humby Holm we have a portion of the river called "Hell's Cauldron," which may not unlikely point to these same Norsemen and their pagan worship. The name of Hel, the mistress of the gloomy under-world, has given name to many places, principally in Yorkshire, such as Hellifield, Hellathyrne, Helwith, two Healeys, Healigh, and Helagh.

COINS.

Between 1815 and 1820 a quantity of coins were found in the chapel-yard in Humbie-holm at the foot of the holm, where there is a green knoll, and where it is evident that the chapel described by Rae stood. Another find of coins was made at Chapel near Durisdeer church, about fifty years ago, when a ploughman turned up a few coins in a moss. There was also another find close to the house at Chapel under a large stone. They were found by James Lorimer, the tenant of Chapel, and his sister Margaret, and were said to be very valuable. Several single coins have been got at different times, but by far the largest discovery of coins in Durisdeer was in 1832, when a horn containing upwards of 1000 silver coins was found at Inglestone. This horn was given to the late Mr. John Shaw of Drumlanrig Park. One of these silver coins was submitted to a distinguished numismatist of Scotland. He says:—"The coin sent is a silver penny or sterling of Edward II., minted at London, reading on the obverse Edward R. Angliæ dominus Hibernie, and on the reverse civitas, London, as the place of mintage. The type is very common, though in most finds other mints, such as Cantor (Canterbury), Eboraci (York), Durems (Durham), occur, and also of coins of the Alexanders and Robert I." These coins were found at a time when antiquarian interest had not yet been excited, and have all been lost.

THE HEADS.

This is the name of a spot now surrounded by a plantation on the left side of the road leading to Durisdeer church, after you pass Jenny Hare's bridge on the Carron. There is a strange tradition respecting the origin of the name, and though there is no certainty as to the time when the transaction took place, we can readily believe that some of the wild and barbarous barons of early times may have been guilty of the tragical act, which has come down to us.

The Castle of Morton is at no great distance, where tradition tells us that a young servant lad of good appearance had captivated the heart of his mistress, who did not know that he was betrothed to one of his own degree on the banks of the Carron. When she found that her advances were rejected, she accused him to her husband of having insulted her in an outrageous manner. The baron threw him into his dungeon to be starved to death, but the mistress repenting of her unjust accusation secretly

EARLY HISTORY OF DURISDEER. 147

conveyed food, and when his betrothed entreated his release, the baron was so enraged to find him alive that he ordered him to be fastened with ropes to two wild horses. They were driven off at full speed and dragged him to this spot, where the head became severed from the body. Hence the name of the Heads. It may be remarked, that it is scarcely possible two wild horses could have dragged a body over such a distance of rough ground without a severance taking place long ere this spot was reached.

POSTAL COMMUNICATION ONE HUNDRED YEARS AGO.

Our ancestors were satisfied with one Post Office for the whole of Upper Nithsdale, which was placed, no doubt for the convenience of the noble family, at New House, the site of the present kitchen-gardens of Drumlanrig. There all letters for the district were directed, the direction being by Drumlanrig, and there they remained till called for, unless some friend was known to be going in the direction, when the postmaster handed the letter to him to be delivered. This was the case in 1776, and how long afterwards I cannot say. The post-boy rode on horseback with his saddle-bags alongside of him, and leaving Edinburgh on a Monday morning, reached Galloway (it is believed Wigtown) at the end of the week, where he remained for a week to rest himself and his horse, when he again started on his way back to Edinburgh, picking up the letters as he went along, and reaching Edinburgh at the end of the third week from the time he had started. I have a letter of date 1776 addressed thus:—

"To Mr. Alex. Mundell, Rector of the Grammar
"School of Closeburn,
   "By Drumlanrig,
   "One Single Intire Sheet: charged 2s."

This is a letter from John Hunter, afterwards Professor of Humanity in the University of St. Andrews, who was at that time secretary to Lord Monboddo. It shows that the Post Office of Closeburn was at Drumlanrig, six miles distant. How different from the present state of matters, when our letters are delivered daily at the house for one penny at eight o'clock A.M., and yet we consider ourselves ill-treated because we are a sub-office to Thornhill.

IMPROVEMENT OF THE PARISH.

The change that has been produced in the appearance of this parish since 1810, when the present noble family came into possession of the property, has been very marked. Sixty years ago the parish was in a very different state as to woods from what it had been a hundred and fifty years before, as is shown by the map of Bleau, published in 1662. There we find a considerable portion of the parish covered with trees. One is called the "Wood of Coshogle," the places nearest its boundaries being Auchensell, Hapland, Kilbryid Kirk, and Coshogill, though towards Durisdeer village the limit is not clearly marked. Another wood is near to Auchintaggart, Dalpeddyre, Ardoch, and Nether Dalpeddyre. There is a third wood of no great extent round Auchinsow. It is curious to find scarcely any trees marked on the district to the south-west of Drumlanrig. All this was changed at the beginning of this century. There were few trees except in the immediate vicinity of Drumlanrig, and the natural wood along the banks of the Nith and Carron; fences could scarcely be said to exist, while herd boys were everywhere required to keep the cattle from straying. The houses of the tenants were built by themselves at the least possible expense, being generally a long row with the dwelling-house in the centre, the byre next to the kitchen, from which there was an entrance, then the stable, and at the other side of the dwelling-house the barn. The houses were thatched with straw, and ropes of straw enveloped the outside of the chimney. In many cases the fire-place was some 5 or 6 feet from the gable, the smoke passing up a wooden chimney called a brace, which came down within 6 or 7 feet of the grate, supported on three legs, and round which the inmates could circulate freely. The wooden vent had a wide mouth to collect the smoke, which rendered it dark and glistening as if it had been varnished. The mode of living was in keeping with the houses.

A native of Durisdeer told a friend of mine "how they got kail-brose to breakfast, sowens to dinner, and porridge to supper." He also gave an old rhyme about the dwellers on the Side, or north slope of Drumlanrig ridge, who seem to have been even lower in the scale of diet than the other parts of the parish. It ran—

"Slaes and butter
mak the
Side folks' supper."

The name Side is still given to that part of the ridge near to Burnmouth, where slaes formerly grew in great abundance. There is likely enough some exaggeration in this statement respecting the mode of living towards the beginning of the century. There was a rough abundance in all farm-houses, where masters and servants fared alike, the dinner generally consisting of broth with meat. How different, however, do the present tenants live, who are paying rentals of five hundred to a thousand pounds per annum. What large capital do such rentals represent! and, though their predecessors were intelligent men, still the working of such capital as is now invested in sheep-farming requires an activity of mind and forethought which was never called forth sixty years ago.

A friend, who is well acquainted with the agriculture of Dumfriesshire, makes the following observations as to Durisdeer:—

"The Galloway breed of cattle, which used to prevail so extensively, has been all but completely superseded by the Ayrshires, there being only one stock of the former variety remaining in the parish. Several of the Ayrshire stocks are of fine quality, notably that on the Home Farm at Holestane of the Duke of Buccleuch. From the time that his Grace's dairy was started his cows have been of a high order, but in recent years, under the auspices of Mr. James Cranston, his Grace's enterprising and skilful manager, by careful selection and general good management, the stock has been brought to such a degree of excellence that it probably contains more really first-class animals than any other herd of Ayrshires in the kingdom. The Duke's Galloway stock at Tibbers (which, though in the parish of Penpont, may be conveniently mentioned in this connection) has long enjoyed a high reputation for purity and general excellence. A few farmers in the parish have paid special attention to the breeding of horses, and have distinguished themselves as prize-takers in this class at both local and national shows."

TOPOGRAPHY.

BOUNDARIES OF DURISDEER.

This parish extends in length from the head of the Wald Path to Druidhill Mill about eight miles, and its breadth on the east side of the river Nith from the head of Enterkine to the foot of Carron, about seven miles, and on the other side of the river it is fully six miles from the foot of the Marr burn to Upper Glenginny. It is bounded on the north-west by the parish of Sanquhar, marching with the farms of Glenim and Dalpeddar, which are on the east side of the Nith, and on the opposite side of the river by the high grounds of Glenwhirn and Farding-Malloch; on the south-west and west by the parish of Penpont, from which it is separated for some distance by the Druidhill burn, then crossing a ridge at Gowkthorn by the Marr burn, to its junction with the Nith; on the north, north-east, and east by the parish of Crawford, from which it is separated by the water-shed on the top of the high mountains running down from the Lowthers to the Scalled Law; on the south and south-east by the parish of Morton, from which it is separated by the Carron in the lower part of its course.

Kirkbride.—This parish lay between Enterkine and Mennock burns, being of no great size, extending, however, to the opposite side of the Nith, according to the old Valuation Roll (Dumfries, printed by Robert Jackson, 1787), and containing "the lands of Craigdarroch, the lands of Twenty Shilling, Hawcleughside, and Rowantreeflat and the lands of Little-Mark, with the pertinents," all now within the parish of Sanquhar. On the north side, from the parish of Crawford in Lanarkshire, by the hills at Enterkine head. Though Rae was for many years minister of this parish, he does not seem to have written an account of it.

The area of the parish of Durisdeer, according to the Ordnance Survey, is 19,852·065 imperial acres. Its general character is hilly and mountainous. It consists of three ranges of mountains, the first of which is the Scalled Law, which lies to the east of the Wald-path, and immediately above the farm-steading of Gateslacks; the second outside of the hills from Troloss to Castle-hill, about two miles in length, rising to a considerable height at the spot called Pittielung (1519 feet). The third range lies close to Enterkine, from the top of the Lowthers to Nether Dalveen, about two miles broad at Upper Dalveen, but not above one mile between Carron and Enterkine. These mountains are excellent sheep pastures, though they are stormy in winter. The portion of the parish to the west of the Nith is equally hilly, though not rising to the same height as on the eastern side.

The following are some of the principal heights:—The highest point is Lowther, 2377 feet; Scaw'd or Scalled Law, 2172 feet; Glenleith Fell, 2003; Well Hill, 1987; Little Scaw'd Law, 1932; all these are on the eastern boundary. The hills to the north of Durisdeer village do not rise to the same height; Steygail, on the extreme north of the parish, 1875; Blackhill, 1740; Dalveen Rig, 1250. Above Coshogle we have Coshogle Rig, 1214, and in the north-western part of the parish, Knockconey, 1341, and in the extreme north, Glenim Craig, 1287.

The height of Durisdeer school-house is 459·08; Enoch bridge, 350·2; Holestane, 250; Birley Hill school, 700; oak tree at foot of hill leading to Drumlanrig, 279; farmhouse of Nether Dalveen, 750; and the boundary between Lanarkshire and Dumfriesshire on the public roads at Troloss, 1096.

ROADS.

In early times the Romans must have had communication with their camp in the Wald-path, and some remains of the road leading forward to Crawfordmuir can still be seen at the foot of the hill, where the camp was situated. For many centuries the roads were mere tracks, which were left in a state of nature. Beginning at the bridge near Carronbridge, which spans the Carron, the road, after passing the cottages near Waulk Mill, struck off through the holm towards Holestane, continued on along the ridge to Drumcruil and Muiryhill, where a road cut off to Durisdeer church and the Wald-path. The main road, however, proceeded forward to the Enterkine-path, known in old times as the "military road," as the officers seem to have considered it safer than that which crossed Crawfordmuir. It was at Enterkine-path that the Covenanters lay in ambush to rescue their friends from the dragoons on their way to Edinburgh. The present line of road from Carronbridge runs on the opposite side of the Carron to Holestane, where it crosses the stream by a substantial bridge, goes on past the site of old Enoch Castle under the railway viaduct to a spot a little way from Durisdeer Mill, where it again passes the stream by a bridge, then proceeds on under Castlehill, up Dalveen pass, and leaves Durisdeer at a height of 1096 feet above the sea level, where it enters Lanarkshire. This road was constructed about 1810, and opened for general traffic about 1813, though the first coach, called the "Commercial," did not run till 1822.

The road from Sanquhar had very much the same direction along the banks of the Nith as it has now, but deviated in some parts in the following way:—From Slunkford it kept the public road until it entered the farm of Ardoch, near Glenarlie bridge, and passing the farm-house descended towards Limecleughfoot, ascended again above the craig, near the retaining wall of the railway, and swept down to Enterkinefoot, keeping farther from the Nith than the present houses. It then took the turn at Hell's Caldron, and kept the present line of road for some time. Then it took the wood of Auchensell, passing behind the gamekeeper's house, again coming to the present road and keeping it to Carronbridge.

There was a kind of road, or rather a mere track, across the ridge of Enterkinefoot to Muiryhill, where in former times there was a house of entertainment. This track is now an excellent road.

There was another road in the parish which is worth being recorded. It crossed the Nith at Slunkford, at the boundary of the parish of Sanquhar (where there is still a ford), passed down the west side of the Nith to Burnmouth, went along by an old ruin called Gateside on the west side of the Marr burn road, on to Crairie-knowe and past Breconside and Balagan, into Scaur water. A branch sent off this road at Burnsands went down by Birleyhill towards the castle.

This western part of the parish is now traversed by an excellent road leading from Penpont up the Marr burn to Sanquhar. There are 32 miles of public roads in the

EARLY HISTORY OF DURISDEER. 155

parish, and several miles of private roads at Drumlanrig which the Duke allows the public to use. The public roads are kept up under the Dumfriesshire Roads Act. The assessment this year (1873) is 5d. per £ of rental, payable equally by proprietor and tenant. Towards the beginning of last century Duke Charles of Queensberry constructed in a great measure at his own expense 22 miles of road through his estate from Thornhill to the borders of Ayrshire. This was the direct road from Dumfries to Glasgow, but all these roads have been superseded to a great extent by the Glasgow and South-Western railway, which passes through the parish, and has a station near Enoch Castle called Carronbridge station. There is a fine viaduct across the Carron, and under the high ground in the neighbourhood a tunnel three-quarters of a mile in length.

The fords across the Nith are the following, but none of them can be passed except when the river is low, viz. :—Slunkford, Auchenbraith Ford, and Castlebank Ford, at the mouth of the Marr burn.

VALUATION OF .PARISH.

The earliest notice of the value of the lands of Durisdeer is in the old Valuation Roll of 1554, in the twelfth year of Queen Mary, when the baronies are valued as follows, in Scots money:—

Barony of Durisdeer, ...	... £31 13 4—	£2 12 0 stg.
Barony of Enoch, ...	... 20 0 0—	1 13 0 ,,
Barony of Drumlanrig, ...	... 120 0 0—	10 0 0 ,,

The Drumlanrig valuation, however, might possibly include the Queensberry lands *in cumulo*. In 1771 the valuation of the parishes of Durisdeer and Kirkbride amounted to 5032 6 8 merks, which is in sterling money equal to £278. In 1827 it had risen to 7094 11 8 merks, equal in sterling money to about £394. Of course, the valuation in merks is an official valuation, which does not enable us to discover the real value of land in 1771 and 1827. It is only within the last twenty years that the actual yearly value of the land has been recorded. This year (1874-75) the Valuation Roll shows the gross value to be—

Railway, ...	£9422 15 0
	3056 0 0
Total, ...	£12,478 15 0

The whole of the parish belongs to the Duke of Buccleuch and Queensberry, with the exception of small portions, which amount to £131.

POPULATION.

According to Dr. Webster's Returns, the population in 1755 was 1019. The number of inhabitants in the year 1794 was 1031. The census of later times gives the following:—

1801,	1148.
1811,	1429.
1821,	1601.
1831,	1488.
1861,	1320.
1871,	1189.

It will be observed that the population has greatly decreased during the last fifty years, and this chiefly arises from the union of farms with the emigration of the inhabitants to manufacturing centres.

Vital Statistics—

1872,	...	Marriages,	7.
,,	...	Births,	31.
,,		Deaths,	18.

Poor.—The amount raised for support of the poor for the year ending May, 1872, was £429 11s. 4½d. The number of paupers on the roll was 36.

School Census.—The school census in 1872 gave 217 children between 5 and 13.

STREAMS.

The river Nith runs down nearly through the centre of the parish, entering the parish at Slunkford on the east, and at March House on the west, and continuing its course till it is joined by the Carron. Its banks are particularly picturesque during its whole course, clothed with natural wood, which must have been there from the earliest ages, and winding its way through precipitous rocks, which have been worn by the water into every kind of curious shape. Along the west bank there is what is known as the "Duchess' Drive," being adapted for riding or driving. It runs from the vicinity of Drumlanrig bridge, and enters the Marr burn road near Burnmouth. Where it enters that road the common juniper grows in great abundance. It has seats at all points where the river presents its most striking views.

The Carron water rises at Upper Dalveen, and enters the Nith near the village of Carronbridge. Though it is small compared with the Nith, its green banks near

Enoch Castle are picturesque, and the viaduct of the Glasgow and South-Western railway, which spans the stream, is a picture of the finest description.

The Enterkine burn is another stream which rises close to the Lowthers, and passing through a mountainous district falls into the Nith at Enterkinefoot, after having been joined by the Fingland and Glen Vallentine burns.

The Marr burn rises in the high ground near Crairieknowe, and passing down runs through Drumlanrig park, where it becomes known as the Park burn, and enters the Nith at the foot of the hill on which the ruins of Tibbers Castle are found. It was along the banks of this beautiful streamlet that Burns is believed to have penned the fine song beginning—

> "Their groves o' sweet myrtle let other lands reckon,
>   Where bright-beaming summers exalt the perfume;
> For dearer to me yon lone glen o' green breckan,
>   Wi' the burn stealing under the lang yellow broom:
> Far dearer to me are yon humble broom bowers,
>   Where the blue-bell and gowan lurk lowly unseen;
> For there lightly tripping amang the wild flowers,
>   A listening the linnet, aft wanders my Jean."

There are many picturesque spots in the parish. How beautiful the hills as seen by the setting sun from the upper windows of Drumlanrig Castle! The pass of Dalveen, with the green sward of its mountains, is acknowledged to equal anything that is found amidst the Apennines or Pyrenees, while for wildness the famous Enterkine Pass cannot be surpassed. Dr. John Brown thus describes it in inimitable language:—"A few steps and you are on its edge, looking down giddy and amazed into its sudden and immense depths. We have seen many of our most remarkable glens and mountain gorges—Glencroe and Glencoe, Glen Nevis (the noblest of them all), the Sma' Glen, Wordsworth's Glen Almain (Glenalmond)—where Ossian sleeps—the lower part of Glen Lyon, and many others of all kinds of sublimity and beauty; but we know nothing more noticeable, more unlike any other place, more impressive, than this short, deep, narrow, and sudden glen. There is only room for its own stream at its bottom, and the sides rise in one smooth and all but perpendicular ascent to the height, on the left, of 1895 feet,—*Thirstane Hill*—and, on the right, of 1875 feet,—the exquisitely moulded *Stey Gail*, or Steep Gable—so steep that it is no easy matter keeping your feet, and if you slip you might just as well go over a *bona fide* mural precipice. 'Commodore Rogers' would feel quite at home here; we all know his merits:—

' Commodore Rogers was a man—exceedingly brave—particular;
He climbed up very high rocks—exceedingly high—perpendicular;
And what made this more inexpressible,
These same rocks were quite inaccessible.' "

The Dalveen Pass, " the lang glen," as Burns calls it, has been immortalised in his song:—

" Last May a braw wooer cam doon the lang glen,
And sair wi' his love he did deave me;
I said there was naething I hated like men—
The deuce gae wi'm to believe me, believe me;
The deuce gae wi'm to believe me."

And in a subsequent verse he takes notice of the farm of Gateslack:—

" But what wad ye think? in a fortnight or less,
The deil tak' his taste to gae near her!

> He up the Gateslack to my black cousin Bess,
>   Guess ye how, the jad! I could bear her, could bear her;
>   Guess ye how, the jad! I could bear her."

¹ The sources of the Menock are found in its high-lying hills. This was one of the four streams where was got the gold, of which King James' bonnet pieces were made, and where hundreds of workmen were in those days employed; the other three being Glengonar, Short-Cleugh, and Wanlock. These four streams were compared to the four rivers in the Garden of the Lord, Pison, Gihon, Hiddekel and Euphrates. The glittering sand is still occasionally to be found, and in Dr. Grierson's museum may be seen fine specimens of the gold.

RAIN-FALL AT WALLACE HALL AND DRUMLANRIG CASTLE.

It may be well to record for future observers the rain-fall during the last twenty years at these two spots, and it will be remarked that considerably less rain falls at Wallace Hall than at Drumlanrig. This may be accounted for from Drumlanrig being in closer proximity to the high hills. To the west rises Cairnkinna (1819 feet), only three or four miles distant as the crow flies, with its spurs Dunduff (1000), Merkland Hill (1210), Craigdashen Acres (1441), onwards to the Tynron Hills. To the east we have the Lowther (2377) range running by Scaw'd Law (2172), Glenleith Fell (2003), Belliboucht (1452), Auchenleck (1392), when the ground falls suddenly, nearly a thousand feet, and for a couple of miles we have the moorland of Threapmoor, &c., with the isolated and conical Queensberry (2279) in the background. It is in that gap that Wallace Hall stands, and the wind, which comes across the Atlantic loaded with moisture, sweeping across the comparatively low hills of Galloway, finds no obstacle in its way, except the slight impediment of Queensberry, till it reaches Moffat, and there fills what I believe is called the "Devil's Punch Bowl," and other such cavities. In the upper part of the valley it is otherwise, for there the moisture-loaded wind is caught first by Cairnkinna Hills, and then by the still higher Lowther range, and the results are seen in the gauges of Drumlanrig and Wanlockhead.

The following is the average fall of each month at Wallace Hall and Drumlanrig during the last twenty years.

Wallace Hall.		Drumlanrig.	
January,	4·6	January,	6·61
February,	3·3	February,	4·48
March,	2·8	March,	3·41
April,	1·9	April,	2·70
May,	1·9	May,	2·61
June,	2·5	June,	3·09
July,	2·5	July,	3·26
August,	3·6	August,	4·12
September,	3·2	September,	4·36
October,	4·7	October,	5·44
November,	3·0	November,	3·62
December,	4·8	December,	5·69
	38·8		49·39

We see that there is an average fall of nearly 1 inch every month more at Drumlanrig. April and May are the months in which the smallest quantity of rain falls, and at Drumlanrig the same proportion holds good.

Wallace Hall.		Drumlanrig.	
April,	1·90	April,	2·70
May,	1·90	May,	2·61

Again, the highest average months are:—

WALLACE HALL.			DRUMLANRIG.		
January,	-	4·60	January,	-	6·61
December,	-	4·80	December,	-	5·69

RAIN-FALL AT WALLACE HALL EACH YEAR.

	Total Quantity during the Year.	Greatest Fall in one Month.		Least Fall in one Month.	
1855,	27·0	August,	5·9	January,	0·0
1856,	31·2	December,	5·9	November,	0·7
1857,	32·3	December,	4·1	August,	2·0
1858,	39·7	October,	5·8	February,	0·7
1859,	38·8	January,	5·1	July,	2·0
1860,	40·5	October,	6·1	April,	0·7
1861,	43·3	August,	8·0	April,	0·2
1862,	45·4	October,	8·2	February,	1·6
1863,	41·6	January,	6·5	March,	1·7
1864,	40·1	September,	6·3	August,	0·4
1865,	34·8	October,	5·8	April,	0·2
1866,	42·5	January,	6·7	May,	1·2
1867,	31·3	October,	4·3	November,	0·3
1868,	51·3	December,	10·8	July,	0·2
1869,	37·6	December,	7·6	May,	0·3
1870,	31·9	October,	6·4	August,	0·6
1871,	33·3	February,	6·0	July,	0·3
1872,	58·5	December,	9·9	June,	0·9
1873,	37·0	August,	7·5	April,	0·1
1874,	38·8	October,	9·8	June,	0·1

At Capenoch, in Keir, close to the end of the spur of high hills running from Cairnkinna to Tynron Doon, an accurate account has been kept by Thomas Stewart Gladstone, Esq., during the last eight years, and though it cannot be altogether compared with the twenty years average of Wallace Hall and Drumlanrig, it is not without interest to observe the difference for these years. The fall of Capenoch is a little less than at Drumlanrig, but much more than at Wallace Hall:—

RAIN-FALL AT CAPENOCH FROM 1867.

1867,	43·35
1868,	59·54
1869,	43·60
1870,	36·98
1871,	44·46
1872,	64·54
1873,	47·27
1874,	48·82

The average fall of these eight years is 48·57, and the average of the same years at Wallace Hall is 40·05. Judging from this comparison, I should expect that the average fall of rain at Capenoch during twenty years will be found to be about 44 inches, being thus about 6 inches more than at Wallace Hall, and 5 less than at Drumlanrig.

EMINENT MEN.

With the exception of the Douglas family, which made its mark by taking a prominent part in the general affairs of the country, there are few of the inhabitants of Durisdeer who have handed down their names to posterity. Possibly the Rev. Peter Rae, minister of Kirkbryde, is the most eminent. He was the son of a clockmaker in Dumfries, and no doubt acquired his mechanical knowledge in this way, so as to enable him to construct a musical clock, which is still to be seen in Drumlanrig Castle. He was translated from Kirkbryde, 11th May, 1732, to Kirkconnel, and died 29th December, 1748, in the seventy-eighth year of his age, and forty-sixth of his ministry. He married Agnes, eldest daughter of John Corsane of Meiklenox. He was the author of several works: History of the Rebellion (Dumfries, 1718, 4to); Gospel Ministers, Christ's Ambassadors (a Sermon, Edinburgh, 1733, 8vo); A Treatise on Lawful Oaths and Perjury (Edinburgh, 1749). In an old volume of pamphlets entitled, "A Glass wherein Nobles, Priests, and People may see the Lord's Controversies against Britain, by Robert Ker, fewer in Gilmertoun, printed in the year 1719," there is an attack on Mr. Peter Rae in doggerel verse. The whole volume is a strange medley of prose and verse of the baldest kind. Rae had just published his History of the Rebellion of 1715, and Ker does not think that printing books is suitable to a minister of the gospel. He says:—

> "If he a right watchman were bred,
> Durst he take up the printing trade;
> Altho' that Paul wrought with his hands,
> The case is different in our lands.
> They have sufficient stipends here
> That may suffice them for their hire."

And he adds—

> "I doubt, then Printer Peter Rae."

When Peter Rae was removed to Kirkconnel in 1732, that parish had been without a resident minister for about fifty years. The first sermon he preached thereafter was from Samuel, chapter 1, verse 2:—"And it came to pass that when the Ark abode in Kir-jath-jearim, that the time was long; for it was twenty years; and all the house of Israel lamented after the Lord."

Besides Peter Rae, there was a clergyman of Durisdeer

of still earlier date, who had been of some literary note, Mr. John Alexander, who was ousted by the people in 1689. He died in Edinburgh, 16th July, 1716, in the eighty-eighth year of his age. He was the author of "Jesuitico-Quakerism Examined, London, 1680, 4to," answered by George Keith, 1682, 8vo.

Nor was Durisdeer without those who had wooed the Muses with some degree of success. The cottage beyond Drumlanrig kitchen gardens, as you approach the castle, is known as the "Poet's Corner," and is likely to retain the name long after its origin has been forgotten. Thomas Edgar resided there about the beginning of this century, and was the author of a book of poems entitled, "Poems on various subjects, but chiefly moral and descriptive, with songs and copious notes, by Thomas Edgar: Dumfries, 1822."

MR. JOHN SHAW OF DRUMLANRIG PARK.

Though Mr. Shaw was a native of Dalkeith, yet he lived so long in the parish of Durisdeer, and by his discoveries in connection with salmon fry acquired such fame that he requires to be noticed in this account of Durisdeer. He was a man of great ingenuity, and devoted his attention for many years to the elucidation of the early history of the salmon. His first paper, entitled "An account of some experiments and observations on the parr and on the ova of the salmon, proving the parr to be the young of the salmon," was published in the *Edinburgh New Philosophical Journal* for July, 1836 (vol. xxi., p. 99). His second paper, under the title of "Experiments on the development and growth of the fry of salmon, from the exclusion of the ovum to the age of six months," was read before the Royal Society of Edinburgh on the 18th December, 1837, and was published in the *Edinburgh New Philosophical Journal* for January, 1838 (vol. xxiv., p. 165). His third paper, entitled " Experimental observations on the development and growth of salmon fry, from the exclusion of the ova to the age of two years," was read before the Royal Society of Edinburgh, and published among their Transactions (vol. xiv.).

He proved by his ingenious experiments, carried on in ponds along the edge of the Nith, opposite to Drumlanrig Castle, what had been previously nothing more than surmised, that the parr remains at least an entire year in the fresh water streams before it becomes a smolt, so that the latter is necessarily not of the same generation as those hatched during the spring, in which it seeks the sea. The essential value of Mr. Shaw's discovery consists in his having proved the identity of that abundant little fish, commonly called parr, with the young or earliest condition of the salmon. He also showed its long continuance in fresh water, and its after conversion into the smolt. Parr every one had known, but it had always been regarded as a distinct and permanent species—that is, a continuous and inconvertible parr. This, however, Mr. Shaw showed by his ingenious experiments to be a mistake, and that the parr was nothing else than the young salmon. Dr. Grierson has in his museum the skins of these young salmon, which he had marked before they went down to the sea.

Mr. Shaw received the *Keith Prize* from the Royal Society of Edinburgh, consisting of silver medal and large silver salver, &c., for his discoveries in regard to salmon. He died 30th March, 1867.

EARLY HISTORY OF CLOSEBURN AND DALGARNOCK.

LIKE other parts of Scotland, these parishes had a period of untold ages, when it was occupied by races respecting whom we know nothing, except what we may glean from the rude instruments of war which are occasionally picked up, or the huge monumental cairns of stone which they raised to commemorate some important event which is now buried in silence. "The account of Time began with Night," says Sir Thomas Browne, "and darkness still attendeth it." Of the stone age Closeburn had till lately furnished no specimen, unless we consider the huge cairns that exist to afford proofs of the race of men that then lived. A stone hammer, however, has been discovered, while digging a drain on the farm of Green. It is of a rude form, without perforation, having only a slight indentation, being 10 inches in length, 4 inches and one-tenth in breadth. It is placed for preservation in Dr. Grierson's Museum. The bronze period is clearly indicated by what has been discovered. A fine specimen of a bronze celt was found by William Rae, April, 1870, in an earth cutting in the wood at the village called the Park. It is 6 inches long and 3 inches across the front, and is considered by Dr. Grierson, who has got it in his museum at Thornhill, to be the finest specimen of a bronze celt in Scotland. There are two other bronze celts in the Thornhill Museum, which were found in Closeburn,—one at Auchencairn in 1853, 3 inches long and $1\frac{1}{2}$ inch across the front, and another at Townfoot, 4 inches long. The museum also possesses a fine bronze pot, or tripod, which was found in Closeburn. In the Antiquarian Museum of Edinburgh there is preserved a bronze pot, though imperfect, which was also found here.

The existence of this early race has often been discovered by what are called *tumuli*,—mounds which have been erected over their dead. These mounds are found in Closeburn, though it cannot be expected, after the uncountable years since they were raised, that many of them can have survived. They are not to be found in the lower grounds, as the plough and other modes of agricultural improvement must have obliterated them long ago. It is in the high-lying parts of the parish that we must look for them, and there they are still to be seen. These *tumuli*, or mounds, exist on the following spots in Closeburn:—one on the Capel, near Mitchelslacks; another not far from Townfoot loch; several in another field of Townfoot, near Knockbrack; one on Threapmoor, beyond Poldivanburn; one beyond Windyhill, one at M'Mount, and several on Glenmaid property. Besides these *tumuli*, which point to a very early race of men, there are evidences of some events which must have taken place long before history or tradition assisted in recording the deeds of our ancestors. There are two roads, which in early times led from the low country to upper Nithsdale,—one ran up the Æ, passing across the hills from Gubhill; the other came from Kirkmahoe, along Gawin Moor, but both passed close to Auchencairn farm-steading. Here some deeds of valour must have taken place among the early settlers, if we may judge from the huge cairns of stone that are found at this spot. The leaders had probably fallen, and their followers had honoured their prowess by those enormous masses of stone which have survived so many ages, though, like the Pyramids of Egypt, they give no record of the names of those for whom they were erected. What is called Mid Cairn is 217 feet in circumference and 12 feet in height; Pottis Shank, 220 feet in circumference and 9 feet high; Whitehill, 182 feet in circumference and 60 feet in diameter; Topach Cairn, 143 feet in circumference; (1) Pottis Cairn, 153 feet in circumference and 6 feet high; (2) Pottis Cairn, 72 feet in circumference. Such enormous masses of stone could never have been collected without the intention of recording some deed which was regarded as highly deserving of being handed down to future ages. What it was, however, is shrouded under a dark veil, which can never be lifted.

Another work of prehistoric times in the parish of Closeburn is the Picts' Wall, or the Deil's Dyke (as it is popularly called), which appears distinctly along Bellyboucht Hill (1296 feet), in the neighbouring parish of Morton, for nearly a mile, and then, crossing the Routon Burn, disappears. It reappears, however, in Closeburn, near Townfoot farm-steading, and can be traced for a mile, close to which is an old camp of an oval form. Then all traces of the dyke vanish till the foot of Watchman Hill on Auchencairn is reached, when the dyke is again seen for a quarter of a mile.

Nor is Closeburn without proofs of having been inhabited by the Druids, whoever they may have been. On Barnmuir Hill there is the appearance of a Druidical circle, though the hand of time and of man has borne hard upon it. The circle is distinctly to be traced, 90 yards in circumference, and the ground within the circle rises 1 foot above the surrounding field. On the sides stones are found, though of no great size, and evidently showing that they had been used as a quarry to build the neighbouring dykes.

HISTORIC TIMES.

We now reach a period in the history of the parish where we have glimmerings of the proceedings that took place between the men who lived and died two thousand years ago. The all-absorbing arms of the Romans had reached Closeburn, where one detachment of their troops had been placed at or close to Wallace Hall, and another somewhat nearer to the Limekilns. These spots in those times would be pointed out by nature as of easy defence against a barbarous people, being enclosed on two sides by a large expanse of water. The ridge in front of the manse, and the little knoll on which Wallace Hall stands, had an extensive loch to the south and west, running from the front of Wallace Hall for a mile down to Kirkpatrick farm-steading. The loch ran up into Wallace Hall garden in front of the house, and the head of the loch is still pointed out by the place-name, Lakehead, belonging to the farm-steading. Then to the east there was another extensive loch occupying nearly the whole meadow from Closeburn Hall to the Limekilns, the remains of which were still to be seen within the last dozen years, close to Closeburn Castle, being known as the Castle Loch.

Wallace Hall knoll and the ridge opposite to the manse

were united by a very narrow neck of land, which could easily be defended on either side as circumstances dictated. These lochs have all disappeared, but the mossy soil and the heavy fogs during autumnal evenings show where they had existed. In 1795, when the late Dr. Mundell was digging the foundation for Wallace Hall, the workmen came upon two cinerary urns, containing the ashes of some Roman officers who had been burned and their ashes placed in these urns. They are now to be seen in the Antiquarian Museum, Edinburgh. Again, when the road running down from Wallace Hall towards the Limekilns was in course of being constructed towards the beginning of this century, the workmen came upon two urns near the bend at the end of the road where it turns towards the Limekilns. Unfortunately, the pickaxe of the workman destroyed them before they were observed, and nothing of them now remains. These urns were found on the grounds of Culfaddoch farm, now Cowfaddoch, which belonged in the middle ages to the Knights Templar.

The detachments of Romans were, no doubt, placed at this spot to guard the approaches from the roads across the hills, to which I have already referred. But in addition to these proofs of the residence of the Romans in the parish of Closeburn, we have distinct traces of a small encampment on the hill above Trigony Cottage, though no remains have ever been discovered in that quarter. It was necessary to guard the communications with the camp at Burnswark, and the road leading to Galloway by Tynron and Moniaive, and therefore these scattered detachments were placed on the most advantageous positions. The course of the Roman road can easily be traced, though no vestiges of it remain. Nature points out where it must have run through Closeburn, and where it continued till the last hundred years. Leaving the Limekilns where it descended to the lower ground, it proceeded along the ridge above the Castle Loch till it reached the manse, in front of which it passed. It then struck out towards Trigony, close to the Roman encampment, and edging along the southern end of the Gait Loch, reaches Dalgarnock Church, continuing its course to the ford leading to Blawplain, on the opposite side of the river. There was no other spot where the river could be crossed so easily for several miles upwards and for one mile downwards, where we find a ford near Barjarg. This was evidently the road by which the Romans kept up their communication with the detachments scattered over Upper Nithsdale. We have no other proofs than those which I have given that the conquerors of the world had been stationed in Closeburn. No Roman coins have ever been discovered, nor Roman implements of war, and this is curious when we cannot doubt that their troops must have occupied various parts of the parish.

MIDDLE AGES.

There comes, however, a blank of a thousand years, when Closeburn sinks out of sight, though during that period men like ourselves inhabited it, and seed-time and harvest regularly occurred. As now, there was marrying and giving in marriage, joys and sorrows in families, but all those events passed away without leaving a mark behind them that has come down to us, if it be not in place-names. To these place-names we must now have recourse, and see if they will assist us to lift the veil and tell us what races peopled the parish during those thousand years (A.D. 100 to A.D. 1100). We know from history that successive waves of races passed over our islands and left their footprints in the names of hills and dales, streams and lochs. Let us try how far Closeburn shows in its place-names the various peoples that had passed their lives amidst its mountains and glens. The Celtic race is the first, of whose existence we have distinct traces. The high hill overlooking the northern part of the parish, and which is mentioned in an old charter, to which reference will afterwards be made, is now known as Auchinleck, the same name it bore six hundred years ago. The word in Gaelic is Achadh-leacach, the field of the bare summit, not a bad description of the hill with its bare rocks. In the same direction, and on the confines of Closeburn and Lanarkshire there is a hill, Penbreck, *i.e.*, Pen-breac, the mottled hill, referring to the mixture of gray rock and heather. Then we have Earncrag, the eagle hill, handing down to us that in early times the king of birds frequented our parish in the high-lying districts; Garrock, answering to Carrick in Galloway and Ireland, meaning rocky, a just description of Garrock and its glens. Even the name of the parish, Dalgarnock is of Celtic origin, derived from Dail-garbh-chnoc, "the field of the rough knoll" not an improper appellation to the ancient state of the ridge above the spot, where the church of Dalgarnock was founded. We find *Dal* prefixed to many place-names, such as Dalbeattie, of which there are several in Scotland, Dalry, Dalkeith. Many others might be added, but these are sufficient to prove that we had a Celtic population in early times. It will be observed that most of these Celtic words are found in the distant parts of the parish, and this might be expected, as the aborigines, when dispossessed by the Saxons, would take refuge in the mountains, and the Saxons would be satisfied with the lower ground, as being the more fertile and most valuable.

SAXONS.

We know, from the general history of our island, that the Saxons dispossessed the Celts; and let us see, therefore, what Saxon place-names we can find. Apart from the Lowland Scotch that now prevails, and which gives names to most of the places at present, there seems little doubt that some Saxon chief of the name of Osbern had large possessions in the parish, from his name being given to the church which he had founded.

In the oldest charters in which the name appears we find Closeburn called Kylosbern, and it has been suggested, with great appearance of probability, that the name is derived from Kil-Osbern, the church of Osbern. In Celtic, Kil means church, and both in Ireland and Scotland, there are several thousand places with this prefix. As to Osbern there is no such saint in the Roman Calendar, but Osbern was formerly a common name; thus in the Saxon Chronicle (ed. Thorpe, 138, 139) we find Asbiorn (Osbern) the Jarl was slain in battle A.D. 871, and again, Earl Siward had a son Osbern. In 1054 this Earl with a large army and a force of ships invaded Scotland, and routed Macbeth; he carried off great booty, both his son Osbern, his sister's son Seward and others being killed on July 27. It is therefore not unreasonable to suppose that some Saxon chief of this name may have had possessions in Closeburn, and founded the church. There is only one other place in Scotland where the name appears, Osbernyston (now Orbiston), in the parish of Bothwell, and it is not without interest to know, in regard

EARLY HISTORY OF CLOSEBURN & DALGARNOCK. 175

to the chapel of Osbernyston, that we find an indenture, dated 1st April, 1253 (Reg. Glasg., p. 162) signed among others by Walterus Scot, probably Scot of Murdostoun, the ancestor of the Dukes of Buccleuch. Then we have Shaws, on the banks of the Nith, the Saxon word for wood, a place-name which appears in many parts of the county; Æ, the stream at Gubhill, the Saxon word for water, and which is found in a variety of forms, as Ea, Ey, Ei, and Ig, but always meaning water: as Ports-ea, the water port; Swans-ea, Sweyn's water; Ey-ton, water town. Then there is Law, a hill above Mitchelslacks, from *hlaew*, a hill.

NORSEMEN.

The only other race that could by possibility have had possessions in this parish were the Danes and Norwegians, whose marauding expeditions made such havoc along the coasts of England and Scotland. They settled, however, in various parts of the country, though chiefly near the coast, and we know from place-names in Annandale that these Norwegian rovers had settlements there. It seems as if some stray settlers had penetrated to Upper Nithsdale, and occupied parts of the parish of Closeburn. Among the place-names we find Auldgirth, which appears in a charter five hundred years old as Dalgarthe. *Garth* meant a place guarded or protected by a fence. It is a word which appears in a variety of Scandinavian compounds, but only in Yorkshire and the Norse colonized districts. Now it is interesting to know that Mr. Black, minister of Closeburn, says:—" Down the river Nith is a ten pound land pertaining to the baron of Closeburn, which marches with the lands of

Claughries and those of Over and Nether Algirth, where hath been a chapel and a *trench* for keeping of a pass at this place." This is the precise meaning of *Garth*, and when we know how close the hills come down to the river Nith at this spot, it may easily be imagined that the inhabitants would regard it as a place where some strong entrenchment ought to be erected to guard the pass. Both chapel and trench have been entirely obliterated since Mr. Black wrote his account, two hundred years ago, but of the truth of his statement respecting the *trench* there can be no doubt. A little lower down, near Dalswinton village, there are evident signs of another entrenchment, and this may very well be the case, as the nature of the country points out how easy it would be to defend the defile.

Not far from Auldgirth there is the farm-steading of Barscar. *Scar* is a Norwegian word, and is a general term throughout the north of England for a steep or precipitous rock, and is derived from old Norse *skera*, to cut, and those who are acquainted with the locality will see how closely it describes the position of Barscar. There is a Scandinavian proper name, *Bardi*, giving name to the town of Bardsey, and possibly some such Norwegian may have taken up his abode on Barscar, and his name has thus been handed down to our days. There seems not the least doubt that these rovers had ascended the valley of the Nith, as we find an unmistakeable proof in the place-name Humby, a farm a little above Drumlanrig Castle, from *Humma*, a Danish name, and *by*, meaning an abode. Wherever we find a place-name so ending we may be sure that it is of Norwegian extraction; thus Deersby (Derby), the deers' abode; Scrooby, Scroop's abode.

EARLY HISTORY OF CLOSEBURN & DALGARNOCK. 177

From these place-names we may conclude that the parish during these thousand years had been peopled by Celts, probably Scoto-Irish, Saxons, and a few Norsemen. In the reign of David I. (1123-1154) we find Closeburn again coming before us in the form of the barony of Kylosbern, belonging to the Crown. We know nothing more respecting it till William the Lion granted it to his son-in-law, Roger de Mandeville, and again Alexander II., grandson of David I., confirms the possession of the barony to Ivan de Kyrkepatric. The history of the parish then becomes closely connected with the fortunes of this baronial family, and will be best told subsequently, so far as it is known, by recording shortly the events in which each individual took a part.

Long before the Douglases of Drumlanrig had been settled (1388) in their Dumfriesshire home, the Kirkpatricks of Kylosbern had made to themselves a name by their patriotic conduct, and earned the honour of being excommunicated by the Pope. They are, even in the twelfth century, found to be the attached friends and supporters of the De Brus family, and had most likely accompanied them from Yorkshire when the Bruces settled in Annandale. They were a powerful family in those early times, having considerable possessions in different parts of the south of Scotland; but unlike the Douglases of Drumlanrig, they gradually sunk in the social scale, and lost, like Francis I., " Tout hors l'honneur," " Everything except their honour." It was thought that it was a chivalrous sense of honour that induced Sir James Kirkpatrick to sell his Closeburn property; but this high feeling has caused him to leave not a stain on the old escutcheon of the Kirkpatricks,

M

though they have meanwhile disappeared from the home of their forefathers.

BARONY OF KYLOSBERN.

This barony was situated in the middle of the parish of Dalgarnock, having Cella Osberni, corrupted in later times into Kylosbern, as its church. It is first mentioned in a charter of William the Lion to his son-in-law, Roger de Mandeville, and again in a charter of confirmation by Alexander II., 1232, to Ivone de Kyrkepatric. In the charter the northern and eastern boundaries are given with sufficient clearness to enable us to fix its limits. It ran from the point where Crichope Linn, called Poldune Larg in the charter, joins the Cample Burn, called Potuisso in the charter, up to its source in Townfoot Loch, then across the hills past a tumulus or cairn, which no longer exists, but which was looking towards (versus) Auchenleck, reaching a runlet or syke (sichcrium) now known as the Straight or Dry Gill. Then the charter tells us to ascend the ridge now known as Din's Rig, which is the water-shed of the waters flowing on one side into the Nith, and on the other into the Annan. Then we are to descend to the stream Poldivan, the Poldune of the charter, which, we are told, separates it from Glengarrock. The charter does not give the boundaries of the barony on the south, but this is accounted for by the lower part of the parish being occupied by the barony of Briddeburg, which seems in later times to have belonged to the Comyns of Dalswinton. There are reasons for supposing that Cairn, Auchencairn, Claughries, and the Auldgirths, Upper and Lower, formed this barony, so then we can see pretty clearly how far Kylosbern barony stretched in this direction. It did not touch upon the

Nith, as the rich holms along the banks of the river belonged to the church, as the place-names, Kirkland, Kirkbog, Templand, and even Cunningholm indicate. The barony Kylosbern was thus of a rectangular shape, about 4 miles from east to west, and $3\frac{1}{2}$ from north to south. In the charter to Ivone de Kyrkepatric it is mentioned as existing, and in the possession of David I., who reigned from 1124 to 1153.

BARONY DE BRIDDEBURG.

In the lower part of the parish there was another barony, though smaller in extent, being only valued at £10, which is known as the barony of Briddeburg.

It comes into notice in the reign of Alexander II., when we find the King granting by charter, dated 7th July, 1247, Inverlunane to Anselm of Camelyne, in excambion for Bridburg in Nithsdale (Book of Caerlaverock). The original charter, which runs thus, is at Ethie:—

Alexander Dei gracia Rex Scottorum &c. Sciant presentes et futuri nos, in excambium terre de Bridtburgh in valle de Nith, quam prius dederamus Anselmo de Camelyne pro homagio et servicio suo dedisse, concessisse et hac carta nostra confirmasse eidem Anselmo terram nostram de Innirelunane, per easdem rectas divisas, per quas Gilbertus Longus firmarius noster eam die huius collacionis de nobis tenuit; salvis eleemosinis nostris et salva Marie, que fuit uxor quondam Nigilli de Ymire, in vita sua, terra, quam ipsa tenet nomine dotalicii, infra dictam terram de Innerlunane &c. Testibus Willelmo comite de Mar, Alano Hostiario, justiciario Scocie, Willelmus de Ros; Roberto de Monte Alto, Willelmo de Huchtirhus. Apud Forfare septimo die Julii anno regni domini regis 33.

"Alexander, by the Grace of God, King of the Scots, &c. Let all present and future know that we, in excambion of the land of Bridburgh, in the valley of Nith, which we had formerly given to Anselm de Camelyne for his homage and service, have given, granted, and, by this our charter, have confirmed to the same Anselm our land of Innerlunnane by the same bounds, &c. Witnesses—William, Earl of Mar, Alan Stewart, Justiciar of Scotland, William de Ros, Robert de Monte Alto, William de Huchtirhus. At Forfar, 7th July, 1247."

A hundred years afterwards it seems to have formed part of the possessions of the Comyns, as on their fall it was divided among the friends of the Bruce. We find (Robertson's Index of M. Charters, pp. 13, 86) that Robert Boyd, ancestor of the Lords of Kilmarnock, got the lands of Duncole in the barony of Dalswinton, and lands of Dalgarthe (Auldgirth), the latter being described as in the barony of Briddeburg (in baronia de Bridburt), and there is a charter still extant, granted by the Bruce at his castle of Lochmaben, on the 14th May, 1319, in favour of Sir Thomas de Kyrkepatric, Knight. It grants a part of Briddeburg—a twopenny land, with the pertinents in the vill of Briddeburg, within the Sheriffdom of Dumfries.

It was not long till the Kirkpatrick family owned the whole, for during the rule of Robert, Duke of Albany, he, as governor, is found granting, in 1409, a charter with a long tailzied destination to Sir Thomas Kirkpatrick, upon his own resignation of the lands and baronies of Kylosbern and Brydburg, without exception of any part being expressed. In the "Articles and Conditions of the Roup and Sale of the Estate of Closeburn" in 1783, by Sir James Kirkpatrick to Dr. Stuart-Menteth, among other lands we find enumerated, "Brigburghfoot Hole, Middle Brigburgh, and Brigburghead," while in an old charter, dated 9th March, 1585, we find the following: "Holmhead in baronia de Brigburg." This Holmhead is situated about a quarter of a mile below Barburgh Mill, at the head of some holm land running along the Nith. The only remnant of the name is this Barburgh Mill, which points out the direction where the barony was situated. There are no documents to show the lands included in it, but it is probable that they were such as have been given above. Mr. Black, minister of Closeburn, in his MS. account of parishes of Upper Nithsdale (Advocates' Library), writing towards the middle of the seventeenth century, says, "Where hath been a chappell." It is not improbable that this chapel was dedicated to St. Bryde, the famous St. Bridget, and that this is the origin of the place-name—Briddeburg. We have Bridlesyke on Auchencairn farm, probably a trace of the same name, as I believe this farm to have formed part of the barony.

BARONY OF TYBARIS.

The barony of Tybaris (Tibbers), which occupied the greater part of Penpont parish, stretches also into Closeburn. All the lands to the north and east of the bounding line, indicated in the charter of Alexander II., belonged to Tybaris, as we find that the Earl of March, who was in possession of it, granted in 1424, to Sir Thomas de Kyrkepatric, the lands of Auchenleck (Townhead and Townfoot) and Newtoun, which are said to be in this barony; while charters in Drumlanrig muniment room show that it also included Locherben, Garroch, Gubhill, Knockinshang, Birkhill, with Dalgarnock Town, no longer in existence, but which was situated near the old church on the banks of the Nith.

CLOSEBURN CASTLE.

This castle is of great antiquity, though we have no data by which we can determine its precise age. In early times the site was pointed out by its insular character for a keep sufficiently strong to withstand any sudden attacks of the marauders of the English border. The beacon on Watchman Hill, a couple of miles distant, would warn them of their approach. The loch has ceased to exist, but it is not difficult to see how easily the water could be brought round, and thus separate it from the neighbouring hill. The piece of ground thus insulated would be between four and five acres. The walls are of extraordinary thickness, being, on the ground floor, 11 feet 11 inches; on the first floor, 8 feet 6 inches; and even in the upper stories six feet thick. They are filled, not with rubble work in the centre, but with large stones throughout, imbedded in mortar, which has been so well prepared that the whole is not less strong than if it were a rock. Originally there had been mere slits in the wall for air rather than light, some of which still remain in the higher floors; but in later times the wall has been excavated to make windows to give what light could be got through such a deep perforation. The ground floor had a well in it sunk so as to supply the inhabitants at all times with water, if they were besieged. It was approached from the upper stories by a stone stair formed in the outer wall. The first floor was the hall, with a side room entered from it. Into this hall there was a door from outside, about 9 feet from the ground, reached no doubt by a ladder which could be pulled up after an entrance had been effected.

The entrance was a circular arch of hard granite, and besides the wooden door, there was behind an iron door, formed of bars of iron, pieced together with considerable ingenuity. This iron door, still existing, is 4 feet 3 inches in breadth, and 6 feet $1\frac{1}{2}$ inches in height. The outer bars of iron are of an average thickness of $1\frac{1}{8}$-inch by 1 inch, while the inner are $1\frac{1}{8}$-inch by $\frac{6}{8}$ of an inch. Grose says "that the door is under a circular arch with zig-zag moulding, rudely cut out of hard granite," but this is now concealed by plaster. Latterly an outside stone stair had been built to approach this door, and this stair still exists, covered over for convenience and comfort so as to connect the castle with the lower buildings. The second floor formed, as it would appear, the principal reception room, and this is adorned with two floral ornaments on the ceiling, and on the wall a curious head and grinning face, of what may be regarded as intended to represent a satyr, such as occasionally is found adorning ancient cathedrals. It is, however, in stucco, and must be of comparatively late date.

On the glass of the window there are some scribblings with a diamond, revealing the feelings of those who have long mouldered in the grave. "Charming Grissie Stewart, J. K.," the initials being no doubt those of Sir James Kirkpatrick, who sold the estate in 1783. Again, "Fine Cristy Kirkpatrick;" and "Miss Jeany Kirkpatrick, a charming creature, 1762;" "Lovely Betty Brown;" "a charming Jade;" "Dear Aggie Clark."

Every floor is arched, and even the roof is a dome-formed arch, covered over with wood, and above are the common flag-stones found in the neighbourhood. The quarry, from which the castle was originally built is found at Crole Chapel, and still supplies stones, as Wallace Hall in 1795 was erected with the same stones. It is of harder material than those supplied by Gateley Bridge quarry. The castle is quadrangular, and rises to a height of 56 feet. It would no doubt only be used in extremities, as there were outside buildings, which would be inhabited more comfortably by the family than such dungeon-like rooms. In some excavations which were lately made for bringing water to the castle, the foundation of buildings was found, showing the direction in which they had stood. They were all taken down in the beginning of the seventeenth century, when the Kirkpatricks built their new mansion at the end of the avenue, which still exists, though all remains of the house have long disappeared. As already stated, it was burnt down in 1748 by some drunken servants, and the Kirkpatricks went back to the old keep, fitting it up as their residence. There they continued till the estate was sold in 1783. The castle was then occupied by "Willie Stewart," the friend and boon companion of Burns, factor to the new proprietor, Dr. James Stuart-Menteth; who was employed by Mr. Menteth to overlook the erection of the new mansion, now known as Closeburn Hall.

Dr. Hill Burton, in his "History of Scotland," remarks "In Mr. Grose's Antiquities there is a drawing of a doorway of Closeburn Castle thoroughly Norman. On a pilgrimage to the spot no such doorway and no vestige of Norman work could be found. The castle is just the featureless Scottish peel tower of the fifteenth or sixteenth century;" and he goes on to say, "It is the less likely that domestic houses were built of stone, as it is probable that, down to the opening of the War of Independence, there were very few castles built of stone in Scotland—that is to say, strong towers, which were alike fortresses and dwelling-houses, according to the Norman and Gothic fashion."

Now it is to be recollected, as I have already said, that the doorway has been long disfigured by plaster, so that its original appearance cannot now be discovered. I confess that I think that the form of the archway is Norman. The Kirkpatricks are from the earliest times found to be closely allied to the De Brus family, coming in all probability with them from England, and receiving through their influence from the Scottish kings the barony of Kylosbern. Nothing is more likely than that they should have at once (1232) set about erecting a manor-house, resembling in some respects what they were accustomed to in the country from which they had emigrated, even if the De Mandevilles had not already founded it in the reign of William the Lion.

TRADITIONS.

There are few old families that have not some strange superstitions connected with their early history. The family of Kirkpatrick were persuaded in ancient times, that when a death was to take place in the family a swan always made its appearance on the loch that surrounded the castle. The last omen of this nature on record saddened the nuptials of Sir Thomas, the first baronet, when marrying for the third time. On the wedding-day his son Roger went out of the castle, and happening to turn his eyes towards the loch, descried the fatal bird. Returning overwhelmed with melancholy, his father rallied him on his desponding appearance, alleging a stepmother to be the cause of his sadness, when the young man only answered, "perhaps ere long you may also be sorrowful," expiring suddenly that very night. Another tradition that has been handed down respecting the Kirkpatrick property is, "that so long as the Kirkpatricks were proprietors of Closeburn, so long should Frizzles (Frasers) be tenants there." I believe that a family of that name continued to occupy a farm till 1783, when the property was sold.

Tradition points out a stone, called Roger's stone, on Barnmuir Hill, where one of the Kirkpatricks shot with his bow one of the English force who was prowling in the vicinity.

HISTORIC FAMILIES.

DE MAGNAVILLA OR DE MANDEVILLE.

This noble family, whose name has been softened in these later times into Mundell, became connected with the parish of Kylosbern as early as the reign of William the Lion (1165-1214). It was of Norman extraction, having come over with William the Conqueror in 1066, as we find William de Mandeville marrying Margaret, daughter and heiress of Eude, High Stewart of William. His son was created Earl of Essex by the Empress Maude, but in these troublous times honours and estates were an unsafe possession, and he was deprived of both, though his son Geoffrey recovered them in the reign of Henry II. He had a son Geoffrey, who was Justiciar of England, in the reign of King John, and it was the second son of this Geoffrey, called Roger de Mandeville, who passed into Scotland, and rose in high favour with William the Lion, marrying his natural daughter Aufrica, and receiving with her as dowry possessions in the South of Scotland, more particularly the baronies of Tynwal (Tinwald) and Kylosbern (Closeburn), with the Temple-lands of Dalgarnock. On his wife's death, her brother, Alexander II., resumed the barony of Kylosbern, and conferred it on Ivone de Kyrkepatrick in 1232. The Mandevilles, however, continued in possession of their Tinwald property for upwards of two hundred years, till it failed in male issue in the middle of the fifteenth century, when the possessions of the Mandevilles were divided among four coheiresses. On 3rd March, 1454, John Menzies of Auchinsel in Durisdeer is one of the Jury to serve Margaret Mundeville, coheiress to her father, William Mundeville, in the fourth part of the lands of Tynwalde. (Inv. Max. Mun., No. 24.) The family also possessed Monreith in the Stewartry.

It was by the marriage of this Margaret Munduele, as she is called in the Terregles charter, to Edward Maxwell, grandson of Herbert, first Lord Maxwell, that Tinwald and Monreith passed into the great Maxwell family. Edward Maxwell, who was now called of Tinwald, subsequently acquired the other portions of the estates of Tinwald and Monreith, which had fallen to the other coheiresses (Invent. Max. Mun., Nos. 39, 43, 44; Lands and Landowners in Galloway, vol. 1., p. 277); and thus sprung the Maxwells of Tinwald, and latterly of Monreith, on the failure of male heirs in the Mandeville family. There is a Sasine on Precept by James III. of Robert Boyd (dated 16th January, 1483), in the lands of Mureth (Monreith), which was formerly possessed by Hawysia Mundwell, grandmother of the said Robert Boyd. Witnesses, Henry and Rolland Vmfrasone and Fergus M'Lympquhay. These Mandevilles were at one time a powerful family in Scotland; Roger de Mandeville, in 1296, was one of the competitors for the Scottish throne, with Baliol and Robert Bruce, no doubt from his grandfather's marriage with Aufrica, though he withdrew his claims and joined the party of Robert Bruce. Sir Thomas, the youngest son of this Roger, joined Edward Bruce in his expedition into Ireland, and there fell in 1216.

The name Munduele, as it appears in the Terregles charter, is a close approach to the form Mundell as it is found in these later times. The family of my predecessor, the late Dr. Mundell, belonged to the parish of Tinwald, and I do not doubt that the blood of the Mandevilles ran in his veins. Branches of old families often continue to linger in a parish long after the main stem has disappeared. Elizabeth, one of the coheiresses, to whom I have already referred, married a William Hepburn, and it is curious to find Dr. Mundell's mother was of this name. In 1610 there was a notary in Dumfries, John Mundeville, who was heritably possessed and seized in two tenements of Templeland, and half an acre of Templand in Torthorwald. In the middle of last century, James Mundell, LL.D., and Professor of Humanity in the University of Edinburgh, was in possession of the small property of Auldgarth (See Appendix, No. IV.) in Closeburn, which had previously belonged to a Johnstone family, a branch of the Wester Hall. This James Mundell was granduncle to Dr. Robert Mundell. There is a charter of resignation, dated 12th Feb., 1752, by James Mundell and his son of the lands of Auldgarth, when they were occupied by Copland, of Blackwood and Collieston. Like the old Mandevilles, all these Mundells have disappeared: I do not know of any relatives of the Mundell family in this part of the world. I have heard that the eldest brother of Dr. Robert Mundell, belonging to the medical profession, emigrated about 1780 to the southern parts of the United States, and that there are still descendants of this branch in America. If this be the case, the blood of the Mandevilles has not yet altogether vanished, though it flows in a world which was unknown when their ancestor became allied to our Scottish kings.

There is, however, I find, another family of this name in Dumfries, represented by Peter Mundell, Esq., of Bogra in Dunscore, whose grandfather coming from Tinwald, settled in Torthorwald, and occupied a large farm on the estate of Rockhill. I have no doubt that this family also is a branch of the same Mandevilles.

It is curious that the family of Mandeville should have nearly died out in Great Britain, so far as my researches have enabled me to discover. One of the titles, indeed, of the Duke of Manchester is Mandeville, but he is not related by blood to the old Norman family; possessing a portion of the property once owned by them, he has assumed the title. In the County Directory of Scotland there are only two Mundells found, who reside in the north, and in the large London Directory only two are recorded.

KIRKPATRICK FAMILY.

The first of this name connected with the south of Scotland, though not said to be Lord of Kylosbern, is "Roger de Kyrkepatric, Miles," who is one of the witnesses to the munificent grant by "Robert, son of Robert de Brus," Lord of Annandale, to the canons of

Gyseburn, of the church of Annand and five other parish churches (including Kirkpatrick) in Annandale, along with the church of Hartlepool with its chapel of "St. Hylda of Hertpol" in Durham, by a charter which must have been dated between 1141 and 1171 (Original Harl. Charters, Brit. Museum, printed in the Appendix No. II., Reg. Glasg.). Here, then, we find that the first notice of a De Kyrkepatric is in close connection with the family of De Brus, and of this family they continued to be warm supporters till they assisted in placing one of them on the Scottish throne. The family may have been of Scoto-Irish origin rather than Norman. The name *Kyrkepatric* points to Ireland, and the Christian name Ivone (Evan) smacks of Celtic, but we have no distinct proof that it was so. Their close connection with the Norman de Brus supports the other side, and it is just as probable that it was of Norman extraction, and had assumed the name of Kyrkepatric from some of the numerous churches or manors in the South of Scotland consecrated to the Irish saint. All this, however, is mere conjecture, as their origin is lost in the mist of bygone ages.

In this early period we find in the troubles of Galloway a Gilpatrick or Kilpatrick, commander of the troops, who was defeated and slain 4th July, 1185. It is thought that he was of the family of Kylosbern, and likely enough he may have been so, though we have no proof of it (Hailes' Annals, vol. I.).

Next there appears an Ivone de Kyrkepatric, to whom this Robert de Brus grants a charter of the fishing of Blaatwode and Eister in Annandale. This same Ivone is witness to the charter of Robert de Brus and his wife Euphemia, granting the fishing of Torduff "Abbati

EARLY HISTORY OF CLOSEBURN & DALGARNOCK. 191

Everardo et conventui et fratribus de Holme" (Holmecultram). This charter was confirmed by Robert, his son. One of these charters is to be found among the writs of the family of Carliel, and the other in extracts taken from the Register of Holmecultram Abbey, both without date; but Everard is a witness to a charter confirmed by William the Lion, of lands in Canonbie, and others in Roxburghshire to Jedburg Abbey in the first year of his reign, that is, 1165. Therefore, if this Ivone be the same as the Ivone who got Kylosbern from Alexander II. in 1232, he must have been very aged when he received the barony of Kylosbern.

In Drumlanrig muniment-room there is a grant of the 20 lib. land of Pennirsax, A.E. (now Pennersaughs in Middlebie), by William de Brus to Yvone de Kyrkepatric* of the lands of Pennirsax, called Thorbeck or Williamby, for military service. This charter was before 1215, when William de Brus died. Their first connection with the lands of Kylosbern, the greater part of which they held for six hundred years, is shown by a charter which the late Mr. Charles Kirkpatrick Sharpe lithographed, and of which the following is a copy:—

Alexander Dei Gracia Rex Scotorum omnibus probis hominibus tocius terre sue, Clericis et Laicis salutem: Sciant presentes et futuri nos dedisse, concessisse, et hac carta nostra confirmasse Ivani de Kyrkepatric pro homagio et servicio suo,

---

* Yvone de Kyrkepatric, witness in a charter of Alexander II. confirming a charter of Maldouen, third Earl of Lennox to Absalon, son of Macbed, of the island called Clarines, 6th April, 1231. Testibus : W. de Bondington, cancellario, Radulfe de Parseleth, capellano, David Cuming, Galfrido de Nova Villa, Yvone de Kyrkepatric, Mychiele de Monte Alto, Roberto de Meiners. (The Lennox, by Mr. Fraser).

Totam terram de Kelosberum per easdem divisas, per quas nos eam tenuimus et Atavus ante nos, excepta terra quæ jacet juxta Auchinleck ex parte boreali subscriptarum divisarum scilicet sicut rivulus, qui dicitur Poldunelarg, descendit in alium rivulum, qui dicitur Potuisso, et ascendendo per Poldunelarg usque ad Macricem Sicherium, qui se extendit per medium musse, ascendendo et sic descendendo ex boreali parte cumuli lapidum versus Auchinleck usque ad rivulum, qui dicitur Poldunii, quæ est divisa inter Kelosberum et Glengarrock. Tenend. et Habend. eidem Ivani et heredibus suis de nobis et heredibus nostris in Feodo et hereditate per rectas divisas ac cum omnibus justis pertinenciis suis in bosco et plano, in terris et aquis, in pratis et morris, et maresiis, in stagnis et molendinis cum furca et fossa, cum socco et sacco, cum thol et them et infangand thef et cum omnibus aliis ad dictam terram juste pertinentibus, libere, quiete, plenarie et honorifice per servicium quarte partis unius militis nomine Albe Firme.

Testibus Gul. de Bondington cancellario, Rogero de Quincay, Waltero filio Alani, Senescalo Justicie Scotice, Johanne di Maccuswell, camerario, Rogero Avenel, Davide Marescallo, Thoma filio Ranulph, Davide de Lyndescia, Rogero filio Glaii, Roberto de Meyners, apud Edinburghum, quarto decimo die Augusti, anno regni domini regis octavo decimo.

"Alexander, by the Grace of God, King of Scots, to all good men of his kingdom, both clergy and laity, greeting: Let present and future generations know that we have given, granted, and by this our charter have confirmed to Ivon (Evan) de Kyrkepatric, in return for his homage and service, All the land of Kylosbern by the same boundaries by which we held it and our great-grandfather (David I.) before us, except the land which lies next to Auchinleck on the northern side of the underwritten boundaries, namely, as the rivulet which is called Poldunelarg (Crichope Burn) descends into another rivulet which is called Potuisso (Cample), and by ascending the Poldunelarg (Crichope Burn) as far as the Macricem Sicherium (the Dry or Straight Gill), which stretches through the middle of the Moss, by ascending [Din's Rig], and thus descending on the northern side of the Cairn of Stones [looking] towards Auchinleck, as far as the rivulet, which is called Poldune (Poldivan) which is the boundary between Kylosbern and Glengarrock: To be held and kept by the same Ivan and his heirs from us and our heirs in Fee and Heritage by its right meiths, and with all its just pertinents in wood and plain (manurit land), in lands and running waters, in hay and moors and marshes, in ponds and mills, with the right of pit and gallows, with soc and sac, with thol (the right to exact custom) and them (frank pledge) and infang thef (right to judge and punish a thief caught within the grantee's jurisdiction), and with all other rights justly pertaining to said land, freely, quietly, fully, and honourably by doing the service pertaining to the fourth part of one knight in the name of Alba Firma (the annual rent paid to the lord).

"Witnesses, Chancellor, Bondington, Roger de Quency, Walter son of Alan, high steward of Scotland, John de Maccuswell, chamberlain, Roger Avenel, David the Marshall, Thomas son of Ranulf, David de Lindesei, Roger son of Glai, Robert de Meyners, at Edinburgh, 14th Aug., in the eighteenth year of our reign (1232)."

It is interesting to look at the witnesses of the charter to Kylosbern, granted by Alexander to Ivan de Kyrkepatric; they were all men of highest eminence in those early times.

The first witness was William de Bondington, Bishop of Glasgow, and Chancellor of Scotland, who died in 1258; styled by Fordun "*Vir dapsilis et liberalis in omnibus.*" Roger de Quency, the next witness, was also an eminent personage, being Earl of Winchester, and, in right of his wife, Elena, eldest daughter and co-heiress of Alan of Galloway, Constable of Scotland. Walter, son of Alan, the third witness, was the third High Steward, who flourished from 1204 to 1246. John de Maccuswell was the ancestor of the great Maxwell family still flourishing among us. Roger de Avenel is said to have died in 1243, and his Eskdale property to have passed with his daughter to a Graham. We find a Laurencius Avenel with his mother Eva jointly make grants to the church of Glasgow out of their "feodom" of Tunregeyth (now Tundergarth), on the borders of Eskdale, between 1258 and 1268 (Reg. Glasg., Nos. 221,277). Robertus de Meyners, the last witness, was a historical personage, the ancestor of the family of Menzies of Enoch in Durisdeer. He was one of the Regents of Scotland in 1255, during the minority of Alexander III. (Hailes' Annals), and frequently appears in deeds of the period in the Balmerino and Glasgow Chartularies.

Adam succeeded his father Ivan, and the only fact respecting him that has come down to us is his dispute with the monks of Kalch (Kelso), respecting the advowson of the church of Kylosbern. The monks applied to the Bishop of Glasgow as the head of the diocese to have the matter inquired into and legally decided. The Bishop appointed his chaplain, John de Lennen, and John, Abbot of Jedburgh, to be arbiters, and, after summoning Adam to appear before them, either personally or by deputy, they declared him contumacious, for treating their summons with contempt, and pronounced the church to belong legally to the Abbot and Convent of Kelso, in a deed dated at Roxburgh in the year of grace 1264. Their words were *dicto Adamo militi presentandi ad eandem ecclesiam perpetuum silencium imponentes et expensas in lite iisdem Monachis adjudicantes.* Thus Adam not only lost the right of presenting to the church, but was saddled with all the expenses that had been incurred (Chart. Kels., 342). Adam evidently continued unwilling to acknowledge the right of the convent, and died without submitting to the award.

He was succeeded by his son Stephen, who, wearied out probably by the persistency of the monks to maintain their hold over the church, at last yielded, and entered into an arrangement with the Abbot. In the deed he is called *Stephanus filius et heres Domini Ade de Kyrkepatric* and it is signed *Die Mercurii proximo post festum purificacionis Beate Marie Virginis,* 1278. Three years afterwards (1281) the convent entered into a business arrangement with a native of Kylosbern, called Adam de Kulenhat, to whom they let *omnes fructus decimarum majores, oblaciones et obvenciones ad ecclesiam de Kylosbern spectantes,* that is, the large tithes and offerings (Chart. Kels., 343).

The death of Margaret, the Fair Maid of Norway, in 1290, a few years after this arrangement respecting the church of Kylosbern, was the commencement of a gloomy period for Scotland. Stephen died about this time, as we find his son Roger the head of the family, and with his brother Duncan assisting Wallace when he was appointed Guardian of Scotland. Roger was with Wallace when he relieved Sir William Douglas at the time he was besieged in Sanquhar Castle. Of his brother

Duncan, the Blind Minstrel thus sings in reference to Wallace:—

> "Ane Kyrk Patrick, that cruel was and keyne,
> In Esdaill wod that half yer he had beyne;
> With Ingliss men he could nocht weyll accord,
> Off Torthorwald he Barron was and Lord,
> Off kyn he was, and Wallace modyr ner."

Roger had, however, to yield to the overwhelming power of Edward I., and, like many other true patriots, swore allegiance to Edward in 1296 (Ragman Roll). It is said that he was trusted so far by Edward that he was made by him, in 1304, Justiciar of all Galloway with Walter Broughton.

The family of De Kyrkepatric, however, had been from the earliest times in close connection with the family of De Brus. It continued to be so at this time, and Roger cast in his lot with the man who was fated to maintain the independence of Scotland against all the power of England. Roger is found six years afterwards (1306) in attendance on Robert Bruce at the Grey Friars Monastery of Dumfries, when the dispute arose between Bruce and the Red Comyn (10th February, 1305-6). Bruce had stabbed his opponent, and on coming out exclaimed, "I fear that I have slain Comyn;" and thereupon Roger, who would have no doubt about such a matter, said, "I mak sikkar," and slew the wounded man outright. This is thought to be the origin of the crest of the family, which is a hand with a dagger erect in pale, dropping blood.

> "Vain Kirkpatrick's bloody dirk
> Making sure of murder's work,"

records the deed in Sir Walter Scott's "Lord of the Isles."

There is certainly some doubt cast on Roger being the instrument of vengeance on Comyn, as in the bull of excommunication by the Pope (Rymer's Fœd., vol. iii., p. 810), he is called Robert; but we hear of no such individual of this name except in this bull, and it is by no means unlikely, in the confusion in which the monks would be thrown, that they might have got hold of a wrong name, and Roger had no interest in undeceiving them, as he would only be bringing himself under the direct ban of the Church. This seems more likely, as even the names of Comyn and of Dumfries, where the murder took place, are so changed in the bull of Pope John (Avignon, 6th January, 1326) that we would have had difficulty to recognize them, if we had not other sources of information. The murder is said to have been *in ecclesia fratrum minor de Dynifis*, and Comyn's brother is called *Robertus de Caymins*. Besides, there is strong proof of the connection of the Bruce with the family of Kirkpatrick in the place-names, which still survive in the parish after an interval of six hundred years. The future king during his manly struggle must often have taken refuge in the wilds of Kylosbern, as we have so many references to him in the hilly country; King's Well, on the farm of Glencorse; Bruce's Well, Rob's Corse (Cross), Kingstand Burn, all on Auchencairn; King's Stone, across the border of the parish on Auchengeith. The presence of Wallace in the parish is also recorded by the place-name Wallace's Kist, near Penbreck Slidders, on the borders of Kirkmichael. Roger occupied a high position among the friends of the Bruce, as we find him one of the Commissioners appointed to treat about peace with the Commissioners of Edward II. at Newcastle-on-Tyne, 1314 (Rymer's Fœd.). Roger left two sons—

Thomas, who succeeded him before 1319; and Roger, who took the castles of Caerlaverock, Durisdeer, and Dalswinton from the English in 1355, and in 1356 was murdered by his friend Lindesay in the castle of Caerlaverock. His character is thus drawn by Wyntoun in his Chronicle (edited by David Macpherson, vol. ii., p. 277):—

> "Kyrk-Patricke Nyddysdale
> Held at ye Scottis Fay all hale,
> Fra ye Castell of Dalswyntoun
> Wes takyn, and syne dwyn down.
> Syne Karlaverok tane had he.
> He was a man of gret bownte,
> Honorabil, wys and rycht worthy:
> He couth rycht mekil of cumpany."

Thomas, who succeeded to his father, Roger, was also in high esteem with Robert Bruce, and obtained as a recognition of his services on the 4th January, 1319, a considerable portion of the barony of Briddeburg, which had been forfeited by the Comyn family of Dalswinton.

The following is a copy from a facsimile of the old charter, which was lithographed by the late Mr. Charles Kirkpatrick Sharpe:—

Robertus dei gracia rex Scotorum, omnibus hominibus tocius terre sue salutem. Sciatis nos dedisse, concessisse et hac presenti carta nostra confirmasse Thome de Kyrkepatric, militi dilecto et fideli nostro pro homagio et servicio suo duas denariatas terre cum pertinenciis in villa de Briddeburg infra vicecomitatem de Drumfries. Tenend et Habend eidem Thome et heredibus suis de nobis et heredibus nostris in feodo et hereditate et in liberam baroniam per omnes rectas metas et divisas suas libere, quiete, plenarie et honorifice cum omnibus libertatibus, commoditatibus, assiamentis et justis pertinenciis. Faciendo inde nobis et Heredibus nostris dictus Thomas et Heredes sui servicium duorum (militum) in (exercitu) nostro et tres (sectas) ad curiam vicecomitatis nostre de Drumfries. . . . Singulis annis ibidem tenendum. In cujus rei testimonium presenti carte nostre sigillum nostrum precepimus apponi. Testibus Bernardo Abbot de Abberbrothic, cancellario nostro, Waltero senescallo Scocie, Jacobo domino de Douglass, Joanne de Meneteth, Roberto de Keith, Marescallo nostro Scocie, et Alexandro de Seton, militibus. Apud Lochmaben vicesimo quarto die Maii Anno regni nostri quarto decimo.

"Robert by the grace of God, King of Scots, to all the people of his kingdom, greeting. Know that I have given, granted, and by this present charter confirmed, to Thomas de Kyrkepatric, our faithful and beloved knight, for his homage and service (to us) a two penny land with its pertinents in the ville of Briddeburg within the Sheriffdom of Dumfries. To be held and kept by the same Thomas and his heirs from us and our heirs in fee and heritage and in free barony on all its proper meiths and marches, freely, quietly, fully, and honourably with all its liberties, conveniences, easements, and just pertinents. The said Thomas and his heirs performing to us and our heirs the service of two knights in our host and three (suitors) at our court of the shire of Dumfries to be held there every year, in testimony of which thing we have caused our seal to be appended to our present charter. Witnesses:—Bernard, Abbot of Arbroath; our Chancellor, Walter Steward of Scotland; James, Lord of Douglas; John of Menteth; Robert of Keith, our Marshall of Scotland; and Alexander of Seton, knights. At Lochmaben, 24th of May, the fourteenth of our reign." (1319.)

This charter of May 24th is granted the year before the Parliament assembled in the abbey of Arbroath, in which the spirited address to the Pope was adopted on 6th April, 1320, remonstrating against the grievous wrongs that had been accumulated on the nation, and asserting the independence of the kingdom. The names of the witnesses to the charter are all of them found attached to the remonstrance except the Abbot Bernard. Walter, High Steward of Scotland, is the husband of Marjory, daughter of Bruce, and whose son succeeded as Robert II. James de Douglas is the "Good Sir James," the attached friend of Bruce, who fell in Spain on his way to the Holy Land with Bruce's heart; while the next witness, John de Menteth, is the friend of Edward I., who is accused of betraying Wallace to the English: he was brother to the sixth Earl Menteth. Robert de Keith commanded the horse at the battle of Bannockburn, 1314, contributing not a little to the success of the Scots. Alexander de Seton was governor of Berwick when it was besieged by the English, 1333. We thus find the witnesses to be all of them men of mark.

There is little else known respecting Thomas on which we can depend. In the Barjarg manuscripts, Mr. Hunter-Arundell queries whether there is not an indenture dated 8th March, 1322, with Sir William de Carleol of Torthorwald, husband of Lady Margaret Bruce, sister to King Robert, by which he promised in marriage his daughter Elizabeth to John, second son of Sir William. He gives no authority for this query, nor have I found any proof of it. In the "Collections for a history of the ancient family of Carlisle," by Nicholas Carlisle (London, 1822), he says (p. 83):—"Among the

Drumlanrig muniments is an indenture between Sir Thomas Kirkpatrick of Closeburne and Sir William de Carlelle of Torthorwald concerning a promise of marriage between John, son to Sir William, and Elizabeth, daughter to Sir Thomas, dated in 1431." I have large notes from the Drumlanrig muniment-room, in which the Torthorwald documents are specially mentioned, and no such indenture is noticed. This indenture seems to refer to the same transaction, and yet there is a difference of a hundred years in respect to the date. In the Kirkpatrick pedigree this alliance is given under Sir Thomas (1319), and another daughter, Margaret, is said to have been married to John Henrisonne of Glasgow, for which marriage a dispensation was obtained from Pope Clement VII. (1342-1352). I do not know the authorities on which these statements are made. At the battle of Neville's Cross, near Durham (17th Oct., 1346), when David II. was taken prisoner, we find a Roger de Kyrkepatric (brother of Thomas) made prisoner by Ralph de Hastings and conveyed to London. Hastings, dying of his wounds, bequeathed the body of Roger to his joint legatees, Edmund Hastings of Kynthorpe, and John de Kyrkeby; and in the same battle Reginald de Kyrkepatric was slain (Dalrym., vol. ii.; Rymer's Fœd., v., p. 535). On 13th July, 1354, Humphrey, son and heir of Roger, was one of the twenty noble youths named as hostages for David II.'s ransom of 90,000 merks, which the Scots refused to ratify (Rymer's Fœd., vol. iii., part 1). Again, on 8th May, 1357, Humphrey was given as one of the hostages for the ransom of David II., being 100,000 merks, when he was delivered by Edward III. to the care of Lord Percy. At this time Roger was one of the commissioners on the part of Scotland. At the Parliament assembled at Edinburgh, 26th Sept., and at the ratification of the treaty there, 6th Oct., 1357, when David II. returned from captivity, Roger was present (Rymer, vol. v.).

On the death of Sir Thomas, his nephew Humphrey, son of his brother Roger, succeeded, but we know nothing more respecting him.

There is here some link of the chain dropped out, as there is an interval of about fifty years before we hear of a head of the family. On 4th Oct., 1409, Sir Thomas de Kyrkepatric receives from Robert, Duke of Albany, a charter of confirmation and tailzie to him and his heir-male, whom failing to his brother Roger, of the lands of Kylosbern. This charter is dated at Ayr. In 1410 his name appears as witness in a charter of certain lands in the barony of Glencairn by Sir Robert Maxwell of Calderwood to Sir Alex. Gordon of Stichell, dated Edin.,— "Domino Thomas de Kyrkepatric, Domino de Klosberne." In 1424 we find a charter granted by George, Earl of March and Dunbar, to his "dear cousin" Sir Thomas, of the lands of Auchinleck and Newtoune, part of the barony of Tybaris, in the parish of Dalgarnock.

In Drumlanrig muniment-room there is a charter by Archibald, Earl of Douglas and Longueville, to his kinsman Sir Thomas, Lord of Kylosbern, of the patronage of the parish church of Pennirsax (Middlebie), 5th May, 1428. He was still alive in 1438, when he was appointed (20th June) one of the commissioners to settle a truce between James II. and Henry VI. (Rymer), and was succeeded by his son George. We find George mentioned in one of the Drumlanrig charters as receiving from the same Earl Douglas, then Duke of Touraine, in France, upon the resignation of his father, the lands of

Pennirsax and the patronage of the church, these entailed to a series of heirs, one after another, in failure of that George and his issue male—13th June, 1432.

This George seems to have been succeeded by Roger Kirkpatrick, who is mentioned in a retour of 10th June, 1445, where his seal is appended bearing his arms, a saltier and chief, charged with three cushions; supporters, two talbot hounds, arg. In 1455 he was commissioner on the Western Borders. He was married to Margaret, daughter of Thomas, first Lord Somerville by Janet, daughter of Sir Alexander Stewart of Derneley. He left two sons, Thomas and Alexander, who is believed to have obtained from James III. a portion of the barony of Kirkmichael as a reward for having taken prisoner James, ninth and last Earl of Douglas, at the battle of Burnswark in 1483, but there is no sufficient proof of this Alexander being of the Kylosbern family.

On the death of his father Thomas succeeded, and took an active part in the stirring events of the period. He is witness to a retour of Robert de Maxwell as heir of his father, Herbert, Lord Maxwell, in the lands and barony of Caerlaverock; the lands of the Garnsalacht and Dursawhen and Spryngkelde, at Dumfries on 14th Feb., 1453 (Terregles Invent., No. 21). He is witness to a seisin in favour of Robert Dalziell of that Ilk of the lands of Bellihoucht in Glencairn, 5th Nov., 1466. In 1470 (15th Oct.) he resigned the baronies of Kylosbern, Briddeburg, with the lands of Auchinleck and Newtoune, obtaining from James III., under the Great Seal, a new charter in favour of himself and wife, Maria, daughter of Herbert, second Lord Maxwell, by Isabel, daughter of William, Lord Seton. He was appointed in 1481 keeper of Lochmaben Castle, and sat in Parliament in 1487. In these warlike times we find on the 22nd April, 1485, Robert, Lord Maxwell, gave assurance for himself and John Maxwell, heir-apparent for Thomas Kirkpatrick of Kilosberne, (original notarial instrument at Terregles). He died in 1502, leaving two sons, Thomas and Henry.

He was succeeded by his eldest son, Thomas, of whom little is known. We find him mentioned in 1509, when Robert, Lord Crichton of Sanquhar, grants to "ane honourable man and his brother-in-law, Thomas Kirkpatrick of Closebern, the ward of Robertmure." He was married to Margaret, daughter of the Lord of Roslin. He left at least one son, Thomas.

Thomas was served heir to his father in 1515, and was among the prisoners taken at Solway Moss in 1542. We are told that he could bring into the field 403 men. These were the days of manrents, as there is one between Robert fifth, Lord Maxwell, and William Kyrkepatric of Kirkmichael (1549-1550), with Thomas Kyrkepatric of Closebern. (Terregles Charters.) This was dated at Closebern, 23rd July, 1550. Again, in 1561, he entered into a contract of manrent with Douglas of Drumlanrig, Crichton of Sanquhar, Sir William Grierson of Lag, Sir John Gordon of Lochinvar, to defend each other against all mortals. He took part at a very early period in the measures of the Reformation, but nevertheless adhered to Queen Mary, signing the bond of 21st Sept., 1565, to assist her. In 1567, when a number of men of property signed a bond of association to support the title of James VI. to the crown of England, we find the following, "Closeburn," "Thomas Kirkpatrick of Ellisland," and "William Kirkpatrick of Kirkmichael with my hand at the pen." But on the 8th May, 1568, at Hamilton, he joined again the association in the Queen's favour. At what time he died is unknown, but he was succeeded by his cousin Roger, of whom we know nothing except that he was married to Jean, eldest daughter of William, sixth Earl of Glencairn (K. Ped.). Roger was succeeded by Thomas, who was in high favour with James VI. We find that the King, understanding that there were continual depredations committed upon the lands of Closeburne, Brigburgh, Auchinleck, Alisland, &c., belonging to Thomas Kirkpatrick, was pleased to constitute him his Justiciary in that part with full powers to take, try, and punish delinquents, according to law, and in the case of resistance from those pursued, to convoke the lieges in warlike manner, and with a full remission, should wounding, mutilation, or slaughter arise from such proceedings. The commission, which was to continue valid for two years, is dated at Edinburgh, 26th May, 1589. In 1592 Thomas Kirkpatrick was cautioner for the appearance of Wilson of Croglin for murder. In 1593 at the battle of Dryfe's Sands, when Lord Maxwell made an attack upon Sir John Johnstone and was killed, though supported by all the powerful barons of Nithsdale, the barons of Lag, Closeburn and Drumlanrig escaped by the fleetness of their horses, which is thus alluded to in the beautiful ballad called "Lord Maxwell's Good Night":—

> "Adieu Drumlanrig false wert aye,
>   And Closeburne in a band;
>   The Laird of Lag from my father that fled,
>   When the Johnstone struck off his hand
>   They were three broken in a band,
>   Joy may they never see."

Again, in 1593, the King issued another dreadful bann

of fire and sword, against certain persons at variance with the Baron of Closeburne, the tenor of which is as follows:—

"James be the grace of God, King of Scottis. To all and sundrie, our lieges subditis, quhome it effieris to quhaes knowlege yir oure Letters sall cum, greeting, forsa mikle as it is understand be us and Lordis of our secret counsale, that upon the xi. day of April last by past, Thomas Grier of Barjarge was orderlie denuncit rebelle, and putt to our horne be virtue of oure utheris letters, rased at the instance of Thomas Kirkpatrick of Closeburne, for not finding of caution and secuertie actit in ye bokis of our secret counsale for the Indempnitie of the said Thomas, his tennantrie and servandis in thair bodyes, and guidis under certain pennall paines mentionat in the saidis utheris Letters, as in the same deulie execute, indorsat, and registrat at lenth is contenit, syke as upoune ye nynetene day of May last by past, Edward Maxwell of Tynwell, Edward and Johnne Maxwellis his sones, Johnne Maxwell, tutr. of Aikinheid, James Maxwell of Porterrack, Johnne Fergussoun of the Isle, Alexander Fergussoun his sone, Johnne Lachlisoun, callid Laird Lachlisoun, Andro Lachlisoun his sone, Cubbie Mellagan in Edgarstoun, John Haning in Glangaber, callit the fouller, Gilbert Griersoun of Drum, and Thomas Griersoun of Barjarg, younger, were lykewayes denunceit rebellis, and putt to our horne be verteu of our utheris twa severall Letters, rased at ye instance of the said Thomas Kirkpatrick, the ane for not finding of caution and secuertie actit in the bukis of oure secreit counsale, for the indempntie of the said Thomas, his tennents and servandis in' thair bodyis and guidis, and the uthir for thair not compeirance personalie before us and our prevey counsale at ane certain day bigane; To have answerit to ane complaint maid be the said Thomas upon thame, toucheing ye making and subscriving of ane unlauchful band, and certain oppressions committit be thame upon him, as oure saidis utheris Letters thane dewlie execute, indorsate, and registrate, shawne to ye Lordis of our secret counsale beiris. At the process of ye quhilkis hornings, the persons theirein forsaidis maist proudlie and contempuaudlie hes remanit sen ye tymes of thair denunciation, lyke as thay do zit unrelaxt, takand na regaird of horning, bot hantis, frequentis and repairis in all publicit partis and placis of oure realme as giff they wer oure frie subjectis, in hie and proud contemption of oure authoritie and lawes, and encouragement of utheris to continew in like rebellioun and disobediens heirefter without remeid be findit. Quhairfoir we have gevin and grantit and be yir porsents gevis, grantis, and committis our full power and commissioun, expres bidding and charge to oure Lovittis, Sir Johnne Gordoun of Lochinvar, Knight; Hew Campbell of ———, Sheriff of Air; Roger Griersoun of Lag; Thomas Kirkpatrick of Closeburne, conjunctlie and severalie to convocat our leiges in armes, and to pas, serche, seik, and tak the saides persouns rebellis quhairever qoy may be apprehendit, and to bring and produce yame before us and oure pravey counsale, to ye effect we may tak order anent their rebellion and disobediens as apperteins. And giff it sall happin ye saidis persouns rebellis or any of yame for eshewing of apprehensioun to flee to strenths or housses, with poure to ye said commissionaries conjunctlie and severalie, to convocat our leiges in armes as said is, and to pas, follow, and persew oure saidis rebellis, assege the saidis strenthis and housses, rais fyre, and use all kynd of force and weirlike ingyne that can be had for wynning and recoverie yairof, and apprehending of oure saidis rebellis being yr untill. And giff in persute of oure saidis rebellis they refuseing to be takin, or assegeing of ye saidis strenthis housses, it sall happin the same persounes oure rebellis or ony of thaime, or ony utheris being in company with thame, and assisting thame, or within the said strenthis and housses, to be hurte, slane, or mutilat, or ony uther inconvenient quhatsumever to follow, we will and grantis, and for us and oure successors decernies and declaris, That ye same sall not be imputt as cryme nor offens to our said commissionaries nor persons assisting them to ye executioun of this oure commission, nor yet no name of thame sall not be callit nor accused quhairfoir criminualie nor civilie be ony maner of way in tyme coming notwithstanding quhatsumever oure actis statutis or proclamacions maid or to be maid in ye contrair ther anent and all paines contenit yr in til we dispense by yir presents and generallie all and sundrie uther things to do, exerce, and use qlk of law or consuetude of our realme or knawne to pertene ferme and stable, halding and for to hald and quhatsumever things sall be lawfullie done yr in charging therfoir for you all and sundrie our said legies and subditis. To concur fortifie and assist oure said commissionaris conjunctlie and severallie in all things tending to ye execution of ys oure commission. And to do nor attempt nathing to ye hinder yr of, as ye and ilkane of you will answer to us upoun yr obediens, at ye uttermost charge and perill. Given under oure signet and subscrivit with oure hand at Haliradhous second day of Juini, and of our Reigne ye XXVI. year, 1593.

         "(Signed) JAMES R."

Peter Rae, in his MS. history of the Presbytery of Penpont, states that he had read a private letter addressed by King James to Thomas Kirkpatrick, whom he had made Gentleman of the Privy Chamber, but the letter was probably destroyed when Closeburn Hall was burned in 1748, as it cannot now be discovered among the archives of the family. He was married to Barbara, daughter of Sir Alex. Stewart of Garlies, by Katherine, daughter of Andrew Lord Herries of Terregles, and widow of John Kirkpatrick of Alisland. The contract is dated at "Haliewode," 17th December, 1614. He obtained a patent of free denizen within the kingdom of England in 1603 from James VI., and he died about the year 1628.

He was succeeded by Thomas, who married Agnes, daughter of Sir John Charteris of Amisfield, Knight, by the Lady Margaret Fleming, daughter of the first Earl of Wigton.

We find in 1592 that he was permitted by King James to pass forth out of Scotland to whatever parts he pleased, and to remain furth thereof for three years, but "the appeirand of Closeburne during his absence forth of our Realme is to behave himself as a deutifull and obedyent subject to us, and to attempt nothing in hurte nor prejudice of neither our Estate and Realme, nor the True Religione presentlie professit within the same, otherwayes this our License to be of nane avail."

He was succeeded by Robert, third son, who married Grizzel, daughter of Sir William Baillie of Lamington, and he again by Thomas, created a baronet of Nova Scotia, 26th March, 1685, for the unshaken fidelity of himself and his ancestors to the Crown. He was succeeded by his eldest son, Sir Thomas, who married, in 1702, Isabel, eldest daughter of Sir William Lockhart, Bart., of Carstairs, by whom he had four sons and a daughter. At his decease he was succeeded by his eldest son, Sir Thomas. This gentleman married Susanna, daughter and heir of James Grierson, Esq. of Capenoch, by whom he had eight children. The mansion of Closeburn, built by the first baronet, partly with the materials of the old residence, of which he left nothing standing save the tower, was burnt to the ground through the carelessness of drunken servants on the night of the 29th August, 1748, and all the family papers, portraits, plates, &c., therein consumed. Sir Thomas died in October, 1771, and was succeeded by his second and eldest surviving son, Sir James, who married Miss Jardine, and was succeeded by his second and eldest surviving son, Sir Thomas, who married a daughter of Charles Sharpe, Esq. of Hoddam, and died in 1844, leaving issue—James, d. s. p., midshipman, R.N.; Charles Sharpe, who succeeded to the title, and died 1872; Eleanor, married to Admiral Sir W. J. Hope Johnstone. Thomas, present baronet, succeeded his father in 1872. Creation—26th March, 1685. Arms—Arg., a saltier and chief arg., the last charge with three cushions, or crest, a hand holding a dagger in pale, distilling drops of blood. The family, it would seem, claims also the following supporters—two talbot hounds, arg.; motto, "I mak siccar."

The property of Kylosbern, though portions of it had from time to time been given to younger children, had in a great measure returned to the head of the family, when difficulties gathered round Sir James, and he found himself compelled to part with an estate which had belonged to his family since 1232. It was offered for sale in 1783, and the value put on it in the deed of sale was the following. It was bought for £50,000:—

£42,150 for Closeburn Barony.
6,300 for Shaws.
1,550 for Kirkpatrick.

It was bought by Dr. James Stuart-Menteth, rector of Barrowby in Lincolnshire, in whose descendants it continued till 1852, when Sir James Stuart-Menteth, Bart., sold the estate to Douglas Baird, Esq., for £225,000, having before sold a portion of it, Kirkland and Dalgarnock Gait, for £7000. This small portion of it has lately (1873) been sold to his Grace the Duke of Buccleuch and Queensberry for £15,500. The estate of Closeburn now belongs to the two daughters and co-heiresses of the late Mr. Douglas Baird, the eldest of whom is married to Frederick Ernest Villiers, Esq., son of the late Bishop of Durham, and the second is married to Lord Cole, eldest son of the Earl of Enniskillen.

FAMILY OF MENTETH.

This family first became connected with the parish of Closeburn in 1783, when the Rev. James Stuart-Menteth, D.D., rector of Barrowby in Lincolnshire, bought the estate from the old family of Kirkpatricks. He married Catherine Maria, fourth daughter of the Rev. Granville Wheler (son of Sir George Wheler, Knight, by Grace his wife, daughter of Sir Thomas Higgins, and a descendant of Sir Beville Granville) of Otterden Place, Kent, by the Lady Catherine-Maria his wife, daughter of Theophilus Hastings, seventh Earl of Huntingdon. Dr. Menteth having been left a large fortune by a near relative of the name of Stuart, assumed the additional surname of Stuart by sign-manual, dated 12th March, 1770, for himself and his descendants.

Sir Charles Granville Stuart-Menteth, Baronet, of Closeburn, born 15th May, 1769, was created a baronet in 1838. He married Ludivina, daughter of Thomas Loughnan by Philadelphia his wife, daughter of Robert Fergusson of Craigdarroch, and by her, who died 6th February, 1852, he had a large family.

Sir Charles was an ardent agriculturist, and by his intelligence and skill rendered the estate of Closeburn an honour to the south of Scotland. He clothed the hills with wood, he drained, he built fences, and at great expense brought down a stream from the hills to irrigate his fields. Unfortunately, his sanguine disposition would not allow him to count the cost, and thus all his improvements were found to be only for the advantage of others. The capacity of his limestone mines was greatly enlarged by the application of water-power; and he bought the estate of Mansfield, on the borders of Ayrshire, to enable him to burn his lime at the smallest cost with the coal found on his own property. He had a strong bent for the science of mechanics, and might, if his fortune had been different, have become an eminent civil engineer. To his ingenuity coachmen owe the drag, which can be worked with the greatest ease at top without the trouble of descending from the seat—a very valuable invention as a means of safety, apart from the relief it ministers to stage-horses over all hilly roads. He died 3rd December, 1847, and was succeeded by his eldest son.

Sir James Stuart-Menteth succeeded his father as

second baronet; married 17th December, 1846, Jane, daughter of Sir Joseph Bailey, Baronet, M.P., of Glanusk Park. He sold the estate of Closeburn, which had become heavily burdened by the expensive improvements of his father, and retired to Mansfield where he died, 1870.

His family claims to be chief of the ancient Earls of Menteth and heir-male of the Stuart dynasty.

THE FAMILY OF BAIRD.

This family, like many in the country, have been the architects of their own fortune, and have raised themselves to importance by their great wealth, which has been acquired not more by their indefatigable energy than by pursuing the high principles of honour of our old Scottish merchants. They are known as the Bairds of Gartsherrie, though they are not proprietors of that estate, but have only their extensive iron-works there. They have been settled for many centuries in Lanarkshire, and the tradition, I believe, of the family is that they are descended from the Bairds of Cambusnethan.

It is believed that the surname of Baird is originally from the south of France, and appearing under several different forms—Bard, Barde, Beard, Byrd—was changed to Baird in later times. We have in 1066 Le Seigneur de Barde mentioned as one of the followers of William the Conqueror. The name first appears in Scotland in the reign of William the Lion, 1178, when Henry de Barde, Mariscallus apud Strivelin, is witness to a charter granted by the king to the Bishop of Glasgow as to some lands in the town of Stirling. The name continues to occur in charters during the whole of the thirteenth century, till, in 1292 and following years, in the Ragman's

Roll we find, according to Nisbet, three of the name of Baird swearing allegiance to Edward I. The first is Fergus de Baird of Meikle and Little Kyp; secondly, John Baird of Evandale; thirdly, Robert Baird, whom Nisbet thinks to be Baird of Cambusnethan, and says that estate went to Sir Alexander Stuart, afterwards of Darnley, by marrying the heiress, Jean Baird, about 1360, and that in 1390 he gave it with his daughter to Sir Thomas Somerville of Carnwath, Lord Somerville's ancestor, upon their marriage. In the patriotic exertions of Wallace we find a Jordan Baird his constant companion; and that Bruce recognized their patriotism is shown by a charter extant, dated 1310, granted in favour of Robert Baird upon the barony of Cambusnethan, which lies in the Upper Ward of Clydesdale, county of Lanark.

The Bairds of Gartsherrie are great merchants, but it is not the first time that this name has appeared before Scotland in the same capacity. In 1328 we are told by Rymer that a treaty of peace was concluded at Northampton between Edward III. and Robert Bruce, by which it was agreed that King Robert should pay to England 30,000 merks for the damage done last year by his army in England. The last payment of this money, being 10,000 merks, fell due at the Feast of John the Baptist, being the 24th June, 1331. Edward is found to have assigned Bruce's obligation to Bartholomew Barde, and others of that name, called the Company of the Bairds trading to Florence, and sends them to Scotland to receive the money from David Bruce, then king; and in a letter written two days after, Edward recommends them to David's special protection. He employs them in several other important transactions

during his reign, and calls them his beloved and trusty
" Bankiers," the Company of the Bairds.

It was, however, not only in peaceful transactions that
the family of Baird distinguished themselves, but in war
they were ready to take their part, as Rymer makes
Peter Baird, in 1338, admiral from the mouth of the
Thames over all the west coast of England, of Kent,
Sussex, Somerset, Dorset, Cornwall, Devon, and Gloucester.

In Scotland many of the name have been distinguished,
though none of them have exceeded the present Bairds
of Gartsherrie in wealth and in the large territorial
possessions which the different members of the family
have acquired. The father of these great ironmasters
was Mr. Alexander Baird, who acquired the estate of
Lochwood, in Lanarkshire, in 1825. He was born in
1765, and died in 1833. By his wife, Jean Moffat, he
left a family of eight sons and two daughters.

1. William Baird, M.P. for the Falkirk Burghs from
1841 to 1846, born in 1796. He bought the estates of
Rosemount, in Ayrshire, and of Elie, in Fife, and died in
1864, leaving a large family.

2. John Baird, born 1798. He succeeded to the
estate of Ury, in Kincardineshire, on the death of his
brother Alexander, and died January, 1870.

3. Alexander Baird, born 1799. He purchased the
estate of Ury, and died in 1862 without issue.

4. James Baird, M.P. for the Falkirk Burghs from
1851 to 1857, born 1802. He bought the estates of
Knoydart in the county of Inverness, and Cambusdoon,
Muirkirk, and others in Ayrshire, and on the death of
his brother Robert, became also proprietor of the estate
of Auchmedden. In 1874 he presented to the Church

of Scotland for the spread of the Gospel £500,000, to be administered by certain trustees, whom he names in the deed of gift. He has been twice married. His first marriage was in 1852, to Charlotte Lockhart of Cambusnethan, who died at Nice, in Italy, in 1857. In 1859 he married Isabella Agnew Hay, daughter of the late Admiral Hay.

5. Robert Baird, born 1806. He purchased Auchmedden in 1854 from the testamentary trustees of the late Sir Charles Forbes of Newe and Edinglassie, Bart., and died in 1856 without issue.

6. Douglas Baird, born 1808. He acquired the estate of Closeburn from Sir James Stuart-Menteth, Bart., in 1852. He married Miss Charlotte Acton, of the old English family of that name, and dying in 1854, left two children, twin daughters, one of whom married in 1870 Viscount Cole, eldest son of the Earl of Enniskillen; and the other, F. E. Villiers, second son of the late Bishop of Durham.

7. George Baird, born 1810. He married Miss Hatton, daughter of Admiral Hatton, and dying in August, 1870, left one son. Mr. Baird purchased the estate of Strichen, in Aberdeenshire, and on the death of his younger brother, David, became also proprietor of the estate of Stitchell, in the county of Roxburgh.

8. David Baird, born 1816. He bought the estate of Stitchell, and died in 1860 without issue. Of the two daughters of Mr. Baird of Lochwood, the eldest, Janet, married first, Mr. Whitelaw, and second, Mr. Weir, by both of which marriages there are families. The second, Jean, married Mr. Jackson, by whom she has a family. The present member for Glasgow, Mr. Whitelaw, is a son of Janet by her first husband.

As landed proprietors, the family have attained a preeminent position in Scotland. William, the eldest brother, bought the estate of Rosemount, in Ayrshire, in 1853, for £47,000, and Elie, in Fifeshire, in the same year, for £155,000. John inherited Lochwood from his father, by whom it was purchased in 1826, while Ury was bequeathed to him by his brother Alexander, who purchased it in 1854 for the sum of £120,000. James Baird purchased in 1853 Cambusdoon, in Ayrshire, for £22,000; in 1857 the estate of Knoydart, in Inverness-shire, for £90,000; in 1863 the estate of Muirkirk for £135,000, besides other properties in Ayrshire of considerable value. On the death of his brother Robert, who died in 1856, he acquired the estate of Auchmedden, Aberdeenshire, which three years previously had been purchased for the sum of £60,000. Douglas, the sixth son, acquired the estate of Closeburn for the sum of £225,000. George, a still younger member of the family, was proprietor of the estate of Strichen, in Aberdeenshire, and Stitchell, in Roxburghshire,—the former purchased in 1865 for the sum of £145,000, and the latter inherited from his brother David, who purchased it in 1853 for the sum of £150,000. The family thus own estates representing in round numbers nearly £2,000,000 of capital, in addition to what they hold as a company in the shape of mineral fields.

VILLIERS FAMILY.

Frederick Ernest Villiers, who married the eldest daughter of Mr. Douglas Baird, and thus became connected with the estate of Closeburn, is son of the late Bishop of Durham, who was brother of the Earl of

Clarendon, a distinguished diplomatist. The family is descended from Thomas Villiers, the first Earl of Clarendon, youngest son of William, second Earl of Jersey, married 1752 Charlotte Capel, eldest daughter of William, third Earl of Essex, by his first wife, Jane, daughter and co-heiress of Henry Hyde, Earl of Clarendon and Rochester, son of Laurence, Earl of Rochester, youngest son of Sir Edward Hyde, Earl of Clarendon. Mrs. Villiers is thus connected with Lady Catherine Hyde, the Duchess of Duke Charles of Queensberry, who has been already noticed for her great beauty.

It is not the first time that members of this old Norman family have come north of the Tweed, as we find that they had penetrated into Scotland as early as the reign of William the Lion (1165-1214). In the Melrose Chartulary (No. 129) "Alexandro de Vilers" is witness to a deed. The family has been widely spread on the Continent as well as in England. The chief and best known families of the name are those of the Dukes de Villars, Dukes de Lauragnais, Marquesses Villers la Faye, Marquess Villers Comte de Grignancourt, Villers de l'Isle Adam. The English Villiers family, Dukes of Buckingham, Earls of Jersey, &c., were of Norman descent, and claimed kinship with the last mentioned, but bore entirely different arms.

COLE FAMILY.

Viscount Cole, who married the second daughter of Mr. Douglas Baird, and thus became connected with Closeburn, is son of the Earl of Enniskillen, an Irish peer. The family is descended from Sir Michael Cole, grandson of the celebrated Sir William Cole of Enniskillen, who defended the town during the war of 1689, resisting and defeating a superior force sent against it by James II. Part of the brave defenders of the town was subsequently formed into a regiment of cavalry, which still retains the name of Enniskillen Dragoons. The present Earl is at the head of the Orange society. The English family of the Coles received large grants of lands in Fermanagh in early times, and have always been staunch supporters of the British rule. In 1760 John Cole was created Baron Mont Florence, and his successor Viscount, 1766, being advanced to the dignity of Earl of Enniskillen, 1789.

CHURCH OF DALGARNOCK.

The earliest church in the parish was no doubt that of Dalgarnock, on the fertile holms of the Nith, founded by the possessor of the barony, whoever he was, who had received from the Crown the privilege of holding fairs, which continued to the end of the last century, and may still be said to flourish in the fairs of Thornhill, to which the Earl of Queensberry got them transferred (1610), calling the spot New Dalgarnock. This name, however, never took root, and has long been forgotten, though the fairs are still continued. The fair or tryste of Dalgarnock has been immortalized in the well-known lines of Burns:—

> "I gaed to the tryste at Dalgarnock,
> And wha but my fine fickle lover was there,
> I glowr'd as I'd seen a warlock, a warlock,
> I glowr'd as I'd seen a warlock."

Mr. Thomson, for whose collection Burns wrote this song, objected to the unpoetic name of Dalgarnock, but

Burns showed true poetic instinct by rejecting the criticism. He assured his critic (Burns' Works, iv., 249) that "Dalgarnock was the name of a romantic spot near the Nith, where are still a ruined church and a burial ground."

Though we do not know the founder of Dalgarnock church, there is no doubt of its existence at a very early period. It was sacred to St. Michael (Gordon's Monast., vol. i., p. 146), and hence the place-name of Mitchel‐slacks. Not many of the churches of Scotland escaped the grasp of the abbeys, and Dalgarnock is no exception. It was granted to the monks of Holyrood by Edgar, son of Duvenald, and grandson of Donegal, a Scoto-Irish chief, who lived in the reign of David I., and seems to have possessed the whole of Nithsdale or Stranid. This Edgar lived in the reign of William the Lion (1165-1214), who confirmed the grant of the church to the monks (Dalrymple's Collection). These monks continued to hold this church till the epoch of the Reformation, and the cure was served by a vicar. Andrew, the vicar of Dalgarnock, having sworn fealty to Edward I., obtained, in 1296, a precept to the Sheriff of Dumfries to restore him to his property. The church was confirmed several times to the monks, as if they had some doubts of the legality of their tenure, first by a charter of William, Bishop of Glasgow, in 1240 (Macfarlane's Coll.); also by John Lindsay, Bishop of Glasgow, in 1322-3, and by a bull of Pope John. (Chart. Glasg.)

The anxiety thus shown to secure the church to the abbey would lead us to suppose that it must have been regarded as a rich prize, but we have no means of determining its value. In the register of assignation and modification of ministers' stipends in 1576 we find the following in regard to Dalgarnock:—"James Williamson, reidar at Dalgarno, his stipend xvi. lib. with the kirkland," &c. In the year 1606, when Dalgarnock and Closeburn were united by the General Assembly held at Linlithgow, we find in the above register the following statement—" Dalgarno is a pendicle of Holyrood House. The teinds whereof (the minister being payed) did belong to the Bishop of Edinbroch; bot efter abolition of episcopacie wer disponed for maintenans of the castle of Edinburgh. The worth of the teinds of this parochin in stok and teind, personage and vicarage, is about 9000 merkis."

Alongside the church of Dalgarnock in ancient times a small village had sprung up, where the fair was held, and its ruins were still to be found towards the end of last century, as an old man who had seen them told my friend, the Rev. John H. Walker, of Greenlaw. The stones would no doubt be employed in building dykes and the neighbouring cottars' houses, and would thus gradually be removed. The old church has long disappeared, but lately the Catholic font for sprinkling holy water was discovered covered up with sods. It is of a very rude construction, being made of the common sandstone of the country, of an oval shape, 7 feet in circuit and 18 inches in height. The hollow for containing the water is rectangular, 13 inches in length and 7 in breadth.

It is strange that the church should have been placed at the very extremity of the parish, at least 10 miles from its eastern boundary; but the holms of the Nith must have been very tempting in those days, when the parish towards the hills was little better than a desert. The church lands lay close to the church, and are now known as Kirkbog and Kirkland. The glebe which belonged to Dalgarnock church was, in later times, situated near Trigony, and was excambed towards the end of last century for land lying close to the glebe of Closeburn. The great proprietors seized everywhere throughout Scotland the church property that lay convenient to them, and in Closeburn the Kirkpatricks followed the example of their neighbours. There is a charter dated at Holyrood, 7th Feb., 1542, of which I have a copy, showing how Robert Stewart, commendator of that abbey, grants to Sir Roger Kirkpatrick *totas et integras terras nostras ecclesiasticas vicarie de Dalgarnock. . . . ad quadraginta solidatas terrarum cum suis pertinenciis in baronia de Dalgarnock, et intra vicecomitatem de Dumfreis.*

Though Roger had thus got himself connected with the property, it had still to pass through various hands before it finally settled in the possession of the family. After the Reformation we find the patronage of Dalgarnock granted in 1591-2 to Sir James Douglas of Drumlanrig, but he was again obliged to resign it in 1594 to Thomas Kirkpatrick of Closeburn (Acta Parl., iv., 90). Thirty years later, on the 5th June, 1621, the King granted to Sir John Spotiswoode of Dairsie the parish church of Dalgarnock, with the tithes and revenues, parsonage and vicarage, and the manse, glebe, and church lands to the same belonging. And this grant was ratified in Parliament, 28th June, 1633 (ib., v., 127). But then comes again another change in its possessors, for a few months afterwards we find Charles I., in his charter, 29th Sept., 1633, establishing the bishopric of Edinburgh, and granting to the bishops of that see the church of Dalgarnock, with the manse, glebe, church lands and tithes, with a number of other churches which had belonged to the monastery of Holyrood House (Keith's Bishops, 33). Its subsequent fate is found when it became bound up with the church of Closeburn.

CLOSEBURN CHURCH.

The same veil hangs over the foundation of Closeburn church which enveloped that of Dalgarnock. It was no doubt erected for the use of the barony of Kylosbern, which we know to have been possessed by the Crown in the reign of David I., but it may have existed at a much earlier period. We know that Edgar, son of Duvenald, who lived in the reign of William the Lion (1165-1214), had inherited large possessions in Nithsdale from his father, and was a liberal benefactor to the church. To the abbey of Kelso he gave in presence of his son Gylconnel the church of Kylosbern (Gordon's Monasticon, vol. ii., p. 479), and also the church of Dalgarnock, as we have before stated, to the abbey of Holyrood. This donation of the church of Kylosbern was confirmed by Walter, the bishop of Glasgow, in 1232, the very year that Ivan de Kyrkepatric received the barony from Alexander II. (Chart. Kelso, No. 278). The Kirkpatrick family, however, did not assent to this arrangement, claiming the right to the advowson. This shows, if we had no other proof, that the grant had been made by another family than the De Kyrkepatric, as they would scarcely have ventured to withdraw from the church what had been given for the benefit of the souls of their ancestors. Adam de Kyrkepatric, son of Ivan, disputed the right of the abbey, and the question was referred to the Abbot of Jedburgh, who decided in 1264 that the abbot and convent of Kelso were the true patrons of the church of Kylosbern (ib., No. 239).

It is not difficult to see why this dispute arose respecting the right to present to the church. It possessed 40 acres of land, and though we do not know the precise position of the church property, there can be little doubt that it was the best land of Kylosbern; and as the Knights Templar had also a large slice of the barony close to the baronial keep, the head of the family would naturally feel aggrieved that he should be so hemmed in by those over whom he had no control. He would also be annoyed that an independent tenant was placed close to him, for the Abbot granted a lease of the tithes to Adam de Kulenhat of Kylosbern for a yearly payment of fifty marks and a half. Adam, the tenant, moreover, was obliged to yield certain services to the Abbot and his attendants when he visited the property, such as fuel, litter (litteragium), hay, grass, and to preserve in their usual state the houses, the *vivarii*, and the inclosed fields (ib., No. 240).

Here, then, we have some idea of the state of Closeburn at that period, and it is impossible not to feel that the monks were real benefactors of the parish. They introduced the system of free tenantry, though the great body of cultivators were neyfs (nativi) or bondmen, who were attached to the soil. The monks pointed out the true road that was to lead to our present civilization. The enclosure of fields, the saving of hay for winter stock, the collection of peat and wood for fuel, the maintenance of the houses of the grange, and, above all, the fish-ponds show the mode of life of these monks. It is curious to find fish-ponds mentioned as among the erections to which Adam bound himself to attend. Such a luxury is not thought of in Closeburn in the present day, even by the richest of the parish. In old documents, Fishers Land, on the banks of the river Nith, close to Shaws Holm, has been a puzzling appellation, but these fish-ponds show how the name has originated, as being the spot where the fish of the monks was caught. The ponds kept them fresh for the table of the abbot. In the fourteenth century these monks estimated their estate, and stated that the church of Kylosbern was worth £26 6s. 8d. yearly; they had besides forty acres of land in the manor of Kylosbern belonging to the church, with a brew-house and other easements, such as have been shown above (Chart. Kelso, p. 23).

The teinds of the church of Closeburn continued to belong to the monks of Kelso till we find them granted, with the church lands, by the Earl of Bothwell, commendator of the abbey in 1580, to a Peter Collace, in order that, as his charter states, they might be improved. How long they continued with him and his heirs we know not, but they eventually came into the possession of the Kirkpatrick family. In the register (1576) of assignation and modification, to which reference has already been made, we find the following:—" Closebern.—Mr. James Ramsay, minister; his stipend, £75 2s. 5d., to be payit out of the third of the personage of Kirmado," &c.; and again, " John Thomsoune, reidare at Closeberne; his stipend, £20 with the Kirkland, to be payit out of the third of Kelso."

REFORMATION.

The principles of a purer and simpler form of religious worship penetrated into Closeburn as into the other parts of Scotland, but in what way, and by whose hands, its ecclesiastical establishments were to be administered was a difficulty here as elsewhere. It is interesting to watch the proceedings of the leading families of the neighbourhood when the valuable possessions of the old church came to be distributed. By a ratification in Parliament, 1594, James VI. confirmed a charter granted by him under the great seal to Sir James Douglas of Drumlanrig, knight, dated in January, 1591, "of the advocation and donation of the paroch kirks and parochins of Kirkbryde, Durisdeir, Glencairn, Penpont, Mortoun, and Dalgarnock;" but the grant was thus qualified: "Provyding alwayes that the said Sir James sall resigne and renounce the advocatioun and donatioun of the said paroch kirk of Dalgarnock to Thomas Kirkpatrick of Closeburne, his aris and assignayes" (Acts of Parl. of Scotland, iv., 90).

We come now to the union of the churches, which took place in 1606 by order of the General Assembly held in Linlithgow. It was thus stated in the register: "Closeburn is a pendicle of Kelso, the teinds whereof wer a part of the rent of the Bishop of Galloway, but Episcopacie being now abolished, is assigned to the Colledge of Glasgow. The worth of this parochin, stock and teind, personage and vicarage, is about 3000 merks." "The two parochins, upon the supplication of the heritors to the Assemblie at Linlithgow, in anno 1606, wer judged fit to be one congregatioun and the union ratified by Parliament." On this subject we find in the register above quoted the following entries:—"1608. Dalgarno, Cloisburn, Mr. David Rodger minister, his stipend, iiij^{xx} lib. money, to be payit out of the lordship of Kelso, or any part thereof, by the Lord his airis and successouris, &c., and mair viij$^{xx.}$, xvij. lib. xvij. for the service at the kirk of Dalgarno, be Sir Thomas Kirkpatrik of Cloiseburne, knicht, takisman of Dalgarno.— 1615. Cloisburn and Dalgarno, Alexander Flemying, minister, his stipend, iiij$^{xx.}$ lib. money, to be payit out of the lordship of Kelso, or onie part thereof, be the Lord of Kelso, his airis and successouris, &c., and viij$^{xx.}$, xvij. lib. xvijs. for the service at the kirk of Dalgarno, be Sir Thomas Kirkpatrick of Cloisburne, knicht, takisman of Dalgarno, with xxxij. lib. out of the prebendaries of Lincluden to be payit be thé takisman and parochinaris of Carlaverock."

How long Peter Collace continued to enjoy the property of Closeburn church does not appear, but the patronage and property are found to have passed into the possession of the Earl of Roxburgh, whom it is curious to find stretching out his hands to such a distant parish. The reason, no doubt, was that he lived close to Kelso, and had sufficient influence at Court to get the whole of the abbey property. Charles I. purchased the whole from the Earl, and transferred it, 13th May, 1637, to the Bishop of Galloway (Acta Parl., vii., 436). Then came the time when Presbyterianism was in the ascendant and had little regard to the private interests of the large proprietors. The Presbytery of Penpont in 1648 took the state of the parishes into their consideration, and examining the rentals, which were produced to them, and after hearing the "information anent the condition of the united kirkis of Dalgarno and Closeburn, wher ther is two standin kirkis with there several manses and gleebs," recommended them to be disjoined forthwith. The following, among other reasons, are given by the Presbytery for the division of these kirks:—" 1. That the said two kirks wer united in the dayes of corruption and Episcopacie, to the great detriment and hurt of the Church. 2. That the two kirks being in rent of stock and teind seventein thousand merks and upwards, may verie convenientlie afford maintainance to two ministers for serving the cure at the said kirks. 3. The number of communicants being seven hundreth or thereabout, may be two flocks, sufficient for two ministers. 4. That the heretours being cited to compeir befor the Presbytrie, most part of them compeired, and could not object any relevant reason (in our judgment) quherfor they might not be disjoyned. 5. That the fabrickes of both churches are now in a gud frame, quhilk will not long continue if they should remain in the present condition," &c.

Then again the chances of Episcopacy came to look more bright on the accession of Charles II. The Parliament of 1662 ratified to the Bishop of Galloway what he had received from Charles I. The Earl of Roxburgh had given up the patronage and tithes, which were probably not much worth, but retained possession of the church lands of Closeburn, which were annexed to his barony of Halydean, and belonged to his successors in the reign of Charles II. and William (Inquisit. Speciales, 270, 313, 347). Church property in those days was subject to great vicissitudes, according as Presbyterianism or Episcopacy came to the surface. We have a proof of this in Closeburn, for about ten years afterwards (1671) we find Sir Thomas Kirkpatrick obtaining a charter of his barony of Closeburn, and with it the patronage of the united kirks of Closeburn and Dalgarnock. The charter was ratified by the Parliament of 1672 (Acta Parl., viii., 154). It shows that the churches had again been united, and from this time the

EARLY HISTORY OF CLOSEBURN & DALGARNOCK. 229

church of Closeburn became the parochial church of the united parish. In 1741 the heritors improved the church by adding three galleries, but it is again in a dilapidated state, and will require such great alterations to fit it for containing the congregation that it has been determined (1875) to build a new church on a different site.

The patronage of the united parishes having been sold along with the estate of Closeburn, belonged to the representatives of the late Mr. Douglas Baird, till the abolition of patronage in 1874. The stipend was augmented in 1856, and was in that year £243 6s. 7½d. The free teinds in the parish amount to £690 0s. 6¾d. The present stipend is seventeen chalders, with £10 for communion elements. The glebe is only nine acres, very different in size from the ancient glebe of Kylosbern alone, which was forty acres. The glebe of Dalgarnock, consisting of four-and-a-half acres, was exchanged in the year 1732 for three acres one rood, lying contiguous to the glebe of Closeburn. In the return to House of Commons (March, 1875) of ministers' stipends in Scotland, the total amount of stipend of Closeburn is given as £309 13s., and the total annual value of living from all sources is £364 13s.

CLERGYMEN OF THE PARISH.

The following is a list of the ministers of Dalgarno and Closeburn:—

DALGARNO.

The parish was supplied by James Williamson, reader, from Betyn, 1568 to 1585.

1593—Richard Brown: translated to Kirkconnel about 1596.

1601—David Rogers, A.M. He was admitted by the Presbytery of Edinburgh, there being no Presbytery in Nithsdale. He was subsequently at Caerlaverock and St. Mungo.

1612—Alexander Flemyng: translated to Morton 1634.

CLOSEBURN.

1574—James Ramsay, having Dalgarno, Kirkmahoe, Kirkmichael, and Garvale also in charge. Translated to Torthorwald about 1585.

1638—Alexander Flemyng: translated from Morton.

1647—William Black, A.M.: admitted a colleague to the above. He was deprived in 1681 for not taking the test; but on petitioning the Privy Council he was allowed, 16th March following, to take it before the Archbishop. He died in 1684.

1688—Thomas Urquhart: had vacated previous to 1689.

1693—Robert Lawrie, A.M.: died the following year.

1694—Thomas Lawrie, A.M.: deposed 1709.

1718—John Lawson: got the church rebuilt in 1741.

1758—James Williamson: translated from Wamphray: translated to Moffat in 1761. Having accepted the Professorship of Mathematics in University of Glasgow, the parish was declared vacant in 1762.

1763—Peter Yorstoun: translated from Kells.

1777—Andrew Yorstoun, son of preceding: translated from Middlebie.

1815—Charles Anderson: translated from Gask.

1830—Andrew Bennet: had D.D. from University of St. Andrews in 1854.

1872—D. Ogilvy-Ramsay: translated from Kirriemuir.

The Rev. Andrew Bennet, D.D., who died in 1872, in a good old age, after forty years' ministry in Closeburn, left behind him the sweet savour of a blameless life, passed in the active discharge of his duties as a parish minister. He was a fine specimen of a true Christian gentleman, who, though full of self-respect, knew what was due to others. He was the son of the Rev. George Bennet, a Presbyterian clergyman in Carlisle, towards the beginning of the present century. Mr. George Bennet was a distinguished Hebrew scholar, and one of the principal contributors to the "British Critic," in which he reviewed from time to time the works of the celebrated English divines. This attracted the heads of the Church of England, and he became at an early period of his life acquainted with many of their most eminent men—with Milner, Dean of Carlisle, and his brother, the historian—with Markham, Archdeacon of York—with Paley, Porteus, Nares, and Horsley, with all of whom he corresponded on intimate terms. It was the learning which he displayed in his reviews of their works that induced Bishop Horsley and other eminent men of the Church of England to inquire of Archdeacon Nares, the editor of the "British Critic," to whom they were indebted for such luminous articles, and they were surprised to find that it was one who laboured in a small Presbyterian congregation in Carlisle.

Bishop Horsley, in his learned work entitled "Hosea, translated from the Hebrew, with notes, explanatory and critical,' by Samuel, Lord Bishop of Rochester" (London, 1801), has recorded the strongest testimony to the merits of Mr. Bennet's work, "Olam Hanashemoth; or a View of the Intermediate State." He also published another work, "A Display of the Spirit and Designs of those who, under pretext of a Reform, aim at the Subversion of the Constitution and Government of this Kingdom, with a Defence of Ecclesiastical Establishments" (Carlisle, 1796). It was published at the moment that we were threatened with a revolution such as had taken place in France, and it brought him at once into the counsel and friendship of all who were supporters of the British Constitution. His friends in the English Church were anxious that he should join them, but he preferred a settlement among his own countrymen, and Archdeacon Markham then applied to his brother-in-law, the Earl of Mansfield, who appointed him to the parish of Strathmiglo in Fife, where he passed many years, dying in 1835, in his eighty-fifth year.

KIRKPATRICK CHURCH.

This church was situated on the slope of Kirkpatrick hill, and opposite to the small village and farm-steading of the same name. Its ruins were still visible towards the end of last century, and the bright verdure of the sward in a field of Brownhill farm still points out where the dust of former ages rests. There is no tradition as to the period when it was erected, but it is not likely to have given a designation to the family, as Chalmers thinks, since we find a witness of this name to a charter of the De Brus long before the family became possessed of Kylosbern. It is more likely to have been erected by the family in honour of St. Patrick, their patron saint, after they had settled in Closeburn. The old font is now to be seen in Dr. Grierson's Museum, Thornhill.

CROAL OR CROLE CHAPEL.

Of this place of religious worship there is no memorial of any kind except the name, which it has handed down to the small village. The village is close to the Lime Kilns, and at the foot of the hill, over which the two roads from the south pass. There is no saint of this name, nor any tradition to throw light on its history. The ruins are still to be seen near the village, at no great distance from the churches of Kylosbern and Kirkpatrick. Behind this village of Croal, and in a field, which was in a state of nature, there was discovered on the 22nd April, 1844, a very large collection of silver coins, which may have been the hoard of the clergy. They consisted of silver pennies and groats. Some of them were of great rarity. Thus, there is one which I possess, and of which the following is a description:—A groat of the second coinage of David II., struck at Edinburgh, obv., head to left, crowned with sceptre in a treasure of six arcs: DAVID D^{ei} GRA. REX. SCOTORVM.; long single cross, with four mullets of six points, VILLA EDINBVRGH.

This is an extremely interesting coin to numismatists, showing, what very few do show, the mullet at the end of the legend on the obverse, no doubt one of the "notable signs" mentioned in the old Act of 1366 (Scots Acts, vol. i., p. 139). A specimen is figured in "Wingate's Illustrations of the Scottish Coinage," pl. 8, fig. 12. Another is a penny of Alexander III., Lindsay's fourth coinage: obv., head to left, crowned with sceptre; ALEXANDER DEI. GRA.—long single cross, with mullets of six points ⊥ REX SCOTORVM. Another is an English penny of Edward II., of the Canterbury mint,—CIVITAS

CANTOR. There is another very rare penny of Edward II., struck at Durham. It is described in "Hawkins' Silver Coins of England," p. 97, and figured in the same work (plate xxiii., fig. 302). The peculiarity is in the form of the cross, and is a highly interesting coin for the English collector. These were the most valuable of the coins that were discovered, but there were hundreds of others. On the English groats there ran:—EDUARD. REX ANGL. FRANC. HYB.; and on the reverse:—CIVITAS LONDINI and POSVI DEVM ADJVTOREM MEVM. Some of the pennies are thus inscribed:—EDW. R. ANGL. DOM^S HIB. On the reverse, CIVITAS EBORACI; and on others, CIVITAS LONDINI. This description of these coins is by a distinguished Scottish numismatist, who took the trouble of examining them for me. How could this large collection have been left here? There was no coin of a later date than Edward II. (1307-1327). Edward passed a night at Dalgarnock in 1307; but these coins, as so many of them are Scottish, could scarcely have belonged to an English marauder. They were found about six inches from the surface, by being turned up by the plough.

In the works of the "Ettrick Shepherd" by the Rev. Thomas Thomson, 1873 (p. 88), the following legend, entitled "The Wife of Crowle," is found:—

"This fragment is a traditionary story put to rhyme without any addition. The woman lived at Crowle Chapel in Nithsdale. It is given more at large in 'The Winter Evening Tales.'

"And aye she sat by the cheek of the grate,
　Pretending to shape and to sew;
But she looked at all that entered the Hall,
　As if she would look them through.

" Her hands she rung, and at times she sung
　　Some wild airs for the dead ;
　Then 'gan to tell a crazy tale,
　　She told it for a meed.

" ' I once had a son, but now he is gone,
　　They tore my son from me;
　His life-blood streamed where the cormorant screamed,
　　On the wild rocks girt by the sea.

" ' So hard his lone bed, and unpillowed his head,
　　For the dark sea cave is his urn ;
　The cliff flowers weep o'er his slumbers so deep,
　　And the dead lights over him burn.

" ' Say what can restore the form that's no more,
　　Or illumine the death-set eye ?
　Yes, a wild mother's tears, and a wild mother's prayers,
　　A spirit may force from the sky.

" ' When the sun had rose high, and the season gone by
　　My yearnings continued the same;
　I prayed to Heaven, both morning and even',
　　To send me my son, till he came.

" ' One evening late by the chimney I sat,
　　I dreamed of the times that were gone ;
　Of its chirrup so eiry and cricket was weary,
　　All silent I sat, and alone.

" ' The fire burnt bright, and I saw by the light
　　My own son enter the Hall;
　A white birchen wand he held in his hand,
　　But no shadow had he on the wall.

" ' He looked at the flame, as forward he came.
　　All steadfast and looked not away;
　His motion was still, as the mist on the hill,
　　And his colour like cold white clay.

"'I knew him full well; but the tones of the bell,
   Which quavered at midnight it rung,
So stunned me, I strove, but could not move
   My hand, my foot, nor my tongue.

"'Blood-drops in a shower then fell on the floor,
   From the roof, and they fell upon me;
No water their stain could wash out again,
   These blood-drops still you may see.

"'His form still grew, and the flame burnt blue,
   I stretched out my arms to embrace;
But he turned his dead eye, so hollow and dry,
   And so wistfully gazed in my face

"'That my head whirled round, the walls and the ground
   All darkened, no more could I see;
But each finger's point, and each finger's joint,
   Grew thick as the joint of my knee.

"'I wakened ere day, but my son was away,
   No word to me had he said;
Though my blood was boiling, and my heart recoiling,
   To see him again still I prayed.

"'And oft has he come to my lonely home,
   In guise that might adamant melt;
He has offered his hand with expression so bland,
   But that hand could never be felt.

"'I've oft seen him glide so close by my side,
   On his grave-cloth the seams I could trace;
The blood from a wound trickled down to the ground,
   And a napkin was over his face.

"'So oft have I seen that death-like mien,
   It has somewhat bewildered my brain;
Yet though chilled with affright at the terrible sight,
   I long still to see it again.'"

BRIDDEBURG CHAPEL.

This chapel, in the southern part of the parish, which is mentioned by Mr. Black, was no doubt the chapel of the barons of Briddeburg, and consecrated to St. Bridget, the only native Irish saint whose name we can trace in the place-names of this country, and who seems to have been a favourite with the Celts of the south of Scotland. In Upper Nithsdale we have the old parish of Kirkbryde; Kirkbride in Keir and in Annandale; Bride-kirk in Annan; Bryde-kirk in Hoddam.

KNIGHTS TEMPLAR.

In addition to the religious bodies which have been noticed, the Knights Templar had secured to themselves large possessions in different parts of the parish. Templand of Dalgarnock points out a piece of ground which had belonged to them, and which is now included in the Queensberry property. Then there is a seisin of Sir Thomas Kirkpatrick, 4th Aug., 1677, in the 40s. land of the Templand of Closeburn, called Cowfaddoch,—in older deeds, Culfaddoch. The name still survives, though the farm of Cowfaddoch no longer exists. It is now the name of a field not far from the Limekilns. There is another Templand mentioned in old deeds, called of Shaws, but its precise site cannot be discovered, though the direction where it lay is indicated by Shaws. These names have handed down the memory of a military order which acquired, by the valour of its knights, immense riches and an eminent degree of warlike renown, but whose vices and cruelty caused the order to be suppressed in 1312 by the Council of Vienne. (See Addison's Knights Templar).

SACRED WELLS AND CROSSES.

Besides these religious places of worship, we have traces left of the old Catholic faith in the consecrated wells. Close to Dalgarnock church there is still known the well of St. Ninian, clear and wholesome, as it was fifteen hundred years ago; at Brownhill, near Kirkpatrick, My Lady's Well, sacred to the Virgin Mary, and which supplied Burns with water in the summer evenings to temper "the barley bree." On Kirkpatrick hill, not far from the site of the old church, there is a well called "Catherine's Strand," sacred no doubt to St. Catherine; and last of all, on Templand farm, close to the wooden bridge over the Cample, there is Moses' Well, an unusual designation, but which some Knight Templar may have given in remembrance of his toils in Palestine.

Then, in regard to crosses, there are few parishes where there will not be found spots marked out by the sacred symbol of our faith. In the distant part of the parish, entering from Kirkmichael, we find Glencorse and Corseburn on the river Æ; and proceeding onward by the road across the hills, there is Rob's Corse, the cross of Robert Bruce. Again, down on the banks of the Nith, near Shawsholm, there is Corsegrip, and near the Limekilns, Corsery hill.

THE BUCHANITES.

Closeburn was the scene of religious fanaticism towards the end of last century, and the monomania has left a place-name, "Buchan Ha'," among us to record a strange proof of the kind of madness which sometimes takes possession of large numbers of the human race, such as we have seen lately in the case of the Mormonites. Not one of the inhabitants of Closeburn joined the sect, so far as I have been able to discover, but the members of it, who came from Ayrshire, took up their residence here for some time. The founder of this sect of strange beings was Mr. White, who was about the year 1770 incumbent of a Relief Congregation at Irvine, in Ayrshire. He is said to have been a popular preacher, broaching new-fangled doctrines, and thus drawing crowds of ignorant persons of the lower orders, who are easily tickled by novelties, without reference to their sense. Among others who came to hear him was Mrs. Buchan, from Glasgow, who became his disciple, and when Mr. White was removed from the ministry by his brethren, she and her friends wandered forth to the number of a hundred, settling at some houses in Closeburn, which acquired the name of "Buchan Ha," from Luckie Buchan, as she was called.

Sir Walter Scott says, "I never heard of alewife that turned preacher except Luckie Buchan in the west."

She gave forth the most blasphemous pretensions, maintaining that she was the Third Person of the Godhead, pretending to confer immortality on whomsoever she breathed, and promising to translate direct to heaven in a body, without their tasting death, all who put unlimited faith in her divine mission. She also personified the woman described in the Revelation of St. John, as being clothed with the Sun and the Moon, and pretended to have brought forth the Man-child who was to rule all nations with a rod of iron (Rev. xii. 1), in the person of the Rev. Hugh White.

It would be a waste of time to follow the vagaries of such a set of foolish beings. My predecessor, who was a young man at the time (1786), recollected that they attempted to ascend in a body to heaven from Templand hill, at sunrise, standing with their faces towards the rising sun, and singing to the air, "the buds of sweet roses," what Burns calls "some of their nonsensical rhymes, which they dignified with the name of hymns." The Kirk-Session of Closeburn fearing that they might become a burden on the parish, compelled them to leave, 10th March, 1787, when they proceeded to Auchengibbert, a wild moorland farm of considerable extent in the parish of Urr and Stewartry of Kirkcudbright, of which they got a lease from John Bushby, sheriff-clerk of Dumfriesshire.

TOPOGRAPHY.

The area of the parish of Closeburn, according to Ordnance Survey, is 29,347·404 imperial acres. It is in its general character hilly and mountainous, with a small portion of level ground towards the banks of the Nith. The hills begin to rise close behind Closeburn Hall, and continue to increase in height till they reach their highest point at Queensberry, which is 2279 feet above the level of the sea. Between this and Auldgirth Bridge Inn there is a marked difference of altitude, as the latter is only 90 feet. The front door of Wallace Hall is 206·78 feet. The following are a few of the heights of the parish:—Ganna, 2157 feet; Mitchelslacks, 700; Penbreck, 1998; Wee Queensberry, 1675; the Law, 1175; the Dod, 1385; Nether Dod, 1150; Garroch Fell, 1939; Loch Ettrick, 908. In these high lying regions, which could give refuge to such patriots as Wallace, when hotly pursued by our "auld enemies," we find a spot called Wallace's Kist, the place of his concealment before he met in bold conflict Greystock, an English commander, whom he defeated and slew at Blue Cairn, across the limits of Closeburn, but close to this spot. The burn is still called Discomfit Gutter. So precipitously do the hills rise close to Auldgirth, that while the inn is only 90 feet, Higher Auldgirth farm-steading is 600 feet.

RIVERS.

The parish rises so high that from its water-shed, Din's Rig, the streams flow on one side into the Solway by the Annan and on the other by the Nith. The Cample burn, joined by Glenleith and Kettleton burns, rises on the borders of Lanarkshire, at the back of Auchenleck hill, and forms the boundary during the greater part of its course between Closeburn and Morton. Its principal tributary is Crichope, which, rising in Townfoot loch, falls over a precipice about 100 feet high, called Grey Mare's Tail, and passes into Crichope linn, one of the most picturesque spots in the south of Scotland. Some violent convulsion of nature has torn asunder the rocks, and the water, taking advantage of the disruption, has worn away the soft sandstone into a strange form, called the Gullet Spout. It continues its course through a curiously contorted channel, till it reaches Hell's Cauldron, close to the Souter's Seat, supposed to be the spot where a shoemaker in the days of religious persecution had concealed himself to cobble the shoes of the Covenanters. At the head of the linn there was a cave where the Covenanters had lain concealed, but it has long disappeared under the operations of the quarryman. Sir Walter Scott had visited the linn, and it is believed that he had got hints for the description of the cave in which he makes Balfour of Burley to be concealed.

The principal stream in the east of the parish, which drains the water into the Annan, is the Æ, forming the boundary between Closeburn and Kirkmichael from its source called the Pot of Æ. The eastern boundary towards Ganna hill and Shank is undetermined, being a wild and barren district. Queensberry hill is not entirely in the parish, which extends, however, as far as Queensberry Shoulder, and then there is a line drawn towards Penbreck, Capel, Yetts, and Berry Rig. The small streams of Garroch, Capel, Poldivan, and Glenleith fall into the Æ.

LOCHS.

In early times the parish was studded over with lochs of considerable size. On the top of Auchenleck hill there is Townhead loch, 1427 feet above the level of the sea; Loch Ettrick, 908, which was enlarged by means of a dam to form a collection of water for the machine to draw off the water from the limestone mines. This dam broke during the month of January, in 1827, and coming down with great fury caused much damage to the lower ground. Townfoot loch still exists, but the Castle loch, which in early times surrounded Closeburn keep, and protected it from the sudden attack of English marauders, has disappeared under agricultural improvements. It was drained by the late Mr. Douglas Baird in 1859; and, hid under a covering of deep peat moss, an old boat was discovered, which now may be seen in the Antiquarian Museum, Edinburgh. It was 12 feet in length, and well preserved by having been sunk in the moss.

In the year 1756 this loch, with some others in the south of Scotland, was agitated by an earthquake, so much so that the people, who were on their way to church (Sunday, 21st February, 1756), felt no inclination to venture within the walls of the sacred building, and Mr. Lawson, the clergyman, conducted divine service among the tombstones. Sir Thomas Kirkpatrick gave the following account of it to the Royal Society:—

"Closeburne, 4th March, 1756.

"About a quarter before nine on Sunday morning we were alarmed with an unusual motion in the waters of Closeburn Loch. The first thing that appeared to me in this wonderful scene was a strong convulsion and agitation of the waters from the west side of the loch towards the middle, when they turned and wheeled about in a strange manner. From thence proceeded two large currents formed like a river, which ran with swiftness and rapidity beyond all description, quite contrary ways, one from the middle to the south-east and the other to the north-east points of the loch. There they were stopt short, as the banks are pretty high, and obliged to turn, which occasioned a prodigious tumbling and agitation at both ends of the body of water. There was likewise a current, which rose sometimes considerably above the surface near the west side, that I frequently observed running with great velocity an hundred yards to the southward, and returning in a moment with as great velocity the other way. What I noticed in the next place was the tossing of the waters in the ponds, which were more or less moved as the agitations of the loch came nearer the side or kept a greater distance from it. But as it is beyond my capacity to give a particular description of all that happened upon this occasion, I shall conclude with telling you that the agitation and current above mentioned continued without intermission for at least three-and-a-half or four hours, when they began to abate a little in their violence, though they were not quite over at sunset. I had almost forgotten to tell you that this strange phenomenon was renewed on Monday morning a little before nine, and lasted for an hour-and-a-half, but the motion of the waters was not near so violent as the day before. What is very remarkable, there was not the least breath or gale of wind on Sunday till one o'clock, a circumstance which balked us not a little in our observations."

MINERAL WELLS.

Near Closeburn Castle there is a strong sulphurous spring, of the same character as Moffat Well, though it flows less fully since the drainage operations in its neighbourhood.

Town-cleugh Well, which is chalybeate, being strongly impregnated with iron. It is called Town-cleugh from its vicinity to a small village called Closeburn Town, the only remains of which towards the end of last century was part of a cross.

Francis Well, on Auchencairn farm, and on Threapmoor there is another mineral well.

EARLY HISTORY OF CLOSEBURN & DALGARNOCK. 245

MINERALS.

The limestone quarry of Closeburn was opened up by Sir James Kirkpatrick in 1770, though the rock had been discovered many years before. It is the most extensive and central in the valley of the Nith, though the mines have long been abandoned from the depth having become too great, and the upper post, as it is called, is the only part that is now worked. The beds of limestone are covered over by a great mass of earth, and the material is now reached only by the removal of this superincumbent earth. The upper post of limestone is about 14 feet thick, being contained within two impure strata of limestone, called by the workmen "dogger." The lower post, which is no longer worked, was about 18 feet thick, and was separated from the upper by strata of sandstone and clay, having the same dip as the upper. The lower post was pure carbonate of lime, ascertained by Dr. Murray's analysis to consist in the 100 parts of 91 of carbonate of lime, equivalent to 50 of pure lime. The upper post is said to be scarcely so pure, being mixed with some portion of magnesia, which is much longer than pure lime in re-absorbing from the air the carbonic acid. Before this limestone was brought extensively into use the land in Upper Nithsdale was covered with heath, barren and unproductive, but by judicious top-dressing the heath has gradually disappeared, and nutritious herbage has taken its place. It is used principally for agricultural purposes, and therefore the quantity sold each year varies very considerably. It is at the commencement of a lease that the tenant top-dresses most liberally, and it is not uncommon to find a tenant laying out as much as £500 in the first year of his lease. The effects of this lime-quarry, and that of Barjarg, may be seen all over the basin of Closeburn, as well as the adjoining straths of Glencairn, Sanquhar, and Dumfries.

When this quarry was first opened up, it was with difficulty that the farmers could be induced to apply the lime to their land, and the proprietor of Closeburn (1775) found it necessary to bind his tenants in their leases to lime a certain quantity of their land yearly, which he furnished gratis, and for which he even paid the carriage; while they, on their parts, were bound to pay five shillings additional rent for every eighty measures, as this was considered sufficient for an acre; yet, though this arrangement was so favourable to the tenant, the greatest quantity any of them would agree to lime was two acres in the year; some of them would lime no more than half an acre, and others could hardly be induced at all to make the experiment. All this unwillingness arose because they believed that the light, dry, sand soil, in place of being improved, would be quite burnt up and rendered useless by lime. Such was the aversion of the people in this country to the use of lime as a manure for land, but this has long passed away, and neither compulsion nor argument are any longer necessary. In 1794 the lime cost ninepence the measure at the lime-works, each measure containing two Dumfries pecks heaped, or about two-and-an-eighth Winchester bushels, and the cause of this high price was the deep cover and the distance from coal. The coal was carted from Sanquhar, which is 14 miles from Closeburn. It cost sevenpence a measure when laid down at the lime-works. The measure is the same with that by which the lime is sold, and one measure of coals is hardly sufficient to burn three of the lime. At present (1873) the price of a measure of lime containing two Winchester bushels is thirteen pence at the lime-works.

The fossils in Closeburn lime strata are interesting, some of which are very rare. Dr. Grierson has a large collection in his museum. *Orthocera gigantica* was first discovered here, and has been described by Professor Buckland.

POPULATION.

According to Dr. Webster's report, the population in 1755 was 999. The number of inhabitants in the year 1778 was between 1000 and 1100. In 1786 it amounted to 1460. The census of late times gives the following:—

	Males.	Females.	Total.	Children at School.	Rooms.
1851,	819	913	1732	...	...
1861,	774	881	1655	310	905
1871,	756	856	1612	313	1013

There was a religious census taken in 1789 by the Rev. Andrew Yorstoun, and he found the number of Dissenters from the Church of Scotland to consist of 98, whom Mr. Yorstoun calls Seceders, now known to us as United Presbyterians. There were 23 Cameronians, now known as Reformed Presbyterians; and lastly, 9 Episcopalians. The Dissenters from the Church were in all 130. The secession from the Church in 1843 increased the number of Dissenters to some extent, but the members and adherents of the Church of Scotland in Closeburn still exceed the Dissenters of all denominations by a considerable number. The Rev. D. Ogilvy-Ramsay, the present minister of the parish, took an ecclesiastical census in 1872-3, and has furnished me with the following results:—

No. of Members and Adherents of the		Church of Scotland,	819
"	"	Free Church,	475
"	"	United Presbyterians,	165
"	"	Evangelical Union,	30
"	"	Church of England,	29
"	"	Baptist Church,	16
"	"	Reformed Presbyterians,	15
Total found by him in the parish, after personal visitation and inquiry from house to house,			1549

There has been a Free Church in the parish since 1843. The first minister of it was the Rev. Alexander Stark, who had previously been a minister of the Church of Scotland in the North. He resigned in 1849, and was succeeded by the Rev. James Hutton, the present incumbent, who was ordained in 1851.

1872.—Marriages in the year,	. . .	11
Births "	. . .	58
Deaths "	. . .	35

VALUATION.

The valued rent of this parish was, in 1671, 5811 merks, and in 1827, 9011 merks 10s. In 1855 the gross valuation was £15,168 18s. 6d., being £12,420 17s. 6d. for lands and houses, and £2748 1s. for Glasgow and South-Western Railway. The gross valuation is now (1875) £20,478 5s. 2d., which is distributed thus:—

The Co-heiresses of Douglas Baird, Esq.,	.	£11,476 16 6
His Grace the Duke of Buccleuch, &c.,	.	5,050 0 0
Charles Copland, Esq., . . .	.	983 8 8
John Mather, Esq., ...	.	90 0 0
Wallace Hall Endowment., . .	.	40 0 0
Roger Kirkpatrick Esq., . . .	.	40 0 0
Railway, ...	.	3,633 0 0
Manse and Glebe, ...	.	45 0 0
Cunningholm, ...	.	120 0 0
		£20,478 5 2

WOODS.

This parish is well wooded, as the late Sir Charles Granville Stuart-Menteth, Bart., devoted much attention to procure shelter by numerous plantations. The woods, however, are of late growth, having been planted within the last eighty years, with the exception of some old beeches round the castle, and one oak, which may likely enough be contemporary with Ivone de Kyrkepatric in 1232. The length of the stem is 31 feet; at its base, 17 feet 8 inches in circumference; 4 feet above ground, 15 feet 2 inches; and at 15 feet above ground, 11 feet. There is a beech, which is one of the finest in Dumfriesshire; length of trunk being 12 feet, thereafter branching into four stems. At $1\frac{1}{2}$ foot above ground it is 17 feet 8 inches in circumference; at 3 feet above ground, 15 feet 4 inches; and at 12 feet above ground, it is 15 feet in circumference. The circumference of each of the two principal stems is $8\frac{1}{2}$ feet. There was a larch at Shaws, which had to be cut down in 1864 from disease at the core, and which was one of the original larches obtained at the same time with those at Barjarg from the Duke of Athole about 1731. Dr. Grierson possesses in his museum a transverse section of this larch, taken at

13 feet from the ground, which is 8 feet 8 inches in circumference, and 2 feet 8 inches in diameter. In this section upwards of 100 rings can be counted. There are 1158 acres of woodlands in Closeburn, as is shown by the return to Government in 1874.

EMINENT MEN.

It is strange how few are found to depart from this life "leaving a foot-print on the sands of time," and of all who have lived and died in Closeburn, with the exception of the old barons of Kirkpatrick, we have only two or three scholars whose names will be handed down to posterity. The Emperor Antoninus truly enough remarks, "The time is at hand when thou wilt forget and be forgotten by all:" "Short, too, the longest posthumous fame, and even this only continued by a succession of poor human beings, who will very soon die, and who know not even themselves much less him who died long ago." The most celebrated scholar of Closeburn was Dr. John Hunter, Professor of Humanity in the University of St. Andrews, who was born in 1746, at Dun's Yett, on Gilchristland farm, though the house has long since disappeared. Dr. Hunter was educated at Wallace Hall school, and became one of the ablest scholars of his day. His ideas of etymology were far in advance of his age, which is shown in his notes to the Latin school books which he edited, and many of which are still used in schools.

Another man of some eminence was the Rev. Dr. Gillespie, minister of Cults, and also Professor of Humanity, having succeeded Dr. Hunter in the Latin chair. He was, like Dr. Hunter, born at Dun's Yett, in February, 1778, and educated at Wallace Hall. Having obtained license in 1813, he was appointed to the church of Cults, through the influence of Dr. Hunter, whose daughter he had married. In 1828 he became Dr. Hunter's assistant, and on the elevation of Dr. Hunter to be Principal, Dr. Gillespie succeeded to the full emoluments of the office. He wanted the learning and solidity of his predecessor, and was best known as a contributor of verses to *Blackwood's Magazine*, which served their fleeting purpose, but have long been forgotten. His second wife was sister of Lord Campbell, Lord High Chancellor of England. Dr. Gillespie died at Dunino, 11th September, 1844, aged sixty-seven.

Closeburn gave birth to another scholar, not less distinguished than Dr. Hunter, though he never reached a professorial chair—Dr. Carson, who was for many years Rector of the High School, Edinburgh. He was first Rector of Dumfries Academy, then was appointed one of the junior masters of Edinburgh High School, and Rector when Dr. Pillans, in 1820, became Professor in Edinburgh University. Dr. Carson was a learned scholar, and has left several works which will maintain his fame.

BURNS IN CLOSEBURN.

The poet was a frequent visitor at the castle of Closeburn about 1788, occupied at that time by William Stewart, the father of Polly Stewart, when he was factor to Dr. Stuart-Menteth. The poet addressed the following poem to "Willie Stewart":—

> "You're welcome, Willie Stewart;
> You're welcome, Willie Stewart;
> There's ne'er a flower that blooms in May,
> That's half sae welcome's thou art.

"Come, bumpers high, express your joy,
   The bowl we maun renew it;
  The tappit-hen, gae bring her ben,
   To welcome Willie Stewart.

"May foes be strang, and friends be slack,
   Ilk action may he rue it;
  May woman on him turn her back,
   That wrangs thee, Willie Stewart."

Mr Wiliam Stewart was son of a publican, who kept a small spirit shop at "Closeburn Kirk brig," but the house has long since disappeared. He was session-clerk for some years, and, like all Scotchmen, was anxious to give his five sons the best education that his means and the time would allow. The result was that they all made their way in the world and rose above their original position. William was born in 1750, beginning life as a packman in England, carrying drapery goods; and the first distinct notice of him is an anecdote which brought him in contact with the Rev. Dr. Stuart-Menteth. Happening to call in the way of his trade on Mr. Menteth in 1783, at Barrowby, in Lincolnshire, he was asked if he knew the Closeburn property, which was then advertised for sale. As it was his native parish, he was well acquainted with it, and his intelligent answers seem to have so won on Mr. Menteth that he was asked by him to accompany him to Scotland to view the property. The result of this visit was, the Closeburn property passed into the possession of Mr. Menteth and Mr. Stewart was appointed factor. Closeburn Hall had been destroyed by fire in 1748, and had never been rebuilt, so that there was no proper dwelling-place on the estate. The old castle had been fitted up by the Kirkpatricks as a temporary abode, and here Mr. Stewart on the removal of the old family ensconced himself to look after the property and to watch the building of the new mansion which Mr. Menteth set about erecting.

It was at this time that Burns seems to have been on intimate terms with Mr. Stewart, and used to visit him at the castle, where they were accustomed to sit late, and often see the sun above the horizon before the company dispersed. Possibly the intercourse of Burns and Stewart was made more intimate from the circumstance that Mrs. Bacon, the landlady of Brownhill Inn, where Burns was only too often found in the evenings, was sister to Mr. Stewart.

Mr. Stewart retired from his office of factor, and in 1793 we find him taking the farm of Laught, Laughtmoor, Bankhead, and Blacknest,—a large tract of uncultivated land in the neighbouring parish of Morton. There Mr. Stewart remained till 1806, when he gave up the farm and retired to Maxwelltown, on the opposite side of the river Nith from Dumfries, dying there in 1812, and being buried in Closeburn churchyard.

The following is the epitaph on his tombstone:—

HIC RELIQUIÆ QUIESCUNT MORTALES
GULIELMI STEWART ARMIGERI
QUI
LOCUM CURATORIS NEGOTIORUM
IN HÆREDIO DE CLOSEBURN
COMPLURIBUS ANNIS FELICITER COMPLEVIT
DIEM OBJIT SUPREMUM
APUD MUNICIPIUM DE MAXWELLTON
19 JULII 1812
ÆTATIS SUÆ ANNO SEXAGESIMO TERTIO
S. T. T. L. *(Sit tibi terra levis).*

"Here rests the mortal remains of William Stewart, Esq., who filled successfully the office of factor for several years on the estate of Closeburn. He died in Maxwelltown, 19th July, 1812, in the sixty-third year of his age. May the earth lie light on thee."

"LOVELY POLLY STEWART."

Polly Stewart, celebrated by Burns for her beauty, was daughter of the above Mr. William Stewart. Her mother was an Englishwoman, the widow of John Lee, Esq., of Luffwich, Northamptonshire, by whom she had a daughter Hannah, who died at Closeburn Castle, 1786, aged twenty-three years. She was married to Mr. Stewart about 1774, and Polly was born about the year 1775; and would therefore be in her sixteenth or seventeenth year when she became known to Burns at Closeburn Castle, her father's house. Some old people who still remember to have seen her in her younger days speak in enthusiastic terms of her beauty and the slimness of her form; and even those who knew her when she had reached threescore say that her youthful figure was such that it was only when her countenance was seen that you could believe that she was advanced in years. She was first married to her cousin Ishmael Stewart, and had by him three sons, William, Charles, and Alexander, who were living with their grandfather at Laught in 1805, and attending Wallace Hall School. Her husband Ishmael was obliged to leave the country under a cloud, and dared not return. At what time he died, and where, is unknown; but Polly in 1801 was, tradition says, obliged to marry against her inclination Mr. George Welsh, granduncle to the late Mrs. Thomas Carlyle—one of the most respected tenants on the Queensberry estate, in whose family the farm of Morton Mains had been for many years. Such marriages are seldom fortunate, and Polly did not find herself an exception. She was of a gay disposition, a lover of pleasure; and Morton Mains is now, and was then still more, distant from the busy haunts of men. Their married life was not happy, and the result was that they separated. She returned to her father's house, who had taken up his abode in 1806 in Maxwelltown. She had two daughters, who predeceased her. Dumfries was at this time full of French officers, prisoners of war, and among them was a handsome Swiss of the name of Fleitz, to whom she became unfortunately attached.

In spite of all remonstrances, she joined her fate to that of Fleitz, accompanying him to France, where Fleitz found employment in the Swiss troops embodied by Louis XVIII. In this service he remained till 1830, and Polly continued with him. In that year Louis Philippe ascended the throne, and dismissed the whole of the Swiss mercenaries, when Fleitz found himself thrown on the wide world. He had for many years been stationed with his regiment in the island of Corsica, but then returned to Switzerland with Polly, where we find her dating the following interesting letters from Lauffenburg, near Basle.

She was now approaching threescore years; and the glamour that had been thrown over her eyes by passion, thirty years before, must have been long dissipated. There is a deep-pent yearning in these letters for knowledge of the fate of those children of whom she could not forget that she was the mother. Her own immediate relatives had passed into the grave, and she writes evidently at a venture to one whom she had known many years before to have been the confidential friend of her youngest son, Alexander. The late Mr. Pagan, to whom they are addressed, was the proprietor of the King's Arms Hotel, Maxwelltown, and one who passed through life highly respected by a large circle of friends. I have to thank his son, Mr. William Pagan, for a copy of the following letters:—

" Feb. 13th, 1831.

" My dear Sir,

" Since the date of your letter, Dec. 24th, 1824, which now lies upon the table before me, no doubt the distance of time admits of many changes. But no consideration of this event or the other accident can discourage me from availing myself of the present occasion to address myself to you; the confidence in my bosom of your *friendship* remains [un]impaired by distance, silence, or absence. That if you can render or afford me satisfaction, join'd with happiness, you will not neglect my present ardent prayer. You was the friend of my two sons: inform me then, my dear friend, of their fate. I observe you was in correspondence with Alexander: say, has he returned to his native land, where or what became of him. Poor Charles! his fate interests me deeply— his heart was good—his kindness to me when last in Scotland made a lasting impression in my *lacerated heart*. Please present the kind regards of his old acquaintance Mr. F. to Mr. Rigg and family, and if he is still at Priestland. I am at present just returned from the island of Corsica, where I was for a very long time. My busy memory visits Maxwelltown but too often. No country, no change of scene, can blot from my bosom my *native land.* Pagan, remember me, and answer my petition. God will reward you for this act of goodness. By the direction you sent me, I try'd to find Alexander. My letters and enquiries were in vain.

"Present our join'd regards to Mrs. Pagan. Accept every warm wish of your old acquaintance—to see you would make him very happy.

"I am sorry to be obliged to put you to the expense of postage, but the different country's occasion this circumstance: from here I can only pay the postage to Calais, as you must pay the inland postage to Dover. Let me beg of you to write me everything you know about him. I have wrote about at the same time as much of news as possible. I am sure I would no more know Dumfries. Direct to me as follows: Mrs. Fleitz, à Lauffenburgh, en Swisse, Canton d'Argavie.

"I am, dear Pagan, yours for ever obliged well wisher and sincere friend,

"M. FLEITZ.

"N.B.—If you know anything of Grace W. there, I am interested also. In course of two weeks you will have this. Adieu!"

"May 29th, 1833."

"Dear Pagan,

"As if writing is permitted from the Elysian fields, I address myself once more to my old acquaintance, not doubting his assistance, and of your still residing in the same place. Formerly knowing your kindness of disposition, the interest you have appeared to take in the immediate departure of my unfortunate son Alexander Stewart for America, persuades me again to the liberty of making my present application—believing, by your correspondence with him, you are enabled to give me the ardent desired information of his fate. The precarious line of my poor Charles produces no hope to learn what became of him; his honest heart was early made to feel the checker'd path that marks *life*. 'Some are made to *mourn*.' Busy memory gives a retrospect to pass'd events. The sudden death of my father proved a fatal stroke to the welfare of Alexander. The volatility of his disposition plunged him into a labyrinth of future misery. Me he deceived in every point, render'd himself wretched and me miserable. Forget my *children* and my country I never can. My dear sir, hear then my solicitation: let charity, the first principle of our true religion, *sway* your mind. Throw not these lines aside, but once more write me. The God who commands the fate of all will bless you and yours for this *benevolence*. Turn not a deaf ear to the petition of the unhappy. The joy your welcome letter will produce, could you behold, would repay the *obstacle* of the inland postage. In the course of ten days this will reach you—in the course of the month I trust the happiness of your letter will arrive. Say if Mr. Rigg is alive. Remember me.

"N.B. Direct as follows: Madame Fleitz, à Lauffenbourg, en Swisse, Canton d'Argovie, p. Basle.

"Our join'd regards to Mrs. Pagan, yourself, and for ever believe me to be

"Sincerely yours welwisher,

"Mary Stewart Fleitz.

"P.S.—I hope, sincerely hope, God will impress your *heart* to answer my ardént prayer with speedy answer and advice. *Adieu!*"

"Lauffenburg, Oct. 6th, 1833.
"Mr. Pagan,

"Considering you truely in the light of a true friend, and not as the mercenary part of mankind, my esteemed friend, sensible am I of the expense of postage; consequently your kind compliance with my ardent prayer is a sufficient inducement for me to value your good heart and well-disposed disposition to render me this essential service. I have spoke to a commercial gentleman, a travelar, who will in the spring go to Glasgow. My intentions are by this medium to refund the postage of your correspondence. It is merely impossible to pay the postage to Dumfries. I have franked this letter through France. The import of this letter is still concerning my son. Your welcome letter, dated 25th June, came safe to hand in 9 days. Immediately I wrote to Alexander under the direction you gave me in yours, paying the expense of inland postage. More than three months are pass'd and no letter from him, notwithstanding you have transmitted my address to him, being upon the point at that epoch of writing to him yourself. I flatter'd myself to have received a letter from him, even if he had not have received mine—a daily disappointment is mine. Nothing could have given me more contentment than a correspondence with him. As I know he is under many obligations to you and Mrs. Pagan, which must ever demand his gratful acknowledgement, you naturaly are his confidential friend, and can solve my questions of anxiety—my astonishment to observe you are ignorant of his employment in procuring his existence since his residence in America.

"Be kind enough to inform me of his intentions. Will he return to Scotland, or does he intend to continue where he is? Who are the trustees at present? Inform me of the ordinary length of time required for letters to go and come from Demerara. Inform me of your just opinion of him in every respect, I am so concerned in everything relating to his future welfare. Will he really be so happy as to be in possession of £1500 after all his misfortunes?—and that information overcame me with joy. He cannot be unhappy with so neat an independance. I have no words adequate to express my joy to have had a letter from him. I am unlucky that I cannot obtain a correspondence.

"Your information concerning my poor Grace is another distraction for me. Inform me if she gets better, and as much as you know about her. By whom was she placed in Moffat to reside? Well, well, my friend, it may go as it will. I am still their mother, and from my father are their *riches derived*. How I would be happy, and wish I could have an hour's conversation with you—to write all is impossible. Inform me of the welfare of your family. I am sure the number is extensive. Your eldest children are quite grown up. Mrs. Pagan is, I hope, in good health, and yourself also. Inform me of the changement in Dumfries and Maxwelltown—the improvements are numerous. Inform me of the price of markets. What tax have you upon port wine and spirits?—taxes were reduced, I should think. I believe the present King is very well liked. The British government is the best and most solid. For these last 3 years I have seen nothing but revolutionary discontent. I was in the island of Corsica when the revolution in France happen'd: since the last of Oct. 1830 I have been here. The present King of France dismissed the Swisse regiment from the service in a very *unhandsome manner*. These last 3 years have not been comfortable. Answer this, my dear friend, immediately—Adieu, adieu!

"Present my sincere regards to Mrs. Pagan, join'd by your old friend and acquaintance Fleitz. Accept of every grateful acknowledgement, and believe me to be always your obliged friend,

"M. FLEITZ."

"Lauffenburg, Nov. 1st, 1833.

"My dear Friend,

"An acquaintance of mine will have the goodness to put this into the general Post Office, and will pay the postage as far as possible. Mr. Pagan, my intentions are good and honest to pay you all the expense of postage. Necessity, my friend, urges me to importune you on the part of Alexander. My wishes cannot be communicated, my pen must be used in a limited manner. Personally, I would speake to you in a confidential manner, but at present prudence must guide my pen. Your friendly advice would aid me. Alexander adheres to silence with me: 4 months are pass'd away without any acknowledgement from him, although I know letters arrive here in due course from all parts of America; even 3 months ago there are letters arrived from those who left this place in the month of March last, &c. My friend, my memory is sound. Contrary to my intentions on my departure from Maxwelltown, on account of Alexander's occupation, which gave me no pleasure. He promised to inform me duely of my mother—that I could immediately be with her, should her health require me. He promised and deceived me, by never informing me in any manner, &c. He persuaded my dear mother to give him possession of what should have been mine. You best know his conduct. His silence towards me shows me I come not under his consideration, although his riches are the partiality of my father, and I am to be deserted. The chagrine of my bosom has no description.

"Tell me, my friend, everything you know. What is his employment in America? Are you of opinon his experience will prove a useful lesson? Is his passion for gambling cured? Have you any information where he means to live? The consequence of his good fortune will change his views. Sorry would I be to think he will by little and little spend his fortune in America: in general the people go to make money, but not to spend, &c. Inform me who are the trustees for him. I am anxious to know who they are.

"A retrospect of busy memory tells me Alexander has used me very ill. Poor Charles suffered also, but he had a kind and good heart for me. Inform me if my dear son will come to Scotland, and what manner he means to employ his money for his future good. My good friend, loose no time in giving me answer pointedly. Tell me if you can, be it good or bad, &c.

"I am at present in a disaggreeable country. The people are not aggreeable. The climate is not bad for the north. They grow much wine, but is weak and sour. Inform me if the confusion in Portugal has had an effect upon the port wine—what is the price of the bottle? The price of markets I would like to know. The taxes are reduced, I am sure, &c.

"N.B.—I hope God will give his blessing to my intentions; and you will not fail to answer, otherways I must believe you have forgot me also. Tell me what family you have—everything is interesting to me. My country is dear to my bosom. And adieu!

"MARY FLEITZ.

"N.B.—Are you acquainted with the trustees? I depend upon hearing from you—prudence prevents me from speaking more plain, &c.

"N.B.—Your friend since three years by the French revolution is no more in the military line; it has been a severe change. My direction is as before: Madam Fleitz, Lauffenburg, Canton d'Argovie, en Swiss, P. Basel. I am, with compliments to Mrs. Pagan, yourself, remain

"Your sincere friend,

"M. FLEITZ."

Polly had still the deep interest of a mother in the fate of Alexander, though he had not treated her well, as she states in her letters. She returned to Scotland in 1834, when she expected that he was to come back; but, alas! when he made his appearance, she found his health so entirely prostrated by the climate of Demerara, where he had resided for many years, that he was unable to walk. The mother and son had been too long separated to have much sympathy with each other. Though Alexander was obliged to be wheeled in a chair, he took to himself a wife, and this induced Polly to return to France. After some years Fleitz died, when Polly took refuge with a cousin in Florence. Her mind at last gave way, and she was removed to an asylum, dying there in 1847, in the seventy-second year of her age. She had survived all her children, who had all died without offspring.

Such was the chequered fate of "Lovely Polly Stewart," of whom Burns sings thus:

> " O lovely Polly Stewart !
>   O charming Polly Stewart !
> There's not a flower that blooms in May
>   That's half so fair as thou art.
> The flower it blaws, it fades and fa's,
>   And art can ne'er renew it;
> But worth and truth eternal youth
>   Will give to Polly Stewart.
>
> " May he whose arms shall fauld thy charms,
>   Possess a leal and true heart;
> To him be given to ken the heaven
>   He grasps in Polly Stewart.
> O lovely Polly Stewart !
>   O charming Polly Stewart !
> There's ne'er a flower that blooms in May
>   That's half so sweet as thou art."

Burns paid great attention to the euphony of his verses, and as a proof of this the late Sir James Stuart-Menteth, Bart., of Closeburn, showed the manner in which he elaborated his lyrics, as is stated by Chambers. " There was then living in Closeburn parish a respectable woman, Christina Kirkpatrick, married to a mason named Flint. She had a masculine understanding; was well acquainted with the old music, the songs and ballads of Scotland; and having a fine voice and good ear, she sang them remarkably well. At a subsequent period, when the poet's mother lived at Dinning, she was on intimate terms with Kirsty, to whom, on removing with her son Gilbert to East Lothian, she gave several little presents; amongst the rest, the low-seated deal-chair, on which she had nursed the poet and the rest of her children. This was obligingly presented to me by Kirsty on her death-bed, and it is now in my possession.

"When Burns dwelt at Ellisland he was accustomed, after composing any of his beautiful songs, to pay Kirsty a visit, that he might hear them sung by her. He often stopped her in the course of the singing when he found any word harsh and grating to his ear, and substituted one more melodious and pleasing. From Kirsty's extensive acquaintance with the old Scottish airs, she was frequently able to suggest to the poet music more suitable to the song she was singing, than that to which he had set it."

This is confirmed by a communication of the late Professor Gillespie of St. Andrews to the *Edinburgh Literary Journal*, 12th December, 1829. He says: "When a schoolboy at Wallace Hall Academy, I saw Burns' horse tied by the bridle to the sneck of a cottage-door in the neighbourhood of Thornhill, and lingered for some time listening to the songs, which, seated in an arm-chair by the fireside, Burns was listening to. Betty (Kirsty) Flint was the name of the songstress. She was neither pretty nor witty, but she had a pipe of the most overpowering pitch, and a taste for song . . . . She sang even to us laddies 'There's nae luck about the house,' and ' Braw, braw lads o' Gala Water,' most inimitably."

Mr. M'Dowall, the author of the interesting volume entitled "Burns in Dumfriesshire," has lately discovered a relic of Burns in addition to the many others that he enumerates in his work. He says: "All who are familiar with the biography of Robert Burns know that when at Ellisland he used to get Kirsty Flint of Closeburn to sing over his songs, in order that he might test them by her rich voice and good musical taste. It is well known, too, that the bard entertained a high respect for Kirsty; but we were not aware till lately that he had, in evidence of this feeling, presented her with the copy of 'Young's Night Thoughts' which he often pondered over, and from which he repeatedly quoted in his correspondence. This volume he gave to Mrs. Flint with the remark: 'Tak that, Kirsty; I hae got more sentimentalism from that book than from any work o' the kind I ever read.' Kirsty, as may be well conceived, treasured the volume, and when at one time asked to dispose of it, declared solemnly, 'I wad juist as sune amaist pairt wi' the Bible itsel' as wi' the beuk gien to me oot o' his ain han' by Mr. Burns.' But to a neighbour who knew her well, and paid much attention to her in her old age, Mr. John Coltart, she lent the volume in 1838, with the assurance that at her death, it was to become his property. Mrs. Flint dying a few months afterwards, it remained with Mr. Coltart, who left it with us a few days back, with a request that we would in his name present it to the Observatory of Dumfries. When suitably inscribed, it will be there deposited among the prized relics of the national bard. On the inside of one of the boards is written, *not* by Burns, but probably by Kirsty herself, the words: 'God give me grace in it to read, and not only for to read, but truley for to understand and always learn to be at God's command.' The book is 18mo size, plainly bound in sheepskin, and bears date, Glasgow, 1764."

In addition to these reminiscences of Burns in Closeburn, it may be stated that there are some traditionary accounts of the fate of the bed on which the poet was born. When Gilbert, the poet's brother, took the farm of Dinning in Closeburn parish, it was brought among his effects from Ayrshire to that place, where it remained till his death. His goods were then sold by public roup, and as Bacon, the landlord of Brownhill, had become known from his connection with Burns about 1790, it was bought by him and occupied by an old groom, Joe Langhorne, well known in the early part of this century to all who were travelling along the Carlisle and Glasgow road. On the death of Bacon (his wife had predeceased him) in 1824, his goods were sold, and Joe, who was a great favourite in the parish, let it be known that he wished to purchase the bedstead with which he had been so long associated. When it was put up, no one offered for it, and Joe got it at his own price. Joe spent the last years of his life in Dumfries, and on his death the bed came into the possession of one of his daughters, who was married to a shoemaker. The bedstead is said to have been cut up and formed into snuff-boxes.

Another relic of Burns, which was sold at this roup, was a snuff-box which the poet had presented to Bacon. It was well known to all those who had resided in Closeburn, and among others to a gentleman who had been boarded in the house of the late Dr. Mundell, and had gone to India, whether in the civil or military service of the East India Service, I am unable to say. This gentleman left instructions with Dr. Mundell that the snuff-box should be bought for him at any reasonable price. Accordingly, Mr. Robert Coltart, then usher of Dr. Mundell, afterwards Presbyterian minister at Demerara, where he died, bought the snuff-box for this gentleman. Who is the possessor of it at this moment is unknown.

Burns had a great power of *impromptu* satire, when provoked by anything which he considered mean. The poet and a reverend clergyman happened to call for their horses at the same time at Brownhill Inn. When the ostler brought them, the minister gave him twopence, and Burns handing him a sixpence turned round to his companion and called out—

> "Black's your coat,
> Black's your hair,
> Black's your conscience,
> And nocht to spair."

Our ancestors were more plain in their language than we are in this refined age, and were not ashamed to call a spade a spade even in the presence of ladies. We must not, therefore, measure Burns altogether by our own standard; and if we find him giving way occasionally, in the exuberance of his spirits with the unpolished class with whom he mixed, to sensuality of language, we must recollect that he was in no way worse than his contemporaries. I think it right to say this much in excuse for some lines of an indecent character which he wrote on the glass of Brownhill window. These were very properly destroyed by the late Sir James Stuart-Menteth, Bart., of Closeburn, that there might be no possibility of the lines seeing the light.

MRS. LAWSON OF NITHBANK.

The late Mrs. Lawson of Nithbank, *née* Agnes Yorstoun, and wife of the late Mr. Lawson of the Royal Mint, used to be a frequent visitor at the house of her uncle, the Rev. Andrew Yorstoun, the much respected minister of Closeburn. On one of these occasions she had been calling at Closeburn Castle, then inhabited by Mr. William Stewart, of whom I have already spoken, when the poet happened to come in, and Miss Agnes Yorstoun, then a very young lady, at his request sung several songs, and among others, "Roy's Wife of Aldivalloch." The song is the following:—

> "Roy's wife of Aldivalloch,
>   Roy's wife of Aldivalloch,
> Wot ye how she cheated me
>   As I came o'er the braes of Balloch?
> For O, she was a canty quean,
>   And weel could dance the Highland walloch!
> How happy I, had she been mine,
>   Or I'd been Roy of Aldivalloch!
>
> "She vow'd, she swore, she wad be mine,
>   She said she lo'ed me best of ony;
> But, oh! the fickle, faithless quean,
>   She's ta'en the carl, and left her Johnnie.
>
> "Her hair sae fair, her een sae clear,
>   Her wee bit mou' sae sweet and bonnie;
> To me she ever will be dear,
>   Tho' she's for ever left her Johnnie."

When the song was finished, Burns said, "Oh, Miss Yorstoun, dinna let him despair that way; let Johnnie sing this," and he at once repeated the following additional stanza:—

> "But Roy's years are three times mine,
>   I'm sure his days can no be monie;
> And when that he is dead and gane,
>   She may repent and tak' her Johnnie."

Many a time and oft did Mrs. Lawson sing this song in after years, and always added the verse of Burns—proud, no doubt, of having received it from the mouth of Scotland's greatest poet. Mrs. Lawson died at Nithbank on

24th January, 1874, and is buried in Closeburn churchyard.

WALLACE HALL ENDOWED SCHOOL.

Wallace Hall School was founded in 1723 by John Wallace, a native of Closeburn, who had made a considerable fortune as a merchant in Glasgow towards the beginning of last century, and who left the larger part of his property for the education of children born in Closeburn. The deed specifies distinctly the object he had in view: "To teach the whole children of the united parish of Closeburn and Dalgarno that shall be put to learn English, Latin, Greek, writing, and arithmetic, or such of these as the scholars or their parents shall desire, and that *gratis*, without any fee or reward other than is hereby provided for him, excepting any gratuity that the parents of the children may, out of their own good will, think fit to give him." He appointed as patrons of the mortification, "John Wallace of Elderslie, Thomas Wallace of Cairnhill, and Michael Wallace, merchant in Glasgow, brothers-german," with the Ministers of Closeburn and the Town-Clerk of Glasgow, who were *ex-officio* patrons. As to the schoolmaster to be appointed, he was to be "a man of good conversation, of Presbyterian principles, and of good literature, and be graduated at some university or college, and be qualified to teach English, Latin, and Greek;" and he gave power to the Presbytery of Penpont "to take trial of these qualifications, and that they do not admit him unless he be found endowed with these accomplishments." He gave powers also to the Presbytery " to inspect and take cognizance of his good behaviour and deportment after he is admitted, and in case of misdemeanour, to remove him from his office." He gave a recommendation to the patrons that "if one of the name of Wallace can, as a vacancy falls out, be found qualified, they present him preferably to all others."

The sum of money that he left was £1400, "*in perpetuam eleemosynam* for settling, fixing, and dateing a school, schoolhouse, and schoolmaster." Of this the sum of one thousand two hundred pounds was to be employed in purchasing a piece of land in Closeburn, or as near to it as might be possible, the rents of which the schoolmaster should enjoy. He also directed that the remainder should be laid out in purchasing five acres of ground in Closeburn, on which the school was to be built, and if the heritors refused to sell or feu, then the whole mortification was to go to the benefit of Glasgow University.

It is interesting to see the steps which the Presbytery took to carry out the intentions of the Testator, and the books of the Presbytery show how much pains and time they bestowed on the matter. The first notice of the mortification in their books is dated "1723, 5th June," when we find "Mr. Lawson (minister of Closeburn) announces to the Presbytery that Mr. Wallace of Cairnhill and his brother wish to meet them respecting a mortification of £1600 left by John Wallace, merchant in Glasgow, in order to settle a school and schoolmaster in the parish of Dalgarno and Closeburn. A committee was appointed to confer with them." "July 3rd.—The committee report that they have met the parties, when the Presbytery direct Mr. Lawson to wait upon the curators of Sir Thomas Kirkpatrick as to the five or six acres of land to be purchased for the use of the schoolmaster." "Sept. 4th.—Presbytery did not find it clear who are to be the purchasers of the five acres, and therefore appoint Mr. Lawson and Carco to consult Mr. Areskine of Barjarg." "Nov. 6th.—Committee report that they have arranged respecting five acres of ground for the use of the school."

"Dec. 4th.—The trustees of Sir Thomas request that two of the Presbytery may be appointed to see the five acres measured, and to write to the gentlemen concerned in Sir Thomas Kirkpatrick's affairs for an allowance of stones, and that the land may be measured so as water may run through it. Mr. Howie and Mr. Bayne appointed to see it measured, and Mr. Lawson is requested to write about the stones and water."

"1724, Jan. 1st.—Report given in as to the ground having been measured. Mr. Lawson is appointed to signify this to the curators, and also to desire them, when the rights are drawn, to see that water may be allowed to the schoolmaster over a little of Sir Thomas Kirkpatrick's ground."

This piece of ground near Closeburn kirk, called Kirkflat, was fued at a peppercorn from the curators of Sir Thomas Kirkpatrick for £550 Scots money. In regard to the water, the Presbytery secured access to the small stream called the Lake, which was the only running water in the neighbourhood, and this the institution still enjoys.

Then came the question as to the appointment of schoolmaster; and as Mr. Wallace in his deed had declared his desire that Mr. Wauch, the schoolmaster of Closeburn (whether he was *parish* schoolmaster is not stated), possibly from old associations, should enjoy the benefit of the money mortified, if he be found qualified, we find the question considered by the Presbytery.

"March 4th.—Presbytery takes into consideration Mr. Wallace's desires that Mr. Wauch should be appointed schoolmaster under the deed of endowment, considers him fit if at next Presbytery he gives in a declaration of his sentiments in answer to that article that requires the schoolmaster to be of Presbyterian principles."

"April 1st.—Mr. Wauch sends an excuse for his absence, which is maintained."

"May 6th.—Mr. Wauch gave in his declaration of Presbyterian principles, but the Presbytery, while accepting the same, instead of the formula of 1711, hereby declares that this shall not be led as a precedent to future entrants into the school of Closeburn. Mr. Wauch is accordingly collated by the Presbytery on condition that he takes his degree before he officiate."

Mr. Wauch had evidently been unwilling to take the oaths to the civil government, and was therefore what was called a Nonjuror; and though the Presbytery agreed to overlook his contumacy, it was not to be taken as a precedent. On the 3rd June Mr. Wauch produced his degree, and is accordingly appointed to enter upon his duties on Monday first. "July the 1st.—The Presbytery received £34 17s. 8d. as produce of sale of Mr. Wallace's books." "August 5th.—William Lukup (son of the builder of Drumlanrig Castle) and John Crocket were employed to build the school, which was to be finished Michaelmas, 1726." "Oct. 7th.—Extract of disposition to the land, on which the school and schoolmaster's house are a-building, is produced. A proposal is made to purchase the lands of Elliock."

The lands of Elliock had been forfeited in 1715 by the Earl of Carnwath, but they must have been in value beyond the sum of money which the Presbytery had to

s

invest. They were afterwards bought by Mr. Veitch, the ancestor of the present proprietor, from the Commissioners of Forfeited Estates.

"1725, Feb. 3rd.—Mr. Lawson reports that he has agreed with a workman to quarry the stones and build the dyke round the five acres for £23." "March 3rd.—There is a proposal to lay out the money on heritable security upon the estate of Cavens, in Kirkbean, or on the estate of the Marquis of Annandale." "April 7th.—The curators of Sir Thomas Kirkpatrick complain that the schoolmaster's house is too little, when it is proposed that the walls should be raised two feet higher for the greater convenience of the garret." "Sept. 1st.—Mr. Lawson and Mr. Wauch are empowered to make various improvements on the original plans. There are to be two gates—one large, opposite to the church, and a small one for Sir Thomas Kirkpatrick's children." "Oct. 6th.—Moderator ordered to write to Mr. Michael Wallace or the executors to send £50 to carry on the buildings of the school of Closeburn." "Dec. 1st.—Presbytery call for half-year's annual rent on heritable bond of £1400 granted by Dr. John Cavens, and appoint the Moderator and Mr. Wauch to give discharge to Cavens." "1726, Jan. 5th.—Moderator reports that £50 had been received from Mr. Wallace to carry on the school buildings. Mr. Lawson reports that he had received £35, one year's interest on £1400 from Dr. Cavens."

This transaction shows the rate of interest in those days to have been $2\frac{1}{2}$ per cent., and it shows also the income which the schoolmaster received from the endowment. The money received by the sale of Mr. Wallace's books had been lent to the Rev. Peter Rae, minister of Kirkbryde, and Robert Jardine of Glencairn, from whom

Mr. Lawson held bills. Mr. Lawson is ordered to receive one year's interest and account for the same.

"Feb. 2nd.—Mr. Alexander Nivison is approved as usher, having promised to teach music, and recommended to teach book-keeping."

"1728, 6th March.—Mr. Lawson proposes that a stone with an inscription should be put up above the schoolmaster's door-head in the vacuum that was left for that purpose, which the Presbytery think reasonable."

The following is the inscription, which is still to be seen built into the porch:—

> JOHN WALLACE
> MERCHANT A NATIVE OF
> CLOSEBURN, WHO DIED
> MAY 1723, MORTIFIED
> FOR THIS AND ANOTHER
> FREE SCHOOL WITHIN
> THIS PARISH THE SVMM
> OF 1400 POUNDS STER.
> MONEY BESIDE ABOUT
> 300 POUNDS STER. FOR
> BUYING AND ENCLOSING
> 5 ACRES OF GROUND AND
> BUILDING THE SCHOOL
> SCHOOLMASTERS HOUSE
> AND OFFICE HOUSES.
>
> NOTUS IN FRATRES ANIMI PATERNI,
> ILLUM AGET PENNA METUENTE SOLVI
> FAMA SUPERSTES.*
>
> Ἡ ἀγάπη οὐδέποτε ἐκπίπτει.

---

* This Latin quotation is found in the second ode of the second book of Horace, and is highly descriptive of Mr. Wallace's character. "Known for his fatherly affection to his brothers, him shall never-dying fame raise aloft on an unflagging pinion." The Greek words are found in 1 Corinthians xiii. 8. "Charity never faileth."

Dr. Cavens, to whom the money of the endowment had been lent at 2½ per cent., got into difficulties, and there seemed some reason to fear that it might be lost altogether. The Presbytery got greatly alarmed, as they might well be, as Cavens was declared bankrupt, and even Mr. Peter Rae was in arrears in the payment of his interest. Mr. Rae is ordered to appear at next meeting of Presbytery and give satisfaction respecting the money. However, the money was at last recovered from Cavens, and, frightened no doubt at what had taken place, they began again to look out for land. They propose to offer twenty-one years' purchase for the lands of Crawford, of Hazelside, in the lordship of Douglas, and to set a tack at the present yearly rent for nineteen or twenty-one years. But they discover that this is beyond their power, as the incumbent can alone grant a legal lease. A very curious circumstance now turns up respecting this money. The Presbytery propose to lend it to Kirkconnel, who is a Catholic; and, doubtful as to its being secure in such hands, they consult Mr. Areskine of Barjarg, who assures them that it will be safely lent, if his eldest son and next Protestant heir concur. Kirkconnel accordingly appears before the Presbytery and promises all they require, upon which they agree to lend him the money.

Their difficulties, however, are not got over, as they receive a letter from the executors strongly protesting against lending the money to a Catholic; and proceeding to a vote whether they should lend the money or not, it was carried in the affirmative with two dissentients, Messrs. Lawson and Howie. At next meeting Mr. Lawson gives in three pages containing reasons of dissent, and one of them is that it is trafficking with the Scarlet Lady.

The Presbytery never gave up the idea of purchasing a piece of land, as the testator directed. They had an offer from Robert Riddel of Glenriddel of the lands of Templand in Closeburn, and also of Auldgirth in the same parish. Many other properties came under their notice in Lanarkshire and Ayrshire, but they at last purchased Baltersan property, in the parish of Holywood, which had belonged to a cadet branch of the great Maxwell family, in December, 1753, for the sum of £1145 sterling. The schoolmaster's right to the rents began from Michaelmas, 1753. This is the property that now belongs to the endowment.

The sum of £255 was lent to Mr. Abercromby of Tullibody at 4½ per cent. on the 30th July, 1756, which was uplifted in 1773, by consent of the Presbytery, and employed in enclosing the property of Baltersan. It is curious to watch the rise of value in the property from 1753.

The money first lent at interest produced	£35
In 1753, rent	45
,, 1762, ,,	55
,, 1795, ,,	145
,, 1815, ,,	580
,, 1844, ,,	440
,, 1863, ,,	630

The size of Baltersan is in Scotch measure 445 acres. The whole piece of ground belonging to Wallace Hall in Closeburn is five acres.

Where John Wallace was buried is unknown, but the tombstone of his family is in Closeburn churchyard, and records the death of his parents. "Here lyes the corps of William Wallace in Hightrees, aged 52, who died January, 1674, and Jannet Kirkpatrick, his spouse, aged

70 years, who died 6th February, 1697 years; also their son, Thomas Wallace, in Dinning, husband to Betty M'Connell, who departed this life upon the 12 day of March, 1700 years, the 47 year of his age; his foresaid spouse, aged 44 years, died March 6, 1697 years. Memento mori."

The following are the incumbents since the endowment was founded:—Mr Wauch, who was schoolmaster in Closeburn at the death of Mr. Wallace, was at Mr. Wallace's request appointed by the Presbytery in 1723, after he had been found qualified. He died in 1744, and on the 6th March, 1745, Mr. Patrick Wallace was appointed. He was succeeded 15th October, 1748, by Mr. Archibald Wallace, who died 17th Nov., 1749, when Mr. Alexander Mundell, a distinguished teacher in Edinburgh, and brother of the Professor of Humanity, was appointed as rector 26th Feb., 1750. He was succeeded by his son, Dr. Robert Mundell, in 1790; and he again, in 1842, by the present incumbent, Craufurd Tait Ramage, A.M., LL.D.

Mr. Alexander Mundell was a first-rate scholar, and at a time (1750) when there were few, if any, boarding establishments where the sons of the higher classes could be educated, Mr. Mundell received young gentlemen into his house. For sixty years the school of Wallace Hall was famed throughout Scotland for its scholarship, and though his son, the late Dr. Mundell, was scarcely equal to his father in learning, as a classical teacher he possibly surpassed him. He pursued a system which, however antiquated it may seem in the present day, gave a knowledge of the classical languages of Greece and Rome which enabled many of his pupils to rise to eminence. In other ways he was a benefactor to the institution over which he had presided so ably for sixty years. He built a house in 1795 at an expense of £1700, a larger sum than the original endowment, and this he left to those who should succeed him, the only memorial of which is the following inscription over the front door of Wallace Hall:—

*Has Ædes Novissimas
Sumptu Proprio Exstruendas Curavit
Robertus Mundell, LL.D.,
Hujusce Academiæ Præfectus.*

At the time when the last Statistical Account of Scotland was published there were ten of his pupils clergymen in the Established Church of Scotland, and three of them were members of Parliament. The following were the clergymen:—The Rev. Messrs. Murray of Mousewald, Barton of Castleton, Rorison of Stair, Wilson of Libberton, Hope of Lamington, Gibson of Lochmaben; Boe, Dunblane; Dr. Brown, St. John's, Glasgow; Dr. Gillespie, St. Andrews; Ferguson, U.P., America.

Mr. Alexander Mundell continued to act till he was struck down by apoplexy in the year 1790. The following poem was written on his sudden death by his friend, Dr. Thomas Yorstoun of Nithbank House:—

"With sad regret the weeping muse may tell
The world and learning's loss, when Mundell fell;
A heart with virtue, head with learning fraught,
This by profession, that by practice taught.
To form the accomplished teacher served the one,
The other graced the Christian and the man.
Performing well his part by heaven assigned
To train and cultivate the youthful mind,

> To those, who knew him his example will,
> Considered well, afford a lesson still.
> Exact, not stiff; and strict, but not severe;
> Learn'd, not pedantic; pious not austere;
> Such were his manners. As a teacher mild,
> He won affection and enticed the child.
> But yet, when vice, or vicious aught appeared,
> His frown was dreaded, and his justice feared;
> Wisely discerning what each case required,
> Some fear restrained, and some due praise inspired;
> For wisdom is alike required to rule
> The subjects of a kingdom and a school.
> And now the labours of his life are past,
> He rests in peace but leaves a name to last,
> Till at the dawning of immortal day
> The sp'rit again shall rouse the sleeping clay.
> As living monuments that far surpass
> The sculptur'd praise of marble or of brass,
> His tutor'd sons in every clime are known,
> And spread their master's honour with their own.
> Engraved upon their minds his memory dear
> Shall long hereafter draw the grateful tear.
> Upright in life the narrow path he trode,
> A man esteemed of men, approved of God,
> Who, when his task was done, recalled him hence,
> With scarce one parting pang of painful sense,
> For ere he felt the stroke, that death had given,
> Ere Nature with Mortality had striven,
> He found, with blest surprise, his soul in heaven.

GROUND AND BUILDINGS OF WALLACE HALL.

When Mr. John Wallace left money to endow Closeburn School, he made it a *sine quâ non* that one of the heritors of the parish should dispose five acres of ground to the Presbytery of Penpont as a small glebe for the master and a site for the intended school; if they refused, the money was to be employed in establishing bursaries in connection with the University of Glasgow. The curators of Sir Thomas Kirkpatrick, then a minor, at once offered to grant a pepper-corn feu of five acres of land at the spot known as Kirkflat, near the church, and the Presbytery accepted the offer, appointing two of their number, the Rev. Messrs. Howie and Baine, to see the ground measured. On 1st January, 1724, the Committee report that they had seen the ground measured, and that they had secured a servitude over the small stream, called the Lake, for the use of the master and the scholars. This is the only water which belongs by the arrangements of the Presbytery to the children, though in later times the rector sunk for the convenience of his family a pump-well at his kitchen door, and for which the present rector paid his predecessor the sum which was placed upon it by the valuators. The late Dr. Mundell sunk another well at the bottom of his garden for the purpose of irrigation, which was removed in 1852 to the vicinity of the stable.

In regard to the buildings, a school-room and master's house were built on the ground, and we find the curators of Sir Thomas complaining that the house is too low. On this complaint being laid before the Presbytery, the Rev. Mr. Lawson and the schoolmaster Mr. Wauch were empowered to make various improvements on the original plans. Among other things, it was arranged "that there are to be two gates—one large, opposite to the church, and a small one for the use of the laird's children."

A school-room was built on the very site where one of them still exists, namely, that occupied by the Senior Assistant, to the east of the playground. It was the school in which Dr. Mundell's father taught till the day of his death in 1790, nor was there any change made till 1795, when the late Dr. Mundell built, at his own expense, the present larger dwelling-house.

The original dwelling-house, built out of the funds of Mr. Wallace, was contained within the walls of the present lower school, nor was there any addition made till about the year 1760, when Mr. Alexander Mundell, who found it too small to accommodate the increasing numbers of his boarders, built the part where the kitchen is now and the stories above, making a large dining-room, which is now the upper school. This was of course built at his own expense, as there were no longer any funds at the disposal of the Presbytery after they bought and paid for Baltersan property, the rents of which belonged to the master. Such was the state of the buildings up to 1795, when the late Dr. Mundell resolved to build a large dwelling-house to give sufficient room for his boarding establishment. This was done at an expense of £1700, part of which he borrowed from the late Mr. Harkness of Mitchellslacks, having no power to burden the estate. I do not doubt that the two Mundells, father and son, expended in new buildings, and the improvement of the old, more than double of the sum which was originally left for the endowment by Mr. Wallace.

When the dwelling-house was built in 1795, a question arose how to utilize the other buildings, which were no longer necessary as a residence, and it was determined to turn the original school-room into a wash-house and laundry, making three school-rooms out of the original dwelling-house and dining-room, of which I have spoken. This was accordingly done, and when I joined the school, 3rd June, 1811, I entered the low school, being the ground-floor of the original dwelling-house; and above there was another large school-room, extending the whole length of the building. The third school-room, where Dr. Mundell taught, was the old dining-room, and is now the upper school. It was thought, however, that three school-rooms were too many, so that in 1812 the lower one ceased to be used.

Such was the state of matters when Dr. Mundell died in 1842. I then resolved to make some improvements on the school buildings, though there were no funds by which my family could be reimbursed if my life were cut short. I employed the late Mr. Newall of Dumfries, an able architect, to assist in carrying out the changes, which I pointed out to him that I wished to make. The whole interior of the original school-room, which had been used latterly as laundry and wash-house, was cleared out. The same thing was done with what had been the original dwelling-house, thus making it into one room the whole height of the walls. The ceiling of the upper school was raised by removing a garret which had been above it. In the lower schools large windows and ventilators were inserted, while what had been the original dwelling-house and the addition to it was re-slated. Thus were constructed three school-rooms, which were considered, thirty years ago, first-rate rooms for the purpose for which they were intended. As there was no proper access to the upper school, I added a new staircase by means of a porch. These alterations gave a much more characteristic appearance to the buildings, impressing upon them something of the features of what is termed the old Scottish baronial style of architecture. As Dr. Mundell had been tenant of Lakehead farm, he had no need of offices at Wallace Hall, and, accordingly, it was necessary to add stabling, coach-house, byre, cart and hay shed, with laundry, wash-house, and coal-cellar. To carry off the water from the wash-house, a drain had to be made to join the sewer leading from the kitchen to the Lake stream; and in the house other conveniences were added, with cisterns and runs on the top of the house to collect the water, with drains to carry off surplus water. All these improvements and additions cost not less than £700.

It may be added that there are no funds to supply school furniture, and each incumbent has paid to his predecessor for the tables and benches that are in the school, as well as for the maps. In regard to heating the schools, in early times each pupil was bound to bring a certain number of peats for this purpose, but for many years the incumbents have done so at their own expense, making no demand on the parents for this item. The deed of Mr. Wallace imposes a payment of £18 for one assistant. The salary at present paid to two assistants is £80 each.

After a lapse of fifty-five years spent in the education of the young, beginning with the early years of Archibald Campbell Tait, youngest son of the late Craufurd Tait, Esq., of Harviestoun, now Archbishop of Canterbury, to whom I had the honour to give lessons in his rudimentary Latin, and of which lengthened period thirty-four have been spent in the service of the parishioners of Closeburn, my round of toil was relieved by a pleasing incident. A number of my old pupils, scattered all over the world, and many of them filling most important positions in the army, the law, the church, medicine, and commerce, spontaneously paid me a mark of respect and affection, which was deeply felt, and must not, from a feeling of false modesty, be omitted to have an acknowledgment in these pages. A handsome sum was raised, and being laid out on a silver salver and other plate, was presented to me at a public dinner in Dumfries on the 9th September, 1873. The salver bore the following inscription:—" This salver forms part of the presentation plate to Craufurd Tait Ramage, Esq., LL.D., by some of his late pupils and a few personal friends, in token of their respect and esteem. 9th Sept., 1873." The dinner was numerously attended, and Dr. Hoggan of Thornhill (in absence of the Hon. W. C. Spring-Rice) took the chair and William Adamson, Esq., was croupier. Among the pupils whose education I either wholly or in part superintended, the following may be given, though some have passed away before their teacher, "not lost, but gone before."

    Archibald Campbell Tait, D.D., Archbishop of Canterbury, Primate of all England and Metropolitan.
    Hoggan, John, Lieutenant-Colonel in Bengal Native Infantry.
    Hoggan, George H. W., Major, Punjaub Cavalry.
    Johnston, William, Esq., Judge in the Bengal Civil Service.
    Kennedy, Alexander, Captain in Madras Infantry.
    Lettsom, Garrow, Esq., late Chargé d'Affaires, Mexico.
    Lushington, Franklin, Esq., C.B., late Lieutenant-Colonel Scots Fusilier Guards.
    Lushington, Frederick, Esq., Judge in the Bengal Civil Service.
    Menteth, Charles Stuart, Lieutenant (deceased).
    Murray, Patrick J., Commander R.N.

Spring-Rice, Hon. Stephen Edmond, late Vice-Chairman of the Board of Customs, London.

Spring-Rice, Hon. Thomas Charles, late Head of the Commercial Department in H.M. Foreign Office.

Spring-Rice, Hon. William Cecil, Registrar of Bankruptcy Court, London.

Spring-Rice, Hon. and Rev. Aubrey, Rural Dean and Vicar, Netherbury, Wilts.

A list has been compiled of Wallace Hall pupils, who have maintained the reputation of the school in the Universities of Scotland, during the last thirty years. Every year since 1844 one or more of them have had their names honourably mentioned in some branch of learning in the University lists. Nine of them are, or lately were, Members of the University Council.

We reprint the list:—

List of Wallace Hall Pupils who have distinguished themselves at the Universities of Scotland since 1844.

UNIVERSITY OF ST. ANDREWS.

Session 1844-5.

John Beck, . . First rank in Junior Latin.
Second rank in Junior Greek.
Second prize for a "Translation of the twenty-third Book of the Iliad, with notes, critical and explanatory."

Session 1845-6.

William Howat, . First rank in the Senior Division of Junior Greek.
First rank in Junior Latin Class.

John Beck, . .   First rank of students of first year in Senior Latin.
Second rank in Senior Greek.

Session 1846-7.

Joseph M'Caig, . .   First rank in Junior Latin.
John Beck, . . .   Distinguished in Senior Latin, Greek, and Moral Philosophy, and gained a prize for a summer exercise on the "Crito" of Plato.
William Howat, . .   Distinguished in Senior Latin and Greek, and gained a prize for a summer exercise, "A Translation of Extracts from various Greek Authors."
John M'Adam, . .   Distinguished in Junior Latin and Greek.

Session 1847-8.

John Beck, . .   Second in the first rank in the Chemical Class.
First in the first rank of students of the third year in Senior Greek Class, the holding of which place entitled him to the Playfair Prize.
Gained a prize for a "Translation of the Agamemnon of Æschylus, with notes, critical and explanatory."

288　EARLY HISTORY OF CLOSEBURN & DALGARNOCK.

William Howat, . Third in the first rank of students of the second year in Senior Greek.
　　　　　　　　　Fourth in order of merit in Senior Latin Class.
John M'Adam, . . Fourth in the first rank of students of the first year in Senior Greek.
Joseph M'Caig, . . Second in second rank in Senior Greek.
　　　　　　　　　First for a Latin poem, elegiac stanza, "Spring."

UNIVERSITY OF EDINBURGH.

Session 1848-9.

John Menzies, . Gained a prize for private studies in Senior Latin Class.
　　　　　　　　Distinguished in the Junior Mathematical Class.

Session 1849-50.

John Menzies,　Gained a prize for summer readings in Tacitus and "Exercise on the First Tusculan Questions," and had the honourable distinction of being selected by his fellow-students as one of five to compete for the Gold Medal in the Senior Latin Class.
　　　　　　　Distinguished in the Senior Mathematical Class.

George Cron, . . Honourably mentioned among the students of the Senior Latin Class.

Session 1850-1.

William Kelly, . Gained a prize for General Excellence by the votes of his fellow-students in Second Greek Class. In the division of merit in First Mathematical Class.

John Menzies, . Gained a prize for an "Essay on the Expedition to Sicily" in Third Greek Class.

Session 1851-2.

George Cron, . . Gained a prize in Junior Mathematical Class.

KING'S COLLEGE, ABERDEEN.

Session 1852-3.

John Milligan, . Gained second prize for General Proficiency, and second prize for Latin verses in Junior Latin Class.

Thomas Fergusson, Fifth in order of merit in Junior Latin Class.

UNIVERSITY OF EDINBURGH.

Session 1852-3.

William Bell, . First prize in Senior Latin for dissertation and exercise on the "Oratio recta into Oratio obliqua."

T

George Cron, . . Eighth prize in Rhetoric and English Literature.

Session 1853-4.
William Bell, . . Prize for Summer Readings in Latin.
Fourth prize in Mathematics.

Session 1854-5.
William Bell, . . Fourth prize in Moral Philosophy.

Session 1855-6.
T. J. Kelly, . Second prize for Elegiac Verse in Junior Latin.
William Bell, . First prize in Junior Natural Philosophy.

Session 1857-8.
Robert Fergusson, Prize for Translation (Latin).
Prize for Private Studies.
William Bell. . . Seventh prize in Rhetoric and English Literature.

Session 1858-9.
A. M'Kinnel, . . Prize for Translation of a passage in Curtius.

Session 1859-60.
William Bell, . . First prize in Natural Science Class in Free Church College.

Session 1860-1.
T. J. Kelly, . . Second prize for Latin Prose in Senior Latin.
Passed in Classics for M.A. Degree.

J. M'Morine, . . First prize for Hexameter and Pentameter Verse in Junior Latin. Subject—"Imaginary Tour in the Mediterranean."
First prize for Prose Translation. Subject—"Abstract in Latin of portion of Curtius."
First prize for General Excellence in Junior Greek.
First prize for Private Readings, 1st Winter Series (Prose), Xenoph. Mem. I.
First prize for Private Readings, 2nd Winter Series (Poetry), Oydssey I.

Session 1861-2.

William Hastie, . First prize for Elegiac Verse in Junior Latin. Subject—"One of the Seasons."
Second prize for Spicelegium, a collection of important remarks during the Session.
First prize for Classical Geography.
Ninth prize in Junior Greek.

Session 1862-3.

Robert Watson, . First prize for Elegiacs in Junior Latin.
First prize for Translation from Curtius, and dissertation and exercise on "Oratio recta into Oratio obliqua."
Seventh prize in Junior Greek.

Robert Dalziel,	Honourable mention for Elegiacs in Junior Latin.
J. M'Morine,	First prize for General Excellence in Senior Greek.
	First prize for Private Readings, 1st Winter Series.
	First prize for Private Readings, 2nd Winter Series.
	Fourth prize in Logic and Metaphysics.
Edward Hoggan,	Certificates of merit in Chemistry and Botany.

Session 1863-4.

John Williamson,	University certificate of merit in Junior Latin.
	Ninth prize in Junior Greek.
Edward Hoggan,	Class medal of Midwifery in Royal College of Surgeons.

Session 1864-5.

John Williamson,	Seventh prize in Second Greek.
William Hastie,	Eighth prize in Second Greek.

Session 1865-6.

Robert Watson,	University certificate of merit in Natural Philosophy.
William Hastie,	Tenth prize in Rhetoric and English Literature.
	University certificate of honour in Senior Latin.

Session 1867-8.

William Hastie, . University certificate of merit in Second Mathematics.
James Thomson, . University certificate of merit in Rhetoric and English Literature.

Session 1868-9.

John Meggat, . . Honorary certificate in Institutes of Medicine.

Session 1869-70.

James Thomson, . Thirteenth prize in Junior Natural Philosophy.
John Williamson, Twelfth prize in Rhetoric and English Literature.
Ninth prize and certificate of honour in Chemistry.

Session 1870-1.

John Meggat, . . University certificate in Midwifery.

Session 1871-2.

John M'Kenzie, . Tenth prize in Junior Latin.
Fourth prize in Junior Greek.

Session 1872-3.

John M'Kenzie, . University certificate of merit in Senior Latin.
University certificate of merit in Senior Greek.

Session 1873-4.

John M'Kenzie, . Passed Class Exam. for M.A. Degree.
Andrew Williamson, Ninth prize in Junior Latin.
Sixth prize in Junior Greek.

Session 1874-5.

Andrew Williamson, Prize in Junior Mathematics.
Certificate of honour in Senior Latin.
Certificate of honour in Senior Greek.
Passed Class Exam. for M.A. Degree.

John M'Kenzie, . Passed Phil. Exam. for M.A. Degree.

James S. Boe, . In Edinburgh School of Medicine.
Certificate of honour for Organic Chemistry.
Certificate of honour in Midwifery at Surgeons' Hall, Edinburgh.

BURSARS.

Beck, John, St. Andrews University Bursary, 1844.
Bell, William, Free Church Bursary, 1856-57, 1859-60.
Howat, William, St. Andrews University Bursary, 1851.
M'Caig, Joseph, St. Andrews University Bursary, 1846.
M'Kenzie, John, M'Diarmid Bursary, 1871.
Milligan, John, Aberdeen University Bursary, 1851.
Williamson, John, Grierson Bursary, 1863-64.
Williamson, Andrew, Grierson Bursary, 1873-74.

GRADUATES IN ARTS AND MEDICINE.

Barrie, Andrew, M.B. and M.C., Dumfries.
Bell, William, M.A.
Brown, Joseph, M.D., Bradford.
Hastie, William, M.A.
Hoggan, Edward, M.D., Thornhill.

Jardine, James M.D., Surgeon to Royal Bengal Fusiliers.
Meggat, John, M.B. and M.C., Durham.
Thomson, James, M.A.
Williamson, John, M.A.
Watson, Robert, M.A.

MINISTERS AND LICENTIATES.

Bell, Rev. William, Free Church, Port-Glasgow.
Cron, Rev. George, Evangelical Union, Belfast.
Cron, Rev. James, Evangelical Union, Langholm.
Fergusson, Rev. Thomas, Preacher, Church of Scotland, Closeburn.
Kelly, Rev. William, Church of Scotland, Newlands.
M'Master, Rev. J., Preacher, Church of Scotland, Aberdeenshire.
Mathison, Rev. John, United Presbyterian Church, Sunderland.
Nivison, Rev. William, United Presbyterian Preacher, Keir (deceased).
Rogerson, Rev. William, United Presbyterian Church, Warkworth, Northumberland.
Thomson, Rev. James, United Presbyterian Church, Greenock.

MEMBERS OF EDINBURGH UNIVERSITY COUNCIL.

Barrie, Andrew, M.B., Dumfries.
Bell, Rev. William, Free Church, Port-Glasgow.
Brown, Joseph, M.D., Bradford.
Fergusson, Rev. Thomas, Preacher, Church of Scotland, Closeburn.

Hastie, William, M.A., Academy, Greenock.
Hoggan, Edward, M.D., Thornhill.
Kelly, Rev. William, Church of Scotland, Newlands.
Watson, Robert, M.A., Rector, Kirkcudbright Academy.
Williamson, John, M.A., Rector, Stiell Hospital, Tranent.

LAWYERS.

Howe, Thomas, Barrister-at-Law.
Leigh, Richard, Solicitor, Wigan.
Murray, Andrew, Solicitor, London (deceased).
Ogle, Hobert Moss, Solicitor (deceased).
Paterson, Robert, Solicitor, Liverpool.
Primrose, John, Solicitor, Dumfries.
Primrose, William, Solicitor, Dumfries.
Sharpe, J., Solicitor, Maxwelltown.

MERCHANTS AND BANKERS, &C.

Adamson, William, Merchant, Liverpool.
Bennet, George, Merchant, London.
Bennet, Richard, Merchant, London.
Dunlop, Charles, Merchant, Bradford.
Evans, John J., Merchant, Liverpool.
Evans, Edward, Merchant, Liverpool.
Gordon, John, Merchant, New York.
Gordon, John, Banker, Rio Janeiro.
Gracie, George, Merchant, Rio Janeiro.
Hyslop, William, Merchant, Liverpool.
M'Lachlan, John, Architect, Edinburgh.
Maclure, Andrew, Lithographer, London.
Macnee, Daniel, Engineer.
Rankin, Henry, Merchant, Liverpool.
Rose, James, Engineer, South America.

To close this account, the following extract from "Men of the Time" may be given:—

"Ramage, Craufurd Tait, LL.D., born at Annefield, near Newhaven, September 10, 1803, was educated at the High School and the University of Edinburgh, where he took the degree of M.A. in 1825. Having travelled three years in Italy, on his return he contributed to the *Quarterly Journal of Education*, the *Penny Cyclopædia*, and the seventh edition of the *Encyclopædia Britannica*; was appointed rector of the endowed school of Wallace Hall, in Dumfriesshire, in 1841; Justice of the Peace for Dumfriesshire in 1848; and the degree of LL.D. was conferred upon him by the University of Glasgow in 1852. An attempt having been made to disconnect the Parochial Schools of Scotland from the Church of Scotland, he wrote several pamphlets in defence of the system; amongst others, one entitled 'Defence of the Parochial Schools of Scotland, in a series of Letters to Viscount Drumlanrig, M.P., the Landowners, the Tenantry, and the Free Church of Scotland;' and has compiled 'Beautiful Thoughts from Greek Authors, with Translations,' 1864, second edition, 1873; 'Beautiful Thoughts from Latin Authors,' in 1864, second edition, 1869; 'Beautiful Thoughts from French and Italian Authors,' 1866, second edition, 1875; 'Beautiful Thoughts from German and Spanish Authors,' 1868; and 'Nooks and Byeways of Italy: Wanderings in search of its Ancient Remains and Modern Superstitions,' 1868."

The Endowed Schools Commission have presented a Report on Wallace Hall Endowment to Parliament (1875), and recommend the following changes in the original deed. After saying that "it is superintended by a headmaster competent to carry boys forward in their studies as far as they can desire to go—a man, moreover, of high character and of great accomplishments," it proceeds thus:—" In considering whether the best use is made of this endowment, I am forced to take note of two prominent facts, viz.: (1) That provision is now made for elementary instruction by the Education (Scotland) Act; (2) That the original endowment has increased beyond what the Testator could have anticipated. We have, therefore, both altered circumstances and a surplus fund to deal with.

" As in many similar cases, the free education given at Wallace Hall is valued only by some. .The great majority, by irregularity of attendance and general indifference, show the slight estimation in which they hold what they get for nothing. Here, as elsewhere, the people themselves would be benefited by the imposition of a moderate fee, except in cases of great poverty.

" It can scarcely be maintained that so large a revenue as £600 a year is properly applied in merely providing for the natives of Closeburn a good parish school. Nor does the will of the Testator himself, apart from other considerations, admit of our maintaining such a proposition. Mr. Wallace intended to provide primarily for the gratuitous *secondary* instruction of Closeburn, requiring, however, that a payment should be made out of the fund left by him in support of elementary schools at Wallace Hall and Gubhill. And it seems to me, that with certain slight modifications, the trust will be administered best in the interests of the parish and its vicinity by being administered in such a way as to carry out Mr. Wallace's original purposes. The modifications I refer to are such as become necessary in consequence of the increase of the fund, the passing of an Education

Act, and the evidence before the Commissioners in proof of the evils attendant on indiscriminate gratuitous instruction.

"Accordingly, I would suggest that a sum should continue to be paid as hitherto for the support of elementary schools at Wallace Hall and Gubhill—a small payment in the latter case, and such a payment in the former as would, along with fees and government grants, secure the services of a competent certificated master. If a proportion of one-third of the pupils, to be selected by the governing body, received gratuitous instruction in these schools, all cases of poverty would be more than met.

"I would anticipate that not less than £500 would then remain for the secondary school alone. The commodious and excellent house and garden might be turned to good use if the master were required to take boarders at a moderate sum. A certain proportion of the fund might be reserved for bursaries, to be competed for by boys from different parts of Dumfriesshire. By these arrangements the benefits of the foundation would be extended in a direction perfectly in accordance with the will of the founder, and the character of the seminary as a secondary school would be raised. Residents in Closeburn who could pass an entrance examination might be admitted to the secondary school gratuitously, and all others on payment of a moderate fee. A Wallace Hall scholarship, open once in two years, to carry promising boys to a University, would also be a good use to which to apply any surplus that might remain. Mr. Wallace, as I have already said, directed the institution of University bursaries until his primary object could be given effect to, and this indicates his leaning towards the higher instruction.

"By this means there might be established a good secondary school in a healthy and attractive rural district; and I think that it is of great importance to Scotland that there should be many such country centres.

"The question of the governing body is one demanding attention. As may be learned from the quotations which I have made from the deed of endowment, the patrons are one body and the trustees are another, while there is no administrative or governing body at all. The trustees are the Presbytery of Penpont. The constitution of the body of patrons is such as to be almost unworkable. The Town-Clerk of Glasgow, the minister of the Parish, and the Laird of Closeburn, are doubtless always available; but it is not at this moment known whether there are at present three male descendants of Mr. Wallace's family; and if there be, which of many possible claimants have a rightful claim to the honour. Were a vacancy to occur in the mastership, it is doubtful if it could be filled up until a litigation had determined who the patrons are.

"I think that a new governing body should be constituted, in whom the trusteeship and patronage should be alike vested, and that it should be composed partly of the present trustees and patrons, partly of new elements. A body composed of the minister and Laird of Closeburn *ex officio*, four members selected by the present trustees (the Presbytery), two members elected by the School Board of Closeburn, and the Lord-Lieutenant and Convener of the county, might be suggested as constituting at once a representation of the present trustees and patrons and of the interests of Closeburn and of the county." This is the recommendation of Simon S. Laurie, Esq., Secretary and Assistant Commissioner to the

Endowed Schools Commission; and I need not say that the reasonable views he has taken of the question, and the changes he has recommended in the administration of the institution, deserve to be maturely considered by those who may hereafter have to carry out some such scheme. Mr. Laurie's large and varied experience of the schools of Scotland peculiarly entitle his opinion to be listened to.

The following is the report of the Committee of the Presbytery of Penpont appointed to watch over the interests of Wallace Hall, in connection with the inquiry being made regarding the institution by the Endowed Schools and Hospitals (Scotland) Commission :—

"Given in to the Presbytery at a *pro re rata* meeting held at Closeburn on 13th March, 1874, and further considered at an adjourned meeting held at Thornhill on 16th March, 1874.

"In Schedule 3, issued by the Endowed Schools Commission, and submitted to the Presbytery some time ago, the Presbytery, as trustees of Wallace Hall, are invited to make any remarks which they consider to be of importance on the government or management or curriculum of the school.

"The Committee of Presbytery had a long interview with Mr. Laurie, Secretary to the Commission and an Assistant Commissioner, during a visit which he paid to Wallace Hall on the 6th February last. They have consulted with parties specially interested in the institution, and they have likewise given the subject a good deal of thoughtful consideration, and they are unanimously of opinion that the following reply to the invitation of the Commission might be forwarded by the Presbytery:—

"'The Presbytery consider that some change, both in

the constitution and administration of the Wallace Hall trust, is desirable; but that any such change must not affect the position of the present incumbent, and should be as far as possible in accordance with the spirit of the trust deed of the founder.

"'I. *As to the Constitution of the Trust.*—In the trust deed there are certain powers vested in the patrons, trustees, the Laird of Closeburn, and others, but there is in reality no governing body. It would be of great advantage, the Presbytery think, were the powers which are vested in these parties centred in one body, to be called the Trustees or Governors of Wallace Hall, and were such additional powers conferred upon that body as would give them sufficient control in all matters connected with the trust. And the Presbytery would respectfully suggest that said body of Trustees or Governors might be constituted as follows: Not less than *four* elected members of the Presbytery of Penpont, as representing the present trustees; the minister of Closeburn *ex officio*, as representing the present patrons; the laird of Closeburn, or, should the estate be under trust, *one* member elected by the trustees under the same; and (should the opening up of the trust to a certain extent be deemed advisable) the Sheriff-Substitute of the county of Dumfries *ex officio;* and *one* or *two* members directly representing the ratepayers of the parish of Closeburn.

"'II. *As to the Administration of the Trust.*—Though the revenue of the trust is large, the Presbytery would strongly deprecate the delocalizing of any of the funds; and they believe that the whole will be required in connection with the due administration of the trust.

"'In the trust deed the teacher is expressly enjoined to

teach Latin and Greek, as well as the elementary branches of education—and that *gratis*—to "the whole children of the parish that shall be put to him" for the purpose. From this it is evident that one great, if not the chief, object of the founder of Wallace Hall was to provide the children of his native parish of Closeburn with a better education than they were otherwise likely to receive. That object has, heretofore, never been lost sight of; and it should, in any change which may be made in the administration of the trust, be kept steadily in view. Nor need, or should, the benefits of such an institution be confined to Closeburn parish. Wallace Hall, from its situation, its wealthy endowment, its accommodation for boarders, &c., may and should not only continue to fulfil the wishes of its founder with respect to his native parish, but also become more and more a centre of higher education, for both girls and boys, to the neighbouring parishes.

"' Elementary education must, of course, be continued in connection with the institution according to use and wont.

"' In the trust deed provision to the extent of £5 is made for the school at Gubhill, a remote district of the parish, which provision should be largely increased.

"' After adequate provision shall have been made for primary and for advanced secondary education at Wallace Hall, and the claims of Gubhill duly met, any surplus fund should, the Presbytery are of opinion, form a bursary fund—the bursaries to be open to pupils attending the rector or headmaster's classes, to be gained by competition, and to be held, some of them at Wallace Hall and some of them at a University.

"' D. OGILVY-RAMSAY, *Convener.*'

"*Thornhill, the 16th day of March,* 1874.—This report was approved of by the Presbytery of Penpont at a meeting held here this day.

                      "DAVID JARDINE, *Pres. Clerk.*"

EARLY HISTORY OF MORTON.

IN Morton, as in other parishes of which I have given an account, the existence of an early race of men in prehistoric times has been shown, by the discovery of several tumuli of stones, which were destroyed almost forty years ago to obtain materials for repairing roads. There is still a tumulus of a small size near to the farm-steading at Burn.

Morton had several ancient pillars in various parts of the parish. On the moor near Morton castle there stood two lofty columns or pillars of hewn stone, and about a mile south of these stood another of the same description, of which we have no tradition, though they were probably erected to record some valorous deed of our ancestors. The Druids had also left their footprints behind them, in a column surrounded by a large circle of coarse blocks of stones, at equal and regular distances, which stood between the old church and Drumcork. One of the pillars was removed about seventy years ago to Friars' Carse by Captain Riddell. A fragment of one of these pillars was found some years ago, and is, I am told, preserved at Dabton. There was another column on the farm of Laught, which was removed at the same time, and is now to be seen at Friars' Carse.

The only other remnant of prehistoric times is the Picts' or Deil's Dyke, which runs along Bellyboucht hill

(1452 feet above the sea level) across the Routon burn, extending for about a mile, and then vanishes to reappear on the opposite side of Cample, near Townfoot farmsteading.

HISTORIC TIMES.

No Roman remains have ever been found within the parish, but there is some appearance of entrenchments, which may have been spots where detachments of their troops had been stationed. At the Gill on the Carron, nearly opposite to the old castle of Enoch, there are evident proofs of a camp, and on the hill (1076 feet above the sea level) above Morton Mains there is another entrenchment, still known as the Deer Camp. Rae says, that upon Morton muir, not far from the castle, is the vestige of the entrenchment of an old camp, called by the inhabitants Kemp's Grave. There is a curious natural knoll at Carronbridge, known as Fairy Knowe. Here, about forty years ago, a cow happened to be grazing on the top of the knowe, when her foot went down through an urn. The urn was about 16 inches in depth and contained bones, but it went all to pieces when it was exposed to the air.

MIDDLE AGES.

There comes a period of a thousand years (100-1100) when we have no records of the events that took place in Morton, or of the people who inhabited it, except what we may glean from the place-names that have come down to us. The Celts have left a few names, which show their presence. The Drum is of frequent occurrence, as the Drum, Drumcork, Drumshinnoch, and wherever it occurs, it is peculiarly descriptive of the physical features of the country around. The literal meaning of the word Druim or Drum is a back, exactly the same as the Latin, Dorsum, with which it is no doubt cognate. It signifies a long, low hill or ridge, and this is precisely the character of the spots where these farm-steadings now stand. The root appears also in Drumlanrig, on the opposite side of the Nith.

Then we have Bellybucht, or more properly Ballyboucht, which appears also in Glencairn, and is a proof of the Scoto-Irish having been in the parish. It is the Irish, Baille-bocht, poor town, referring to the poorness of the soil. There is a village near Dublin of this name, and it gives an appellation to some town lands in Antrim, Kildare, Cork, and Wexford.

That, however, which is curious is that, while we have few words that show the presence of the Anglo-Saxons, we have not a few that indicate that the Norsemen or Scandinavian rovers had penetrated and been settled in the parish. Thus Ridding is from the Norse rydia, to rid or clear. It refers to the cutting down of trees to make a clearing, much of the same character as thwaite, which signifies cleared land for the purposes of agriculture in the midst of a forest. The Gill is old Norse gil, meaning a small ravine, and is the name of a glen opposite to Enoch castle, where the site of a Roman camp is found. There is How Gill, leading from Morton castle to the Burn, and Gill-head wood, near East Morton. Even Kettleton may record an old Norseman, Chatel, as there are many place-names in England where the name appears—Kettleburgh, now Kettleborough (Suffolk), Chatel's fortified town; Chatel-worth, now

Chatsworth (Derby), Chatel's well-watered estate. Then we have Fell, the old Norse name for a hill, which is pure Scandinavian, and is found often in the English lake district, which we know to have been peopled by a colony of Norsemen. With the exception of Shaw, meaning wood, there seems to be no pure Anglo-Saxon word in Morton parish. Besides these we have Dry-gill, and the ravine between the village and the school-house is known as "the Gill." There is also Hungill, near the Curling Loch.

MORTON BARONY.

At what period and in whose favour this barony was first erected we have no documents to show. In the reign of David I. (1124-1153) the parish, along with the whole of Nithsdale, is found in the possession of Dunegal, a Scoto-Irish chieftain, whose family will be spoken of afterwards, so far as the scanty materials of these early times allow. The barony occupied nearly the whole of the parish, consisting of the following lands, as is shown by the charter of alienation and seisin granted by William, Earl of Morton, to Sir William Douglas of Coshogle (Drumlanrig Charters). "The mains of Morton, with the mill and mill lands, and the castle, tower, manor, and other pertinents; the lands of Eris-Morton, White-fauld, Gallow-flat, Hall-gill, Dabton, Carronhill, Drumcork, Broom-rig, Thornhill, Upper and Nether Laught, Gallow Bridge (Gately Brig), Upper Kirkland and Langmyre, with a proportionable part of the common, called Morton Muir, and the other dependencies, all lying in the barony of Morton. 22nd October, 1608."

MORTON CASTLE.

A castle must have existed here as early as the beginning of the twelfth century, when the Scoto-Irish chieftain, Dunegal, ruled over the whole of Nithsdale, and had his manor-house at this spot. The present building, however, is evidently of a much later date, from its resemblance to the Norman castles of England. The ornamentation of the principal door, which is still perfect, would induce us to place it in the times of the Edwards. It is a massive structure even in its ruins, and when it was complete must have been able to withstand the imperfect modes of siege of early times. It was defended on all sides, except the south-west, by a loch, which must have been formed by a dam, as it is at the present time. A deep fosse, no doubt crossed by a drawbridge, though now filled up, would protect it on the south-west, and enclosed a piece of ground, which would be used as a garden. It stands on the south side, on the brow of a deep glen, which extends to a considerable distance south-east and north-west.

The south wall of the castle is quite entire, and shows the strength of resistance which had to be overcome by those who attacked it. There are two towers of different sizes, one to the west being 32 feet, and the other to the east being 28 feet externally; between these towers the outward wall extends 96 feet and is 36 feet in height. This seems to have been nearly its original height, though some of the top layers of stone may have been displaced. The towers are 8 or 10 feet higher. The walls at the foundation are about 8 feet, in some places 10 feet thick.

While there was no doubt an outer fosse to be

crossed, the castle had a gateway with a portcullis, which has long disappeared, but the groove along which the portcullis moved can be traced on the north-west tower. The northern part of the castle has disappeared, except the foundations, which are so evident that an architect could have no difficulty in presenting the precise form of the original building. It was in this direction that there must have been an outer court, which would be entered after passing the gateway; and a stair, of which nothing now remains, led to the upper reception-room, of large dimensions. The ornamental doorway still exists.

Passing into the interior, you come upon what must have been a huge kitchen, and possibly dining-hall for the retainers, extending at present, where there are no divisions, 88 feet by 30. The room originally was about 70 feet, as there is a portion cut off in connection with the north-west tower. The huge kitchen grate, of a rude construction, would be at the east end, and to the right leading into the tower was a narrow entrance, scarcely admitting the passage of one person, where a postern door was placed to admit of safe communication with the outside. The huge stone across this entrance has strange fossil marks, which may yet exercise the ingenuity of geologists. They might be regarded by the ignorant as hieroglyphics, but the neighbouring quarry of Morton Mains, from which the stones have been got for building the castle, furnishes such strangely marked stones. Can the marks be what earth-worms would make in the sand before it hardened into stone?

Above this lower chamber there was one large reception-room, entered by a stair from the outer court, and above this there were garrets. The engraving in "Grose" shows that there were in his time (1790) outer buildings, which no longer exist, and these probably formed the domicile of the family of Archibald Douglas, the chamberlain of Duke William, whom we know to have been married here in 1670.

The vicissitudes of the castle are unknown. In early times it was regarded as one of the strongholds of the kingdom, and it was one of those castles which David II. was suspected of having been willing to come under a secret engagement to dismantle, as the price of his freedom. Whether the barons of Dalkeith, to whom it belonged, lived here in later times I have seen no records to prove. A cadet branch of that family certainly possessed a considerable portion of land in the parish of Morton towards the end of the sixteenth century, as will be shown hereafter, but the castle and barony of Morton did not belong to them. The interior of the castle was cleared under the directions of the Duke of Buccleuch; nothing, however, of importance was found. A cannonball, with pieces of a spear, was turned up, and there was some charred wood, as if the buildings had been destroyed by fire.

There are place-names in its vicinity which show that the possessor of the barony had the right of pit and gallows. At some little distance on the hill east of the castle stood an aged thorn, which was uprooted many years ago by a hurricane of wind, but which was known as Judgment Thorn, and the tradition of the country still points out the spot where it grew; while close to the farm-steading of Morton Mains are Gallows Flat and Hangingshaw, where doom of judgment was carried into execution. The approach of an enemy was seen from a hill to the west of the castle, which is still known as Watchman Knowe. When the embankments of the loch had gone to decay, towards the beginning of last century, in the mossy soil at the bottom a boat was dug out, which had been formed, like an Indian canoe, out of one solid piece of wood. A short time after this there was dug out of the same moss a small copper camp-kettle, and in the year 1728 there was also found a fine copper tea-pot stroup quite entire (Rae's MS.).

The late Miss Clerk-Douglas of Holmhill used to say that her great-grandfather was the last inhabitant of Morton castle, with the exception of an old woman, a servant of the family, who had lived so long within its walls that, when the great-grandfather of Miss Douglas found it necessary to abandon the castle from its ruinous state, she refused to do so, and continued to find shelter there till her death. This would be toward the beginning of last century.

FAMILY OF DUNEGAL OR RANDOLPH.

The earliest possessor of this castle of whom we have mention is Dunegal, supposed to be of the race of the Dougalls or M'Dowalls of Galloway, who were of Celtic extraction. This Dunegal of Stranid or Nithsdale occupied the castle as one of the chief seats of his power in the beginning of the twelfth century, during the reign of David I. (1124-1153), and his possessions seem to have spread over the whole of Nithsdale, as is shown in the following charter of David I., granting Strathannand (Annandale) to Robert de Brus. *Charta Davidis regis Scocie Roberto de Brus, totam terram de Estrahanent* (Strathannan) *a divisa Dunegal de Stranit usque ad divisam Randolphi de Meschines et ut illam teneat cum omnibus consuetudinibus quas Randolphus de Meschines unquam habuit in Cardivil* (Carlisle) *et in terra sua de Cumberland, illo die quo unquam meliores et liberiores habuit. Testibus, Eustathio filio Johannis, Hugo de Morvill, Alano de Perci et Willelmo de Somerville, Berengers de Engamo, Randolpho de Scales (Soulis?), Willelmo de Morvil, Henrico filio Warin, Edmund de Camera. Apud Sconam.* "Charter of David, King of Scotland (grants) to Robert de Brus all the land of Annandale from the boundary of Dunegal of Nithsdale to the boundary of Randolph de Meschines, and that he should hold it with all rights which Randolph ever held in Carlyle and his land of Cumberland, on the day when he held it best and most free, &c. At Scone." He was to hold it under the same tenure as Randolph enjoyed his estate (Dugdale, i., p. 447).

Dunegal left four sons, and in these early days the feudal system does not seem to have prevailed, as his great possessions were divided among his sons, though the eldest Rudolph or Randolph received the largest portion, and became still more powerful by marrying an heiress called Bethoc, through whom he got the lands of Bethocrule and Bughchester (Beucastle) in Teviotdale. Randolph and his wife granted to the monks of Jedburgh a carucate (sixty acres) of land with common of pasture in the vill of Bughchester, and this grant was confirmed by William the Lion (1165-1214). The original charter has been engraved by the munificence of the Duke of Buccleuch. Randolph also granted to the monks of Kelso some lands within Dumfries town, thus showing how extensive his possessions in Dumfriesshire must have been (Chart. Kelso, No. 11).

Rudolph and his brother Duvenald witnessed several charters of David I. to the see of Glasgow (Chart. Glas., 9, 12, 13, 17). The other sons of Dunegal were Duncan and Gillespie.

The family now assumed the surname of Randolph, and is known from this time by that name, though there is a blank here in their history which we are unable to fill up. In Fordun (l. x., c. 26) we find Thomas Randolph as Sheriff of Roxburgh in 1266, and Chamberlain of Scotland from 1269 to 1278. There seems, however, to be a generation missed between Randolph, son of Dunegal, and this Thomas. Besides, it may be doubted whether Thomas Randolph, who married Isobel, eldest daughter of the Earl of Carrick, the sister of Robert Bruce, the restorer of the monarchy, may not be the son of the Chamberlain rather than the Chamberlain himself. The succession during the twelfth and thirteenth centuries is doubtful. Be this as it may, the son of this Isobel was the celebrated Sir Thomas Randolph of Stranith, "Dominus Vallis de Nith" as he is called, who obtained from his uncle the earldom of Moray, the lordship of Annandale, with the barony of Morton and other estates for his great services. His daughter Agnes carried, through failure of male heirs, his property to the Earls of March. In course of time the barony of Morton came into the possession of the Douglases of Dalkeith.

We are able also to trace the history of Duvenald, the second son of Dunegal. He obtained a considerable portion of his father's extensive lands in Nithsdale, which he transmitted to his son Edgar, who lived under William the Lion and Alexander II. He granted to the monks of Kelso the church of Morton, with a carucate of land, and this grant was confirmed by William the

Lion (Chart. Kelso, No. 344, 401). He also granted to the monks of Holyrood house the church of Dalgarnock, a grant which was also confirmed by William the Lion. His daughter Affrica possessed the lands of Dunscore during the reign of Alexander II. She granted to the monastery of Melrose a fourth-part of the territory of Dunscore, and the grant was confirmed by a charter of Alexander II. in 1229 (Chart. Mel., No. 103, 104, 105).

The scanty records of these times prevent us from being able to trace the succession of this family, but in the thirteenth century they assumed the surname of Edgar. During the reign of Robert Bruce, Richard Edgar possessed the castle and half of the barony of Sancher (Regist. Mag. Sig., 1. 27). He also held the lands of Ellioc in the parish of Sanquhar, the lands of Bartenonade, Lobri, Slochan, Glenabekan, and part of the lands of Kilpatric in the same shire, of all of which he obtained charters from Robert Bruce (Robertson's Index, 12, 13, 21).

Families of the name of Edgar continued to flourish in the south of Scotland; and an interesting little work, containing a list of such families, and ably edited by Dr. Charles Rogers, 1873, has been published by the Grampian club. They have all probably Duvenald as their common progenitor. The place-name of Edgarstoun in Dunscore hands down to us the site of their manor-house.

Returning to the descendants of Rudolph, eldest son of Dunegal, we have shown that after the battle of Bannockburn, 24th June, 1314, the barony of Morton was granted by Robert Bruce to his nephew, Sir Thomas Randolph. At the fatal battle of Durham, 17th Oct., 1346, Thomas, Earl of Moray, being killed, his heroic sister Agnes,

Countess of Dunbar, became sole possessor of his vast estates, and the Earl of Dunbar now assumed the additional title of Earl of Moray, although it was a male fee. Besides the earldom of Moray and other possessions, he obtained the baronies of Morton and Tybaris (Douglas Peerage, vol. ii., p. 170).

In 1396 the barony was in the possession of Sir James Douglas, Earl of Morton (Douglas Peerage, p. 266), and his son Sir James Douglas had a charter of Morton barony from Robert III., 29th April, 1401, and again on resignation, 20th February, 1433 (p. 267); on 30th May, 1459, another to William de Douglas on resignation of James, Earl of Morton; and an Act of Parliament was passed at Perth, 9th October, 1459, confirming to Janet, Countess of Caithness, Lady of Dalkeith, and William de Douglas of Morton, knight, her son, the possession of the lands of Morton.

The property was thus disjoined (1459) from the main branch of the family, the Douglases of Dalkeith, and passed into a cadet branch, Sir William Douglas of Morton and Whyttingham. His wife's name was Euphemia, but of what family we do not know, nor is it easy to trace the early links of his descendants. The greater part, however, of the barony of Morton must have gone back to the head of the family, the Earl of Morton. Rae in his MS. account of the parish of Morton, which was written about the beginning of the eighteenth century, tells us that Sir William Douglas of Coshogle bought from the Earl of Morton the estate of Morton.

This was the culminating point in the fortunes of the Coshogle family, but it was only a sunny blink, at once overcast by a dark cloud. Sir William descended from the hills, where his fathers had hitherto resided, and Rae tells us that he built a house below Thornhill, to the south-westward of that place, and sometimes resided there. This was called the Red House. Adversity seems to have followed close on the heels of his prosperity, for we find, ten years after he had got the property from the Earl of Morton, a deed of resignation and a contract of sale to the Earl of Queensberry of the Mains of Morton and the rest of the lands mentioned above, 2nd Dec., 1618. These lands thus came into the possession of the Drumlanrig branch of the Douglases, and were merged in the Queensberry property. (Drumlanrig Charters.)

There is, however, a difficulty in regard to the Mains and Castle of Morton, which we are unable to clear up. We see that they were sold, by the charter to which reference has been made, to the Queensberry family, and yet Rae tells us in his MS. that the Mains and a small farm called Blairfoot belonged to another branch of the Douglas family, "being a very pleasant place, worth 1200 merks per annum, and very fertile both for corn and pasture." Now there was certainly a family of this name, and respecting which we have gathered the following authentic information from the Drumlanrig charters. The first of the family who is mentioned is Hugh Douglas, who has a charter and seisin of the £5 land of Bellybucht, in the barony of Morton, called Burn, and that part called Bus from Dalziell of that Ilk, afterwards Lord Dalziell, with fealty and service to Dalziell as superior against all offenders, their sovereign the King, the Earl of Morton, and the Lords of Drumlanrig excepted, dated 23rd April, 1593. There is next a seisin of these lands to James Douglas of Morton, as son and heir of the above Hugh, 20th July, 1624; and again another seisin of these lands to William of Morton, as son and heir to the above James, 30th October, 1652. Next we have their names mentioned with Auchinsell, Muirhill, and Blackmyre, which Robert Menzies of Enoch resigns to James Douglas of Morton, 21st April, 1636, and again as superior to William of Morton, as son and heir of the above James, 19th July, 1653. William Douglas seems to have got into difficulties, as we find him parting with all the foregoing lands and also with Bus and Burn, together with the barony of Lochrinny, in the parish of Dalry, to the Earl of Queensberry, 1672. We have also a disposition granted to his Lordship by the above William of Morton, and also by his eldest son, James, his two brothers, Archibald and Samuel, and by Fergusson of Craigdarroch and Menzies of Auchinsell, two of his creditors. The lands are passed from him in perpetuity, namely, those already mentioned, and also the Mains and Castle of Morton, 16th January, 1683. We thus see that the Mains and Castle of Morton remained in the possession of this family till this late period, and this agrees with what Rae states. A friend well acquainted with Scottish law has suggested that our difficulty in regard to the Mains of Morton, &c., may be satisfactorily explained in this way. When Sir William Douglas of Coshogle sold to the Earl of Queensberry, in 1618, the barony of Morton, the whole barony would be conveyed, but there might be others in the possession of lands, who held of Sir William as superior, and the superiority of those lands would no doubt be included in the conveyance. The conveyance, if this were the case, would not only assign the rents but also the feu-duties and casualties. The warrandice clause also would except the feus and other rights of property granted by the seller or his predecessors, and other technical clauses necessary would be introduced.

When the Queensberry family acquired the Mains, &c., on the 16th January, 1693, the right of property then acquired would be consolidated with the right of superiority by the purchasers executing a deed of resignation *ad remanentiam* of the *dominium utile* in his own hand as superior. Even such a deed was not necessary, as the superiority title, which would be a good title to the lands, would work off the base infeftment upon the *dominium utile*, and the two fees would be effectually consolidated by prescription, there being in this case more than forty years' possession in the superiority title before the right of property was acquired. This, I think, is a satisfactory explanation, and solves the difficulty that had occurred to me in regard to the Mains, &c., of Morton, which seemed to have been twice bought. After the purchase there were found to be feudatories scattered over the parish, whose rights had to be acquired by the Earl. These feudatories (1621) were found at Carronbridge, Dabton, Drumcork, and Thornhill, which show that the rights of superiority were acquired with the barony.

It is not without interest to trace the history of the family of Douglas of the Mains of Morton. James Douglas married Christian Lockhart of Lee, and had two sons—William Douglas of Morton (1666), who married Esther Elliot, and Archibald Douglas of Fingland, whose marriage to Marion Kennedy of Auchtyfardell is recorded to have taken place at "the Castell of Mortoun, the tent day of May, 1670." This Archibald Douglas was the father of William Douglas of Fingland, the suitor of "Bonnie Annie Laurie."

The following is their pedigree, as far as it can be carried back authentically by the Drumlanrig charters:—

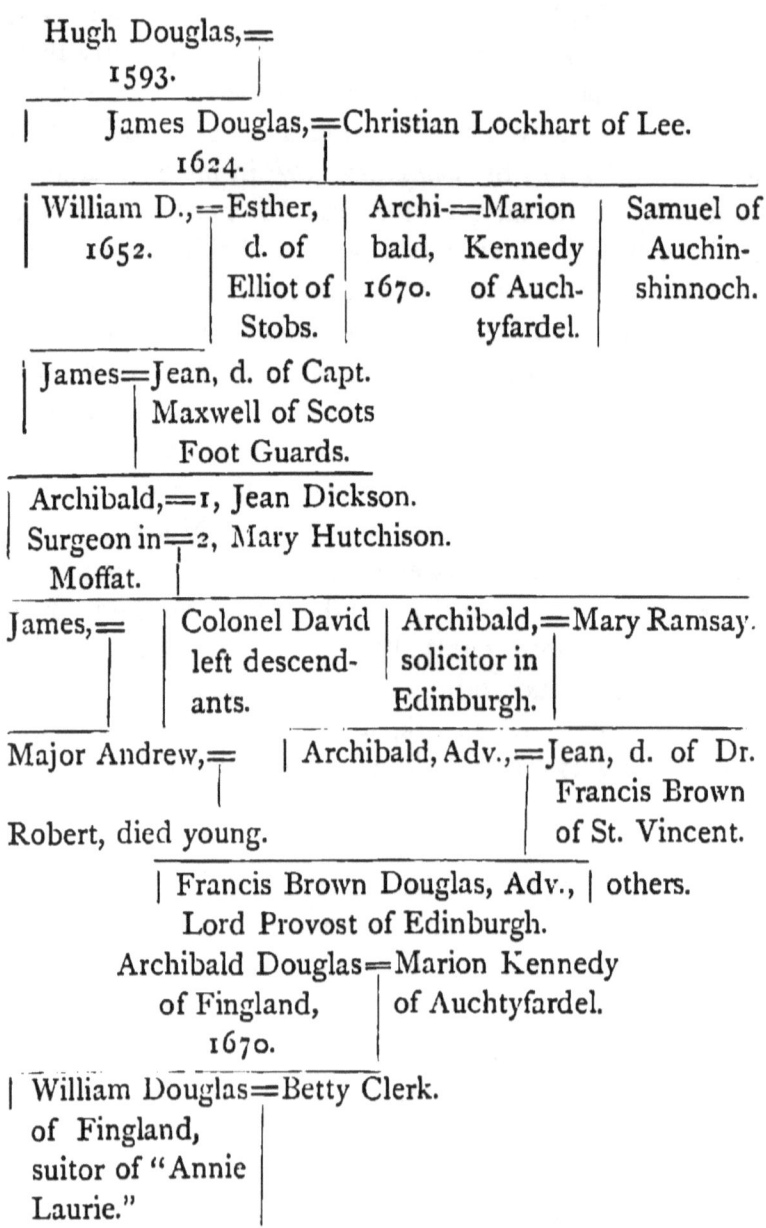

Hugh Douglas,= 1593.

James Douglas,=Christian Lockhart of Lee.
1624.

William D.,=Esther, | Archi-=Marion | Samuel of
1652. | d. of | bald, | Kennedy | Auchin-
| Elliot of | 1670. | of Auch- | shinnoch.
| Stobs. | | tyfardel. |

James=Jean, d. of Capt.
Maxwell of Scots
Foot Guards.

Archibald,=1, Jean Dickson.
Surgeon in =2, Mary Hutchison.
Moffat.

James,= | Colonel David | Archibald,=Mary Ramsay.
| left descend- | solicitor in
| ants. | Edinburgh.

Major Andrew,= | Archibald, Adv.,=Jean, d. of Dr.
| | Francis Brown
Robert, died young. | of St. Vincent.

Francis Brown Douglas, Adv., | others.
Lord Provost of Edinburgh.

Archibald Douglas=Marion Kennedy
of Fingland, | of Auchtyfardel.
1670. |

William Douglas=Betty Clerk.
of Fingland,
suitor of "Annie
Laurie."

EARLY HISTORY OF MORTON.

Archibald=Elizabeth	Alexr.=Janet	Chas.=Eliz-
Douglas, Lt.- Gen. and Col. of 13th Dragoons & M.P. for County of Dumfries.	Burchard, m. 1761.	John- stone. Sarah.	abeth Vernon.

Robert,=Frances Jeffreys,
Rector of Salwarpe & Hampton Lovett.	1787, d. of H. Vaughan of Worcester.

Frances Anne=Rev. D. Morgan.	Helen=Very Rev. Thos. Gaisford, D.D., Rector of Wickham and Canon of Durham.	Henry=Eleanor Birt.
Robert Archibald=Rebecca Maria assumed the name of Gresley in addition to that of Douglas.	Harvey.	Mary=Rev. Richd. Lowndes, who assumed on the death of his mother the name of Garth only.

The following letter by Archibald Douglas, surgeon of Lockerbie, confirms the pedigree that is given above:—

"Lockerbie, 16th Oct., 1782.
"Loving son,
"My great grandfather, James Douglas of Morton, who married Christian Lockhart, second daughter of

x

James Lockhart of Lee, had three sons and three daughters, and either by disposition or according to marriage contract, William Douglas, the eldest son, my grandfather, was to give each 10,000 merks of patrimony.

"To Archibald, his brother, therefore, he gave Fingland, being £100 a year.

"To Samuel, the lands of Auchenshinnoch, of nearly the same rent, according to inventory; Janet=Johnstone of Corehead; —— =Ferguson of Craigdarroch; —— = Gordon of Trochain.

"My grandfather married Esther, daughter of Elliot of Stobs, and was named as one of the Convention of Estates for Nithsdale, 2nd March, 1668. His brothers, Archibald and Samuel, were buried in the family ground in Morton between 1714 and 1723. I buried my first wife, Jean Dickson, aunt of David of Hartree, in 1756, in said aisle, built in the wall of the church. I was born 24th June, 1703, so I was major when I granted bond to my cousin, William Douglas of Fingland.

"(Signed)   A. D."

The brother of General Douglas was Charles Douglas, who died at Holmhill, in 1788, and whose family of five daughters lived to a great age, and were well known in Upper Nithsdale.

Charles Douglas=Elizabeth Vernon of Musselburgh.
1. William, capt., 103 Reg., m. Henrietta Nicholson.
2. Archibald, surgeon, 44th Reg., who died at Portsmouth.
3. Thomas, capt., who died at Holmhill, 1826.
4. Alexander (in the navy), drowned off the American coast.

5. Margaret.
6. Sarah, died at Holmhill, 1841, aged 93.
7. Hyde, died 1839, aged 90.
8. Elizabeth, died 1841, aged 91.
9. Clerk, died 1859, aged 99.

William Douglas=Henrietta Nicholson, granddaughter of Lady Henrietta Sandford, d. of William, third Earl of Inchiquin.

| Charles, drowned, with 300 rank and file of his Regiment (59th), in 1815, in Tranmoor Bay, Waterford. | Harriet=Mossman of Auchtyfardle. | Emily=Thos Whyte. |

Harriet = Adam Mossman of Auchtyfardle, merchant, Liverpool.

| Harriet, resides in Liverpool. | Sarah, dead, 1875. |

Emily = Thomas Whyte of Upper Gleneslin, in Dumfriesshire.

| James C. Douglas,=Harriet, resides in France. | dead. | Emily, dead. |

George. | Helen Rosalie Marie=Nath. Kemp of Patcham Place, Sussex, (20th Feb., 1875).

CHURCH OF MORTON.

At what time the church of Morton was founded is unknown, but it is likely to have been in existence as early as the reign of David I. (1121-1153). We hear of it first before the end of the twelfth century, when it was granted with a carucate of land which belonged to it by Edgar, grandson of Dunegal of Stranid, to the monks of Kelso (Chart. Kelso, No. 344). This grant was confirmed by William the Lion (ib. 401), and both these grants were confirmed by Walter, Bishop of Glasgow, in 1232 (ib. 278). When these monks formed an estimate of their property in the fourteenth century, they stated that they possessed the church of Morton "in rectoria," which used to render by the year £10. The monks received the rectorial tithes, and the cure was served by a vicar. It is interesting to trace the history of these church lands at the time of the Reformation. There is first a charter and seisin to Archibald Douglas in Carronhill (possibly one of the Coshogle family) and his heirs, by the vicar of the church of Morton, Mr. Archibald Menzies, for the payment of £14 Scots yearly and 20d. more *nomine feudi firme*, 23rd January, 1569; then another by James VI., when the temporalities of the church came into the crown, the rent then £2 Scots yearly and 40d. more, 13th March, 1587, and 16th July, 1590. There is another crown charter, precept, and seisin of these lands granted to William (afterwards Sir William) Douglas of Coshogle, and Sir William's disposition to the above Archibald in Carronhill, giving back the lands to him, 13th June, 1622. Precept and seisin of the same lands by Robert, Earl of Roxburgh, to another Archibald Douglas, son and heir of Archibald in Carronhill, 9th Aug., 1623; then a disposition of these lands by Archibald, the son, and a confirmation of the Earl of Roxburgh, the superior, in favour of the Earl of Queensberry, at that time Baron of Drumlanrig, and his heirs-male, the rent £2 3s. 4d. as formerly, dated 5th Aug., 1629; and the church lands thus merged in the Queensberry property (Drumlanrig Charters). Kirkfield is now valued at £40 per annum.

The old church was situated on rising ground about a mile and a half from the castle of Morton; but as the population had congregated in the village of Thornhill in later times, the Duke of Buccleuch and Queensberry removed it to the vicinity of the village in 1841, and built a handsome church at a cost of £3553 16s. 8d. It affords accommodation for 1200 persons. The glebe is about twenty acres in extent, and is valued at £25 yearly. The stipend is nineteen chalders, with £10 for communion elements. In the return to the House of Commons (March, 1875) of Ministers' Stipends in Scotland, the total amount of stipend of Morton is given at £360, and the total annual value of the living from all sources as £420.

The Duke of Buccleuch and Queensberry was patron of the church till the abolition of patronage in 1874. The following is a list of the ministers of the parish:—

1580—Thomas Maxwell, reader at Dumfries, and minister at Redkirk (now part of Gretna parish), is stated to be minister here in 1580, while it is also said "he cannot serve at sundrie places, makes no residence, but is a Jackman with Drumlanrik" (wore a steel jacket and defended Sir James Douglas of Drumlanrig).

1607—John Douglas, reader at Penpont, from 1593 to 1601.

1601—Alexander Flemyng, translated from Dalgarno: translated to Closeburn about 1633.

1635—William Kay.

1638—John Weir, A.M.: translated to Carluke in 1640.

164 —Adam Sinclar, A.M.: translated to Sanquhar before 1650.

1648—George Clelland, A.M.

16 —Luke Greenshiels, A.M.: translated to Ardrossan before 1687.

1687—Thomas Henderson, A.M.: ousted by the people at the Revolution, but was received into Communion by the Commission of Assembly in 1701.

1691—Patrick Flint, A.M.

1693—John Pasley, A.M.

1714—John Howie.

1734—Archibald Little: translated to Kirkpatrick-Irongray in 1759.

1760—Robert Aitken: got the church rebuilt in 1781.

1790—John Yorstoun, son of the Rev. Peter Yorstoun: translated to Torthorwald in 1808.

1809—David Smith.

1839—John Murray: translated from Abbotshall.

Besides the Church of Scotland, which is numerously attended, the population is scattered among a variety of sects. There is a chapel in the village formerly of the Anti-burgher persuasion, now belonging to the United Presbyterian body; and the members of the Evangelical Union meet in the Mason Hall. The Reformed Presbyterians have representatives in Morton, and the Free

Church, of Virgin Hall in Penpont, are not without adherents in the same parish.

UNITED PRESBYTERIAN CHURCH.

The Secession congregation of Thornhill was connected with that of Moniaive till 1805, when it was disjoined from it and organized as a separate congregation. First church built, 1784; second church built, 1816; sittings, 480. The following is a list of the ministers:—

1788—James Pattison: ordained as minister of the united congregations of Moniaive and Thornhill. At the disjunction of the congregations in 1805 he made choice of Thornhill. Died in 1816.

1817—William Rogerson. Died in 1857.

1860—Robert Wishart.

The following copy of the letter announcing the grant of a site for the first church of this body is sufficiently quaint to warrant its insertion here:—

"PICCADELLY, 10th Feby., 1784.

"Sir,—I have orders from the Duke of Queensberry to send you the enclosed Petition, and to tell you that as He formerly promised, so He now agrees to give the Petitioners a Bit of Ground at Thornhill whereon to build them a meeting-house, and the Duke desires you will set off to them a Bit of Ground for that purpose, but His Grace is not inclined to contribute anything more towards it, thinking it would be better to conform themselves to the Established Church.—I am, your most obt. servant,

(Signed)   WM. MITCHELL.

" Mr. John M'Murdo." (See Appendix No. VII.).

EVANGELICAL UNION INDEPENDENTS.

There is a handsome chapel now (1874) building for this religious body, to be seated for 312, and of which the probable cost will be from £850 to £900.

First Minister, —Rev. James Pearson.
Second ,, —Rev. John M'Ilveen: he was pastor-elect, but being in bad health, his ordination never took place. He died in Nov., 1860.
Third ,, —Rev. Alexander Nairn.
Fourth ,, —Rev. R. J. Gray.
Fifth and present—Rev. Robert Mitchell, Dingwall.

SACRED WELLS AND CROSSES.

There are several sacred wells, as "St. Patrick's Well," in a field to the south-west of Thornhill; and on a hill at East Morton farm there is "Mary's Well." The end of the hill where the new manse is situated was in early times known as Corsehill-end, evidently pointing out the site of an ancient cross.

SCHOOLS.

There are several schools in the parish. Besides the National School in Thornhill, there are two subsidiary schools and schoolmasters' houses, built and supported by his Grace the Duke of Buccleuch and Queensberry—one at Carronbridge, the schoolmaster of which receives £35; and another at Gateleybridge, with a salary of £25. The following is the abstract of census, 24th May, 1873, taken by Mr. Joseph M'Caig, officer of School Board:—

No. of children from	5 to 13 years of age,	.	379
,, ,,	2 to 5 ,,	.	146
,, attending school from	5 to 13 ,,	.	319
,, ,, ,,	2 to 5 ,,	.	3
,, private tuition ,,	5 to 13 ,,	.	5
,, not attending school ,,	5 to 13 ,,	.	55
No. of male children, . . ,,	2 to 13 ,,	.	269
,, female ,, ,,	2 to 13 ,,	.	256
,, male ,, . ,,	2 to 5 ,,	.	81
,, female ,, . ,,	2 to 5 ,,	.	63

Children receiving education.	Parish School, .	106	Absent through neglect,	18
	Mr. Black's adventure,	104	Ill-health or bodily infirmity,	8
	Miss Forbes' adventure,	29	5 years of age, . .	10
	Carronbridge School,	51	Considered complete, .	6
	Gatelawbridge ,,	28	Temporary absence, .	13
	Durisdeer F.C. ,,	4		—
	Private tuition, ,,	5		55
		327		

POPULATION.

The population of the parish was in 1755, 435; 1792, 908; 1801, 1255; 1841, 2167; 1871, 2098. Year ending 31st December, 1872—Births, 69; marriages, 13; deaths, 45.

POOR.

The amount raised from assessment for the relief of the poor for the year ending May, 1872, was £603 10s. 9d. The number of poor on the roll was 63, with 46 dependants, of whom 9 were insane or fatuous persons. The average number receiving relief about 1834 was 30.

TOPOGRAPHY.

The parish is irregular in its form. It is bounded on the west, north-west, and north by the parish of Durisdeer, from which it is separated by the waters of Carron, the Shieldhouse burn, and the head of Glenaggart; on the north-east it is bounded by a part of Crawfordmuir, in Clydesdale, the march running eastward along the watershed of the mountain called Glenleith; on the south-east and east by the united parishes of Closeburn and Dalgarnock, from which it is separated by the Cample; on the south-west by the river Nith, which divides it from the parish of Penpont, with the exception of about 120 acres, called Cowl and Morton-holm, lying on the western bank of the Nith. The extent of the parish from south-west to north-east is about 6 miles, and its mean breadth about $3\frac{1}{2}$ miles.

The area of the parish, according to Ordnance Survey, is 8126·819 imperial acres. The external surface of the parish is diversified by ridge and valley, rising gradually from the banks of the Nith, ridge after ridge, till it reaches the high mountains of Bellybucht and Glenleith. Along the banks of the Nith there is some holm land of extreme fertility. Then, the ridge on which Thornhill is placed is, like most of the parishes around, of a light and gravelly soil; while on the high ridge, running south from Morton Castle, the soil is damp and wettish, lying on a clayey bottom. A good deal of this high ground has been laid out in plantations, for which it is better suited than for corn or pasture. At the foot of the hills there is a considerable extent of meadow land of a rich alluvial soil, and very productive. The ranges of the ridges and rising grounds of the hills and mountains run across the parish from south-east to north-west. The greater part of the arable land lies on a red sandstone bottom under the clay or gravel, and the mountains rest on the primitive and whinstone rocks.

The highest point of the parish is found on Bellybucht, 1452 feet above the level of the sea, and of the others the following may be given:—Bar hill, 1381 feet; East Morton hill, 1255 feet; Morton Mains hill, 1076 feet; Cog's Dish, 700 feet; Morton Castle loch, 602 feet; Old Church, 363·5; New Church, 280·2.

STREAMS.

There is only one stream, Kettleton burn, which can be said to belong wholly to the parish. It rises to the north-east, near the march of Clydesdale, running in its course first straight west, then, turning southwards, it falls into the Cample, a little below the Burn farm-steading. It is joined by the Shielburn and the Routon. There is another small stream called Glenleith, which falls into the Cample. There is only one loch, Morton Castle loch, which is of considerable size, but it has been increased by artificial embankments. Whitemoss and Dabton lochs, near Thornhill, are used for curling. Near Waterside Mains there is the Physic Well, which is chalybeate.

WOODS IN MORTON.

The woods of this parish have been chiefly planted since the property came into the possession of the Dukes of Buccleuch. There is only one remarkable tree, a silver fir, growing in Morton Mains wood, which must be somewhere about the same age as the Barjarg silver fir in Keir, which is known to have been planted in 1731, and is now in girth, at $4\frac{1}{2}$ feet from the ground, 11 feet. By measurement of this tree at different times it is known that it has grown at the rate of 12 inches every ten years for the first ninety years, and then only at the rate of $3\frac{1}{2}$ inches every ten years. The following are the dimensions of this Morton fir:—Height, 95 feet; length of bole, 59 feet; girth of base, 25 feet; do., 4 feet from ground, $12\frac{1}{2}$; spread of branches, 58 feet. In the return to Government in 1874 of the acreage of woodlands, for Morton there appear 1167 acres.

ROADS.

The old Glasgow road from Dumfries entered the parish by the wooden bridge over the Cample, at the bottom of the hill leading from Templand farm-house in Closeburn. This bridge was originally built of stone with money left by Mr. Wallace, who endowed the school of Wallace Hall. When the road was changed to its present course, the stones of this bridge were removed to build the present bridge over the same stream, on the new line of road, about the year 1788. The old road continued up the hill, passing in front of the U.P. Chapel, forwards past the present girls' school, straight on through the fields, passing behind Langmyre, Meadow Bank, and then in front of Dabton, to Carronbridge, where the road passed into Durisdeer. The new line of road enters the parish at the stone bridge above-mentioned, and continues straight to Thornhill. The Holmhill road was constructed early in the century to save the hills leading to Thornhill. There is a good road past King's Quarry to Morton Castle, and another leading to Thornhill Station, past Drumcork. The road to the station on the Glasgow and South-Western Railway from Thornhill was greatly improved in the year 1850. There are about 21 miles of public roads in the parish, maintained under the Dumfriesshire Roads Act. The assessment for the current year (1873) is sixpence per pound, payable equally by proprietor and tenant.

NITH BRIDGE.

Where this bridge now stands there was originally only a ford, which was passed by boat, giving name still to the Boat Brae on the side of Morton, and to Boatford property on the side of Penpont. The necessity of a bridge was proved to the county by a melancholy accident which took place on the evening of a Thornhill Candlemas Fair, 23rd February, 1773, when six persons out of thirteen were drowned by the upsetting of the boat. The following were the names of the parties who met this sad fate, and it will be observed that there were three men with the name "James," and three women called "Jean." They were :—

James Ferguson, farmer, Glenwhargen.
James Geddes, blacksmith, Knowkelly, Tynron.
James Gracie, Penfillan, Keir.
Jean Kirkpatrick, Penfillan, Keir.
Jean Rorison, from Moniaive.
Jean Hairstens, Moniaive. (?)

The boatman was William Fingland, grandfather of the present respected tenant of Laught, and it is handed down that he was saved by his son Thomas, who was riding across on the horse of James Gracie, and was just in time to save his father. The boat was upset by a gust of wind, but the superstitious are always ready to ascribe such accidents to other causes. It got abroad that a strange man in black rushed into the boat as it was pushing off, that he went down with the boat and was never seen more, so that it was inferred that Satanic agency had brought about the catastrophe. James Ferguson of Glenwhargen was remarkable for strength, and it was supposed that he must have been kept down by the death struggles of the women. In those days money could not be raised by the county so readily as at present, and much of the funds had to be got by voluntary subscriptions. The bridge was thus not built till 1777, as the inscription on it shows.

VALUATION OF PARISH.

The valued rental of the parish was £846. The real rental was thought to be in 1792 about £1500, if the farms had been let at the rate usually paid for similar lands in this part of the country, but the rental of the parish at this time was only £751, as large grassums or fines were always received at granting new leases. In 1815 assessed property was £3030; in 1855 the valuation was £5064; and now, in 1875, it is £7061 12s. 6d., exclusive of the railway, which is valued at £3189. The parish of Morton belongs wholly to the Duke of Buccleuch, with the exception of some small portions, amounting to £347 2s. It is only just to his Grace to show the noble manner in which he has administered this trust, and that cannot be more clearly done than by giving the expenditure during the last few years on the public buildings which he has erected, and by pointing out the various other ways in which he has improved the parish:—

Cost of parish church,	£3,553 16 8
Cost of manse,	1,755 11 0
Cost of schoolmaster's house,	888 13 1
Cost of school-house,	1,297 17 6
School at Carronbridge,	180 0 8
School at Gateleybridge,	234 17 11
Expense of bringing water into Thornhill,	2,324 15 8
Expense of drainage in Thornhill,	1,309 6 4
Fire-hose,	89 19 0
	£11,634 17 10

Besides the above expenditure for the erection of buildings, &c., large sums are annually paid for keeping them in repair.

MINERALS.

Gateleybridge quarry is excellent freestone, having a high reputation, not only supplying the wants of the whole district, but sending large quantities for quay walls and public buildings in Scotland, England, and Ireland.

THORNHILL.

This flourishing village has increased greatly during the last hundred years, and has obtained, through the kind attention of the Duke of Buccleuch, to whom it belongs, everything that could render it a desirable residence. Some fifteen years ago a row of beautiful lime trees was planted on each side of the main street, which are all in a thriving state, giving it the appearance of an English village. In 1779 the population was 325; in 1791, 430; and in 1871, 1348—of whom there were 615 males and 733 females. The Duke of Buccleuch introduced a plentiful supply of water in 1867, and effected a complete system of drainage at the same time. Fire-hose was also provided in case of fire. The village was lighted with gas by a joint-stock company about 1840 or 1841; price at present, 10s. 10d. per 1000 cubic feet.

AMUSEMENTS.

The inhabitants are not without the means of amusement, according to the season of the year. A bowling-green was commenced in 1837 on what was at that time a piece of waste ground, which had hitherto been covered during the larger portion of the year with stagnant water. It was opened in 1832, and is now one of the finest greens in the south of Scotland. Its length is 60 yards, and breadth 35. The number of members is between forty and fifty, and the annual subscription is 6s. A cricket club was commenced a few years ago, and meets by kind permission of his Grace in a field at Boatford, but it has not a large roll of members. Quoiting is and has been

EARLY HISTORY OF MORTON.

for many years abandoned in the parish. The curling club is well patronized and in a flourishing state, having a first-rate pond, close to the village. The library was once in a flourishing condition, but is now reduced to about 800 volumes, mostly old. There are very few members. Annual subscription, 4s. 4d. A reading-room existed for a number of years, but was given up from want of support. Daily papers are so numerous and cheap that parties prefer to purchase and read at home.

SOCIETIES.

A soup-kitchen during winter and spring months has been in existence for upwards of thirty years, disbursing annually upwards of £40 in soup and coals among the necessitous classes.

There are three benefit societies, viz. :—1. The Brotherly Society, instituted in 1870, which is conducted on a limited scale; 2. The Oddfellows Society, which has a large roll of members, and is in a flourishing state; 3. The Masonic Friendly Society, in connection with St. John's Lodge of Freemasons, which is also in a flourishing state.

SAVINGS BANK.

The National Security Savings Bank was instituted in 1843, "to provide for the safe custody and increase of savings belonging to the industrious classes, to receive deposits of money for the benefit of the depositors, and accumulate the produce at compound interest on Government securities." The bank is under the patronage of the Duke of Buccleuch, and managed by gentlemen connected with the district. The rules provide that there shall be not less than twenty managers, including six trustees. All the managers and trustees act gratuitously, and all office-bearers entrusted with the funds, or receiving any salary, find security by granting bond with sufficient caution. A return is sent weekly to the commissioners for the reduction of the national debt, signed by the treasurer, actuary, and two trustees or managers specially appointed for that purpose, stating the amount deposited and withdrawn. The annual balance papers are all prepared by the commissioners, and when filled up a copy is sent to them in terms of Act of Parliament. The funds at the annual balance on 20th November, 1872, amounted to £11,236 12s. 2d., invested (with the exception of a working balance of £239 4s. 4d., in the hands of the treasurer and actuary) with the commissioners for the reduction of the national debt. The total number of depositors on 20th November, 1872, was 716, with a balance at their credit amounting to £10,812 5s. 6d. Four friendly societies and one charitable society have at their credit £341 16s. The interest paid to the depositors during the year amounted to £280 11s. 10d. Rate of interest allowed, £2 15s. per cent.

THE NITHSDALE AGRICULTURAL SOCIETY.

This Society, which holds its annual show in a field close to the village, was instituted in September, 1827, and held its first show in September, 1828. It has always been vigorously managed. Prizes are offered annually to the amount of £117. It consists at present of 120 members, and the funds on hands are upwards of £240.

CATTLE SHOW PRIZES OFFERED ANNUALLY.

Horses,		£19	0 0
Cattle—			
Ayrshire,	£20 15 0		
Galloway,	17 15 0		
Shorthorn and cross-bred,	7 5 0		
		45 15	0
Sheep—			
Cheviot,	£21 5 0		
Blackfaced,	13 0 0		
Leicester, &c., tups and half-bred lambs,	5 10 0		
		39 15	0
Swine,		3 0	0
Dairy produce,		10 5	0
Total,		£117 15	0

RUSSELL PRIZES.

In connection with it, prizes were founded in 1857 by James Russell, Esq., of Breckonside, for "The Oldest Working Man who is still following his usual employment," and to the "Agricultural Servant, male or female, who has been longest in the same service." The prizes were at first 5 guineas each, but have been increased to 6 guineas.

The age of the oldest man who has received the prize was 86; the age of the youngest was 78; and the average of the whole 82. The longest time of service by any of the servants who received the prize was 54 years, the shortest, 38 years, and the average of the whole 44 years.

Candidates must be resident within the district consisting of the Presbytery of Penpont, with the addition of any of the adjoining parishes in which shall reside at the time not less than five members of the Society.

Candidates must also be persons of unexceptionable moral character, members of some Christian church, and regular attendants of public worship.

Candidates must never have been on the roll of paupers, and must always have supported themselves by their own labour. These prizes are continued annually, but no person having obtained either the one or the other will be at liberty to compete again for the same prize till after three clear years; and should it so happen that any one man may have a just claim for both prizes at the same time, only one of them shall be awarded to him in one year.

FLOWER SHOW.

The Thornhill and Upper Nithsdale Cottage Horticultural and Practical Gardeners' Society hold their annual exhibition on the third Tuesday of September, when prizes to the amount of upwards of £12 are offered for competition. The Society has been very useful in developing and extending a taste for the cultivation of flowers, fruits, and vegetables, and great interest is taken by the community generally in the annual exhibition.

COURTS, &C.

Sheriff Circuit Courts for small debt causes not exceeding £12, and for causes under the Debtor's Recovery Act, 1867, are appointed to be held in Thornhill three times a year, generally in February, June, and October. For a number of years very few causes have come before these courts, and of late none at all. Creditors, instead of waiting for them, avail themselves of the privilege now allowed them of taking their causes before the weekly courts at Dumfries.

J.P. SMALL DEBT COURTS.

Small Debt Courts were also appointed by the justices to be held in Thornhill in April, August, and December, but they have been in abeyance for several years.

J.P. COURTS FOR POLICE CASES.

Justice of the Peace Courts for Police cases were held for many years regularly in Thornhill, but for a few years none have been held, the public prosecutors preferring to take the cases before the Dumfries Courts.

Thornhill is the polling place for Upper Nithsdale at parliamentary elections; the meeting place of the justices for granting hotel licenses, &c.; and is the place of meeting of the trustees of the sixth division of the public roads of the county. An auction for the sale of live stock has been in existence for several years, and is held every fortnight. The hiring fairs of the district are also held in Thornhill.

FREEMASONS.

This lodge was first mooted 23rd December, 1813, when a meeting took place, and initiatory steps were taken to organize the lodge. It was placed, 7th February, 1814, on the roll of daughter lodges by the "name, style, and title of St. John's Lodge, Thornhill, No. 328," but now numbered as 252. At the consecration of St. John's, the Rev. Edward Dobbie, the minister of the Relief congregation at Burnhead, offered up an appropriate prayer. It is not without interest to see the first office-bearers. They were as follows:—Robert M'Lachlan, Master; John Borland, Senior Warden; James M'Kerrow, Junior Warden; David Bryden, Secretary; Robt. Shankland, Treasurer; John M'Math, Clerk; Jas. M'Myn, Chaplain; Alex. Rae and Wm. Dickson, Senior and Junior Deacons; Thomas M'Lachlan and James Laidlaw, Stewards; John Turner, Tyler. It is noteworthy that of the several treasurers of St. John's, Brothers William M'Caig and Wm. Brown, saddler, held office, the former for twenty-two years, the latter (who still continues in charge of the funds) for the same number of years.

The election is by ballot, and takes place on the day (27th Dec.)—

> "Made festive to the zeal
> In his Great Master's cause of one expert—
> Saint John the Evangelist!"

There is a benefit society connected with it, "to grant relief to members during sickness and for funeral expenses." It was instituted in February, 1842, with a membership of 33, and a fund of £31 6s. At the present date (January, 1874) it has a membership of 180 and funds to the amount of £208 16s. 3d. During the last twenty years it has expended in sick allowances and funeral expenses about £500, while the lodge has supplemented that amount (from its own masonic fund) one-third, making a total of nearly £670.

This lodge has always shown itself ready to aid in the promotion of schemes of public benevolence, and of such patriotic objects as the repair of the public mausoleum of Robert Burns and the erection of the Wallace Monument at Abbey Craig. The care taken in the selection of members can have no stronger proof than that there is only one instance on record of Thornhill St. John's being called upon to "exclude" and "admonish" for irregular conduct any of its members, and that expulsion has never yet had to be resorted to. The number of members on the roll is 224. A handsome masonic hall has been erected in South Drumlanrig Street, costing £700; the lodge possessing shares in the hall to the value of £244. The lodge-room is 43 feet by 24 feet. The first foundation-stone laid under the immediate auspices of St. John's, Thornhill, was that of its own hall, 4th April, 1834, and they have subsequently planted the foundation-stone of the new parish church of Morton, 11th May, 1840; the Cample viaduct, 10th Sept., 1847; the keystone of the Cample viaduct, 24th March, 1849; the Thornhill railway station-house, 7th June, 1850; the Union Bank at Thornhill in 1852; the parish school-house of Morton, 23rd Aug., 1864. Of the foundation-stones which the Lodge of Thornhill has aided in planting the following is a summary:—That of a church at Lochmaben, April, 1818; bridge at Annan, April, 1825; bridge over the river Milk at Lockerby, July, 1834; St. Mary's church, Dumfries, May, 1837; manse at Lochmaben, April, 1839; Caledonian railway station-house at Lockerby, May, 1847; Victoria bridge over the Clyde at Glasgow, March, 1851; bridge at Lockerby, July, 1851; bank at Lochmaben, May, 1852; new Poorhouse at Dumfries, July, 1853; Freemasons' Hall, Edinburgh, June, 1858; Wallace Monument at the Abbey Craig, near Stirling, June, 1862; new bridge over the Nith at New Cumnock, August, 1863; Mechanics' Institute at

Lockerby, January, 1865; Greyfriars' church, Dumfries, 1866; parish church, Penpont, 30th July, 1867; Museum, Thornhill, 22nd June, 1869; Royal Infirmary, Dumfries, 16th Sept., 1869; Royal Infirmary, Edinburgh 13th Oct., 1870. The following is a list of the present office-bearers of the lodge (January, 1874):—Douglas Dobie, R. W. Master; Andrew Glendinning, Depute Master; Joseph M'Caig, Past Master; Chas. Brown, Senior Warden; John Waugh, Junior Warden; Wm. Brown, Treasurer; Peter Brown, Secretary; David Hastings, Chaplain; Peter R. Brown, Senior Deacon; James Bennet, Junior Deacon; David Maxwell, Standard Bearer; Robert Corson, Senior Steward; James Graham, Junior Steward; Alexander Wallace, Inner Guard; Wm. Callander, Tyler; Proxy-Master, F. A. Barrow, Glasgow.

CROSS AND JAIL OF THORNHILL.

This cross was erected by Duke Charles in the year 1714, at the same time that the new line of road leading from Dumfries through Thornhill was constructed, chiefly at his own expense. He built, also, according to tradition, an inn, the house now occupied by Dr. Hoggan, and which has the inscription of 1714 upon its front. It was constructed principally from the stones of the Red House, built a little way to the south of Thornhill, in the holm land near the bridge leading to Templand farmhouse, by Sir William Douglas of Coshogle, and which had come into the possession of the Douglases of Drumlanrig when the barony of Morton was bought by the Earl of Queensberry in 1618. Duke Charles built at the same time a jail, which no longer exists, but which stood on the opposite side from the inn, where the stables of the George Hotel are now found. The place of execution was in the field now occupied by a nursery, and which is still known as the Gallows Flat, though only one felon is said to have been executed here.

ANTIQUITY OF THORNHILL.

Before passing from this village, it is interesting to know that it is mentioned under the appellation of *Thornhill* in a charter of George de Dunbar, Earl of March, passing the barony, or part of the barony, of Morton to James de Douglas, "dominus de Dalkeith" (Registrum Honoris de Mortoun, vol. ii., pp. 77-79), in the reign of David II. (1329-1370). The charter says :—" *Omnes et singulas terras nostras de Mortoun, Castrum ejusdem, et locum castri, parcum ejusdem, Erechemorton, debtoun, drumcork, et Thornhill, cum pertinenciis infra baroniam de Mortoun.*" It is curious to find a name which has all the appearance of being modern carried away back five hundred years, giving it thus the respectability of hoary age.

This charter is not dated, neither is another as to the Mill (Morton Mill) within the barony of Morton, which is granted by the same Earl to Sir James, " *molendinum nostrum infra Baroniam de Mortoun, cum multura et sequelis ejusdem, reddendo inde nobis et heredibus nostris dictus dominus Jacobus et heredes sui unum denarium argenti nomine albe firme apud Mortoun*" (vol. ii., 78). We are able to get an approximation to the dates, as there is a confirmation of the *first* mentioned by David II., characterized as "*donacionem illam et concessionem,*" which is dated at Melros on the 27th day——, in the fortieth year of his reign (1369).

The death of John, Earl of Moray, at the fatal battle

of Durham, 17th Oct., 1346, without issue, had caused, as we have already stated, his large estates, and among them the barony of Morton, or the half of it, to pass into the possession of his sister, Black Agnes, who was married to Patrick de Dunbar, Earl of March.

Agnes, sister of George de Dunbar, and daughter of Black Agnes, was the first wife of Sir James Douglas, and it was near her remains, in the abbey of Newbotil, that he directed his body to be laid. "*Corpus meum sepeliendum in monasterio B. V. de Newbotyil juxta corpus quondam Agnetis mee.*" We are in this way able to see how the barony, or part of the barony, of Morton would naturally come as heirship into the Douglas family. George de Dunbar had a charter from David II. of the *half* of the baronies of "Tybris et Mortoun," which Patrick, Earl of March and Moray, and *Agnes* his spouse, had resigned, to be given out in his favour. This charter is dated 28th June, in the thirty-fourth year of the King's reign (1363).

UPPER NITHSDALE COMBINATION POORHOUSE.

The Poorhouse is situated about two miles from Thornhill, a mile from Thornhill station, and close to Gateleybridge quarry. It was built in 1854-55 for the use of nine parishes, whose proportionate interest is thus represented:—Closeburn, 12 billets or shares; Morton, 20; Durisdeer, 10; Sanquhar, 25; Kirkconnel, 15; Penpont, 10; Keir, 10; Glencairn, 12; Dunscore 12—in all, 126 shares or billets. It cost £5218 9s. 9d., borrowed from private parties, and was paid off by ten yearly instalments in 1864. The following table shows (leaving out shillings and pence) the proportions of this sum of

£5218 paid by the different parishes in the combination, viz. :—

Parishes.	Principal.	Interest.	Total.
Keir,	£351	£63	£414
Penpont,	351	63	414
Durisdeer,	351	63	414
Closeburn,	421	76	497
Morton,	702	127	829
Kirkconnel,	526	95	621
Sanquhar,	877	158	1035
Glencairn,	421	76	497
Dunscore,	421	76	497
Total,	£4421	£797	£5218

Equal to--per billet or share—
Of principal,   35
Of interest,   6

Total, ... 41

The average number of poor in the house has been as follows:—

Average maximum number of inmates, 45 in 1 year.
  ,,   minimum ,,   ,,   25 ,,
Number of inmates per last return,   27

The cost weekly of the maintenance of the inmates has much increased of late years; for last year, 16th May, 1873, it was 3/7 2-12ths, that including food, clothing, and medicine. This is the highest weekly average that it has ever reached, and it is not without interest to contrast it with the cost of maintenance per week for the first eight years. It has been caused by the increased cost of every article of food. The average number of paupers in the Poorhouse, and the cost of maintenance per week was as follows during the first eight years:—

			Number Dec.	Rate per Week.
For the year ended May 14,	1857,	16·389	3/6 5-12ths
,,	,,	1858,	24·197	3/3 1-12th
,,	,,	1859,	25·065	3/1 7-12ths
,,	,,	1860,	32·706	3/1 7-12ths
,,	,,	1861,	39·860	3/1 3-12ths
,,	,,	1862,	36·526	3/0 4-12ths
,,	,,	1863,	43·676	3/0 4-12ths
,,	,,	1864,	45·699	2/11 4-12ths

The house is well adapted for the purpose, being well supplied with every convenience necessary for such a body.

EMINENT PERSONS.

The Douglases of Morton.—There are two members of this family who deserve to be particularly noticed in this account of Morton, William Douglas, who inherited Fingland, in the Stewartry; and his son, Archibald Douglas, a distinguished cavalry officer.

William Douglas.—He is best known as the suitor of Annie Laurie of Maxwelton, in Glencairn, and the author of that pathetic lyric, "Bonnie Annie Laurie," in which he depicts her charms in such beautiful language.

> "Her brow is like the snaw-drift,
> Her neck is like the swan,
> Her face it is the fairest
> That e'er the sun shone on;
> That e'er the sun shone on,
> And dark blue is her ee;
> And for bonnie Annie Laurie
> I'll lay me doon and dee."

She was, however, obdurate to his passionate appeal, preferring Alexander Fergusson of Craigdarroch, to whom she was eventually married. William Douglas is said to have been the hero of the well-known song, "Willie was a wanton wag." Though he was refused by Annie, he did not pine away in single blessedness, but made a runaway marriage with Elizabeth Clerk of Glenboig, in Galloway, by whom he had four sons and two daughters. He was one of the best swordsmen of his time, and was quick in quarrel. He fought a duel with Captain Menzies of Enoch, which had nearly proved fatal. At the instigation of the Duke of Douglas he fought a noted professional swordsman, wounded and disarmed him, less, as the other maintained, by skill in fence than by Fingland's "fierce and squinting eyes." There is a tradition in the family that when the Duke of Douglas had, in a quarrel, stabbed his cousin, Captain Kerr, and was obliged to fly to the Continent, Fingland conveyed the Duke away under the guise of his servant.

General Douglas.—Archibald Douglas, son of the above William of Fingland, entered the army at an early age, and rose to the rank of lieutenant-general. His first regiment was the 4th Dragoons, of which he became lieutenant-colonel, 4th Feb., 1746. He was present at the battle of Dettingen, 26th June, 1743, having three horses shot under him, and one of his eyebrows shot away. The first brunt of the battle fell on the horse, who were hard pressed by the French cavalry, but the infantry of the allies stood firm and the battle was gained. In 1747 he was appointed aide-de-camp to the King, George II. On the 18th October, 1758, he obtained the colonelcy of the 13th Dragoons, and commanded that regiment at Minden, 1st August, 1759, and he was gazetted as major-general on the 15th September following. He was subsequently commander-in-chief of the forces in Ireland. General Douglas was elected M.P. for the county of Dumfries, first in 1762, and secondly in 1768. He died in 1778.

George Ferguson, A.M., LL.D.—Dr. Ferguson, though a native of Tynron, having been born about 1798, properly belonged to Morton, where he received his education at the parish school from Mr. Hamilton, who was a distinguished teacher in the early part of this century. He was appointed to the parish school of Dunscore in the year 1816 or 1817, which he retained for some time, but proceeding to the University of Edinburgh he distinguished himself so as to attract the attention of the late Professor Pillans. By his recommendation he became tutor in the family of Mr. Loch, M.P. for the Wick Burghs, and in 1824, when the Edinburgh Academy was instituted, he was appointed one of the classical masters. There he continued till 1847, when he succeeded to the Professorship of Humanity in King's College, Aberdeen, and on the union of King's College with Marischal College he retired on a pension. He died in 1866. Dr. Ferguson was a distinguished classical scholar, and edited many school books, which have proved by their scholarship so useful that they have never yet been superseded.

His elder brother, Alexander, A.M., was also an eminent teacher, having commenced his career at a small school at Burnhead, in the parish of Dunscore, in 1814. In 1818 he was elected parochial schoolmaster of Mouswald, and in 1823 he was transferred to the parish school of Dryfesdale at Lockerby, where he continued till 1873, thus completing fifty years' service in that parish. In 1868 a jubilee entertainment was given to him by his old pupils, to mark their high appreciation of their obligations to him.

His third brother, Robert, A.M., became minister of Fenwick, in Ayrshire, and in 1843, leaving the Church of Scotland, was appointed to St. David's Free Church, Edinburgh. He died in 1866.

His fourth brother, James, M.D., received the earlier part of his education at the parish school of Morton, and afterwards at the Edinburgh Academy under his brother. He entered the University of Edinburgh as a medical student, and after completing the ordinary course took the degree of M.D., but not liking the medical profession, and being an excellent classical scholar, especially in Greek, he started a classical seminary in Aberdeen, known as the West-End Academy, and for many years was very successful. He died when comparatively a young man in 1864. He edited the first and second books of Xenophon's Anabasis, with Vocabulary, which is still popular among teachers. He published also "Grammatical Exercises on the moods, tenses, and syntax of Attic Greek, with Vocabulary."

His younger brother, John, is now Free Church minister at Barr, in Ayrshire. This family is a fair specimen of what the old parochial schools instituted by the Church of Scotland could produce, and I trust that the change that has lately taken place may not reduce Scotland to the dead level of commercial clerkships.

Alexander Reid, A.M., LL.D.—Dr. Reid was born in Thornhill about the end of last century, and after being educated partly at Morton parish school, and partly at

Wallace Hall Academy, proceeded to the University of Edinburgh. He was for many years a teacher in the Circus School, Edinburgh, and subsequently founded the school called the Edinburgh Institution, which was for a long time highly successful. He compiled a valuable English pronouncing dictionary, which still continues to be an authority in the schools of Scotland. Dr. Reid published several elementary books on English Grammar, Composition, Geography (Modern, Ancient, and Physical), which are still used in schools.

"*Old Mortality.*"—Another person connected with this parish, who has earned for himself a niche in the temple of fame, though he is not a native of it, is Robert Paterson, better known as "Old Mortality." He was the tenant of Gateleybridge quarry for many years, and his history is full of interest, from having suggested the novel of "Old Mortality" to Sir Walter Scott. His history is thus told by his son Robert, in a short memorial addressed to Joseph Train, the Galloway correspondent of Sir Walter:—" My father, Robert Paterson, was the youngest son of Walter Paterson of Haggieshall, in the parish of Hawick, and within less than a mile of the town. His mother's name was Margaret Scott. He was the youngest of a numerous family, and his elder brother Francis had taken a lease of Corncockle freestone quarry from Sir John Jardine of Applegarth. He built a dwelling-house for himself at a place called Caldwell, beside the quarry, and very near the old Spedlins Castle, which still remains entire and in tolerable habitable repair. Here he got good encouragement in his business as a freestone mason and stone-cutter, and brought up his family in a respectable way. My father was by this time come to the time of life that was proper to choose some way of doing for himself, and he served an apprenticeship with his brother Francis, and continued with him as a journeyman for some considerable time afterwards. My mother's name was Elizabeth Gray, daughter of Robert Gray, gardener to Sir John Jardine of Applegarth; the place of his residence, Jardine Hall, close by the east side of Annan water, and within loud speaking of Spedlins Castle, on the west side, and in which my mother and her parents dwelt. My mother was cook to Sir Thomas Kirkpatrick of Closeburn in the year 1740, still memorable for frost; and I think not long after that year my father and mother had been married. Soon after this Sir Thomas took a lease for them from the Duke of Queensberry of the freestone quarry of Gateleybridge. Here my father built a substantial and comfortable house for himself and family, with ground that kept one horse and one cow, at a moderate rent, in the parish of Morton, near Thornhill. In the year 1745, as the army of Prince Charles Stewart was on their retreat from England, their road was through Thornhill; but a party of them—and I think it had only been a straggling or foraging party —came to my father's house. They took my father prisoner along with them. My mother got a very great fright. She, no doubt, thought she would never see him more; but they took him only a mile or two, asked many questions, and made him show them a smithy where they could get their horses shod, and then set him safely at liberty. He had at this time two children. He had now got plenty of business as builder and hewer on the Duke's estate and for Sir Thomas, and employment for a number of men occasionally at least. At last he found that Galloway was a place destitute of freestone—and, as a consequence, of grave-stones—or any to work them.

After repeated trials of carrying grave-stones into Galloway and selling them, answered his expectations of a profitable concern. About this time one Sandy Rae, from somewhere in the Highlands, was frequently in the country in and about the parish of Morton as a wandering boy, friendless and nearly destitute of clothes. He was often admitted to a night's lodgings when he came that way to my father's house. After acquaintance he came to be employed to do an errand and other services he could do; and finding a considerable amount of sharpness in him, he gave him new clothes and made him an apprentice to himself. He learned the trade well. My father brought him along with him in several trips into Galloway, and sometimes my father would return and leave Rae to finish the stones. Some time about August, 1758, my father neglected to return to his family, and made but few remittances. His son Walter, when a boy about ten or twelve years of age, came into Galloway in quest of him, and with some difficulty found him out. He did not allow him to return, but put him to school, and afterwards learned him the trade of stone-cutter, in which he was expert. Sandy Rae settled in Galloway, in the parish of Crossmichael. He married, and had a family. There are two of his sons still alive—one a schoolmaster in Wigton, the other a surgeon in Gatehouse-of-fleet. In 1768 my father made us a visit, after an absence of ten years, brought us into Galloway, and took a house for us in the village of Balmaclellan, near which some of us resided ever since. As his business lay now entirely in the churchyards, it could not last long in one place, and it therefore behoved him to travel; and I believe there are few churchyards in Galloway, and especially in Wigtownshire, but he wrought in, and large portions of his handycraft are yet to be seen. When himself through age not so fit to travel as formerly, he kept a pony to carry him and his tools. He purchased his grave-stones at Dumfries, Locharbriggs quarry, or Whitehaven, as he found most convenient. In the year 1800, or 1801, he went to Dumfries, in order to get some grave-stones at Locharbriggs quarry. After stopping there five or six days, and all that time complaining of a pain in his bowels, he set out for Bankend, in the parish of Caerlaverock, where there is a freestone quarry, and where the stones would be made much more convenient for water-carriage, as I suppose they were intended for Wigtownshire. He was got within a very short distance of the house of Bankend, where some persons at the door observed him approaching, apparently in an uneasy posture, or some rather strange appearance about him. While they were looking at him, he fell from the horse. They came to him immediately, the white pony standing beside him. They carried him into the house. He was able to speak, and told who he was, and where his sons lived. He was born in 17(12?), died on the 29th January, 1801."

It will be observed that his son does not refer to his Covenanting propensities as the reasons which led to his irregular and wayward mode of life. The air of romance which Sir Walter Scott has contrived to throw over his character is somewhat dimmed. Sir Walter was anxious to have erected a stone to his memory, but though he made an attempt to find out the place of his burial, he was unsuccessful. This, however, has now been accomplished by the Messrs. Black of Edinburgh, who possess the copyright of the *Waverley Novels*. A neat memorial stone has been erected by them in Caerlaverock churchyard, with the following inscription:—

ERECTED
TO THE MEMORY
OF
ROBERT PATERSON,
THE
Old Mortality
OF
SIR WALTER SCOTT,
WHO WAS BURIED HERE,
FEBRUARY, 1801.

Why seeks he here with unwearied toil,
  Through Death's dim walks to urge his way,
Reclaim his long-asserted spoil,
  And lead oblivion into day.

This is not the only one to the memory of "Old Mortality," as the following is found in the churchyard of Balmaclellan, which contains, however, some dates which do not agree with the statement of his son Robert. This memorial stone was erected in 1855 by Thomas Paterson, who is still alive, son to the above Robert. The following is a copy of the tombstone in Balmaclellan churchyard:—

TO THE MEMORY OF

ROBERT PATERSON, Stone-engraver, well-known as "Old Mortality," who died at Bankend of Caerlaverock, 14th Feb., 1801, aged 83. Also of Elizabeth Gray, his spouse, who died at Balmaclellan village, 5th May, 1785, aged 59. Also, of Robert, their son, who died 30th April, 1846, aged 90. Also, of Agnes M'Knight, his spouse, who died 5th August, 1818. Also, of John, their son, who died 29th January, 1810, aged 13. Also, of Alexander, who died at Wakefield, 26th October, 1837, aged 42. Also, of Robert, their son, who died at Liverpool, 3rd February, 1865, aged 65.—Erected by Thomas Paterson, 1855.

This Thomas Paterson married Jane Murray, a grandniece of the famous Dr. Alexander Murray, the linguist, and her issue is a son, Robert, and a daughter. "Old Mortality" had five children—three sons, Walter, Robert, and John; two daughters, Margaret and Janet.

"Old Mortality" is not forgotten by the old people of Balmaclellan. One old lady, eighty-three (1870), Mrs. Janet Clement M'Lellan, remembers seeing him just once. Her father, who lived at the present post-office, across the road from their (the Patersons') house, brought them out to see the old man. He was a gey, droll-looking auld body. He was riding on a wee bit white pony, had on an auld hat hanging over his lugs, and the pony was ganging unco slow. She never saw him but once. She was then a young bit lassie. She knew Robert Paterson, late shoemaker here. "Robert was not very well liked—bad-tempered, but very honest and truthful." She says that they had all dure tempers.

In regard to the arrest of "Old Mortality" by the Highlanders, there are some additional particulars handed down by tradition in the parish of Closeburn, which give point to the anecdote, and seem not unlikely to be correct, as they are in keeping with his character. It is stated that when the Highlanders reached Gateleybridge, they entered the house of Robert Paterson and became very insolent to his young wife, who sent a message to her husband at the quarry that the Highlanders were plundering his house. On his arrival he showed no fear, telling them that they had been served right, and that they could expect nothing but calamity, as the hand of the Almighty was against them, and all the bloody house of Stuart. This excited their wrath, and they carried him off prisoner, keeping him under arrest till they reached Glenback, when he contrived to escape.

As stated above, Robert was a respectable shoemaker in Balmaclellan, dying in 1846 at the age of ninety. Walter was, like his father, a stone-mason, and I find a tombstone in Balmaclellan churchyard to the following effect:—

"Erected to the memory of Walter Paterson, stone-engraver, who died at the Holm of Balmaclellan, on the 9th May, 1812, aged 63 years, and Mary Lock, his wife, who died at Balmaclellan Kirk, on the 16th September, 1819, in the 69th year of her age.

"As a tribute of affection, gratitude, and respect by their sons Nathaniel and Walter, ministers of the Free Church of Scotland."

In regard to these affectionate sons it may be stated that Nathaniel was minister of Galashiels, in Selkirkshire, but left the Church of Scotland at the secession of 1843, and was, till his death in 1871, Free Church minister of St. Andrew's, Glasgow. He is the author of a very popular work, "The Manse Garden," and was Moderator of the Free Church in 1850. His brother Walter, sometime a professor in a Prussian University, was minister of Kirkwood, in Peeblesshire, but seceded in 1843. He is author of the "Legend of Iona."

Round John, son of "Old Mortality," who emigrated to America, there gathered a strange romance, which has only lately been dissipated. He was believed to be a John Paterson, who rose to be a wealthy merchant of Baltimore, and whose daughter, Elizabeth, married Jerome Bonaparte, youngest brother of Napoleon I., and subsequently King of Westphalia. The widow of Robert, brother of Elizabeth, became Marchioness of Wellesley, and, if this had been a correct statement, it would have brought "Old Mortality" in connection with the late Duke of Wellington. No doubt there is a curious mingling of the families of the human race, where we find rich and poor often jostle each other in closest proximity, but in this case it is altogether a myth; and the question has been lately settled by the great-grandson of "Old Mortality," the son of Dr. Paterson, the Free Church minister of St. Andrew's, Glasgow. He happened to be in Baltimore, and, naturally interested in the question, was courteously permitted to examine the will of Madame Jerome's father. From this document, which is prefaced by a short autobiography of the testator, it appears that Madame Bonaparte's father's name was William; that he was a native of Tanat, county Donegal, Ireland, and brought up in connection with the Episcopal Church. After settling in Baltimore, he had seven sons and one daughter, whom he mentions under the name of Betsy, and as the wife of Jerome Bonaparte. There seems to be no reason to doubt the statement made in the will, especially in view of the scanty evidence for the truth of the story so long and so widely circulated. This statement is found in a volume lately published (1874), "Letters to his family by Nathaniel Paterson, D.D.," with a Memoir by the Rev. Alexander Anderson, West Free Church, Helensburgh.

Janet Douglas Fraser.—This old lady, though of an

eccentric character, would have made some impression on the sands of time if she had received a proper education and been regularly trained. Even in her uncultivated state there were gleams of cleverness in her sayings and doings which attracted the attention of her neighbours. She was a native of Closeburn, one of that family of which it was said, "that so long as the Kirkpatricks were proprietors of Closeburn, so long should Frizzels (Frasers) be tenants there." When the adherents of the Free Church had some difficulty in procuring a central site for their church, she presented them with a piece of ground on which Virgin Hall is now built, and the deed of gift was expressed in these quaint words, in her own handwritting: "The deed of gift is to be as free from henceforth to the Free Church as I wish the heavenly mansion to be made to me, and to last the property of the Free Church while Sun, Moon, and Stars endure.—Signed by my hand this 18th of August, 1845." Janet was an authoress, having written "Poems on Religious Subjects," two small volumes, 1853; "Predestination, Election, on God's decrees, and the Restoration of the Creature," two poems; "The Proverbs of Solomon in Metre." She died in Thornhill, 30th July, 1855, aged seventy-six years.

BURNS IN MORTON.

William Stewart, as we have already stated, removed in 1793 from Closeburn Castle to the farm of Laught, in the parish of Morton, and there Burns continued to cultivate his society. Once while he was there, "Sandie Spence," as he was called, the ploughman of Mr. Stewart, one of whose children had become seriously ill, was sent for by his wife to be present at the death of his child. The father proceeded to his master, whom he found to be enjoying himself with Burns, and begged that he would come and offer up a prayer for his child. To this Mr. Stewart at once assented, and said to Burns, "Come awa wi' me." When they entered the house, Mr. Stewart asked Burns to offer up a prayer, with which request he at once complied, and it was so affecting, and spoken in such earnest and heartfelt terms, that the mothers around, who had come in to comfort the afflicted parents, wept audibly. The grandson of Alexander Spence is now the respected tenant of Blackpark, in Holywood parish.

The late Professor Gillespie of St. Andrews, and of whom I have already spoken in my account of Closeburn, tells another anecdote of Burns in connection with Morton. The Professor remembered seeing the poet on a fair-day in August, 1790, at Thornhill, where a poor woman, Kate Watson, was in the habit on that day of keeping a shebeen for her drouthy neighbours. "I saw the poet," he says, "enter her door, and anticipated nothing short of an immediate seizure of a certain greybeard and barrel, which, to my certain knowledge, contained the contraband commodities our bard was in search of. A nod, accompanied by a significant movement of the forefinger, brought Kate to the doorway, and I was near enough to hear the following words distinctly uttered: 'Kate, are you mad? Dinna you know that the supervisor and I will be in upon you in the course of forty minutes. Good bye t'ye at present!' I had access to know that the friendly hint was not neglected. It saved a poor widow from a fine of several pounds for committing a quarterly offence, by which the revenue was probably subject to an annual loss of five shillings."

DR. GRIERSON'S MUSEUM.

There is a valuable museum in Thornhill, belonging to Dr. Grierson, and which contains a large number of curiosities, not only collected in Dumfriesshire, but sent to him by his friends from all parts of the world. He has been at great pains in securing antiquarian objects that are occasionally discovered in Upper Nithsdale, and which, unless there is such a place of deposit, would be either lost altogether, or perhaps never heard of, being thrown aside as worthless by the ignorant. Dr. Grierson advocates the founding of such collections in every district, and we quite agree with his views on this point. Such places are the means not only of saving objects of interest to the antiquary and naturalist, but have the effect of exciting a taste among the people, especially among the young, for scientific and antiquarian pursuits. This is the idea which Sir John Lubbock has advocated with much eloquence, and it is no doubt the right light in which we should regard it. A museum of this kind is not a mere collection of strange, old-world objects, but every item has a peculiar history that sets the mind of even the unlearned to meditate sometimes on the curious works of God, and sometimes on the kind of world that was around the spot in which he lives, thousands of years ago. Even the dullest boor, when he looks on the stone celts, or even the rude querns with which our ancestors ground their oats, cannot but draw a contrast between those primitive times and the high civilization which now surrounds him. Dr. Grierson has, by great perseverance, succeeded in making his noble objects to be appreciated by the whole district in which he resides, and nothing of any moment is now found in Upper Nithsdale that does not come into his possession.

At the meeting of the British Association, and of the Social Science Congress, held in Glasgow in 1874, he brought forward his views with much earnestness, and received the cordial sympathy of the leading men in science and social improvement. The progress of Dr. Grierson's museum shows how much can be done to diffuse a taste for objects of science among the people, and especially among the young. No object, as we have stated, that is strange or that has any unusual appearance, if discovered within the district, but finds its way to the museum. Not only is this the case, but the museum has many other tributaries than its native rills. Youths, who have been imbued with a taste for natural objects in the early days of the museum, though scattered in distant lands, never forget the lessons they have learned from Dr. Grierson. They send from time to time specimens of anything curious which they find, to add to the interest of the collection in their native vale.

One character of the museum which ought to be specially noted is its identification with the people, and the desire to bring together all that possesses a local interest—the old baptismal basin of the parish—the old village drum—George Menzies' bugle—Jenny Fraser's chair—old spinning wheels—cups and saucers that belonged to great great-grandmothers, and then come the priceless relics of Robert Burns, such as the poem of the "Whistle," as it first came from his pen—an excise permit filled up and signed by Burns—glasses and various other objects once handled by the poet—a portion of the flooring of Mossgiel and, alas! a portion of the bed on which he died. Then there are relics of what pertained to his history—an oil painting of his widow, once the "Bonnie Jean," and still in the portrait comely— almost all the photographs and facsimiles that have been made of his poems and other writings. When Scotland repented of her neglect of her bard, and set about to erect a mausoleum to receive his dust, Mr. Hunt of London supplied the plans and drawings. These original plans and drawings are in the museum, and there is an autograph letter of Sir Walter Scott, dated 1822, declaring Burns to be "The Great National Poet." Then there is a cast of the skull, and surmounting this and the other relics of Burns is a cross formed from a splinter that fell from the coffin of Burns as it was being deposited in the Mausoleum. There are several relics of the Covenanters, and a number of very old bibles, several of which are in black letter, the date of the oldest being 1563. Need we mention autographic letters of noted individuals, besides many ancient deeds and other manuscripts, with a series of newspapers, dating so far back as 1705?

In fact the local relics are too numerous to be recorded, but we cannot in loyalty omit to mention a cast from the mould that was taken of the skull of King Robert Bruce, which was obtained many years ago, when his tomb was opened at Dunfermline.

The gallery of the museum is devoted to the works of man's hand, divided into works of art, manufactures, and antiquities. The latter department is specially interesting, beginning, as it does, with the earliest period—the stone period of antiquaries. Then we have stone celts, not only those found in the south of Scotland, but from distant lands, showing how like is the early working of untutored man when placed in similar circumstances. Then come the bronzes, that would seem to overlap and to have succeeded to the age of stone, prior to the sterner age of iron, which was not obtained from refractory ore till the blast of Vulcan's furnace made it yield. Iron succeeded bronze, and in the museum are numerous warlike weapons, which, from their rude and primitive form, would seem to be among the first productions of Tubal Cain, or Vulcan's trials of the metal. As men found out many inventions, the forging of iron weapons was improved, until war produced the skilfully and elegantly formed weapons, inlaid with silver and gold, many of which are in the museum. Dresses, and objects of personal ornament, domestic utensils, all such are more or less represented, besides some objects of high art in porcelain and crystal. The industrial series of specimens is being rapidly added too. The collection of coins and medals is considerable, though from want of glazed cases they cannot be exhibited.

By an ingeniously constructed winding-stair the gallery communicates with the ground-floor, on which and on the walls are arranged the natural history collections. It may be noted that the gallery is supported by six oaks as brought from the forest, being among the last of the natural woods of Nithsdale. They are adorned by heads of deer and other animals, and among them the most remarkable is the skull of the ancient ox, already mentioned in the description of the park of Drumlanrig. The specimen in the museum is one of the largest that has been found in the peat mosses of Scotland. There are numerous skulls of dogs and sheep, particularly of the black-faced ram, with curling horns of a gigantic size.

Among the birds are many rare species met with in the district. Among the fish there is an interesting series of specimens, formed by the late Mr. Shaw, of Drumlanrig, when engaged in investigating the natural history of the salmon and sea-trout. The reptiles are numerous, one snake measuring 20 feet in length, while a crocodile measures 12 feet. The collection of smaller animals is very perfect, special care being taken to have all the species met with in the district to be represented. The collection of fossils is considerable, as far as the local species are concerned, and there are specimens to illustrate all the recognized formations in this country, and many from abroad. Among the fossils are many very fine specimens. Although scarcely fossil, we may mention the greater part of the bones of the great New Zealand bird, the *Dinornis*, or Moa, which must have had the colossal height of about 14 feet. The minerals are numerous, but here, as in other parts of the museum, there is a want of glazed cases to exhibit them. The vegetable productions from various countries are often of very strange forms—a large collection of woods, both in transverse and longitudinal sections. There is a nearly complete herbarium of British plants. One case may well be styled the "Chamber of Horrors," filled with monsters, lambs, calves, pigs, dogs, cats, chickens with double heads, double bodies, extra limbs, strange and abnormal forms, most unearthly-looking, all of which are objects of deep scientific interest to the initiated.

The grounds that surround the building are filled with trees, shrubs, and plants, some of which are rare. The mode in which the grounds are laid out may be called the natural style of gardening, where art conceals art. Such was the style of the garden of Pope at Twickenham. Large mounds have been thrown up, and hundreds of carts of rough stones afford location for the various forms of vegetation, among which some species of animals have been introduced, and have become naturalized, though all are harmless. The grounds also contain various objects of antiquity, and several ancient stone crosses. Lastly, we may mention the entrance, where there are four stone pillars, each with a remarkable stripe of a light colour running through their whole length. These stones were obtained at Gateleybridge quarry, where no such marked stones had before been found. It is difficult to give a geological explanation of these curiously marked stones, and no one has yet done so satisfactorily.

Although the building of the museum was commenced in June, 1869, it was not till July, 1872, that it was open to visitors. The building and the laying out of the grounds, the mounting and arranging of specimens, necessarily occupied a considerable time, more especially as much of the work was done by Dr. Grierson's own hands; indeed, everything that it was possible for himself to do. Since it was opened, a continued stream of additions has been flowing into the museum and grounds. The sources have been various. Many most interesting specimens have been sent by those who have gone from Thornhill and the neighbourhood to distant lands, while numerous specimens have been the result of searching at home after things previously unheeded or unknown. Strangers, also, have not been unmindful of the museum, when they returned to their own homes, and have sent contributions. Most willingly does Dr. Grierson give everything that he can spare from his store of duplicates to those who can make use of them, and this extends to the plants in the garden as well as to the objects in the museum, in which visitors on their *first* visit inscribe their names; though this is restricted to the first visit, up to September, 1875, the number of names entered is nearly four thousand. Some curious statistics might be made out as to the classes or condition to which the visitors have belonged, there being a preponderance of certain classes, and a comparative absence of others; but it would be invidious to particularize, as many who have not yet indicated an interest in the museum may yet come to do so.

Considering the small amount of attention given by the bulk of the people, and the small amount of science that is among them, the success of this institution has been beyond expectation, and we trust it will prove a means of raising the mental standard of the people. A society in connection with the museum, which is named the Society of Inquiry, has been well attended by young men in the district, and has been productive of the best results, stimulating inquiry, and giving the minds of the young a bent towards intellectual pursuits. The special feature of this society is original observation. Its first meeting was in September, 1872, and its meetings, which are monthly in the museum, have been continued with little or no intermission up to the present time.

The following document was deposited in the memorial stone when the foundation of the building was laid: —"Unto them who shall live in the ages of the future, and into whose hands this writing may come, know that the building in which this is deposited was erected with the view of being an auxiliary to education, and to promote in the minds of the people a taste for intellectual pursuits—one of the means for that end being a museum of the works of nature and art. The building was erected by Thomas Boyle Grierson, from money saved by him while in the practice of medicine in the village of Thornhill and surrounding district, and the collections in the museum were formed by him. Walter Francis Montague Douglas-Scott, fifth Duke of Buccleuch and seventh Duke of Queensberry, granted the land on which to build, together with stone. The memorial stone was laid with masonic honours, in presence of the people, on the twenty-second day of June, in the year of our Lord one thousand eight hundred and sixty-nine, by Samuel Sibbald, Master of St. John's Lodge of Freemasons of Thornhill. The architect was Charles Howitt, and the contractor and builder was John Black. May the God of our fathers, our God, the God of every succeeding generation, grant His protection, guidance, and aid; and may all that is done be in His name and to His glory. Written by my hand, T. B. Grierson." It is only right to add that Dr. Grierson is most liberal in regard to admission to his museum and grounds, ready to receive with the utmost kindness and patience all who present themselves—young and old, rich and poor;—willing also to pour out from his well-stored mind the knowledge which he has been gradually accumulating for many years. The museum is open to all gratis from one o'clock to evening on Saturdays, when the sons of labour are supposed to have most leisure, while the payment of a small sum on other days enables all to have entrance.

APPENDIX.

No. I.

QUEENSBERRY ESTATE.

SIR WILLIAM DE DOUGLAS, FIRST BARON OF DRUMLANRIG.

1388.—He received the barony of Drumlanrig from his father, who fell at Otterburn in 1388.

1412.—Confirmation of this gift by James I.

SIR WILLIAM, SIXTH BARON OF DRUMLANRIG.

1492.—A merkland in Humbie, and a merk or the third of a merk in Crairie, from Lyndesay of Crairie, a feudatory of Sir William.

1500.—Lands of Dalgarno town and Land Croft, making 10 merks (O.E.): 40 shilling more lying in the east part of the same town of Dalgarno, from Adam de Kyrkepatrick of Pennersax, and grandson of Sir Thomas of Kylosberne, in 1423.

1502.—Three merks of Maccumflat (O.E.), in the barony of Drumlanrig, from Kirkpatrick of Maccumflat.

1506.—Twenty shilling land of Dalgonar; 20 shilling of Powgoun (Polgown); 20 shilling of Douchra; 20 shilling of Dowrochack; 40 shilling of Glenmannoch (Glenmanna) ; 50 shilling of Dowzarne; and 4 libland of Woodend, Corlynstane, Little Dunduff, with the 2 merks (O.E.) of Craylay, from Campbell of Wester Loudon, the son and heir of Campbell of that Ilk.

1507.--The 5 merkland of Ardoch: 20 shilling land of Nether Crairie ; and one merk (O.E.) of Humbie, from William Crichton of Ardoch.

1509.—The Tower of Tybris, with the mayns and mill; the lands of Glengarrock, Auchengassel, Auchynbany, Dabbillay, Clauchyngar, and Knockbayn; lands of Penpont, with the mill; and the lands lying on Schar and Schynell croft, Castle Moat of Tybris, reserved in original grant by the Earl of March—all these from William Maitland of Lethington.

1512.—Lands of Glencorse and Dalquharzen (afterwards Drumfadzen), from Peter Denom of Crikan.

SIR JAMES, SEVENTH BARON OF DRUMLANRIG.

1533.—The lands of Craigenbaith (afterwards Craigmay), in the stewartry of Kirkcudbright, from the Crown.

1540.—The 10 merkland of Upper Garroch, in barony of Tibbers; 6 merkland of Glenym; the 5 merks of Dalpeddar; the 20 shilling land of Powgoun; and the merkland of Dalgonar—all in the barony of Drumlanrig, and redeemed at this time from Menzies of that Ilk.

1544.—The Castle, Moat of Tybris, and two acres of ground belonging to it, from John Maitland of Auchengassel, the son-in-law of Sir James.

1545.—Part of Schanlokfute and Deizar.

1552.—The lands of Kirkhope and Whitecamp, from Patrick Hamilton of Shawfield.

1557.—The merkland of Polvadach (O.E.), in the barony of Grenan, in the stewartry of Kirkcudbright, from Alexander Stewart of Garlies.

1562.—Half the barony of Mouswald, and half the lands of Raffelgill, from Janet, eldest daughter of Simon Carruthers of Mouswald, and her husband Rorison, of Barndennoch, in Glencairn.

1573.—The 40 shilling land of Glenmaid (O.E.), in the barony of Dalswinton from Roger de Kyrkepatric of Ross.

1573.—The lands of Ross, in barony of Kirkmichael, viz.:—The lands of Knock, Auchenskew, Meikle Holm, Dalfebil, Nether Garvel, and Ross, from the Crown, by forfeiture of Earl Bothwell.

1573.—The 20 shilling land called Templeland, in stewartry of Annandale, from William Johnstone of Elschieshiells.

1573.—The third of the 20 shilling land (O.E.) of Redhall, in the same stewartry, from William Johnstone.

1573.—The 10 lib. land (O.E.) of Carruthers, Dounanby, Kirtleclock, in the same stewartry, from the Crown, by forfeiture of Earl Bothwell.

SIR JAMES, EIGHTH BARON OF DRUMLANRIG.

1587.—The 10 lib. land of Almorines, in the stewartry of Kirkcudbright.

1589.—The whole of the above lands incorporated into one barony, called the barony of Drumlanrig.

1589.—5 merkland of Airds, and 5 merkland of Auchendolly, in barony of Crossmichael; patronage of the parish church of Glencairn, parsonage and vicarage, from Douglas of Penzierie.

1591.—The £20 land of Penersax with the churches (Acta Parl. iv. 90).

1606.—The 13 merks and half merk of Branrig; 13½ merks of Mitchellslacks; the 8 merks of Tibbers, with fishing and other dependencies; the 2 merks of Malloch-ford; the 4 merkland and mill of Balgrays; the 2 merks of Balgray hills; the 3 merks of Auchenwraith; the 6 merkland and manor of Auchengassel; 6 merks of Glenfravoch and the lands of Whitehill and Clongar; those of Farding-Allan and Auchconey; the 40 shilling land and mill of Clauchan Holms; 5 merkland of Auchinbrack; 6 merkland of Mid-Schynelhead; and the lands of Craigencoon, Denary, Benan, Killiewarren, and Corfarden, with the mills, woods, fishings, and other appurtenances, from John Maitland of Auchengassel.

1606.—The lands of Cleughhead, in the barony of Tibbers, from the Rev. Robert Hunter of Sanquhar and his wife Marguerite Hamilton.

1609.—The lands of Locherben, Garrock, Gubhill, Knockenshang, and Birkhill, from John Maitland of Auchengassel.

1613.—The other half the barony of Mouswald from Janet, heiress to Marion Carruthers, her sister.

Patronage of the parish church of Penpont, parsonage and vicarage, a free gift from the Crown.

WILLIAM, FIRST VISCOUNT OF DRUMLANRIG, AND AFTERWARDS EARL OF QUEENSBERRY, VISCOUNT DRUMLANRIG, AND LORD DOUGLAS OF HAWICK AND TIBBERS.

1619.—The barony of Morton, containing the mains of Morton, with the mill and mill lands, and the castle, tower, and manor; the lands of Erismorton, Whitefauld, Gallowflat, Halgill, Dabton, Carronhill, Drumcork, Broomrig, Thornhill, Upper and Nether Laught, Gallowbridge, Upper Kirkland, and Langmyre, with a proportionate part of the common called Morton Moor, and the woods, salmon-fishings, the lands of Bellybucht and Drumshinnoch, from Sir William Douglas of Coshogle.

1633.—The church lands of Morton. Parts of the barony of Morton called Cowl and Mortonholm.

1633.—Upper and Nether Dalveen, Gateslack, Halfpennyland (Hapland), with mill of Durisdeer; the merkland of Muirhouse; 2 sixteenth parts of the church lands of Durisdeer, from Douglas of Dalveen.

1634.—The church lands of Kirkbryde and mill, Coshogle, Ingliston and Anniston, otherwise Collin and Chapelhill, Thirstane, from Douglas of Dalveen.

1636.—Ashtrees, in the barony of Lag, from M'Lellan of Nether Mill; Margarady, in the the barony of Glencairn, from Lag.

1636—5 merkland of Auchensow, with the corn and wauk milns thirled to the same; the 6 merkland of Auchengreach; the 5 merkland of Castle Gilmour and Muirhead; and the 4 merks of Upper and Middle Dalpeddar, from Alexander M'Math.

1639.—The whole barony of Sanquhar, containing the 8 merkland of Glenmucklochs, the 2 merks of Farding, the 3 merks of Guffockland, 6 merks of Knockengig, and the 3 merks of Corsenook, with the patronage of the parish, and of all chapels and churches thereto belonging; Ryehill, from William, first Earl of Dumfries.

JAMES, THE SECOND EARL OF QUEENSBERRY, VISCOUNT DRUMLANRIG, ETC.

1641.—The lands of Kyninmount, Locherwood, Muirhouse, Cummertrees, Brydekirk, Dalbank, with the fishings, lands, and mill of Dornock; the 10 merkland of Torduff; 23 merkland of Middlebie; 10 lib. of Lus; 21 lib. of Kirkconnel; 42 lib. of Rokilhead, Kendilhead, Holmshaw, and Cogry; the 5 merks of Marjorybank; 20 lib. of Auldcats and Belorchard; 5 merks of Todhillmuir and Redhead, and the 20 merks of Kirkpatrick with the 20 merks of Pettynane, in the shire of Lanark, and the patronage of the several churches of Dornock, Middlebie, Lus, and Kirkconnel; Templelands of Torthorwald, from Sir Robert Douglas, afterwards Lord Belhaven.

1641.—Birks, Cleuchfoot, Knowe, Auchennaught, 6 merks of Auchenbenzy, and the 20 shilling land of Eightcrosses.

1666.—Lands of Barpark, Maynes, Kill and Ullyside, the two hills, Upper and Nether, the two Drumbayensies, Glenmady, Glenhead, Glenbarry, Freuchoch, Glengar, Crafford, Carvas, Burnfoot, Connelbuies, Kilside, Drumbuy, Glendog, Clarkleith, Duntercleugh, and Coig, called King's Coig, also Nether Coig, called Aiken's Coig, Coighead, Marchdyke, Glengover, Wanlockhead, Kinkenar, Cowrig, Boag, Browlies, Burnhead, Lockley, Auchuntaggart, the lands called Quarters, and those of Lochburn, Ryehill, Kirkland, Townhead, and both the Carcos.

The glebe and church lands of Morton, patronage of the parish churches of Morton, Kirkmichael, Kirkbryde, Glencairn, Durisdeer, Tynron, Garvell, Cummertrees, Ecclefechan, Terregles, Lochrutton, Kirkbayne, Cowend (Colvend), Caerlaverock.

WILLIAM, THIRD EARL AND FIRST DUKE OF QUEENSBERRY.

1673.—The 20 shilling land of Templand, in parish of Lochrutton, from Walter, Lord Torphichen.

1673.—Lands of Bus, Burn, Blairfoot, Riddings, and Drumshinnoch, in the barony of Morton, from William Douglas of Morton.

1679.—The lands of Stanebut and Burngrains, in the barony of Durisdeer, from Agnes Douglas, heir of Walter of Baitford and her husband, Fergusson of Craigdarroch.

1686.—The lands of Blackmyre, in parish of Penpont, with the manor and other pertinents, from Douglas of Stenhouse.

1693.—The lands of Auchensell, in the barony of Enoch; those of Lochrinery and Trosten, in the parish of Dalry, from William Douglas of Morton.

1693.—The lands of Balagan, Drumcruil, the Kirkland, manse, glebe, bank, and acres of ground in the Holm of Penpont and of Lochar Meadow, Boatford, and Glen-Whapenoch, in the same parish, from Hunter of Balagan; lands of Selthorn and Kirtlehead, in Annandale, from Henry Scott; a quarter of the church lands in the town of Durisdeer, from the Prebend of Durisdeer; the 8 lib. land of Denzery, Benans, and Corsfarding, in the barony of Drumlanrig, from Isabel and Mary Douglas. The castle of Niedpath, and a considerable estate in the county of Peebles, was bought from the Tweeddale family about this time.

1694.—The lands of Glencorse, in the parish of Closeburn, from the heirs of John Alison of Glencorse.

JAMES, THE SECOND DUKE OF QUEENSBERRY AND FIRST OF DOVER, ETC.

1698.—The estate of the Earl of Nithsdale, parts of it in Annandale, from Earl of Nithsdale.

1703.—The two merks of Porterstown and Porters Carse, the poundland of Bush, and the poundlands of Penfillan; the merkland of Penmuirty; the 2 lib. land of Beuchan; Upper Barndennoch, including Clariston, Farthing-James; the mill of Allanton; the patronage of the church of Keir, from William, Earl of Nithsdale.

1704.—The barony of Enoch, from Captain James Menzies, eldest son and heir of James Menzies of Enoch, at 24 years' purchase, besides a handsome allowance to old Enoch and his wife during their lives.

1707.—Lands of Turmuir, Manta-rig, Robert-Hill, and Tukesholm, in the parish of Dryfesdale, from Douglas of Dornock.

1708.—Barony of Airds in Tynron, along with Dalgarnock holm, Blawplain, Kirkbog, Rosehill, Cunningholm in Closeburn, from Sir Robert Grierson of Lag; and Peter Rae observes all his purchases were free, without restraint, and most just and equal.

CHARLES, THE THIRD DUKE OF QUEENSBERRY, ETC.

1714.—The lands of Arkland and Burn, in the parish of Penpont, from Douglas of Balagan.

1741.—Barony of Craigs, from the four daughters of Hairstens of Craigs. The 40 shilling land of Halliday hill, in the parish of Dunscore; the 20 shilling land of Grennan, otherwise Messinger's land, in the parish of Penpont, from Grierson of Lag.

1743.—Lands of Loch-house and Thornick, in the parish of Kirkpatrick-Juxta, from William Stewart.

1746.—Lands of Castle-Robert, in the parish of Kirkconnel, from Alexander Crichton of Gairland.

1752.—Lands and houses in Sanquhar.

1753.—The 10 lb. land of Newton and Paschgilfoot, in the parish of Moffat; lands of Bishop's Cleugh, in the parish of Dryfesdale, from Johnstone of Beerholm.

1753.—Windyhill, in Closeburn, from George Gillespie.

1754.—Parts of the barony of Gilston, in the stewartry of Kirkcudbright, from Carruthers of Inglestone. Parts of the barony of Amisfield, from Dalziell of Glenæ.

1758.—The lands of Templand, in Closeburn, from Riddell of Glenriddell.

1759.—The barony of Tinwald, from Charles Erskine of Barjarg.

1763.—The lands of Scotsbridge, in the parish of Middlebie, from William Bell of Scotsbridge.

LANDS ACQUIRED SINCE 1810 BY THE DUKE OF BUCCLEUCH AND QUEENSBERRY.

Parts of the Eccles estate in Penpont; Killiewarren, from John Gracie, and Stenhouse, in Tynron, from Mr. M'Turk.

Crairepark and Burnmouth, from James Veitch of Eliock, about twenty years ago.

Durisdeer town, from Matthew M'Kerrow, about 1868-69.

Kirkland, in Closeburn, in 1872, from Mr. Schlinder Edgar; Boatford, in Penpont, from John Maxwell.

Boggs and Stepends, in Penpont, from Pringle's Trustees, in 1871, through Mr. Hope Johnstone, who purchased, but who excambed with his Grace, getting some lands in Annandale for these lands which he had purchased.

Grovehill in Penpont, in 1875, from Mr. John Thompson.

Bank and Euchanhead, in Sanquhar, from James Veitch of Eliock, about twenty years ago. Portion of Sanquhar Moor, when divided, in 1830.

Subjects leased by Burgh of Sanquhar to M'Nab of Holm, and now part of the farm of Heuksland.

Carcoside, in Kirkconnel, from Alexander Hamilton, about twenty years ago.

Holm, in Kirkconnel, from Mr. M'Nab's representatives.

Auchenhessnane, in Tynron, from Samuel Moffat of Grovehill, about 1853.

It may be observed that his Grace holds the right of property, or *dominium utile*, of almost all the lands described, but in several instances he is only owner of the superiority, receiving small feu-duties and the usual casualties of the feus. Then, again, many pieces of land are let on building leases or feued, or it may be held as tenant-at-will for a small rent. Of course, the greater part of such cases must be that of houses and gardens.

No. II.

FAMILIES OF YORSTOUN AND EWART.

These families became possessed of a portion of the Tinwald barony in later times, and are now represented by Morden Carthew Yorstoun, Esq., of East Tinwald. The Yorstoun family is of Norwegian origin, being in early times found in the Shetland islands. The first of the name that I have met with is in the chartulary of Glasgow (vol. ii., p. 446), where two of this family are mentioned as witnesses to a charter of David Craufurde, burgess of Edinburgh, of date 16th July, 1484, in the reign of James III., granted to the Dean of Glasgow; "Domino Jacobo Yorkstoun cappellano et Willelmo Yorkstoun" (Yorkstoun), "Sir James Yorstoun, Chaplain (of Bishop of Glasgow), and William Yorstoun."

The founder of the family in Dumfriesshire, which has now extensive and highly respectable connections, was the Rev. Peter Yorstoun, minister of Kells in Galloway, who came from Shetland, and was educated at Glasgow University towards the middle of last century. In those primitive days it was a custom among divinity students, during the summer holidays, to make tours through the provinces, and to call at the manses on their way, where they were generally received with much kindness. It seems that Mr. Yorstoun had followed this custom, and in his tour through Galloway visited the manse of Kells, where he was kindly received by the Rev. Andrew Ewart, then far advanced in years, and on whom he made such a good impression that he was eventually appointed assistant and successor, marrying Miss Agnes Ewart, and succeeding to the full cure in 1754.

This arrangement was not agreeable to some of the congregation, who thought that they had not been sufficiently consulted, and the result was that a considerable number seceded, and attended a neighbouring church, separated from them by a stream, which required to be passed by boat. As soon as this became known to Mr. Yorstoun, he gave directions to the boatman to make no charge to the recusants, but to keep a note and he would pay the amount. This pleased the parties so much that they gave up their opposition and returned to the church. Mr. Yorstoun became a great favourite, and was deeply regretted when he was transferred to Closeburn on the death of the Rev. Mr. Lawson in 1763. Here he continued to officiate with much acceptance till his death in 1776, aged seventy, leaving four sons, Thomas, Andrew, James, and John.

Thomas, the eldest son, became an able medical practitioner in the upper vale of the Nith, and acted as chamberlain to William, fourth Duke of Queensberry, from 1797 to 1810. He married his cousin, Catherine, eldest daughter of James Ewart of Mulloch in the stewartry. He died at Thornhill in 1810, leaving one son and several daughters.

Andrew Yorstoun, second son, was appointed minister of Middlebie in 1774, and translated to Closeburn on the death of his father in 1776. Here he continued an efficient and much respected clergyman till his death in 1814. He married his cousin, Agnes Ewart, but died without issue.

James Yorstoun, third son, was minister of Hoddam, marrying Miss Currie, but died without issue.

John Yorstoun, fourth son, was first appointed minister of Morton, on the death of the Rev. Mr. Aitken in 1790, and then transferred to Torthorwald in 1808, dying without issue. He accumulated a considerable fortune, and bought from the Marquis of Queensberry the property of East Tinwald, which is now inherited by his relative, Mr. Morden Carthew-Yorstoun.

THE FAMILY OF EWART.

This family, with which the Yorstouns became closely connected by intermarriages, can be traced to a very early period. The following charter under the great seal of Robert II. (1370-1390) shows that they had their possessions in Annandale.

Robertus &c. Sciatis nos approbasse &c. donacionem illam et concessionem, quas Georgius de Dunbar, Com. March. et Dom. Vall. Annandie fecit et concessit Nigello Ewart de terris de Smallgyllis et de Syftinhowys cum pertinenciis in dict. Vall. de Ann. Ten. et hab. &c.

"Robert king of the Scots, &c. Know that we have approved of, &c., that gift and concession, which George de Dunbar, Earl of March and Lord of Annandale, made and granted to Nigel Ewart of the lands of Smallgyllis and Syftynhowys, with its pertinents, &c." Dated at Methven, 26th June, 1373.

The name continues to occur in charters from this time. Thus, in the Terregles charters (No. 45), of date 25th April, 1485, we find the name of John Ewart, chaplain. Coming down some hundred years, the Burgh Records and Register of Deeds in the stewartry of Kirkcudbright show an Andrew Ewart in Grange, between the years 1576 and 1591, who is the first of the family in the stewartry of whom we have notice. He was appointed treasurer to the burgh of Kirkcudbright in October, 1583.

His son, John Ewart in Grange, was admitted freeman of the burgh in 1601, filling the offices of councillor and bailie several times between 1611 and 1635. The estate of Mulloch in Galloway, which had belonged to the abbey of Dundrennan, and had passed with other parts of the property to the Maxwells of Terregles, came into the possession of John Ewart. His son, John Ewart, younger of Mulloch, was member of the Town Council in 1611, being bailie various times between that period and 1630. He was chosen provost in 1649, and repeatedly filled the office of chief magistrate.

John Ewart, son of the foregoing, was bailie in 1653, and in the month of May, 1663, when a riot took place in Kirkcudbright respecting a curate to whom the inhabitants were greatly opposed, the Privy Council appointed a Committee to make inquiries respecting it, and the result was that Lord Kirkcudbright, with John Ewart, John Carson of Senwick, and several others, were committed to prison in Edinburgh, some for being concerned in the riot, and others for not using proper means to quell the disturbance. The charge brought against John Ewart was, that having been chosen provost of the burgh, he had refused to act, and was thus chief cause of the disturbance. On the 13th August the Privy Council passed the following sentence upon him :—" Likeas the said Lords banish John Ewart forth of this realm for his offence, and ordains and command him forth of the same betwixt and this day twenty days, not to be seen therein at any time hereafter, without licence from his Majesty or the Council, at his highest peril." He, however, obtained a mitigation of his sentence. A new election of councillors and magistrates was ordered by the Privy Council at this time, and William Ewart, a younger brother of John, was chosen provost.

John Ewart, at the revolution in 1688, when the Presbyterian party was reinstated in powers, was again chosen provost, and represented the burgh in King William's first Parliament. He appears to have died about 1697, for Sir Andrew Home is then mentioned in the Burgh Records as having been elected Commissioner to Parliament in the room of the late John Ewart.

His eldest son, the Rev. Andrew Ewart, was the first minister of the parish of Kells after the Revolution. He married Agnes Grierson, daughter of John Grierson of Capenoch by Marion, daughter of Wm. Brown, son of the Rev. John Brown of Glencairn. This Agnes was aunt to Susanna, who married Sir Thomas Kirkpatrick, Bart., of Closeburn. Of their children Agnes, sixth daughter, married the Rev. Peter Yorstoun, who succeeded to Kells on the death of Mr. Ewart in 1754. His second son, James, succeeded to the property of Mulloch. John, his fourth son, became minister of Troqueer, whose eldest son, Joseph, was minister plenipotentiary for Great Britain at the Court of Berlin; and his second son, William, was an opulent merchant in Liverpool. The two sons of William represented Liverpool in Parliament, and one of them, William, was M.P. for the Dumfries Burghs from 1841 to 1865.

The representative of these two families in Dumfriesshire may be considered to be Morden Carthew-Yorstoun, Esq., of East Tinwald, who is descended in the female line from the Ewarts of Mulloch. He is the eldest son of Lieut.-General Morden Carthew, C.B., of the Madras Army, by his first wife, Jemima Borland, daughter of John Ewart, Esq., of Mulloch, b. 1832; married, 1854, Maynard Eliza Charlotte Rochfort, only daughter of Major-General Sir Archibald Bogle. Mr. Carthew-Yorstoun, who entered the Indian army in 1848, is Captain in the Scottish Borderers Militia; he assumed the additional name of Yorstoun in 1860, on succession to the East Tinwald estate. He contested with great spirit, though unsuccessfully, the Dumfries Burghs in 1874 in the Conservative interest.

No. III.

DOUGLAS VAULT.

1. Coffin with bones of the ancestors of the Dukes of Queensberry.
2. Coffin with inscription, "Isabella Douglas, Duchess of Queensberry." She was wife of William, first Duke, created 3rd November, 1684, and sixth daughter of William, first Marquis of Douglas.
3. Coffin with inscription, "Lord George Douglas." He was third son to William, first Duke, and died unmarried at Sanquhar, in July, 1693. His father presented the books belonging to this young nobleman to the library of the Faculty of Advocates at Edinburgh, where the presses containing them are thus inscribed:—

"*Libb. incomparabilis adolescentis D. D. Geo. Douglas, quos pater, Guil. Dux de Queensberrie, illo mortuo, Facultati Advocatorum donavit, hisce tribus for. inclusi.*"

4. Lead coffin with inscription, "James Douglas, Duke of Queensberry and Dover." He was born at Sanquhar Castle, 18th December, 1662, and educated at Glasgow University. He is the Union Duke, and died in 1711.

5. Coffin of Mary Boyle, Duchess of Queensberry and Dover, wife of the second Duke. She was fourth daughter of Charles, Lord Clifford, eldest son of Richard, Earl of Burlington and Cork. She died 2nd October, 1709.

6. Coffin inscribed "Charles, Duke of Queensberry and Dover, Marquess of Dumfriesshire and Beverley, Earl of Drumlanrig and Sanquhar, Viscount of Nith, Torthorwald, and Ross, Lord Douglas of Kinmount, Middlebie, and Dornock, &c., Baron Rippon, died October 12th, 1778, in the 80th year of his age." He and his Duchess having given offence by their patronage of the poet Gay, were forbidden to appear at Court by George II. He died in London, and was buried in this vault.

7. Coffin with the inscription, "Her Grace Catherine, Duchess of Queensberry and Dover, died July 17th, 1777, aged 76 years." Catherine Hyde was wife of Charles, third Duke, and second daughter of Henry, Earl of Clarendon and Rochester.

8. Coffin inscribed, "Henry Douglas, Earl of Drumlanrig, died October 19th, 1754." He was the eldest son of Charles, third Duke. After passing some weeks with his newly-married wife, Lady Elizabeth Hope, eldest daughter of John, second Earl of Hopetoun, at Drumlanrig, they proceeded to England, when Lord Drumlanrig, riding before the carriages, was killed by a discharge of one of his own pistols, near Bawtry, in Yorkshire, in his thirty-second year.

9. Coffin inscribed "Elizabeth Hope, Dowager Countess of Drumlanrig. Born March 1st, 1736; died April 7th, 1756." The Countess never recovered the shock which was occasioned by the sad death of her husband, and died two years afterwards.

10. Coffin inscribed "Charles Douglas, Earl of Drumlanrig, died October 24th, 1756, aged 30 years." He was second son of Duke Charles. Being in delicate health, he was obliged to leave Britain for a warmer climate, and was in Lisbon on November 1st, 1755,

when the fatal earthquake happened. Returning home next year, he died at Ambresbury, in Wiltshire.

11. A coffin inscribed, "*Natus* 18, *Mai Anno,* 1696, *October* 21, *decessit, Anno,* 1696." This is, no doubt, William, Earl of Drumlanrig, born May 18th, 1696, dying an infant seven months old.

12. "Lady Isabel, daughter of James, Duke of Queensberry; born August 11th, 1691, died July 17th, 1695." In the vault there are other lead coffins without any inscription; also, some small lead cases, measuring about 15 inches by 16; also, a round lead case 24 inches by 9; also, a large lead case, in which are portions of wood and three skull caps that have been cut off with a saw.

No. IV.

TOMBSTONES IN DALGARNOCK CHURCHYARD.

Here lys the corps of William Harkness, in Mitchellslacks, who died Sept., 1691, aged 45 years.

Also, his son Thomas, who died Nov., 1702, aged 21 years.

Here is interred the corps of Isabel Currie, spouse to William H., in Mitchellslacks, who died in Sept. 11, 1714, and her age 26 years.

Also, the corps of Catharine Ferguson, his spouse, who died March 30th, 1727, aged 33 years.

Also, the corps of Grizzel Ewart, his spouse, who died Nov. 15th, 1755, her age 61 years.

Also, here is interred the corps of William H., in Mitchellslacks, who died August 14, 1769, his age 80 years.

In memory of Janet Scott, daughter of Archibald Scott and Margaret Cranston in Hoprig, who died in Nov., 1782, aged 54 years.

Also, Thomas H., her husband, son of the late William H. and Catharine Ferguson, who died at Mitchellslacks, 25th May, 1797, aged 80 years.

James Harkness of Locherben narrowly escaped martyrdom. The more prominent of his descendants are here given.

Here lyes the body of James H., in Locherben, who died 6th Dec., 1723, aged 72 years.

Belo this stone his dust doth ly
Who indured 28 years
Persecution by tyranny—
Did him pursue with echo and cry,

> Through many a lonesome place,
> At last by Clavers he was taen—
>   Sentenced for to dy;
> But God, who for his soul took care,
> Did him from prison bring,
> Because no other cause they had
> But that he ould not give up,
> With Christ, his glorious King,
> And swear allegence to that beast,
> The Duke of York, I mean,
> In spite of all there hellish rage
> A natural death he died,
> In full assurance of his rest
> With Christ ieternalie.

Here lyeth Kettrin Hoatson, spouse to William H., Locherben, who died 20th May, 1744, aged 68 years.

Here lyes the body of William H., in Locherben, who died 23rd June, 1767, aged 70 years.

In memory of John H., in Holestain, who died the 3rd June, 1790, in the 80 year of his age.

Also, William H., of Holestain, son to the above John H., who died 12th Feb., 1811, aged 57 years.

Also of William H., son to the above William H., of Holestain, and Mid^m. on board H.M.S. *Owen Glendower*, who died 29th April, 1810, aged 19 years.

Also to the memory of John H., son of the late William H., in Holestain, who died 11th Nov., 1832, aged 53 years.

Here lyes Margt. H., who died June 12, 1770, in the 23 year of her age.

And also Isabell H., who died Aug. 7, 1770, in the 16 year of her age. Children to John H. and Margt. M'Cormick, in Holestain.

No. V.

AULDGARTH IN CLOSEBURN.

The earliest notice of this property, which belonged in early times to the barons of Briddeburgh, mentioned in a charter of Alexander II. (1214-1249), is found in a charter (18th August, 1581) to John Ferguson, nephew and heir of Brice Ferguson of Algarth, and Janet Kirkpatrick his spouse, of the lands of Algarth, Blackcrag. This was in the reign of James V. Some fifty years afterwards there is a charter of confirmation under the great seal of James VI., in favour of Roger and Robert Kirkpatrick of these same lands, dated 4th February, 1583. Then we have Janet Kirkpatrick, one of the daughters of Robert Kirkpatrick of Auldgarth, mentioned in a decree of exhibition in 1638, and a registered extract of revocation by the late Thomas Kirkpatrick in the following year (1639). Next, 27th April, 1669, there is the marriage contract of Thomas Kirkpatrick of Auldgarth with Elizabeth Ferguson of Isle in Dunscore, a relative of the Fergusons of Craigdarroch. In 1670 (2nd February) there is a contract of marriage between Janet Kirkpatrick and John Johnston of Gallobank, and the same year, 5th August, there is a retour of Thomas Kirkpatrick of Auldgarth as heir and grandson of Janet Kirkpatrick in the half of the 3 merkland of Auldgarth, viz., 1 merkland Auldgarth; 1 merkland of Blackcrag; 1 merkland of Netherhaugh, parish of Dalgarnock.

Part of the property seems then to have been sold and came into the possession of a neighbouring proprietor, as we find, 25th March, 1690, Retour of John Johnstone, son and heir of John Johnstone of Clauchrie, an adjoining farm in Closeburn, in the $2\frac{1}{2}$ and $10\frac{1}{2}$ penny land of the 5 merkland of Auldgarth, and the 40 penny land of Dunduiï.

Then, in 1699 (8th March), we have the retours of Helen Kirkpatrick, daughter and co-heiress of Thomas Kirkpatrick of Auldgarth, and John Pasley, son of Mary, daughter and co-heiress of Thomas Kirkpatrick, in the half of Auldgarth, extending to 3 merks, viz., 1 merk of Auldgarth, 1 merk of Blackcrag, and 1 merk of Netherhaugh, A. E.

In a deed by James, Commendator of Melrose, to infeft, 7th December, 1585, John, son and heir of Thomas Kirkpatrick of Alisland (a neighbouring property in Dunscore, and famed as the residence of Burns), we find one of the witnesses to be Roger Kirkpatrick of Auldgarth.

John Pasley in the above retours was son of the Rev. John Pasley, minister of Morton. In Durisdeer churchyard there is the following inscription on a tombstone:—" Here lyeth Robert Pasley, son to Mr. John Pasley, minister at Morton, and Eupham Scot, who died April, 1702, aged scarce two years. Also Mary Pasley, who died March, 1726, aged 4 months, and John Pasley, who died February, 1728, aged 13 months, and Thomas Pasley, who died the 14th of December, 1729, aged six years, children to John Pasley, son to the said Mr. Pasley."

No. VI.

KIRKPATRICKS OF ALISLAND AND FRIARS' CARSE.

At what period and which of the younger sons of the Kirkpatricks of Closeburn settled at Alisland there are no documents to show, but the family was here on the 13th September, 1465, as we find a commission by Cardinal Antonius, dated at Rome, confirming a charter from the monastery of Melrose to John Kirkpatrick of Alisland of the following lands of Dunscore, which belonged to the monastery, viz.:—The £36 land of Dalgonar, including the lands of Killielago, Bessiewalla, Over and Nether Bairdwell, Dempstertown, Over and Nether Lagan, Over and Nether Dunscoir, Ryddingnis, Edgarstoune, Mulliganstoune, Culroy (Kilroy), and Ferdinmottithill; and also the £4 land of Friars' Carse.

The commission is addressed to the Archdeacon of Sodor, the Dean of Restalrig, and the Provost of ——— in the diocese of St. Andrews, proceeding on the narrative that "Andrew the Abbot and the Convent of the Monastery of Melrose of the Cistercian order in the said diocese, in augmentation of their rental and for certain sums of money paid to them by John Kirkpatrick of Alisland, had granted these lands to him and the heirs-male of his body lawfully procreated or to be procreated, whom failing to his nearest and lawful heirs-male, bearing the name and arms of Kirkpatrick, whom failing to the eldest of the heirs-female whatsoever (without division) of the said John. The said lands to be held in fee farm of the said Convent of Melrose within the diocese of Glasgow, paying 46 merks, 6½ lib. stg., or 40 ounces of pure silver, at least 11 pence fyne, and doubling the same the 1st year of each entry to said lands.

"The said John Kirkpatrick and his heirs are bound to receive and entertain each year the Abbot, Convent and their horses, once in summer for three days and three nights, and the same length of time in winter in their dwelling of Friars' Carse, and to provide them with meat and drink and all other necessaries.

"Moreover, the said Abbot and Convent for the good and faithful service done and to be done by the said John Kirkpatrick and his heirs grant him and them the office of Baillery of the £36 land of

Dalgonar, with all the profits, &c., thereof, with power to hold Baillie Courts, paying yearly for said office one penny Scots of Blanch farm. Therefore grants confirmation to the above-named persons or any two of them to call for protection and to grant confirmation by Apostolical authority of all charters and letters in favour of said John Kirkpatrick. Given at Rome, Eight Ides of Sept., 2nd year of the Pontificate of Pope Paul II." (No. 824, Ant. Society of Edinburgh.)

The Kirkpatrick family had thus got possession of large possessions in Dunscore, which had belonged to the monastery of Melrose, and they kept firm hold of them for upwards of two hundred years. We hear nothing more for a hundred years, but on the 9th August, 1565, there is a tack to Thomas Kirkpatrick of Alisland by the monastery of the tiends of the over part of the parish of Dunscore for the feu of £20 Scots.

The same Thomas obtains, a few days after, 30th August, 1565, a charter from Michael Balfour, Commendator of Melrose, of the 24s. 6d. land in Dunscore, viz., 6s. 3d. in Edgarstoun, occupied by John Muirhead; 6s. 3d. in M'Cubbinstoun; 5s. in M'Chainstoun-riddings, occupied by Roger Haining; and 7s. in Fardinwell, occupied by Andrew Muirhead. Sas., 30th Aug., 1565. Witnesses, Rich. Kirkpatrick in Friars' Carse, And. Muirhead in Fardinwell, and Gilbert Greer in Amulligantown.

In 1581 we hear of the marriage of John, heir-apparent to Thomas Kilpatrick of Alisland, and Barbara Stewart, wherein Alex. Stewart of Garlies, her brother, and Dame Cath. Herries, her mother, burden themselves with her tocher, 700 merks from Alexander, and 400 merks from her mother on the one part; and on the other part, Thomas, the bridegroom's father, engages to maintain them in his house and give them 100 merks yearly to buy clothes. Dated at Kirkcudbright. The witnesses are Wm. Maxwell, Master of Herries; Roger Kirkpatrick of Closeburn; Roger Grierson of Lag; Robert Herries of Mabie; Gavin Dunbar of Baldoon; Alex. Cunningham of ———; John Weir of Bargetoon; John Crichton, apparent of Carco.

Twenty years later (7th Dec., 1585) James, Commendator of Melrose, infefts John, son and heir of said Thomas, in the above-mentioned lands, with the following witnesses:—Roger Kirkpatrick of Auldgarth; Thomas Greer, brother of Roger of Barndennoch;

Robert Kirkpatrick of Rockellhead, and John, son of George Muir in Hallmyre. On the 21st Feb., 1607, there is a charter to the same John of the lands of M'Chainstoun and Bessiewalla. A few years afterwards, in 1612, John Kirkpatrick, younger of Friars' Carse, grants charter to Robert (Roger?) Kirkpatrick of the lands of Alisland. John Kirkpatrick of Friars' Carse, the son of Roger, in conjunction with John his son, younger of Friar's Carse, disponed these lands to John Maxwell of Shaws, 16th March, 1628.

```
Thomas K. of Alisland       =
                            |
John K. of Friars' Carse,   =
         1619.              |
Roger K. of Alisland,       =
         1621.              |
| John K. of Friar's Carse, =
  along with his son, disponed |
  Friars' Carse in 1628.    |
| John K., younger of Friars' Carse.
```

It is not possible to trace clearly the history of the lands of Friars' Carse. In 1638 there is a retour of John Rome, son and heir of John of Dalswinton, to half of the £4 land of Friars' Carse, and again a retour of John Hay of Aberlady, son and heir of William of Aberlady in the same lands, and again in 1668 a retour of John Hay of Aberlady, heir of William Hay, his grandfather, who had been clerk of Session.

The lands of Friars' Carse seem to have been divided, and a portion of it at this time (1664-1710) had belonged to Provost Irvine of Dumfries, who made them over to Robert Laurie of Maxwelltown, to whom the rental from 1675 to 1710 was paid.

ALISLAND.

In the fifteenth and sixteenth centuries Alisland, as we have seen, belonged to a branch of the Kirkpatrick family, but in what way it was connected with the main branch I have not been able to discover. As time passes on, however, we begin to see that it was so, as in 1684 there is a sasine of Roger Kirkpatrick, second son of Thomas Kirkpatrick, first baronet of Closeburn, 1685 (the Roger who saw the swan predicting the death of one of the family) in the lands of Alisland and Templand of Closeburn. In this sasine are mentioned Thomas, younger of Closeburn, and John Kirkpatrick of Barnmuir. This Roger died young and unmarried, when the property would again revert to the head of the family. We find it in the possession of William, the third son of the second baronet of Closeburn, who was an advocate at the Scottish bar, and is called of Alisland. He married Jean, daughter of Charles Areskine, Lord Alva, Lord Justice-Clerk, great-grandson of John, Earl of Mar. The son of this William was Charles Kirkpatrick, who took the surname of Sharpe, according to the will of Matthew Sharpe of Hoddom, who bequeathed him all his estates, and from him is descended the present Wm. Sharpe, Esq., of Hoddom and Knockhill. The above Charles had a large family: 1, Matthew, General in the British army; 2, Charles Kirkpatrick Sharpe, the antiquarian, and well known to literary circles in Edinburgh in the first quarter of the present century; 3, Alexander, Admiral in the Royal Navy; 4, William, now of Hoddom. Daughters—1, Susan, married James, second son of John Erskine of Mar, representative of the Earls of Mar; 2, Jane, married Sir Thomas Kirkpatrick, Bart., of Closeburn, Sheriff of Dumfriesshire; 3, Eleanor, died unmarried; 4, Isabella, married G. Orde, Esq.; 5, Elizabeth Cecilia, died unmarried; 6, Grace, married the Rev. Robert Bedford.

KIRKPATRICK FAMILY OF ROSS.

The old Kirkpatrick family of Closeburn was spread over the whole of the southern part of Dumfriesshire. There were two branches in the parish of Kirkmichael, the Kirkpatricks of Kirkmichael and Kirkpatricks of Ross. The history of the Ross family may be followed with tolerable accuracy. Adam de Kyrkepatrick of Kylosbern, who had a dispute with the Abbey of Kelso respecting the advowson of the church of Kylosbern, and which was settled against him in 1264 (Chart. Kelso, 342), had two sons, Stephen, who succeeded him, and Duncan, who married Isabel, daughter and heiress of Sir David de Torthorwald, and thus inherited the barony of Torthorwald. This Sir David was a witness to a donation of "ane mark out of the lands of Maybie and Auchincook" by Michael, son of Durant of Maybie, in 1289. Upon the resignation of Duncan and Isabel, Robert Bruce granted a new charter of the lands of

Torthorwald. Their son Humphrey got another charter of confirmation, 16th July, 1326 (Writs of Carliel). Sir Robert, possibly the son of Humphrey, was taken prisoner at the battle of Duplin in 1333, and was succeeded by Sir Roger, who, in 1357, got a charter from Sir John de Graham, of an annual rent of 40s. out of Over Duff, and had also a donation from John de Corrie of the lands of Wamphray and Duntreth, with church of Wamphray, dated 16th June, 1357. We are told that this Roger exchanged the lands of Torthorwald for the barony of Ross. It was in this way that the Kirkpatricks came into possession of the Ross barony.

Now there can be no doubt that Sir William de Carleol received the lands of Cruzeantown. In the collections for a History of the Ancient Family of Carlisle, by Nicholas Carlisle (London, 1822), he says:—

"This charter of the Bruce is preserved in Lord Haddington's manuscript collections.

"*Carta Willielmi de Karliolo, militis et Margarite sponse sue, sororis regis Roberti, de terris de Crunnyantoun et Munygip in baronia de Kirkmichel forest, &c., faciendo domino capitali feudi illius servicium debitum et consuetum.*"

The date of this charter is not preserved. It was recorded in Rotulus C. of Robert I.'s register of Great Seals, which is now lost. This is given on the authority of the late Mr. Thomas Thomson of the Register Office.

These lands were not in the barony of Ross, for we find the lands of Ross enumerated in a retour of 11th Feb., 1656, of Robert Grierson of Lag, son and heir of Sir John: "The Mains, 40s.; Knock, 20s.; Skirling, 30s.; Urias, £4; Reidhill, 20s.; Courance, 23s. 4d.; Over Carrel, 56s.; Cumrue, 20s.; Nether Garrel, £4." In whatever way the Kirkpatricks came into possession of lands in Kirkmichael parish they were certainly settled there about this time, as we find William Kirkpatrick of Ross granting a charter, dated 22nd April, 1372, to John of Garrock of the "2 merkland of Glenys and Garrelgill within the tenement of Wamphray." There is a Roger of Ross, granting, after 1400, liberty to Johnstone of Elschieshiels to carry off water from the river Æ, which passes through the barony into the Annan.

There comes now, however, a period of one hundred years (1400-1500) when I can find no references to these Kirkpatricks; and it is only towards the end of the fifteenth century that they again come into notice by means of the Drumlanrig charters. These documents (No. 43) mention three members of the family, in seisins (1552-1558) of the name of Roger. The first Roger, the grandfather of the last, must have lived about 1500. There are three grants of the last Roger of Ross by charter, precept, and seisin to Sir James Douglas of Drumlanrig; one of the land of Knock, and the other lands of the barony of Ross, with a charter of confirmation by Earl Bothwell, as superior, Sept., 1558. We thus see that they sold the Ross barony to Douglas of Drumlanrig, and it is now merged in the Queensberry estate of the Duke of Buccleuch. What became of the family is unknown to me.

KIRKPATRICKS OF KIRKMICHAEL.

We have thus seen that there was a branch of this family in possession of the barony of Ross at an early period, but it is a matter of considerable doubt whether they possessed any other part of the parish before an Alexander Kirkpatrick obtained from James III. part of the barony of Kirkmichael in 1484, by a charter under the great seal, as a reward for having taken prisoner at the battle of Burnswark in 1483, James, ninth and last Earl of Douglas, who ended his days at the abbey of Lindores. This Alexander is supposed to have been second son of Sir Roger Kirkpatrick of Closeburn, and Margaret, daughter of Thomas, first Lord Somerville, but the Kirkpatricks were certainly settled in Kirkmichael before the above grant, as I find so early as the 28th August, 1472. Henry de Kyrkepatricke of Knock is witness to a charter of Sir Edward de Crechton of Sanchar, to his son Edward, of the lands of Kirkpatrick in Glencairn. Here, then, we have these Kirkpatricks settled in the barony of Kirkmichael before Alexander got his grant from James III., and it is by no means unreasonable to suppose that this Alexander might be of the Kirkmichael branch rather than of the Kylosbern. The following are the lands granted to Alexander under the great seal (B. xi. 80): "*Tot. et integ. terr. ville de Kirkmichell cum le Plewlands; tot. et integ. terr. de Molin. Raahill, Crumzeantoune, Monygep, cum pert. jac. in bar. de Kirkmichell inf. vic. de Drumfreis; tot. et integ. terr. de Drifeholme, Bekhous, villam de Drivisdale, Torwood, Belhill, Beltone, et Quawis cum pert. jac. in Senescallatu Vallis Annandie infra vic. de Drumfries; tot. et integ.*

terre. de Lochbirgeame et octodecim librat. terrar. de Dons cum pert. jac. in domin. Marchie infra vic de Berwic."

It is stated in the charter that these lands are granted on the forfeiture of William, formerly Lord Creichtoun, and his brother, Gawin. Most of these lands can still be traced, and are now in the possession of J. J. Hope Johnstone, Esq., of Annandale. Where the Ville de Kirkmichael and Plewlands were I cannot discover, but I see that the barony of Kirkmichael stretched into the old parish of Garrel (Garwald), and Alexander Kirkpatrick's portion seems to have lain chiefly in Garrel. Raahill (Raehills) is now the seat of Mr. Johnstone, and is valued, with its park and holm-farm, at £920; and in the valuation roll of 1671 I observe Crumziertoun mentioned, which has dropped out of later rolls, no doubt being included in the cumulo of Raehills. Molin and Upper and Nether Minygap are valued at £600. All these lands are now in the parish of Johnstone.

Looking back into the history of these lands, I find (Robertson's Index, 47) that Adam de Johnstone had a charter from David II. (1329-1370) of the lands of Crumantoun (the Crumzeantoune of 1484), Molyn, Monykipper (now Minygap), and Rahill, in the barony of Kirkmichael. Of these lands there seems to have been a constant change of proprietors, for in 1477 we find Gavin Crichton, brother of William, Lord Crichton, has a charter of these same lands from his said brother, and now again they are forfeited, and come into possession of Alexander Kirkpatrick. But this is not all their vicissitudes, for I find a charter under the Great Seal to Patrick Hepburn, Earl Bothwell and third Lord Halys, dated 13th of October, 1488, only four years after Alexander Kirkpatrick had got them from James III., granting to Lord Halys:—" *Over Kirkmichael, Nether Kirkmichael, le Rahill, Molynnis, Monygip et Crumzanitoun, et generaliter omnes alias terras ad dict. dom. et bar. de Drivsdale et Kirkmichael pertinen.*"

Still, we find the Kirkpatricks in possession of the lands of Kirkmichael during the sixteenth century. In 1548 William Kirkpatrick of Kirkmichael is summoned with others before Parliament. Then, 9th June, 1575, there is a charter confirming Margaret Charteris, spouse of Alexander K. of K., in an annual rent out of the lands of Kirkmichael. We have then, 13th April, 1621, a retour of William Kirkpatrick, heir to his father Sir Alexander, and

1st October, 1629 (Inq. Gen.), William K. as heir to his great-grandfather, William Kirkpatrick of Kirkmichael. It was this William, who seems to have sold about this time the lands of Kirkmichael to Sir John Charteris of Amisfield, as we find them disposed of by Sir John in 1636 to John, Earl of Wigton, and from this nobleman they passed, in 1659, to James Johnstone, Earl of Hartfell, and with the descendant of this nobleman, Mr. J. J. Hope Johnstone of Annandale, they now rest.

No. VII.

FAMILY OF M'MURDO.

This family, of Scoto-Irish extraction, was no doubt originally Murdoch, and first comes into notice in this part of the south of Scotland towards the end of the sixteenth century, where it seems to have acquired a portion of ecclesiastical property in the parish of Dunscore belonging to the Abbey of Melrose. Here it gave its name to the property of M'Murdiestoun. The Commendator of Melrose grants a charter, dated 25th July, 1565, to John M'Murday and his heirs of the lands of M'Cubbingstoun and Ferdingmakrary, possibly Farding-makrary, referring to the valuation of the land, as we have in the parish of Durisdeer a farm called Farthingbank. Among the lands paying feu-duties to the Abbey, M'Cubbingstoun is mentioned, but not the latter, though Farthingwell is given. His son Robert succeeded him, as we find the following retour, dated 27th October, 1602:—"*Robertus Macmurdie hæres Joannis Macmurdie in Dunscoir, patris—in 6 solidatis, 3 denariatis terrarum (6s. 3d. land) de Cubbentoun et Ferdene Macrerie, nunc vulgo vocati Macmurdestoun, A. E. infra parochiam de Dunscoir.*" From him sprang two sons, Robert, who died without issue, and John. From this John, we believe, sprang the Dumfries members of the family. James, the eldest son of John, succeeded, and it was from this elder branch that Robert M'Murdo of Drungans was descended, whom we find to be chamberlain to Charles, Duke of Queensberry from 1763 to 1766. He became connected with the Douglas family of Drumlanrig, by marrying, in 1740, Philadelphia, daughter of James Douglas of Dornock. This branch of the Douglas family was descended from the Hon. Archibald Douglas, third son of the first Earl of Queensberry; and there are some curious and interesting letters in possession of Robert M'Murdo of the Whittern, Herefordshire, grandson of Philadelphia, addressed by William, first Duke of Queensberry, to his cousin and confidential commissioner, Douglas of Dornock. This Robert M'Murdo was born 7th June, 1716, and died 25th June, 1766, aged fifty years. On the tombstone of Philadelphia Douglas, in St. Michael's churchyard, it states that "she having lived in this frail world xxxi. years, adorned with innocence and the most amicable virtues, was called to immortality by the great Rewarder of the good, upon the vi. of February, MDCCLIV. This monument is erected by her disconsolate husband.

> "Nor herb, fruit, flower,
> Glist'ning with dew, nor fragrance after showers,
> Nor grateful ev'ning mild, nor walk by moon
> Or glittering star-light, without thee is sweet.
> —Milton, P. L., b. iv., l. 644."

His son John M'Murdo was appointed chamberlain by William, Duke of Queensberry (old Q.), and is found to be acting on the Queensberry property from 1780 to 1797. Mr. M'Murdo was the kind friend of Burns, who was often entertained at his hospitable table at Drumlanrig from 1788 till the time of the poet's death in 1796. His son, Lieutenant-Colonel Archibald M'Murdo, was an officer in the British army, whose history is thus condensed on a tombstone in St. Michael's churchyard—"Sacred to the memory of Lieutenant-Colonel Archibald M'Murdo, formerly of H.M. 27th Regiment of Foot, and latterly of the Dumfriesshire Regiment of the North British Militia, who died at Dumfries on the 11th October, 1829, aged 54 years." His son John, born 1815, served for some years in the Madras Infantry, and became in later years Lieutenant-Colonel of the Dumfries Militia, dying in 1868. Other sons are Vice-Admiral Archibald M'Murdo of Cargenholm, whom we believe to have accompanied Sir John Ross on his expedition to the North Pole, and was honourably mentioned in that bold attempt to solve a question which still remains undecided, and Major-General William Montague M'Murdo, C.B., known as a distinguished officer, having attracted the attention of the late Sir Charles Napier, by his personal intrepidity and great zeal in the Scinde war, more particularly at the battle of Meeanee, and whose daughter he subsequently married. "Sir Charles," says *Men of the Time*, "appointed him his Assistant Quartermaster-General, and on many occasions expressed in very emphatic terms the high opinion he entertained of his conduct and services. He became Major in 1848, Lieutenant-Colonel in 1853, and Colonel in 1854. At an early period of the campaign in the Crimea, when the inadequate means of land conveyance for the service of the troops had become apparent, he was entrusted with the formation and command of the Land Transport Corps—since designated the Military Train—which new branch of our military establishment he rendered efficient, and for this service was made C.B. Not long after the volunteer movement of 1859 assumed a permanent character, Col. M'Murdo was selected as the fittest officer for the important and responsible post of Inspector-General of Volunteer Forces for the term of five years, towards the expiration of which the most active and influential promoters of the movement took immediate steps to mark their high appreciation of his zealous and valuable services in the organization of the force by appointing a committee to raise a subscription for the purpose of presenting him, on his retirement, with a suitable testimonial of their respect and regard. In February, 1865, the honorary Colonelcies of the Inns of Court Volunteers and the Engineer and Railway Volunteer staff corps were accepted by him."

Robert M'Murdo of Drungans had another son, Colonel Charles M'Murdo, who entered the army as ensign in 1760, became Major 1794, Lieut.-Colonel 1795, and Colonel in 1802, when, as his health gave away from the climate of Jamaica, he was obliged to retire, and was appointed Inspector of Yeomanry and Volunteers corps. He served his country for forty years in various parts of the world. In 1795 he was at Zutphen, and having been left in charge of the Military Hospital, when the French occupied the town, he was at first regarded as a prisoner of war, but was eventually released, and allowed to return to the army. He was present with the troops under Sir Alured Clark at the taking of the Cape of Good Hope. He married Isabella, daughter of John Coffin, Esq., of Quebec, and by her had Robert M'Murdo, Esq., of the Whittern, Herefordshire, born 1806, who married, 1829, Sarah Anne, daughter of the late Henry Robert Whitcombe, Esq., of the Whittern. He was educated at Edinburgh, and served for some years in the Bengal Army, having entered the service in 1822. He is J.P. and D.L. for the county of Hereford.

The eldest son, H. R. Douglas, entered the Royal Navy, acting as Flag-Lieutenant to Admiral Austen at the taking of Rangoon. He afterwards proceeded up the river as second in command to Commander (now Vice-Admiral) Sir Walter Tarleton, being mentioned in his despatches by that officer as having done good service, and receiving the medal and clasp for the war in Burmah. He was subsequently appointed to command the tender to the *Fox* frigate, and lost his life off Rangoon by the sinking of a boat belonging to the tender.

His second son, Charles Edward, was first appointed to the 79th Cameron Highlanders, serving with them at Balaclava and in the trenches at Sebastopol, being then appointed as aide-de-camp to his cousin Colonel M'Murdo, then in command of the Land Transport Corps. He then returned to his own Regiment, the 79th, and proceeded with them to India, being present with that regiment in all the actions in which they were engaged, receiving the Indian medal and clasp for Lucknow. He has also the medal and clasp for the Crimean, and the Turkish medal. He married, in 1870, Mary Cathleen, eldest daughter of Major Bernard.

It will be seen that this branch has chosen the military profession, and has furnished many distinguished officers both for the army and navy; but there was another branch, which has come down the stream of time *pari passu*, and which devoted itself to advance the spiritual interests of their countrymen. Going back to the middle or end of the seventeenth century, for we do not know the precise date, we find John M'Murdo, second son of a John, whom we have before mentioned, entering the church and becoming minister of Torthorwald, the charge at present occupied by his great-great-grandson, the Rev. Joseph R. Duncan. William, son of this John, had a daughter Anne, born 1745, who married, in 1770, the Rev. George Duncan, minister of Lochrutton. This George was the father of Dr. Henry Duncan, the founder of the savings banks. We may mention that John M'Murdo, minister of Torthorwald, married first, Mary Muir of Cassencarrie, and thus became connected with the Sharpes of Hoddom; and secondly, Alice Charteris, a member of the Amisfield family.

The family of M'Murdo possessed at one time the property of Killielago-craig, in Dunscore, as we find a retour, dated 25th May, 1675, of Bessie M'Murdo as heir of Thomas of Killielago-craig, her grandfather, in the 6s. land of the same, and again, 19th June, 1691, sasine upon charter under the great seal (6th March, 1691) in favour of John Maxwell of Middlebie, among others, in the 6s. land of Killielago, &c., sometime possessed by Thomas M'Murdo.

We have thus seen that the M'Murdos have done good service to their country both in war and peace; but there is another old worthy, who, though we are unable to connect him with this branch, deserves to be recorded as a benefactor to his country in another way—the architect or overseer, it would appear, of many of the ecclesiastical buildings of Scotland, more particularly of that magnificent abbey of Melrose, the ruins of which are still the wonder and admiration of the present generation. A tablet, near a small door leading to a gallery on the west side of the south transept of Melrose abbey, contains the following inscription:—

> "John Murdo sometime callit was I,
> And born in Parysse certainly,
> And had in keeping al mason werk
> Of Sant Androy's, ye Hye Kerk
> Of Glasgow, Melrose, and Paslay,
> Of Nyddisdayll and of Galway,
> Pray to God and Mary baith,
> And sweet Sanct John to keep
> This holy Kirk fra scaith."

DOUGLAS FAMILY OF DORNOCK.

The family of Douglas of Dornock, with which Robert M'Murdo of Drungans became so closely connected by marrying Philadelphia Douglas, was descended from William, first Earl of Queensberry (died 1640), whose third son was Archibald Douglas, to whom the Earl gave the estate of Dornock, which remained in the possession of the family till 1707, when it was bought by Duke James of Queensberry, and thus merged in the Queensberry estate. This Archibald Douglas was succeeded by his son William Douglas, who was employed by his cousin, Duke William, first Duke of Queensberry, as his confidential commissioner and agent, to whom he addressed the curious and interesting letters on his private affairs which are given below. William was succeeded by his son James Douglas, who was twice married, first to Isabella Man and secondly to Philadelphia Johnstone, daughter of Sir John Johnstone, first baronet of Westerhall. James left a son, Archibald (who died S. P.), and two daughters—Philadelphia, married to Robert M'Murdo, and Clementina, married to Robert Fergusson, a younger son of the Craigdarroch family, and whose grand-daughter Ludivina became Lady Menteath of Closeburn.

The originals of the following letters of Duke William to his cousin of Dornock are now, as I have said before, in the possession of Robert M'Murdo, Esq., of the Whittern, Herefordshire, whose grandfather married Philadelphia, great-grand-daughter of Archibald Douglas, third son of William, first Earl of Queensberry.

These letters are particularly interesting, as they show the character of Duke William without a mask, and in a way of which he need not be ashamed. While he attends closely to his private affairs, it is evident that he desires nothing but justice, and in some instances he even prefers to be a loser than be hard on those whom he regarded as trying to injure him. The Covenanters did not like him. Here, however, we find that he pitied what he considered their folly, and was anxious to save their families from the calamities they were evidently bringing upon them. He talks of the whole country being quiet except within his own bounds, and without doubt he thought so, and yet Scotland was at the moment seated on a volcano which burst out within a couple of months from the date of his last letter, and scattered the Chancellor Drummond and his satellites to the four winds of heaven. Duke William had refused to concur in the repressive measures of government, and had retired to private life, but he was aware that he occupied too prominent a position in Scotland to allow of his being altogether forgotten by an adverse government. His large property would be looked on with envious eyes by many, and if he could be brought within the meshes of the law, little mercy would have been shown by his old friends, from whom he had conscientiously separated. His son James was, we see by the letters, in London, where he would be anxiously watching what turn public affairs might take, and when James II. fled in December to France was one of the first to join in welcoming William of Orange. It does not appear that Duke William subsequently took a prominent part in public affairs. There was much to be done in laying out the grounds round Drumlanrig, and the castle, we know by the dates on the towers, was still unfinished. His time would thus be more pleasantly employed than in the anxieties of public life.

In referring to the proprietors, with whom he had disputes, he mentions them by the names of their properties, Springkell, Lag, Kelhead, Boytath, &c., as was usual in those early times, much in the same way as farmers are now known to their friends by the names of their farms.

Of all the servants whom he employed Wm. Lukup is the only one who has come down to us. It was believed that he was clerk of the works to oversee the erection of the castle, but these letters show that he was contractor for the work, and, as is often the case now, disputes arose as to overwork. Duke William evidently thought Lukup was only too ready to charge more than was due, yet even then he was prepared to enter into the question and pay whatever was reasonable. Lukup was afterwards employed in 1703 to repair Drumlanrig bridge, and his son was one of the contractors in 1724 to erect the buildings of Wallace Hall. He was buried in Durisdeer churchyard, where a tombstone records the death of two of his children.

"Edinb., 28th June, 1688.

"Cussing,

"Since my last I have both yours of 18 & 25 current from Bodsbeg, to which I had given this retourne sooner, bot that I had not occasion. I'm verrie weill satisfied with the account you give me of the bussines of Crowdiknow, and doe wonder how Geo. Bell came to trouble me soe much in the bussines. I wish with all my heart the Marches wer cleared, and since Geo. Bell concernes himself soe much, it will be fitt to have witnesses, and all things also prepared against I come to the Country, and the privater this be done, the better. Assure yourself Jo. Bell shall not suffer for the offer he made at Coatsbrigs Mailling, which affaire I expect you'll have prepared against I come to the country. And I doubt not bot you'll attend to all the other particullars both relating to Dornock and otherwise, that I bad you speak to Coatsbrig. The money you sent to Mr. J. Rich is receav'd, and I doubt not bot David Reid will bring you receat therrof, who will certainly be at home on Saturdey night, and he is now in Fyfe at my old Lady Carnewaith's buriall. I'm sory for the bad account you give me of Marketts, upon which soe much depends. I doubt not bot befor this the Marchants will be retourn'd, and in which case I expect account from you about easiest way of remitting Money for my son (afterwards Duke James), bot he is now heir and remembers you verrie kindlie: he resolves to returne the next week or the begining of the following to bring home his wife; she shows now big with Child. In this I will not advise, whatever the consequences be, bot Dr. Hay and others say, ther's noe hazard (there was hazard, for there was a miscarriage). I receav'd the box with the papers in drumlanrig, and I doubt not bot long agoe you have the letter about Stewart of Ardoch: your bussiness with Mr. Dowglas will be reported on Tuesday, in which I'm to sollicit all the Lords on Monday, and what comes of it, you shall know in due tyme. You ar sure I'm not weill satisfied at Kellhead's bourning my tennants peits, bot its lyke the rest of his wise bargaines. Lag assures me, it wes not Kellhead, bot one Carlyle that brunt them, and that the ground the tennants made use of, was not ther oun, nor did they even pretend priviledge ther befor, so lett the bottome of all this be gott befor the thing be brought in publick, or farther mov'd in, which I beg you take effectual wayse to doe, and put all in wreating, whereof I expect account in due tyme: withall speak fully with Kellhead and the Carlyles in the thing, and inform yourself, if what Kellhead wreats in the inclosed to Coatsbrig be true, and tell Geo. Bell I'm not weill pleas'd he should lett my tennants meit with those injuries; if they wer his own, he would protect them better, and withall assure Kellhead he will not find his account by such Methods. Young Brodkirk was latly with me about the bussiness with Kellhead and the Carlyles, in which I cannot alter the Measure I have still followed in that Matter. As to Wm. Lucup's Affairs (contractor or clerk of the works at Drumlanrig) I find your Compt exact, and his lyke a Taylor's Bill, whereof the one halfe may be weill cutt off. Tell him, when I come to the Country, all those little pretensions of his shall be considered, and what's just, he shall have, bot more is not to be expected in the way he takes, and tell him withall that when his Indenture is consider'd, it will in my opinion be found that I have paid him as much as he is oblidged to by the said Indenture, even though he aledges to have done over, bot nothing can be mor said of this, till Meiting, till which tyme you may keep both the accounts, and tell him to to be bussie, and when I come to the country, he shall have his Cloathes, which Ja. Weir this day tells me he has not yet gott. I shall be glad to hear you have gott Albie's paper, tho' Sprinkell (Maxwell) sayes it's not worth a farthing, Albie

having caused inhibit Blackshous several yeeres before signing of the
said paper, and what is in this faill not to try both at Albie and others,
and if the Inhibition be duly registrate. The sooner you send in Mr.
Douglass, the better, James now being desyrous to be gone. I hear
noe mor of Brakensyde's preferment in the country, only I'm told My
Lord Annandaille pretend he'll pass from it, nor am I inclined to
meddle in it or anie thing else relating to his Concernes. Befor my
Lord Annandaille parted from this, I spoke with him about the
bussines betwixt him and me, wherein I found him verrie fair, and if
he alter not his resolution we'll certainly agree in the Matter, for I
have promis'd to give in his Charge and the state of that wholle
affair in wreating. The wholle Heritours of the Country, who wer
heir, ar gone to the Meeting at drumfries in obedience to the
Counsell's Commands; what's proposed and passes at the Meeting
I expect you first will hear. As to J. Dalzell's affair with my
tennants, he spoke nothing of it to me, and befor I receav'd your
last letter, he was gone, soe I must referr the Matter to you, and
doe desyre you speak him fully in it, in which ther's nothing to be
said, bot that business lay as they ar till my coming to the country,
and then I'll press, as much as he, to have all things clear'd, and I
am sure its mor my interest, for I have these many yeares been much
wrong'd by these Marches, which my unwillingness to be heard
(hard) with old Jo. & Ro. Dalzell made me sitt with, bot now that
the bussiness is begune on ther syd, I will not lett delay, and shall
bring to the country such papers as shall clear all, little to ther
advantage, for I'm sure I have them, with full informations by Mr.
Geo. Blair, bot all this only to yourself, and in the Meantyme gett
the best information you can both as to the Marches themselves, and
witnesses to be made use off, thereof Make a state, soe that at my
coming to the country everything may be right done. And with the
Minister of Kirkmahoe, as my former directs, tho' my —— and I ar
lyke to part without ending the bussiness of Kirkmahoe; this I find
is Ro. Alexander's Influence, who may soon doe him a better office,
bot you shall know mor of this at Meeting. I desyre you take all
wayes to clear yourself about the bussiness of Kirkmahoe, whereof
I suppose Cariol knowes most, and what you learne take in wreating,
soe that at Meiting clear resolutions may be taken in that affair.
Tell And. Dowglass I receav'd his of 14 from Thornhill with a state
inclos'd of some late discoveries he has made in Compting with the

tennants of ommissions out of Wm. Menzies's Charges, about which I shall speake with the said Wm. who is heir. In the meantyme it will be fitt you gett by the first occasion, and send me a state of what's due by Wm. Menzies's bond, and of former discoveries he made against him, whereof he acquainted me, when he was at London, soe that I may be in a condition to comune with the said Wm. as to the wholle. When the Minister of Moffat was heir, he made Dr. —— speek to me about my Teynds in that paroch, to which I delay giving a positive answer, till I come to the country. In the meantyme I desyre you informe yourself, and make a State of it in wreating. what teynd he getts out of my interest in that parish, als weill in Coreheads possession as otherwayse. Lykewise inform yourself what's payd by the vassalls, particullarlie Brechensyde, for if we settle at all, I incline that it be for the wholle, for I doe not incline that any bodie bot myself have my own or my vassall's money any longer for reasons verrie obvious, but all this only to yourself till Meiting. As to Geo. Charteris wife's Affair, tho' I have condiscended to noe bodie to Allow her to stay till Mertinmas. yet I'm Content you speak with her as to the rent she will give, next as to the difference betwixt her and me at last Compting, and in the last place, if she will take the house in Sanquhar again at the rate her husband bought them, and as I shall be satisfied with her answers in these particullars, it shall be order'd, and it may be a longer tyme, soe lett you first heer account of this Matter, soe that I may resolve upon and order things accordingly. You'll receave this from Mr. Th——, who has from the Colledge of Glasgow a right for the halfe years vaccant stipend 1686, in which for all that nothing is to be done till my coming to the country. In the meantyme you would informe yourself if the Church was then vacant, lykewise Consider this Minister's presentation, since possiblie he may be presented to it. The Minister complained to me that the Church and Manse ar in disorder, which you would cause timously right, and helpe them in tyme, ther being noe advantage in delay: when the Manse is repaired, the Minister ought to be oblidg'd to keep it without troubling the parish. The Minister has lykewise been speaking for his Stipend, whereof you ar to order him to be payd in terms of his back-bond, which, if you have not, lett me know, and it shall be sent by the first, and being upon the subject of Manses, I remember in Wm. Lucup's wise accounts, he charges for the reparations of the Manses of Deisdeir and Sanquhar, both which wer payd in my opinion by Geo. Charteris, at least I'm sure a considerable part of them was, and I'm sure more than he deserved, for they were both verrie insufficientlie built, especially that of Deisdeir. When Lag was last heir, he proposed to me to take a Tack of Tothorall and Musewall and Roehellhead and severall other of my Lands in Annandaille, in which Affair ther ar both Conveniences and Inconveniences, and the last may doe mor than Ballance the first. Howiver at my coming to the country I'm resolved to hear him: in the Meantyme this only to yourself, and faill not to have your thoughts of the thing, soe that I may know what to doe, and what Clauses to putt in the Tack, in case we settle: I find he desyres and . . off a part of the . . rent, which I have and only offers him terms of payment. I wonder in your bussiness of Annandaille, you say nothing of Albie's offers as to his own lands. In which Springkell tells me verrie pleasant stories, particullarlie that he devyded his little interest amongst all his sones and has made them all Lairds. Springkell lykewise tells me that he is to Make a bargain with Blacketthouse for some of his lands for a park; what's in all this faill not to try, soe at Meiting you may be able to informe me in how far these little projects are consistent with my interest, soe expecting you'll Mind these things, and all my other Concernes, and longing much to see you in the Country. I am.

"Your most affectionat Cusin and faithfull friend

"QUEENSBERRIE."

"Edinb., 16th July, 1668.

"CUSSING,

"Since my last I have yours of 3rd and 9th, to which you had gott this returne sooner, bot that I have in all this been huried with my son's being heir, and his dispatch back: he parted on Thursday last and goes to Inchine? to bring his wife down before she be brought to bed, which for all that I apprehend he will not gett done. However I'll have an account of it in few dayes, whereof you may expect to be acquainted in due tyme. Ja: Weir is now delyvering his charge to Wm. Dowglass, which had been done sooner, bot that Ja: Weir stayed a week in the country after he came, how

I shall be glad Wm Dowglass proove proper for that trust whereof noebodie can make Judgement without tryall. In the Meentyme you may be confident I shall spare no paines to Advise and instruct him and give him memorialles of every thing in wreating. The Account you gave me of Marketts, and what I hear from others on that subject is verrie unpleasant. I howp befor this things goe better, and what prospect you have of getting my Son Ansuered Money at London, I long to know, and whether he stay or come down, ther will be use for considerable soumes to be got wher they will. As to the Goods of Torthorwald the sooner you get them off, the better, which I doubt not. Instruct Tho. Kennedy and order him to take all wayes for this. As to Lag's proposal, he has sayd noe more of it, since his coming last to town, and if it be done at all, it must be done in the country. Meanwhylle if you meet with Lag, you may speak with him about it, and try what Method he resolves to follow, you may lykewise speak with Hallaithes, what you judge fitt in the thing bot let it goe noefurther. As to the bussiness of Echolfegell, after considering your information and hearing the tennants at great lenth, I judged fitt to raise Counsel Letters and Law borrowes against Kellhead and all the others, which the tennants shall bring home with them, they will go straight to you with a note from Mr. Ja. Richardson, and faill not to expedite the letters tymouslie, and as he shall advise. Lett your first bean what's done in Albie's affair. You may be sure I'll not allow Sprinkell to medle with Blacketthouse. And in the meanwhyle inform yourself of Albie of the value Sprinkell would have and of everything relating to it. The Cancellour [Drummond, Earl of Perth, of whom a portrait is said by Pennant to be in Drumlanrig Castle] and Counsell ar verrie weill satisfied at what the Heritours did at ther Meeting. And as to the justice of . . . . . they may assure themselves of favourable judgement from me, tho' I know others would not doe the lyke. I am glad you and Sir John Dalzell ar lyke to settle the matter you wrott off for I shall be very sorry to be heard [hard] with him, and I am sure some in the Government will think us verrie weill wear'd upon one another. E. Annandaille and your Minister ar not yet settled, and I'm told the bussines is to be reported the morrow. It's said my Lord of Annandaille has gained the Bishop, which soures the minister extremely. I expect you'll get me a state what my Lands and my vassalls in that paroch pay, for whatever way bussines goe, I'm resolved to have that in my own hands. You did weill to keep the Minister of Torthorwald's back-bond ther being no use for it heir. As to Wm. Lukup's affair, it's not possible to proceed further in the account till I come to the country, and then he needs not doubt to have all justice done him. In the meantyme advise him to be busie and putt the work as fast bye as possible. Just now one Walter Bell comes heir with a complaint of Albie, and tells me of a pursuit intended against him befor the Stewart court, bot I could medle in none of these Matters, having heard nothing from you. I have spoke with Wm. Menzies in the bussines of his compt, but can come to noe close. I said he is trusted by the Colledge of Glasgow in the bussines of the vacant stipends, which must be my payment in soefar. As to Margaret Angus answers, they doe not at all satisfie me, so lett imediatly decreet be taken against her, for I'm positively resolved, she shall not stay, and besyd you ar not to allow her to live in any place of my interest. Receave enclosed Mrs. Hume's Compt and discharge of Stipend, which keep with my other papers till meeting. And will you meet and advise with Carlioll in the bussines of Kirkmahoe at Convenience. As to Gullihills Affair (in Holywood) I shall speak with Mr. J. Rich this day, and possibly ere the bearer goe may have his thoughts, both about that and Mrs. Patersone. As to Wm. Wilson's affair, I have told David Reid all I can say in the thing, he is certainly a clamorous, cheating fellow, but such ought never to gaine by these methodes, nor can I understand why he should have a soume for six hundredth merk, which constantly both before and since he had it, payed sooner. Of all this you may give David Reid my thoughts. Remember me to the Cominishers and tell him I receaved his letters and shall speak with Bishop C—— about it. Tell Mr. James Alexander and the Minister of Hoddam I receaved thar letter about the bussines of Ackollfegell (Ecclefechan) and doe thank them for ther kindness to my tennants. Being to send a great deal of furnitur from this place to Drumlangrig, faill not imediatly to wreat to David Reid and Archibald Douglass, that they have heir soe soon as possible sixteen or eighteen carriage horse with ropes and packsaddles for carrying things, for the rest will come in carts—Wreat to Will Johnstoune that he send out with the Carriadge horse wholle Ropes and cords about the house, lykewise that he gett from Wm Lukup the whole ropes came about the boxes of Marbles and other things latly sent from this place.

And order Will Johnstoune or Wm Lucup to send a state of what Ropes comes. As to my own being in the Country, I design it as soon as possible after the Session. And cannot till then be positive, and wreat too Wm Johnstoune or David Reid, and withall that they need Make noe more preparations for me, till they have my particullar directiones, which they may Expect in due tyme. As to Mr —— Affair its he occasions noe small noise and trouble. I howp it shall goe well enouch, but I'm sure it cannot close this session. Stenhous (Douglas in Tynron) stay heir upon that account was judged needless, soe he went home last week. My affair with Spanoh is lykewise determined, and tho' I have not earnd the halfe of what I have just right to, yet I fancie what is done will make him uneasy. I intreat you try if you can gett a discreat servant for a padge, or such a footman as may rune after my Coach heir, and ryde with me in the Country, and wait &c. Constantly upon my Chamber, wherever I am: he should be a handsome fellow and honest and sober, the sooner you Mind this the better. And if you can gett such an one, haist him heir with a line from you. I much rather incline to have him a useful servant than a padge, being weary of those Cattle. And if you fall in upon any ther, haist him heir, and I shall cause putt livery upon him, for I have verrie good use for him. This at present is all I Mind, and as bussines occurs, you shall still hear from me. So expecting your cair in every thing, and that you'll keep the Chamberlands in Mind of their duty, I am with great Confidence

"Your most affectionate Cussing and faithfull friend
"QUEENSBERRIE."

"Edinb., 17th Aug., 1688.
"CUSSING,
"Last night brought me yours of July 30 and touching the affair of Ecclefechen I wonder how Kellhead or any body else can blame me or any other body except themselves for what's past, since they forced me to it, much against my will. And that it was never to be shuned without Exposing my Interest for a prey to every body. All I can add to my former letter on this subject is that Mr. J. Rich and others advise me, that in regaird that the day of Apearance is soe long, and that it's uncertain if the Counsell sitts

then, that you and any other Kellhead pleases call the tennants and
witnesses, and try both the natur of the laite ryot, and the natur of
the tennants possession, and whether they payed any thing for it or
not. All which send account heir soe soon as possible, that further
Advice may be given in the Matter and propose and Manadge this
with Kellhead as from yourself, which if he shune lett it fall, in
which case try and informe me exactly of the natur of the bussines
yourself, both as to what's past, and of what natur the tennants
possession was that's to say, if they had it by right or by tollerance
or payment. And this is all I need say on the subject. I saw a
letter last night from Kellhead to Mr. Jo. Richardsone, wher, efter
he has given him soe foolish accounts of this affair, he charges
Coatbrig and others of great villanies against me particullarly, that
Kirkconell, Irving and one Caneg and severall others thereabout
have been allowed to possess considerable parcells of ground, formerly belonging to Woodhouse and in his possession, as part of
the lands of Ecollfechan, when I recovered decreet against him, and
tho' Kellhead's information does not with me give great authority
to anything, yet Coatsbrig's actings in my Affaires and his relation
to Kirkconnel Makes me Consider this probable enouch, soe what's
in it and of what value the lands are, I intreat you be at the paines
to try, and show they'll be proven parts and pendicles of these lands,
of all which Make a State in wreating : he lykewise insinuetes that
others thereabouts have the same Advantages both ther and in
Middlebie, whereof faill not to take all wayes to informe yourself,
And to procure discoveries promise what gratuities you please.
Several others have informed me of this Matter long agoe, bot I
could never gett anything clearly made out, and I fear thus prove
lyke the rest, howiver take all possible wayes to be at the bottom of
it. I'm sory Marhetts Continue soe bad, when you ar in Niths-
daille faill not to meet with And. Douglass, David Reid and Wm.
Lukup and order what's necessary in my concernes. And. tells me
of a field Conventicle has been lately in the head of Sanquhar, I'm
to speak to the Chancellor in it this evening. In the Meantyme I
have ordered Andrew to try who was at it, especially my tennants,
and send me an account of all so soon as possible. And it's
wonderfull that these rascalls, tho' they regard not my prejudice,
will need destroy themselves and their poor families. And when
nothing of that kind is heard in the Country, that it should be in

my interest, and my tennants only Chargeable with it, you ar sure cannot be verrie pleasant to me. And what use my Enemies will Make of it both heir and above is sufficiently obvious. As to Wm. Lukup's affair keep all wayes to keep the workmen together, bot more Money is not to be expected till I be ther. I wonder to hear from Stenhouse that the worke people has not gott the victuall at the Rates of the Country, which they take not; it seemes ther Money is not soe scarse as they pretend. I have now wrot to And. Douglass about this, so you and he orders what you judge fitt. As to boitath you have done all that's necessar, till I be there, And in the Meantyme cause Tho. Kennedy gett exact information, and be able at Meiting to advise me, who shall be trusted in the perambulation, for it's fitt the thing be taken absolutely away to free thes unhappy people from mor clamours. Cause tell Crowdiknow I take verrie ill he insists in that bussines before any other Court than Myne, which is certainly occasioned be Coatsbrig's Advice, which lykewise lett him know he will not gain by such Methods at the long runne. I have long agoe account of the Carcheshage bussines from And. Douglass, to which I gave answers and Caused show the Information to the Chancellour, with which he seemed verrie weill satisfied. Since my last one Bratton, a Mousald Drover, came heir on his way to St. Johnstoun (Perth), he sayes he'll be able this begining of October to Answer a 1000 lib. sterling, bot cannot be positive as to the Exchange; He has promised to call heir towards the end of the week, as he returnes from St. Johnstoun. And that he will speak more fully, whereof you shall have account in due tyme. Meanwhylle I doubt not you'll take all Imagenable paines to Make settlements with others at the easiest rate; whereof give me full account that I may Acquaint my son accordingly. I cannot yet be positive as to my coming from this, which you are sure shall be as soon as I can. The Chancellour parts towards close of the week. And at present I have tyme to say noe more, but that I trust everything to your cair, and design to hear frequently and fully from you,

"And am unalterably,
"your most Affectionate Cussin and
"faithfull friend   QUEENSBERRIE.
"poor Mr. Jo. Rich has been verrie ill
"but is this day much better."

"Ed. 31 Aug., 1688.

" CUSIN,

Yesterday Morning the bearer brought me yours of 27 Current, and I had dispatched him last night, but I was so taken up with James —— affairs and wreating to my son that I had not one spare miniut, but now you shall hear from me as to all things. As to Mr. Rose's offer, I will by no means accept of it, for I may have the same heir, bot if he'll settle for 4 or 4½ or at most 5 per Cent, you may make the bargaine, bot I'll only be oblidged to pay the Money heir. Bring it as low as you can, for ther will be a considerable soume to Remitt, which is not to be shuned. Try Lykewise if upon receat of Money here, he can give me bills upon Berwick, and upon what Rate. Of all this it Concernes me extreamly to have a speedy and distinct account, which I long for, soe pray Mind it, and if you can make the bargain at 4 or 4½, it will do weill. Receaved Littleparks letter, which is just of the natur I expected. As to the 100 lib. sterling Mr. Rose desyred you to answer to the two Drovers, you doe weill not to do it without sufficient security, but having that the more money you get up ther upon these soumes, the better. As to the vaccancy of Dornoch you shall hear fully, when Mr. Reid comes out, and the delay of his presentation now is that I have forgott whether I have been in use to present to the Tythes or Modified Stipend of that Church. And the late Minister wants the presentation. However I'm taking wayes to Clear it by my own papers, whereof you shall have account. In the meantime Mr. Finnie has intimate to me an act of Counsell in his favours for halfe a yeares Stipend mor than he formerly got, so you see Godliness is still a great gain. Howiver I contend it's not at the Counsell's dispose and am resolved to speak verrie firmly to the Chancellour about it, when he comes heir, which I'm told will be tomorrow. You would acquaint my sone what Money you give in to be answered at London and when. I doubt not you'll Mind the letter and bussines with Mrs. Alison [wife of John Alison, Chamberlain, proprietor of Glencorse in Closeburn] whereof lett Mr. Jo. Richardsone and me have account soe soon as possible. Mynd the list of the disorderly people in my Bounds, and see that it be exact, but it requires no great haist, only I wish it be ready against my coming to the Country. As to Wm. Lucup's affair I'll allow noe mor money till the supply at Drumlangrig be exhausted nor can they have use of any soe long as it lasts, which I'm sure will be till I come to the Country. In the Meantyme tell him to be bussied and assur him that James Smyth shall come along, and the first bussines I fall upon shall be to clear with him in every thing both as to whats past and to come. And till then advise him to be bussie and Cairfull, and tell both Stenhouse and him that they remember cairfully, what my Instructions bears in those Matters, particullarly about having the officehouses ready for me and all the rest of the House made clean and Locked up, and Lykewise what's ordered about the gardens planting and hedges. By your first letter to Drumlangrig, send the enclosed list of seeds in a line to the Gairdiner ordering him to consider exactly if he gott them all, and have a state for me against I come to the Country of what was wanting. Lykewise Mind him that September is the properest tyme for sowing the grasses lately sent, and that he make use of proper ground in the park for them, which order And. Douglass to see made soe as the Gairdiner thinks fitt, who I find a verrie usefull servant, and Tell Wm. Lukup I will not allow him to be runne down especially for doing his duty, pray take paines in the bussines of the Carchshago, in which I'm sure your Passing Boarholme may be of use. I wish you have got thos papers for Springkill in that affair: bot his information's are not always stood to the back. I know nothing of his being in this place, nor have I seen or heard of him. Earl Annandaille went from this last week, and he and I parted in very good termes, and what his pretensions may be ther, My sone, I believe, may give account. In the Meantyme assur yoursel he promises verrie fair, bot all this about him only to yourself. Soe soon as possible wreat to David Reid (to whom ther's noe occasion going from this) that imediatly he meit with Wm. Lukup, and cause him send some of his men to Sanquhar to take in the Chimneyes of my Chamber, the Drawing roume and hall, which ar by a great deall too large, and by taking them in as they ought, will both make the Roumes warmer and prevent smoaking. This is to be done with the tile there and cannot take up much tyme or charges and I'll not be pleased if I find it not done when I come. Lykewise tell David to take exact notice to the ovens, both in the Kitchen and Bakehouse, and if they be any way faultie that they be presently helped and made sufficient, for it will not be proper those things be doing when I'm ther. Tell him Lykewise that he & Wm. Johnstoune consider what useless Broken pouder [pewter] is there and unfitt to be made use off, and that he send it in by the first occasion heir with the weight of it. And new pouther [pewter] shall be sent out in place of it and that he may doe this more exactly, tell him goe throu the wholle Roumes and Wardrobes, and see if they have the Keyes of the Wardrob at Drumlangrig, that the old washbasins and what useless peader [pewter] he finds ther, send it out, and if there be any usefull pewter ther, send it to Sanquhar and keep it ther. James Weir tells me there is ane old brewing Lead at Sanquhar quyt useless and that it is not possible to mend it, order David and Wm. Johnstoune to consider it, and if it be soe, lett the said Lead be sent heir with one of the Retourned Carts from Drumlanrig, that it may be disposed off, Bot if it can be usefull at Drumlanrig or Sanquhar, it's still to be keept. Tell David & Wm. Johnstoune to cause cleer the Bartisans of Sanquhar, and that the doors be made sufficient and locks putt upon them. Tell Wm. Johnstoune that I have lost the state of provisions to be sent to Sanquhar that he gave me when he was heir, soe order him by the first occasion to send me ane exact note of every thing to be provided and sent from this, and that they have ther thoughts how all things shall be provided to the best advantage in the country, and that they remember former directions and have every thing in order. Tell David that he kill presently both the old Bucks and send them heir eased up, as James Weir used to doe: I would not putt them to this, bot that David in his letter assured me that they can do it as weill as James Weir, bot tell them I'll take it verrie ill, if they kill the wrong deer, soe if they have the least distrust of themselves, tell them not to Medle with it, but send me word and I'll wreat to James Weir to go ther. James Weir tells me one of the bucks to be killed is whyte and the other brown.

www.ingramcontent.com/pod-product-compliance
Lightning Source LLC
Chambersburg PA
CBHW051727300426
44115CB00007B/494